The Diaries of
GEORGE WASHINGTON

Volume III

1771–75, 1780–81

ASSISTANT EDITORS

Beverly H. Runge, Frederick Hall Schmidt,
and Philander D. Chase

George H. Reese, CONSULTING EDITOR

Joan Paterson Kerr, PICTURE EDITOR

THE DIARIES OF
GEORGE
WASHINGTON

VOLUME III

1771–75, 1780–81

DONALD JACKSON, *EDITOR*

DOROTHY TWOHIG, *ASSOCIATE EDITOR*

UNIVERSITY PRESS OF VIRGINIA

CHARLOTTESVILLE

This edition has been prepared by the staff of
The Papers of George Washington,
sponsored by
The Mount Vernon Ladies' Association of the Union
and the University of Virginia
with the support of
The National Endowment for the Humanities
and
The National Historical Publications
and Records Commission

THE UNIVERSITY PRESS OF VIRGINIA

First published 1978

Frontispiece: Washington before Yorktown, by Rembrandt Peale.
(Corcoran Gallery of Art, gift of the Mount Vernon Ladies' Association)

Library of Congress Cataloging in Publication Data

Washington, George, Pres. U.S., 1732–1799
The diaries of George Washington.

Includes bibliographies and indexes.
1. Washington, George, Pres. U.S., 1732–1799.
2. Presidents—United States—Biography. I. Jackson, Donald Dean, 1919—   II.
Twohig, Dorothy.   III. Title
E312.8 1976   973.4′1′0924 [B]   75–41365
ISBN 0–8139–0721–7 (v. 3)

Printed in the United States of America

Administrative Board

David A. Shannon, *Chairman*   Mrs. John H. Guy, Jr.
W. Walker Cowen

Advisory Committee

John R. Alden   Charles McC. Mathias, Jr.
C. Waller Barrett   L. Quincy Mumford
Francis L. Berkeley, Jr.   Merrill D. Peterson
Julian P. Boyd   Saunders Redding
Comte René de Chambrun   Stephen T. Riley
James Thomas Flexner   James Thorpe
Merrill Jensen   Lawrence W. Towner
Wilmarth S. Lewis   Nicholas B. Wainwright
Lewis A. McMurran, Jr.   Charles C. Wall
John O. Marsh, Jr.   John A. Washington, M.D.
Esmond Wright

Contents

Map

Illustrations

Illustrations

Editorial Procedures and Symbols

Transcription of the diaries has remained as faithful as possible to the original manuscript. Because of the nature of GW's diary entries, absolute consistency in punctuation has been virtually impossible. Where feasible, the punctuation has generally been retained as written. However, in cases where sentences are separated by dashes, a common device in the eighteenth century, the dash has been changed to a period and following word capitalized. Dashes which appear after periods have been dropped. Periods have been inserted at points which are clearly the ends of sentences. In many of the diaries, particularly those dealing with planting and the weather, entries consist of phrases separated by dashes rather than sentences. Generally if the phrase appears to stand alone, a period has been substituted for the dash.

Spelling of all words is retained as it appears in manuscript. Errors in spelling of geographic locations and proper names have been corrected in notes or in brackets only if the spelling in the text makes the word incomprehensible. Washington occasionally, especially in the diaries, placed above an incorrectly written word a symbol sometimes resembling a tilde, sometimes an infinity sign, to indicate an error in orthography. When this device is used the editors have silently corrected the word.

The ampersand has been retained. The thorn has been transcribed as "th." The symbol for per has been written out. When a tilde is used to indicate either a double letter or missing letters, the correction has been made silently or the word has been transcribed as an abbreviation. Capitalization is retained as it appears in the manuscript; if the writer's intention is not clear, modern usage is followed.

Contractions and abbreviations are retained as written; a period is inserted after abbreviations. When an apostrophe has been used in contractions it is retained. Superscripts have been lowered, and if the word is an abbreviation a period has been added. When the meaning of an abbreviation is not obvious, it has been expanded in square brackets: H[unting] C[reek]; so[uther]ly.

Other editorial insertions or corrections in the text also appear in square brackets. Missing dates are supplied in square brackets in diary entries. Angle brackets ⟨ ⟩ are used to indicate mutilated material. If it is clear from the context what word or words are missing, or missing material has been filled in from other sources, the words are inserted between the angle brackets.

A space left blank by Washington in the manuscript of the diaries is indicated by a square bracketed gap in the text. In cases where Washington has crossed out words or phrases, the deletions have not been noted. If a deletion contains substantive material it appears in a footnote. Words inadvertently repeated or repeated at the bottom of a page of manuscript have been dropped.

If the intended location of marginal notations is clear, they have been inserted in the proper place without comment; otherwise, insertions appear in footnotes.

In cases where the date is repeated for several entries on the same day, the repetitive date has been omitted and the succeeding entries have been paragraphed.

Because Washington used the blank pages of the *Virginia Almanack* or occasionally small notebooks to keep his diaries, lack of space sometimes forced him to make entries and memoranda out of order in the volume. The correct position of such entries is often open to question, and the editors have not always agreed with earlier editors of the diaries on this matter. Such divergence of opinion, however, has not been annotated.

Bibliographical references are cited by one or two words, usually the author's last name, in small capitals. If two or more works by authors with the same surname have been used, numbers are assigned: HARRISON [2]. Full publication information is included in the bibliography for each volume. The symbols used to identify repositories in the footnotes precede the bibliography.

Surveying notes and dated memoranda kept in diary form have not been included in this edition of Washington's diaries, although the information contained in them has often been used in annotation.

Editorial Procedures and Symbols

Individuals and places mentioned for the first time in this volume have been identified in the footnotes; those which have been identified in the first two volumes may be located by consulting the indexes of those volumes. A cumulative index will be included in the last volume of the *Diaries*.

The Diaries of
GEORGE WASHINGTON

Volume III

1771–75, 1780–81

Mount Vernon Flour, Western Bounty Lands

1771

[January]

Where & how my time is Spent

Jany. 1st.   Rid to my Mill in the forenoon and afternoon.

2.   Did the same thing again. Met Colo. Robt. Fairfax there, & upon my return home found Mr. Piper, Mr. Muir, and Doctr. Rumney here who dined & lodged.

Robert Fairfax was preparing at this time to return to his home in England, Leeds Castle, where he lived until his death in 1793 (GW to Jonathan Boucher, 3 Feb. 1771, CSmH). He became the seventh Baron Fairfax when his brother Thomas died in 1781.

Rumney apparently brought a quantity of the "Best Bark" for Patsy Custis. Peruvian bark, also called cinchona, was one of the popular eighteenth-century remedies for epilepsy as well as for malaria. Before Rumney left Mount Vernon, he also furnished Patsy with a fresh assortment of pills, powders, and drops (receipt from William Rumney, 24 June 1772, ViHi: Custis Papers).

3.   The above Gentlemen stayed all day and Night. My Brother John and Mr. Lawe. Washington came here to Dinner.

4.   After Breakfast Mr. Piper, Mr. Muir and Doctr. Rumney re-turnd to Alexa. My Brothr. Mr. Lawe. Washington & self went to the Mill.

5.   My Brother & Mr. Lawe. Washington set of for Frederick. I went a hunting with the two Mr. Triplets and Mr. Peake but killd nothing.

6.   At home all day alone.

7.   The Two Colo. Fairfaxs and Mrs. Fairfax dined and lodged here.

Besides the Fairfaxes, Dr. George Steptoe (d. 1784), of Westmoreland County, apparently visited Mount Vernon about this time; on either 7 or 8

Jan., GW paid him £2 3s. for examining Patsy Custis and giving her a pre-
scription (LEDGER A, 333; CUSTIS ACCOUNT BOOK). Steptoe had graduated from
the University of Edinburgh in 1767.

8. The Same Company dined here again but went away in the
Evening.

9. Rid to the Mill in the forenoon and Afternoon.

10. Mr. Robt. Adam & Mr. Josh. Watson dined and lodged here.
Before they came I had rid to my Mill in the forenoon.

Robert Adam had recently entered into a business partnership with two
friends, Matthew Campbell (d. 1782) and James Adam (died c.1787), both
merchants of Alexandria. Known as Robert Adam & Co., this firm dealt in
several agricultural commodities including wheat, corn, flour, and fish and
had plans to import goods from Great Britain and the West Indies for sale
in Alexandria. The partnership lasted until the end of 1776, when it was
dissolved because of "Declining Business," but Robert Adam continued to operate his own milling and baking enterprises until his death in 1789 (LEDGER
A, 324, 326, 341; *Va. Gaz.*, D&H, 14 Feb. 1777; Robert Adam to GW, 10 April
1778, DLC:GW).

Joseph Watson (d. 1773), burgess for Dunmore County 1772–73, was a
friend of both GW and Robert Adam (Adam to GW, 16 Sept. 1773,
DLC:GW; *Va. Gaz.*, P&D, 23 Sept. 1773).

11. The above Gentlemen dined here again to day and went
away in the Afternoon. In the forenoon we all went to the Mill.

12. Went a huntg. with the two Mr. Triplets Mr. Manley and
Mr. Peake. Run a Deer to the Water but killed nothing.

13. Mrs. Washington Patcy Custis & myself Dined and lodged at
Belvoir.

14. Dined there this day also and Returnd home after it.

15. Rid to the Mill & Race in the forenoon and afternoon.

16. Rid to the Mill and up the Mill Race in the Afternoon.

17. Rid to the Mill &ca. in the Afternn. and went up to Alexa.
with Mrs. Washington & Patcy Custis in the Afternoon.

18. Rid to my Mill and the Race above it in the forenoon—at
home afterwards.

19. Went a hunting in Compa. with the two Mr. Triplets, Mr. Manley & Mr. Peake. Killed a Fox after two hours Chase. In the Afternoon rid to where my People were at work on the Mill Race.

GW's workers were now extending the millrace a few hundred yards northeast to a point on Dogue Run, a short distance above the mouth of Piney Branch.

20. Went to Pohick Church with Mrs. Washington and returnd to Dinr. Mr. Ball dined here.

21. Went up to Court Mrs. Washington & Patcy Custis with me. Returnd in the Afternoon & Mr. Hr. Ross with us.

The January court met only today. At this session Lund Washington and James Wren, two witnesses to the signing of Valinda Wade's deeds to GW 17–18 Dec. 1770, took oaths verifying those deeds, and the justices ordered the documents to be certified (Fairfax County Order Book for 1770–72, 169–72, Vi Microfilm).

22. Dined at home and afterwards went to Colcherster with Mr. Ross on my way to Dumfries on the Arbitration between Doctr. Ross & Co. and Mr. Semple.

This arbitration, which had been begun in Colchester 27 Aug. 1770, was in GW's opinion "a very disagreeable" one (GW to Charles Washington, 25 Jan. 1771, CSmH). The arbitrators were obliged to meet in Dumfries for a third session beginning on 28 Mar. to settle it.

23. Waited at Colchester till 2 Oclock for Colo. Mason. Dined at Courts's & went to Dumfries afterwards & to the Play of the Recruitg. Officer. Lodgd at Mr. Montgomeries.

William Courts kept an inn, commonly called the Stone House, at the ferry landing in Colchester (*Va. Gaz.*, P, 8 Sept. 1775). *The Recruiting Officer: A Comedy,* by George Farquhar, was a genial satire about the British army and its brutal recruiting system. First performed in London in 1706, the play was a great favorite of English and American audiences throughout the eighteenth century (FARQUHAR, 2:33–112). This production was staged by the American Company of Comedians, which had recently left Annapolis and would soon return to Williamsburg for the spring court days.

24. On the Arbitration.

25. Ditto – – – Ditto.

26. Ditto – – – Ditto.

27.   Receivg. News of part of my Mill Wall's falling in I came home to Dinner and found Miss Molly Manley here.

Excavation of the mill site in 1932 revealed a layer of "soft aqueous sand" under the wall separating the water pit, where the waterwheel stood, from the cog pit in which the gears needed for transmission of power were located. It was also discovered that there were "bad subsoil conditions generally under the southeast corner of the building," where the raceway exited (BURSON, 10). The wall that fell today was probably one of the two walls meeting at this corner or the wall between the water and cog pits.

28.   Returnd to Dumfries on the above Arbitration.

29.   Employd therein. In the Evening went to a Play.

30.   Employed as above and abt. [   ] Oclock at Night finished all the business we coud at this meeting.

31.   Returnd home by my Mill & the Dam where my People were attempting to stop water.

The Dogue Run dam at the head of the millrace was apparently under construction, but the heavy rain that fell 29–30 Jan. had swollen the stream, making the job more difficult.

Acct. of the Weather in Jany.

Jan. 1.   Calm & very pleasant—being clear with all.

2.   Clear and very pleasant with but little Wind and that Southwardly.

3.   Still clear but a little Cooler Wind Shifting to the Northward.

4.   A little cool but pleasant notwithstanding being clear.

5.   Frosty Morning but clear with the Wind rather fresh from the Southwd.

6.   Clear forenoon & pleasant but gloomy Afternoon.

7.   Very Raw, Cold & Cloudy in the forenoon but clear afternoon.

8. A little Cool but clear and tolerably pleasant afterwards.

9. Clear and pleasant with but little Wind & that Southwardly.

10. Very pleasant and warm with but little Wind.

11. Much such a day as yesterday only a little Warmer.

12. Clear, Mild, and pleasant in the forenoon but lowering afterwards.

13. A little Rain last Night but clear again with the Wind at No. West.

14. Cold Morning, and hard frost. The Afternoon somewhat milder the Wind having got about to the Southward again.

15. A little Raw and Cold in the Morning altho the Wind was Southwardly. Afternoon very cloudy and threatning.

16. Constant Rain the whole day with the Wind high from the Eastward. In the Evening it Shifted to the Southward.

17. Clear & pleasant, the Wind what little there was of it being still Southwardly.

18. Ground froze—the Wind being tolerably fresh from the No. West and at times Cloudy. It was cold & Raw.

19. Ground very hard froze. Morng. clear & Cold. Wind (tho not much of it) at No. West. Midday and Afternn. clear & pleast. Wind Southwardly.

20. Ground hard froze. Morning Cloudy & Cold tho the Wind was Southwardly. Afternn. clear & pleast.

21. Clear and Calm forenoon with frozen Ground. Afternn. very lowering and like for falling Weather.

22. Rain the preceeding Night, and Snowing till near 2 Oclock with the Wind varying from East to North.

23. •Calm and Cloudy but not very cold. No frost this Morning.

24. No frost but calm and Cloudy all day.

25. Much such a day as yesterday but somewhat colder & Rawer.

26. Clear and a little Cool in the Morning. Ground frozen and wind (tho not much of it) Northwardly.

27. But a Slight frost and tolerably pleasant. Eveng. somewhat Cool.

28. Hard frost Wind Northwardly clear and Cold.

29. Very hard frost Afternoon lowering Cold and like for Snow.

30. A Great quantity of Rain fell last Night—a good deal the forepart of the day. Afternoon misting and tolerably warm.

31. Morning calm, clear, warm and pleasant but the Afternn. Cloudy cold and Windy from the No. West.

[February]

Where and how my time is Spent

Feby. 1st. At the Mill in the forenoon and afternoon. Doctr. Rumney came here before Dinner & stayd all Night.

2. At the Mill and where my People was at Work on the Race in the forenoon & afternoon. Mr. Rutherford & Price Posey came here in the Evening.

Robert Rutherford (1728–1803) was a prominent landowner and burgess from Frederick County. During the French and Indian War he had served for a time as a deputy commissary for the Virginia Regiment and in the fall of 1757, on the recommendation of GW, raised a partisan company called Rutherford's Rangers (GW to Robert Dinwiddie, 5 Oct. 1757, DLC:GW). After the war he married Mary Daubigny Howe, widow of a British army officer, and settled on Flowing Springs farm near Evitt's Run (BUSHONG, 436–37).

John Price Posey (d. 1788), a son of Capt. John Posey, began working about this time in Thomas Lawson's iron and flour business on Neabsco Creek. He was able to obtain the job because GW persuaded Lawson to hire him (Posey to GW, 25 May 1771, DLC:GW).

3.   Val. Crawford came this Afternoon & Price Posey went away in the Morng.

Young Posey was going to Annapolis and apparently carried a letter from GW to Jonathan Boucher, in which GW asked the tutor on behalf of Mrs. Washington to buy two ounces of ether for Patsy Custis, "if such a thing is to be had in Annapolis," and to send it by Price Posey on his return to Virginia (3 Feb. 1771, CSmH). Ether, like valerian and musk, was thought to be a strong antispasmodic, useful in treating epilepsy when taken internally in small doses (HOOPER, 383). It was not employed as an anesthetic until the next century.

4.   Mr. Rutherford Went away After breakfast. I rid to my Mill &ca. Docter Rumney came to Dinner & Doctr. Craik in the Afternoon. Both stayd all Night.

5.   The Gentlemen all went away. I rid to my Mill in the forenoon & Afternoon.

6.   Rid to my Mill by the Ferry in the forenoon, & afternoon. Price Posey came here this Evening.

THE FERRY: Capt. John Posey's ferry which GW had begun to rent 23 April 1770.

7.   Price Posey went away. I rid to the Mill, & Dam at the head of the Race in the forenoon & Afternoon.

8.   Rid to my Mill & Tumbling Dam in the Forenoon & Afternoon. Doctr. Rumney dind here & went away afterwds.

GW today paid the millwright John Ball the balance of his account, £66 4s. 3d., plus a bonus of 5 guineas. Ball's total bill, the other part of which had been advanced in installments during August and December, amounted to £101 2s. 6d., including £31 2s. 6d. for the wages of Ball and his five workmen. The remaining £70 covered the cost of several items of mill equipment that Ball sold GW: two pairs of millstones, hoisting gear for lifting barrels of grain and flour to upper floors of the mill, and two bolting chests, devices in which flour was sifted through fine-mesh cloth to separate it from bran and other impurities (LEDGER A, 324, 333).

9.   Attempted to go a hunting, but prevented by Rain. Rid to the Mill in the fore and Afternoon.

10.   At home all day. Mr. Val. Crawford came to Dinner.

11.   Rid by my Mill and Dam at the head of the Race on my way

to an Arbitration between John Graham and the Estate of Allan Macrae decd.

For the Graham-Macrae arbitration, see the main entry for 19 Dec. 1770.

12. At Colchester on the said Arbitration.

13. Ditto—at Ditto—on Ditto.

14. Ditto—at Ditto—on Ditto.

15. Ditto—at Ditto—on Ditto—in Company with Colo. Mason & Colo. T. Lee the other Arbitrators—Mr. T. Mason & Mr. Mercer the Attorneys.

Thomas Ludwell Lee (1730–1778), of Stafford County, one of the sons of Thomas and Hannah Ludwell Lee of Stratford Hall, lived at Belleview plantation on the south side of Potomac Creek, near the Stafford County court house (FITHIAN, 23). Educated in London at the Inns of Court, he was a burgess 1758–65 and was said to be "the most popular man in Virginia, and the delight of the eyes of every Virginian" (John Adams to Richard Bland Lee, 11 Aug. 1819, ADAMS [2], 10:382). But he had no desire to play a prominent role in public life, being by nature a man of "extreme indolence, especially in affairs th[a]t require some little trouble" (William Lee to Anthony Stewart, 1769, LEE [1], 219–20).

16. Still at Colchester upon the same business and in the same Company till 8 Oclock at Night.

17. Returnd home to Breakfast by my Mill Damn. Found my Brother Charles & one Mr. Thompson here who came on Friday last.

Mr. Thompson is probably William Thompson (d. 1793), of Stafford County, son of Rev. John Thompson (d. 1772) of St. Mark's Parish, Culpeper County. He was a student at the College of William and Mary 1762–63 and married Sarah Carter, daughter of Col. Charles Carter of Cleve, King George County (SLAUGHTER [2], 174–77; ST. PAUL'S, 141).

18. Those two Gentlemen went a Gunning & I rid to my Mill in the forenoon.

19. They went a Ducking and I again Rid to my Mill in the forenoon.

20. Rid to my Mill. Colo. Thos. Lee came here to Dinner. My Bro. & Mr. Thompson a Ducking.

21.   At home all day. Colo. Lee still here. The other Gentn. went a Ducking.

22.   Rid to my Mill in the forenoon. All the Gentlemen went away after Breakfast. Doctr. Rumney came in the Afternoon and stayed all Night.

23.   I rid to the Mill before breakfast and returnd to Dinner. Doctor Rumney went away after breakfast.

On the following day Rumney charged a package of valerian and "a vial of drops" to Patsy Custis's account (receipt from William Rumney, 24 June 1772, ViHi: Custis Papers).

24.   At Home all day—alone

25.   Rid to the Mill in the forenoon and Afternoon. Colo. Robt. Fairfax made a Morning Visit here.

26.   Detaind at home all day by bad Weather.

27.   Rid to my Mill in the Forenoon and Afternoon. Colo. Robt. Fairfax dined here.

28.   Rid to the Mill in the Forenoon. Mr. Ross and Mr. Peter Waggener came here in the Evening and stayed all Night.

Acct. of the Weather in Feby.

Feby. 1st.   Ground hard froze & day Cool, Wind being fresh from the No. West.

2.   Ground froze but not so cool, nor the Wind so fresh as yesterday. The Morng. Cloudy after a white frost but the Eveng. Clear & Wind South.

3.   Ground a little froze—day clear & pleasant with but little Wind.

4.   Wind pretty fresh & somewhat Raw from the Southward.

5.   Ground but little froze this Morng. but the Wind getting to No. West & blowing fresh it turnd very Cold.

6.   Very hard frost & keen Wind from the No[rth]ward, in the Morning. Midday tolerably pleasant Wind being Southwardly. Afternoon rather cool again the Wind getting to the East. The whole day tolerably clear.

7.   Ground hard froze. Morning very Cloudy with a fine mixture of Snow & Rain. Eveng. Clear calm & pleast.

8.   Frozen Morning & Cold. Midday Clear & Pleasant. Afternoon very Cloudy & Raining from the Eastward.

9.   Much Rain fell last Night, & some this Morning. About 9 Oclock the Wind Shifting to No. West blew violently all day & grew very Cold being sometime Cloudy.

10.   Wind still fresh and Cold from the No. West. Ground very hard froze.

11.   Ground very hard froze. The Weather Cool and Clear but not so Cold as yesterday.

12.   Rain in the Night. Wind exceeding high from the No. West & towards Evening very Cold.

13.   Last Night Colder than any Night we have had this year. Ground exceeding hard froze. Day clear & Wind still at No. West but not so Cold.

14.   Weather clear and frosty but more moderate Wind getting Southwardly.

15.   Tolerably calm and Still—what little wind blew was from the Southward. Weather clear, yet frosty.

16.   Snow about 3 Inches deep in the Morning & snowing all day from the Northward.

17.   Light Snow all the Morning with but little Wind. About 10 Oclock it came out of Northwest blew violent hard & dispersd the Clouds.

18.   Exceeding Cold and frosty with the Wind still at No. West but not so hard. Evening more moderate.

19.   Morning not very Cold. Midday pleasant but Evening Cold, Wind getting to No. West again.

20.   Exceeding Cold, & freezing Wind being high and piercing from the No. West.

GW on this date wrote Jonathan Boucher that it was "quite impossible . . . to cross the River in these Storms of wind." Ice was also hindering travelers (20–25 Feb. 1771, DLC:GW).

21.   Colder than yesterday—Wind being still in the same place & higher. River & every place closd blockd up.

22.   Wind still in the same place but not so fresh nor so cold.

23.   Day moderate with but little Wind but that Northwardly in the Morning—Southwardly afterwds.

24.   Morning Mild & lowering. Wind (what little stirg.) Southwardly. River opening fast. Afternoon Cloudy & sometimes dropping with Rain.

25.   No frost—forenoon clear, Warm & very pleasant. Afternoon very Cloudy but still warm. Wind Southwardly. Snow almost gone.

GW informed Jonathan Boucher in a postscript of this date that "now the River is so much choked with Ice as to render . . . passage precarious" (20–25 Feb. 1771, DLC:GW).

26.   Began Raining in the Night & kept constantly at it all day with the Wind fresh from No. East. Snow quite gone, and Ice also.

27.   Pleasant Morning but cloudy afterwards and sometimes Raining slowly. In the Evening clear, Wind blowing fresh from the Westward. No frost.

28.   Wind hard from the No. West, & growing very cold. Weather clear, & in the Evening Freezing, but no frost in the Morning.

[March]

Where & how my time is disposd of

Mar. 1.   Messrs. Ross and Wagener went away after breakfast. I rid to my Mill and Ditchers in the forenoon. In the Afternoon Doctr. Craik came.

Hector Ross today settled his current account with GW, paying him £89 9s. 5d. cash, much of which was owed as a result of an arrangement made at John Posey's sale in Oct. 1769 (LEDGER A, 276, 327, 333).

2.   The Doctr. & I set of for Winchester. Dined at Triplets and lodgd at Wests.

GW had called a meeting of the officers of the Virginia Regiment at Winchester on 4 Mar. to report on the trip down the Ohio River that he had made the previous fall (*Va. Gaz.*, P&D, 31 Jan., 7 Feb., and 14 Feb. 1771, and R, 31 Jan. 1771).

   TRIPLETS: the ordinary of James and William Carr Lane at Newgate (now Centreville). Since GW had last stopped there on 12 Sept. 1769, William Carr Lane had died, leaving the tavern and the other family enterprises to the care of James Lane and James's son-in-law Simon Triplett. A second cousin of Thomas and William Triplett of Fairfax County, Simon Triplett had married James Lane's daughter Martha in 1765 (MCDONALD, 474–76, 487–88).

3.   Dined at Barry's (on Shanondoah) and reached Greenway Court in the Afternoon where we stayd all Night.

Berry's ferry was on the Shenandoah River about eight miles east of Greenway Court. Joseph Berry had moved into this area about 1759, and by April 1767 he had taken over the ferry and a nearby ordinary from Joseph Combs. He continued to operate both until at least 1795. The Joshua Fry and Peter Jefferson map of 1755 and the Thomas Jefferson map of 1786 refer to the ferry as Ashby's ferry, but the Ashby family apparently was never connected with it (BERRY'S FERRY, 11–12).

4.   Reachd Winchester to Dinner according to Appointment with the Officers &ca. claimg. part of the 200,000 Acs. of L[an]d.

Before GW left Greenway Court, he obtained a grant from Lord Fairfax for the unclaimed land on Dogue Run he had surveyed on 24 Mar. 1770, a total of 20½ acres (Lord Fairfax's grant to GW, 4 Mar. 1771, Northern Neck Deeds and Grants, Book I, 187, Vi Microfilm). This land gave him control of most of the area around his new dams and upper millrace, but a portion of the race still infringed upon William Harrison's patent, a problem that was not resolved until he exchanged some small strips of land there with William Triplett 18 May 1785.

5.   At Winchester all day. Dined with Lord Fairfax.

Although scheduled for 4 Mar., the officers' meeting was actually held today. Besides GW and Dr. James Craik, only four officers or their representatives were present. After hearing GW's report and learning that William Crawford had begun to survey along the Great Kanawha River, they unanimously agreed that he should be instructed to finish his work there and then proceed as soon as possible to survey lands on the Tygart Valley River, a branch of the Monongahela. To cover Crawford's expenses, GW was authorized to advance him £80, collecting money for that purpose not only from officers but now for the first time from former rank-and-file members of the regiment also. Each field officer was assessed £11 5s., each captain £6 15s., each subaltern £4 10s., and each common soldier a fourth of a subaltern's share (minutes of the officers of the Virginia Regiment, 5 Mar. 1771, DLC:GW).

6.   Dined at my Lodging which was at Mr. Philp. Bushes and went home with my Br. Mr. Saml. Washington in the Eveng.

Philip Bush (1732–1812) reputedly offered the best accommodations in Winchester at his Golden Buck Inn, a handsome two-story stone building on Cameron Street. He was born in Mannheim, Germany, and settled in Winchester about 1762 (NORRIS [1], 178; GREENE [3], 127).

7.   At my Brothers all day writing Instructions & dispatches for Captn. Crawford the Surveyor of our 200,000 Acs. of Land.

8.   Ditto–About Ditto.

9.   Finished Ditto for Mr. Marcus Stephenson–who was to be the bearer of them. Mr. Dick & the two Mr. Nurses dined at my Brothers today.

Marcus Stephenson of Frederick County was a half brother of William Crawford. Mr. Dick is probably Charles Dick of Fredericksburg, who owned land on Patterson's Creek in Hampshire County (*Va. Gaz.*, P&D, 17 Oct. 1771). THE TWO MR. NURSES: James Nourse (1731–1784) and his son Joseph Nourse (1754–1841), who lived at Piedmont, about two miles east of Harewood. James Nourse was born in Herefordshire, Eng., and in 1753 married Sarah Fouace in London. They left London with their nine children in 1769 and settled at Piedmont a year later (LYLE, 8–10, 24).

10.   Dined at Mr. Nurses, & returnd to my Brother's in the Evening.

11.   Set of from my Brother's for Mr. Warnr. Washington's on my return Home.

12.   Left Mr. Washingtons, & crossing at Snickers's (where I eat an early Dinner) reach'd Leesburg betwn. 4 & 5 Oclock in the Afternoon.

Leesburg, founded in 1758, was the county seat of Loudoun County. The English traveler Nicholas Cresswell described the town in 1774 as "regularly laid off in squares, but very indifferently built and few inhabitants and little trade, tho' very advantageously situated, for it is at the conjunction of the great Roads from the North part of the Continent to the South and the East and the West" (CRESSWELL, 48).

13.   Reachd home, after being obliged to Ferry over goose Creek at Houghs Mill & coming Round by Ellzeys. Found Doctr. Craik here.

Hough's mill was owned by John Hough (d. 1797), of Loudoun County, a well-known surveyor who had settled in the area about 1744 (DLC:Toner Collection; WILLIAMS [1], 82). He was one of the original trustees of Leesburg, an agent for Robert Carter of Nomini Hall 1767–77 and collector of quitrents for Lord Fairfax from 1764 until at least 1773 (HENING, 7:236; MORTON [1], 279; LEDGER A, 199, 257; LEDGER B, 53).

ELLZEYS: probably the home of Lewis Ellzey, father of William and Thomasin Ellzey. Lewis, who was the first sheriff of Fairfax County, served as a Truro Parish vestryman 1744–48.

14.   Rid to my Mill & came home by Posey's. Captn. Adam dined here.

Although Robert Adam of Alexandria had been appointed a captain in the Fairfax County militia during 1768, GW usually refers to him in the diaries as Mr. Adam (Fairfax County Order Book for 1768–70, 36, Vi Microfilm). The Captain Adam who came today was probably Thomas Adam, who commanded the brig *Adventure* on several trading voyages out of the South Potomac Naval District 1766–68. The *Adventure* had apparently been owned jointly by Thomas and Robert Adam until this year, but now the two men were having a new vessel built to replace the *Adventure:* the ship *Martha,* which on 23 Dec. 1771 would make her maiden voyage from the South Potomac under the command of John Thomas Boucher (P.R.O., C.O.5/1350, f. 51; P.R.O., C.O.5/1449, f. 83; P.R.O., C.O.5/1450, ff. 10–12, 40; see main entry for 14 April 1771).

15.   Surveyed the Plantation at Posey's & came home to Dinner Plotting the Courses afterwards.

16.   Rid by Posey's to the Mill in the forenoon—at home afterwards.

17.   At home all day alone till the Evening when Doctr. Rumney came here.

18.   Rid to Posey's to lay of a fence before Breakfast & went to Court afterwards & stayd all Night.

The court met 18–22 Mar., but GW attended only the first two days. On this date Harrison Manley appeared before the justices as a third witness to GW's deeds from Valinda Wade, and the documents were ordered to be officially recorded in the county deed books (Fairfax County Order Book for 1770–72, 172–75, Vi Microfilm). However, GW was unable to take immediate possession of the land he had bought because John Barry refused to let the 193-acre tract be divided and soon planted his own crops on most of it. GW hired two lawyers to represent him against Barry and his son, but the case did not come before the court until 20 Aug. 1772 (Robert H. Harrison to GW, 10 Jan. 1772, DLC:GW).

19.   At Court all day. In the Afternoon came home, and found Majr. Jenefir, Mr. Boucher, & Jacky Custis here.

Jacky and his tutor had come at Robert Fairfax's request to see him before he returned to England. Fairfax shared Boucher's opinion that Jacky should tour Europe, and he had invited him to vacation at Leeds Castle during his stay abroad. The matter was probably discussed over dinner at Belvoir two days later, but still no definite decision was made about it (GW to Jonathan Boucher, 3 Feb. 1771, CSmH).

20.   At home all day (except before Breakfast when I rid to the Mill) with the above Company.

21.   Went with the above to Belvoir to Dinner & returnd in the Evening with Mr. Boucher and Jacky Custis.

22.   At home all day.

23.   Mr. Boucher went away after Breakfast. I rid to the Mill by Muddy hole & Doeg Run. Majr. Jenefir Mr. Saml. Gallaway & Mr. Thos. Ringold dined & lodgd here, as did Mr. B. Fairfax.

Samuel Galloway (d. 1785) was a prominent merchant from Anne Arundel County, Md. He lived with his invalid wife, Anne Chew Galloway, at Tulip Hill, an elegant house on the West River about ten miles south of Annapolis. A Quaker, he was, nevertheless, reputed to be "a man of opulence" and a great lover of horseflesh (TAYLOE, 90). Galloway's companion on this visit was either Thomas Ringgold (c.1715–1772), of Chestertown, Md., or his son Thomas Ringgold (c.1744–1776), also of Chestertown. The elder Ringgold had married Anna Maria Earle and was an active merchant who sometimes joined Galloway as a partner in the West Indian or Portuguese trades. Both he and Galloway dealt in a wide variety of commodities including tobacco, grain, lumber, wine, and slaves (BARKER [1], 98–100, 114, n.118). The younger Ringgold was married to Galloway's daughter Mary and was a merchant like his father.

24.   At home all day. Majr. Jenefir & Mr. Ringold went away after Breakfast & Mr. Fairfax after Dinner. Mr. Robt. Adam & Mr. M. Campbell dined here.

25.   Mr. Gallaway went away after Breakfast. I rid to my Mill and Dam both in the fore and afternoon.

26.   Rid to My Mill and Mill dam at the head of the Race in the forenoon (after going a hunting in the Morning). In the After-noon Rid to Posey's.

GW today provided Jacky Custis with £5 10s. for traveling expenses to An-napolis and Baltimore. A decision had been reached to allow Jacky to go to the latter place to be inoculated, but upon his departure sometime within the next few days, he had "so many doubts and difficulties" about the matter, that GW and Mrs. Washington "concluded nothing was more foreign from his Intention" (LEDGER A, 335; CUSTIS ACCOUNT BOOK; GW to Jonathan Boucher, 20 April 1771, CSmH).

27.   Dined at Colchester in my way to Dumfries on the Arbitra-tion between Doctr. Ross & Compa. & Mr. Semple. Supped at Grahams & lodgd at Mr. Montgomeres.

Graham's is probably the home of Dumfries merchant Richard Graham, but may be John Graham's home about 1½ miles southeast of town (MASON [2], 1:iv; VERME, 49, 126; W.P.A. [1], 94). GW recorded no tavern expenses for this stay in Dumfries.

28.   Upon the Arbitration all day with Colo. Mason—Mr. Mun-dell & Mr. Ross.

29.   Upon the Arbitration with the above Gentlemen as above.

30.   Ditto—Ditto—Ditto.

31.   Ditto—Ditto—Ditto.

Acct. of the Weather in March

Mar. 1st.   Ground hard froze. Wind fresh & Cold in the fore-noon—clear, calm, & warmer in the Afternoon.

2d.   Lowering & Cloudy Morning (with the Ground frozen & Wind at No. East) —all the Afternoon Snowing.

3.   Clear & Cool Wind being at No. West. Ground a little frozen.

4.   Still, Cool, & frosty. Weather clear & Wind at No. West.

5.   But little frost—day calm & the fore part of it clear, & very pleasant.

CALM: In the manuscript this word reads "clalm."

6.   Scarce any Frost. Morning clear, calm, & pleasant but the afternn. very lowering & like for Rain.

7.   Snowing all this day, and Night also, Wind appearing to be abt. No. Et.

8.   Still Snowing more or less all day. In the Night it began to Hail & sometimes Rain.

9.   Fine Snow with a mixture of Rain & then Snow. In the Night it Haild & Raind.

10.   Fine Misting Rain all the day with the Wind pretty fresh at No. Et. but thawing (it never having yet froze).

11.   Misting till abt. 12 Oclock then clearg. with the wind westwardly.

12.   Wind at No. West & pretty fresh, tho neither Cold & freezing.

13.   No Frost. Wind still continuing at North West pretty fresh with some Clouds. Snow all gone.

14.   Still Cloudy and the Wind fresh from No. West but no Frost.

15.   Pleasant Morning, but Cloudy afterwards With the Wind at No. West & cool but no frost in the Morning.

16.   Ground very hard froze. Morng. clear, and Wind cold from the No. West which blew hard all day & very piercing.

17.   Still at No. West & cold but neither so high or piercing as yesterday. Ground however froze hard.

18.   Ground but little froze, Wind still in the same Quarter but moderate, and tolerably pleasant.

19.   White frost but the Ground not froze. Morning clear, calm & pleasant, but Evening very lowering with the [wind] at South.

20.   Smoky, and more or less Cloudy with but little Wind and pleast.

21.   Clear and pleasant forenoon, with but little wind. Afternoon very cloudy & like for Rain.

22.   Raining more or less till the Afternoon, then tolerably clear but in the Night heavy Rain with thunder.

23.   Clear and pleasant with the Wind pretty fresh from the Northwest but not cold.

24.   Clear & very pleasant with but little Wind and that from the Southward.

25.   Clear, Warm, and pleasant with but little Wind and that Southwardly.

26.   Very Pleasant, clear, and Calm forenoon. Lowering Afternoon with great appearance of Rain but none of consequence fell.

27.   A little Cooler than yesterday but tolerably pleasant.

28.   Warm forenoon, and Afternoon With Rain, thunder, Lightning, & Wind.

29.   Flying Clouds with the Wind pretty fresh from the No. West & Cool.

30.   Wind Eastwardly & Cool with Rain more or less all day.

31.   But little wind. Misting & sometimes Raining all day.

Remarks & Occurs. in March

20th.   Began to Manufacture my Wheat with the Water of Piney Branch, which being insufficient to keep the Mill constantly at Work, & Country Custom coming in no great progress coud be made.

COUNTRY CUSTOM: Farmers from the local countryside were bringing their grain to GW's mill to be ground in exchange for a one-eighth toll (HENING, 6:58).

[April]

Where & how my time is Spent

April 1st.   Still at Dumfries upon the Arbitration between Doctr. Ross and Compa. & Mr. Semple, which was finished about 9 Oclock this Night.

2.   Got home to breakfast about 9 Oclock. Mr. Robt. Adam dined & lodgd Here. In the Afternoon, I rid to the Mill Race, Mill, & Posey's.

3.   At home all day. Lord Fairfax, the two Colo. Fairfax's, and Mr. Chas. Alexander dind here & went away afterwards.

4.   Lowering with the Wind very high from the Eastward wch. contd. all Night. Rid to my Mill—the Mill dam & fishing Landing in the forenoon & the two first again in the Afternoon. Mr. Hadan lodgd here.

5.   Rid to the Mill Dam and contd. there all day. Returnd home by the Mill.

6.   Rid to the Mill, the Mill Dam, & Fishing Landing before Dinner. Doctr. Rumney dind here.

7.   At home all day. Doctr. Rumney dined here and went away afterwds.

8.   Rid to my Mill Race & Mill before Dinner. Mr. Carson dined here.

Mr. Carson is probably Thomas Carson (died c.1772), merchant of Alexandria.

9.   Rid to the fishing Landing before Dinner, in the afternoon Doctr. Craik came here, and stayd all Night.

10.   Doctr. Craik went away in the Morning. I rid to the fishing Landing at Poseys. Mr. Magowan came here to Dinner and stayed all Night.

11.   Rid by Muddy hole to Doeg Run & from thence to the Mill. Mr. Magowan went this Afternn. to Colchester.

12.   Rid into the Neck & returned home by Muddy hole & Posey's.

13.   Rid to the Mill and to Poseys in the forenoon at home Afterwards.

14.   Went to Pohick Church & came home to Dinner Mr. Magowan with us. Found Mr. Adam, Mr. Campbell & Captns. Conway & Adam who Dined and went away afterwds.

Richard Conway (died c.1808), of Alexandria, had commanded merchant vessels sailing out of the Potomac River since 1765 and at this time was captain of the *Friendship,* a schooner owned by John Williams & Co. of Alexandria. The *Friendship* had returned from the West Indies on 3 April with a cargo of rum, molasses, and sugar (P.R.O., C.O.5/1449, f. 82; P.R.O., C.O.5/1450, f. 11; P.R.O., C.O.5/1349, f. 207).

15.   Went to Alexandria to Court. Stayd all Night. Mr. Magowan w[en]t.

The court met only on this day in April (Fairfax County Order Book for 1770–72, 205–8, Vi Microfilm).

16.   Came home to Dinner. Mr. Magowan & Mr. Pierce Baily came with me the latter went away afterwds.

Before returning to Mount Vernon, GW attended a meeting of the Fairfax nonimportation committee. At the request of two merchants, Alexander Henderson of Colchester and William Balmain of Alexandria, the committee examined the invoices for cargoes that had recently arrived from Glasgow and ruled that the merchants could properly accept them (*Va. Gaz.,* R, 18 July 1771).

17.   Rid to the Mill and fishing Landg. at Posey's in the forenoon. Majr. Wagener dined here & went away aftds.

GW today gave Hanson Posey 16s. drawn on the account of his father, John Posey, who was now living in Maryland (LEDGER A, 256, 335).

18.   At home all day.

19.   Rid to Muddy hole—Doeg Run, the Mill, & Posey's in the forenoon. Mr. Campbell dined here with Mr. Magowan.

20.   Rid to Muddy hole, Doeg Run & the Mill & came home by Posey's to Dinner. Mr. Magowan went away after Breakfast & Mr. Campbell dind here.

21. At home all day. Mrs. Fairfax din'd here and went away in the Afternoon.

22d. Rid by Muddy hole & Doeg Run to the Mill—from thence to the Fishing Landing at Posey & home to Dinner.

23. Rid to the Fishing Landing at Poseys & home to Dinner.

24. Rid with Mrs. Washington & Patcy Custis to the Fishg. Landing at Poseys & from thence I rid to the Mill & home to Dinner. Mr. Campbell dined here. Mr. Robt. Alexander came in the Evening.

25. Mr. Alexander & I rid to my Mill & then to the Fishg. Landing at Posey and came home to dinner after wch. he went away.

26. At home in the forenoon. In the Afternoon Rid by Muddy hole to Doeg Run from thence to the Mill & so home by the fishing Landing at Poseys.

27. Set out with Mrs. Washington & Patcy Custis on my journey to Williamsburg. Dined at Colchester & Suppd & lodgd in Dumfries.

Setting out only one day later than planned, the family traveled south in GW's chariot. The burgesses were not meeting this spring because they had no pressing business to consider. But GW had to go to Williamsburg to give the General Court his annual report on the administration of Jacky and Patsy Custis's affairs and to collect interest on various Custis bonds (CUSTIS ACCOUNT BOOK).

28. Dined at my Mother's and lodgd at Colo. Lewis's. Supped at my Brother Charles's.

29. Dined at Caroline Court House and lodgd at Hubbards Ordinary.

GW today recorded paying 2s. 6d. for repair of his chariot (LEDGER A, 335).

30. Breakfasted at Todds Ordinary and after making some considerable stop at Ruffins Ferry, occasioned by a Sick Horse—reachd Colo. Bassetts a little in the Night.

Acct. of the Weather in April

April 1st. Morning Calm, & Warm. Afternoon a little Windy from the No. West & cooler—day clear.

2d. Morning Cool Wind still Northwardly, the Weather clear, & tolerably pleasant.

3. Clear and the Wind variable, being Northwardly in the forenoon & Easterly afterwards.

4. Wind high and boisterous from the Eastward with great appearances of Rain (except being cold).

5. Wind in the same place all last Night & till 10 Oclock to day & as high. In the forenoon 2 or 3 hours close constt. Rain—then clear & pleast. Wind getting Westwardly.

6. Clear & tolerably pleasant Wind being Westwardly in the forenoon but Southwardly afterwards.

7. Clear in the forepart of the day but lowering afterwards. Wind very fresh from the So. West.

8. Rain in the Night and the Wind exceeding fresh from the No. West all day & Night & very Cold.

9. Ice this Morning & very cold. The Wind continuing all day in the same place but lying at Night.

10. Wind Southwardly and not fresh. Day Cloudy, & every now & then Raining tho' but little fell. In the Evening the Wind got to Northwest and blew fresh all Night.

11. Wind hard at No. West all day and Cold.

12. Wind still fresh and Cold from the West & No. West With a Muddy Sky.

13. Very Raw and Cold with but little Wind. Cloudy all day & sometimes Snowing, sometimes hailing & at other times Raining but little of any fell—most however of Rain.

14. Lowering in the Morning and calm. Clear afterwards with the Wind at No. West and tolerable fresh.

15. Clear and very Cold. Wind very high from the same point as yesterday.

16.   Wind still in the same quarter & high—also very Cold.

17.   Wind till about an hour or two by Son in the Morning was Southerly—then hard at No. West but not very cold—clear also.

18.   Calm and Cloudy in the Morng. then high Wind from the So. West after that at So. Et. with Rain.

19.   Calm & lowering Morning—every now and then dropping Rain, and Warm. Afternoon high Wind from the No. West & Cold.

20.   Cold, & boisterous Wind from the North West.

21.   Clear with the Wind at No. Wt. till the Afternoon then Calm & more moderate.

22d.   A Pleasant day & Warm—the Morning Calm. In the Evening Wind at So. East & somewhat threatning.

23.   Warm and very pleasant with the Wind Southerly & clear.

24.   Warm and very pleasant with but little Wind and that Southerly.

25.   Clear & very warm in the forenoon with but little Wind. The Afternoon Cloudy with the Wind fresh & Cold from the No. West.

26.   Cool all day Wind hanging to the Northward till the Afternoon when it shifted to the Eastward.

27.   Still Cool tho the Wind was Southerly & weather clear.

28.   Cool in the Morning, & Cloudy all day, with Appearances of Rain but none fell. Afternoon warmer.

29.   Cloudy Morning, but clear and Warm afterwards, with the Wind Southwardly.

30.   Lowering & like to rain all day but none fell. Wind Southwardly & Warm.

Remarks & Occs. in April.

5th.   Turn'd the Water of Doeg Run into my Mill Race, which seemd to afford Water enough for both Mills. One of which constantly employd in Grinding up my own Wheat.

With the new millrace and dams finished GW now had a gravitational force of water sufficient for his needs, but his water supply remained undependable. The millrace often froze in the winter and dried up in the summer. At other times freshets broke his dams and the sides of the race. The new mill could run only about half of each year. The two mills to which GW here refers are the two sets of millstones, each technically constituting a gristmill by itself, although both are in the same millhouse. When GW says "mill," he usually means the millhouse including both sets of stones or the small plantation surrounding the millhouse.

10.   Began to Haul the Sein, tho few fish were Catchd, & those of the Shad kind, owing to the coolness of the Weather. Many Shad had been catchd on the Maryland Shore.

11.   Obligd to send a hand to the Mill to Assist in Packing &ca.

GW's flour was being packed into large barrels and small casks for sale to Virginia merchants (LEDGER A, 326, 341; see "Remarks" entry for 6 June 1771).

17.   Began to Plant Corn at my Mill Plantation.

20.   Began to Plant Ditto at Muddy hole.

25.   Began Ditto at Doeg Run.
    The Herring began to run in large Shoals—but were checkd again by the Cool Weather.

Fishing on the Potomac must have soon improved, because by the end of May, GW had delivered 679,200 herring and 7,760 shad to Robert Adam's company. Despite the fact that some of the herring spoiled due to improper packing, he was credited with £134 4s. 3d. for the fish and £12 for rent of fish houses (LEDGER A, 326). This year Adam shipped GW's herring to Jamaica on board the brig *Adventure* now owned by Judson Coolidge of Maryland (P.R.O., C.O.5/1349, f. 208; Adam to GW, 24 June 1771, DLC:GW).

[May]

Where & how my time is spent

May 1st.   At Colo. Bassetts all day.

2.   Set out with Colo. Bassett for Williamsburg and reachd Town about 12 Oclock. Dined at Mrs. Dawson's & went to the Play.

At the theater, GW saw a performance by the American Company of Comedians, which had been in Williamsburg for more than a month (LEDGER A, 335; RANKIN, 159). Mrs. Campbell, with whom he lodged as usual, had by this date moved down Duke of Gloucester Street to "the COFFEE-HOUSE . . . next the Capitol." Owned by the heirs of Nathaniel Walthoe, late clerk of the General Assembly, it was soon to be offered for sale at public auction by the executor of the estate (*Va. Gaz.*, P&D, 16 May 1771). Mrs. Campbell's old place in the second block from the Capitol had been bought during the previous year by James Anderson, a blacksmith and gunsmith (GIBBS, 152–54; WILLIAMSBURG, 24–25).

3.   Dined at the Speaker's and went to the Play—after wch. Drank a Bowl or two of Punch at Mrs. Campbells.

4.   Dined at Mrs. Campbells (& paid for Dinner & Club) and went up to Eltham with Colos. Bassett & Lewis.

5.   At Eltham all day.

6.   Returnd to Williamsburg by 11 Oclock with Colo. Bassett & Colo. Lewis. Dined at Mrs. Vobes and Suppd at Anderson.

Robert Anderson (b. 1743) had opened a public house near the College of William and Mary in the fall of 1769 but in March of this year had moved to the Wetherburn Tavern, succeeding James Barrett Southall as its innkeeper. Anderson leased the tavern from Wetherburn's heirs and operated it until 1779 (GIBBS, 145–47).

7.   Dined at Mrs. Dawson's and Spent the Evening at Anderson's.

8.   Dined at Southalls with Colo. Robt. Fairfax & some other Gentlemn. & went to the Play &

In March, James Barrett Southall had moved his place of business from the Wetherburn Tavern across Duke of Gloucester Street to the Raleigh Tavern, which he bought from the executors of Anthony Hay's estate. Southall operated the Raleigh for at least the next ten years, and under his management it continued to be a popular place for social events, meetings, and auctions (GIBBS, 196–97).

The "&" at the end of this entry seems to connect it to the entry for the following day and may indicate that both entries, and possibly others for this trip, were written at a later date from memory or notes (DIARIES, 2:17).

9.   Dined at Mrs. Campbell's and Spent the Evening at Southalls with the Treasurer &ca.

10.   Dined at Mrs. Campbells & went to Bed early.

11.   Returnd to Eltham with Colo. Bassett, after dining at Mrs. Campbells.

12.   At Eltham all day except Ridg. to Colo. Bassetts Meadow at Roots's with him.

On this day Lund Washington sent GW the unhappy news that the mill was "once more in a bad way." The wall between the water and cog pits was falling down, allowing the floor of the mill, the forebay, and one of the waterwheel's supports to settle several inches. Grinding had to be stopped while the wall and forebay were temporarily braced with timbers. But, Lund reported, the wheat fields looked more promising than usual (ViMtV).

13.   Rid to the Brick House with Colo. Bassett and returnd to Dinner.

14.   Went into the Fields with Colo. Bassett a shooting–killd sevl. Hares &ca.

15.   Went up to the Plantations about Rockahock. Dined at Mrs. Chamberlaynes with Mrs. Washington & returnd to Colo. Bassetts in the Eveng.

Rockahock was the New Kent County neighborhood in which the Custis White House was located (John Parke Custis to GW, 11 Sept. 1777, ViHi). The Custis plantations in New Kent were Rockahock, Brick House, Old Quarter, and Harlow's, all belonging to Jacky Custis ("An Inventory of the Stocks As given in by the respective Overseers in the Month of December 1771, after the decease of Mr. Valentine," ViHi: Custis Papers). Rebecca Chamberlayne, widow of Edward Pye Chamberlayne (1725–c.1769), lived on the Pamunkey River about a mile from the White House.

16.   Dined at Mrs. Dangerfields with Colo. Bassetts Family & returnd in the Afternoon to Eltham.

Mrs. Hannah Daingerfield of New Kent County appears on Burwell Bassett's census list of 1782 as head of a household consisting of 2 whites and 33 blacks (HEADS OF FAMILIES, VA., 36). She was conducting her own financial affairs before 1776 (*Va. Gaz.*, D&H, 3 Aug. 1776).

17.   Visited my Plantation in King William. Dined at Colo. Bd. Moores & returnd to Colo. Bassetts in the Afternoon.

MY PLANTATION: Claiborne's plantation (see entry for 24 April 1760). Bernard Moore was now able to support his family only through the charity of friends. Having finally disposed of all his property to pay his debts, he had obtained use of some land at no cost and was working it with slaves who had been bought with money lent by several acquaintances, including GW who had provided £100 (Moore to GW, 12 Jan. 1771, and GW to Moore, 23 Jan. 1771, DLC:GW).

18. Rid to the Brick House with the Family. Hauld the Sein & returnd to Dinner after which went to Mr. Davis's & Drank Tea.

19. Went to Church & returnd to Colo. Bassetts to Dinner with other Compy. among whom were the two Mr. Dandridges.

The two Mr. Dandridges are probably William and Bartholomew Dandridge, Mrs. Washington's brothers.

20. Rid to the Brick House to see my Chariot & Horses (which were sent round to my Quarter) cross.

The Brick House ferry crossed the Pamunkey River to West Point in King William County (RICE, 2: pl. 104). MY QUARTER: Claiborne's plantation.

21. Set out for my Brothers at Nomony—crossing over to my Quarter, & so by Frazer's to Hobs Hole where we dined, & then crossing the [Rappahannock] River lodged at Mr. Josh. Lanes.

MY BROTHERS: John Augustine Washington's home, Bushfield. Joseph Lane (d. 1786), a younger brother of James and William Carr Lane of Newgate, lived at Nomini Forest in Westmoreland County and was the deputy collector of customs for the South Potomac Naval District (MCDONALD, 468–77; *Va. Gaz.*, P&D, 25 Feb. 1773).

22. Reached my Brothers pretty early in the day.

23. Rid with him to his Mill, and to Mr. Carters New Mills at the head of Nomony. Returnd to Dinr.

John Augustine Washington's mill stood on a branch of the Nomini River, about six miles upstream from Bushfield and about half a mile east of Robert Carter's house, Nomini Hall (FITHIAN, 109). It was during this month that Carter returned from Williamsburg with his family to resume living at Nomini Hall. He had decided recently to expand his flour-manufacturing facilities, and a short distance west of his house, where another branch of the Nomini flowed, he was apparently having a "Double Mill"—that is, a mill with two waterwheels—built or rebuilt along with a two-oven bakery (*Va. Gaz.*, R, 19 Nov. 1772; EATON, 55; MORTON [1], 178–80).

Nomini Hall, home of Robert Carter. (Colonial Williamsburg Photograph)

24. Dined at Mr. John Smiths at Cabbin Point. Returnd to my Brothrs. in the Afternoon.

25. Dined at the Revd. Mr. Smiths and returnd to my Brother's again in the Evening.

26. Dined at Mr. Booths and proceeded to Mrs. Washington's of Popes Creek in the Afternoon.

27. Stayed there all day.

28. Set out after Breakfast. Dined at Mr. Burdett Ashtons and continued on Afterwards to Mr. Lawrence Washington's.

Burdett Ashton (1747–1814) was a son-in-law of Anne Aylett Washington, having married her daughter Ann Washington (1752–1777) in 1768.

29. Stayed at Mr. Washington's all day. Good deal of Company dining there.

30.   Reachd home—crossing at Boyd's hole to the Widow Martin's Landing & pass by Nangemoy Church & the Widow Elbecks to my own Ferry. Found Jacky Custis there.

WIDOW MARTIN'S LANDING: In 1774 Nicholas Cresswell visited "Mrs. Marsden, a widow lady in the neighbourhood" of Nanjemoy, Md. (CRESSWELL, 17). The Nanjemoy (Durham) Parish Church, built 1732–36, stood a few miles northwest of Nanjemoy, near present-day Ironsides, Md. (RIGHTMYER, 142–43). Sarah Edgar Eilbeck (d. 1780), widow of the merchant and planter William Eilbeck (d. 1765) and mother-in-law of George Mason, lived at the head of Mattawoman Creek about three miles southeast of present-day Mason Springs, Md. (W.P.A. [2], 489).

Jacky's presence at Mount Vernon was an occasion for some rejoicing. Without informing his mother or GW he had changed his mind about smallpox inoculation, had been inoculated in Baltimore 8 April, and was now fully recovered "without hardly one Mark to tell that He ever had it" (Jonathan Boucher to GW, 9 May 1771, DLC:GW).

31.   Rid to Muddy hole—Doeg Run & the Mill before Dinner. In the Afternoon Vale. Crawford came here & went away again in the Morning.

Acct. of the Weather in May

May 1st.   Wind tolerably fresh from the South East, with appearances of Rain but none fell.

2.   Cloudy Morning and Warm with the Wind fresh from the Southward.

3.   Warm, with appearances of Rain but none fell. Wind Southerly.

4.   A little Cool. Wind Northwardly.

5.   Clear & Cool. Wind in the same place.

6.   Clear—the Wind getting Southerly again the Air grew warmer.

7.   Warm (but not Hot) —the Sky Muddy & thick.

8.   Raining in the Morning, & more or less all day. With but very little Wind.

9.   Clear and pleasant Morning with the Wind Westwardly. In the Evening thunder Lightning & Rain.

10.   Clear and pleasant with the Wind Westwardly.

11.   Clear forenoon—little like Rain afterwards with the Wind Eastwardly & cold.

12.   Cold all day, and Cloudy.

13.   Still Cold with the Wind fresh from the Northward.

14.   Much such a day as yesterday Wind being in the same place.

15.   Morning clear, but Afternoon like for Rain; Wind fresh from the Westward.

16.   Clear, Calm, and Warm. What little wind stirrd was from the Eastward.

17.   Wind still Eastwardly & pretty fresh.

18.   Wind in the same place and somewhat cooler. In the Eveng. a great appearance of Rain but none fell at this place.

19.   Warm with but little Wind. In the Afternoon great appearances of Rain, but none fell here. Thunder & lightning in the Night.

20.   Wind still Southerly and Warm with great appearances of Rain but none fell here. In the afternoon the Wind blew very fresh from the Southwest.

21.   Still warm, with the Wind Southerly and showery in places.

22.   Morning lowering but clear afterwards, and warm. In the Afternoon showers.

23.   Cloudy, & like to Rain—also warm wind being still Southerly.

24.   Wind in the same place. The Weather clear and pleasant, but a little Warm, especially in the Afternoon.

25.   Wind very fresh from the So. West all the forenoon. In the afternoon it was Easterly and Raining.

26.   Cloudy all the Morning with the Wind Eastwardly & cool. Afternoon something clearer & warmer.

27.   Wind Southerly & Morning Raining. Afternoon clear & warm.

28.   In the Morning early, Rain–then clear & warm. After that Rain with the Wind at No. & Cold.

29.   Wind Northwardly & very Cold notwithstanding the weather was clear.

30.   Clear, & not so cool as yesterday, being calm & still after the Morning.

31.   Clear and Warm–Wind being Southwardly.

[June]

Where & how my time is Spent

June 1st.   Rid into the Neck and to the Mill before Dinner. In the Afternoon a Mr. Debutts of Maryland came & stayd all Night.

John De Butts was a wealthy planter from St. Mary's County, Md.

2.   After Breakfast Mr. Debutts went away, and in the afternoon Mr. Wagener the younger came here & stayed all Night.

3.   Mr. Wagener went away after Breakfast. I rid to the Mill & Plantation at Posey's before Dinner.

4.   At home all day without Compa.

5.   Ditto. Mr. Matthw. Campbell came in the Afternoon & stayed all Night.

6.   Mr. Campbell went away after Breakfast, & Jacky Custis re-turnd to Annapolis. Mrs. Washington Patcy Custis & myself Dined at Belvoir.

Jacky's departure from home had been briefly delayed so that his laundry could be done. He returned to school with £2 8s. Virginia currency to use as personal pocket money and £50 Maryland currency from which the bills for his inoculation and living expenses at Baltimore were to be paid (GW to Jonathan Boucher, 5 June 1771, WRITINGS, 3:42–46; LEDGER A, 337).

7.   Rid to Muddy hole, Doeg Run and the Mill before Dinner.

8.   Rid to the Plantn. at the Ferry—then into the Neck, & so home to Dinner, by Muddy hole.

Henceforth, GW usually refers to Capt. John Posey's former plantation, all of which he now controlled either by purchase or rental, as Ferry plantation, the ferry there being its most distinctive feature.

9.   At home all day.

10.   Rid to Ferry Plantation—Mill—Doeg Run & home by Muddy hole to Dinner.

11.   At home in the forenoon. In the afternoon Rid by the Ferry Plantation to the Mill and back.

A nineteenth-century drawing of the new mill, probably completed in late 1770, and the miller's house built in 1771. (National Archives)

12. At the Mill in the forenoon & Afternoon Inspecting and delivering Flour to Messrs. Robt. Adam & Co.

See agreement with Adam & Co. under "Remarks" entry for 6 June 1771.

13. At the same place as yesterday & on the same business till Dinner. Colo. Fairfax & Lady dined here.

14. Clear & Cool. Rid to the Mill and the Plantation at the Ferry. In the afternoon Doctr. Craik came here.

15. Doctr. Craik went away after Breakfast. I rid as far as the Ferry with him afterwards was at the delivery of Flour at my Fish Ho[use] Landing.

16. At home all day. My Brother Jno. Came here to Dinner & Majr. Waggener in the Afternoon.

17. At home all day both the above Gentlemen here—the last of whom Sick.

18. Went up to Alexandria & returnd in the Afternoon Mr. Magowan with me. My Brothr. went in the Morning.

GW went to Alexandria for a meeting of the Fairfax nonimportation committee, which had been asked by Alexander Henderson and William Balmain to judge two new shipments of goods. Only 12 hats sent by mistake of the manufacturer were found to be unacceptable, and the committee was convinced that Henderson and Balmain had "strictly adhered to the spirit and intention of the association" for their part. But the two merchants complained "that they found so little regard paid to the association by others . . . that they should think themselves obliged for the future" to protect their businesses by sending "their orders in the same manner with other importers; restraining themselves only from importing tea, and other taxed articles" (*Va. Gaz.*, R, 18 July 1771).

19. Major Wagener went away this Morning. I rid to Muddy hole & Doeg Run Plantation's.

20. Rid to the Mill and Ferry Plantations. Mr. Magowan went to Colchr.

21. Mr. Robt. Adam came here in the Morning to Breakfast & went with me to Mr. French's Funeral. Mr. Magowan came here with me to Dinner where we found Mr. Stedlar.

Robert Adam today brought GW an initial payment of £300 for the flour he had agreed to buy on 6 June. Further cash payments totaling £201 6d. were made in October and November, and the balance was credited to GW's general account with Adam's company (LEDGER A, 340, 345, 347).

Although Daniel French had died 25 May, the public funeral sermon was apparently not preached until this day. The services may have been held at the still-unfinished new Pohick Church, the construction of which French had been directing before he died. French's grave is in the churchyard there.

22.   Mr. Magowan returnd to Maryland. I rid to Muddy hole and into the Neck.

23.   Went to Pohick Church and returnd home to Dinner.

24.   At Home all day—writing.

25.   Rid by the Ferry Plantation to the Mill from thence to Doeg Run Quartr. & home by Muddy hole.

26.   At home all day Writing.

27.   At home all day Writing. Miss Nancy McCarty came in the Afternoon.

28.   Rid by the Ferry Plantation & Mill to Doeg Run Quarter & Meadow. Returnd home by Muddy hole Plantn.

29.   Rid to Ferry Quarter Mill and Muddy hole.

30.   At Home all day. Miss Nancy Peake &ca. dined here as did Price Posey & went away in the Afternoon as Miss Nancy McCarty also did.

Acct. of the Weather in June

June 1st.   Clear and Warm—Wind being Southerly.

2.   Also clear and pleasant—with but little Wind and that Southerly.

3.   Warm, but clear, with little Wind & that Southerly.

4.   Wind Easterly & pretty fresh. Evening Cool.

5.   Very foggy Morning, then Rain with thunder and Lightning. Afternoon very Cloudy.

6.   Clear but very Warm with the Wind Southerly. Foggy Morning.

7.   Very warm in the forenoon with Thunder & lightning & great appearances of Rain every[where] but none fell here. This Morning also.

The manuscript reads "great appearances of Rain every Rain every but none fell here."

8.   Lowering Morning, and very warm day with Clouds & appearances of Rain in the Evening.

9.   Dull foggy Morning & Afterwards warm—with black clouds & a little Rain in the Afternoon.

10.   Clear & Warm—with very little [wind] & that Southerly. Appearances of Rain but none fell here.

11.   Clear and tolerably pleasant with but little Wind.

12.   Pretty smart & constant Rain in the forenoon. Afternoon clear with the wind Northwardly.

13.   Clear and Cool—Wind Northwardly.

14.   Clear and Cool—wind being still Northwardly but pleasant Notwithstanding.

15.   Clear in the Morning, but Cloudy afterwards and Warm, with appearances of Rain. Wind Eastwardly.

16.   Rain in the Night, & till 8 or Nine Oclock this Morning; then clear, and Warm. Wind Eastwardly.

17.   Misting, of and on all day with the Wind still to the Eastward.

18.   Much such a day as yesterday, till the Evening then the Wind Shifting to the Northward it grew cool.

19.   The Morning Cool—the Afternoon warm, there being little or no Wind; day rather Cloudy & Lowering.

20. A good deal of Rain fell last Night and this Morning. Wind Easterly.

21. Clear & Warm. Wind Southerly. In the Night Rain again.

22. Clear and something Cooler—Wind getting Westwardly.

23. Clear and Warm wind Southerly in the Night Rain.

24. Cloudy & Lowering. In the Evening Raining moderately.

25. Cloudy and like for Rain all day, but none fell. Still and very Warm.

26. Calm & very warm the first part of the day. The Latter part Raining with variable Wind.

27. Foggy Morning—close & still day, & very warm.

28. Dewey Morning, close still and Smoky—also very warm.

29. Dewey Morning and very Warm in the Afternoon two or three Showers of Rain.

30. Cool Morning with the Wind at North West. All the Afternoon showery.

Remarks & Occurs. in June

June 1st.   Morris at Doeg Run Quarter Planted his Swamps with Corn.
Finished breaking up Corn Ground at Muddy hole.
Only half done in the Neck but quite finishd at Doeg Run.

6. Sold all the Flour I have left to Robt. Adam & Co. at the following Rates—fine flour at 12/6 Midlings at 10/. & Shipstuff at 8/4 pr. Ct. £300 of the Money, to be paid in Octr.—the residue in April with Int[eres]t from Octr.

In May the company had bought about 13,500 pounds of GW's flour for £60 7s. 10d., and during June it bought about 128,000 pounds more for £765 3s. 7d. (LEDGER A, 326, 341). Over three-fourths of this flour was of fine quality, that is, finely ground and relatively free of bran and impurities. The rest consisted of middlings, a coarse medium-grade flour containing some bran, and ship stuff, the lowest quality of flour, containing much bran. Adam & Co. may have used some of GW's flour for local sale or for making bread at the company's bakery, but much of it, especially the fine flour, must have been exported as it was. The brig *Adventure* sailed from the Potomac for Jamaica with 200 barrels of flour on 8 July, and the ship *Nancy* of Philadelphia, which left for Lisbon on the same day, carried 2,269 barrels of flour (P.R.O., C.O.5/1349, f. 208).

During the spring GW also sold flour to two Norfolk merchants. Philip Carberry, a baker, bought 1,432 pounds of ship stuff for £5 19s. 4d., and William Chisholm, who traded with the West Indies, purchased 36,997 pounds of fine flour for £236 19s. 8d. (LEDGER A, 336, 338; Lund Washington to GW, 12 May 1771, ViMtV).

7.   Agreed with Mr. Pendleton of Frederick for all the Land to be Included by a Line to be run from the No. West C[orne]r of Owen Thomas's Patent to a Corner of the Land on which James McCarmick lives in my Line supposd to contain abt. 180 Acres for £400 the Money to be paid in two years with Int[eres]t from the 25th. of next Decr. This years Rent to be paid to me & only a special Warrantee to be given with the Land.

Got done breaking up my Corn Ground at the Mill.

GW is agreeing to sell Philip Pendleton (1752–1802) a small part of his Bullskin plantation. A contract was not signed until 7 Dec. 1771, but the terms remained unchanged. Owen Thomas's patent for 400 acres, which GW had surveyed 3 April 1750, adjoined GW's land on the south and east. Pendleton had previously bought all or part of this patent from Thomas (Northern Neck Grants and Deeds, Book-H, 88, Vi Microfilm; CHAPPELEAR [2], map facing p. 56).

9.   The Appearances of the Weather, for sevl. days past, has given the greatest room to apprehend the Rust—the Mornings close, foggy, and Calm; the Evenings Cloudy & sometimes Raining—Heavy Dews at Nights & Warm Sultry days.

11.   Finished Breaking up Corn Ground at the Ferry Plantation.

15.   Finished Ditto in the Neck.

24.   Began to cut grass at Doeg Run Quarter.

25.   Discoverd the Rust bad in the Wheat at the Mill. My Wheat every where being much Injurd by the Speck or Spot.

Finished Cutting the Meadow at Doeg Run—6 Scythe men being employd each day.

27. Finishd Plowing over my Corn at Muddy hole a 2d. time and got all over it with the Hoes at the same time.

28. Finishd Securing my Hay at Doeg Run.
    Also got over all but the last Cut of Corn in the Neck with the Plows and Hoes.

29. Got over all my Corn at Doeg Run twice with the Hoes and Plows.

[July]

Where & how my time is Spent

July 1. Rid into the Neck to my Harvest People, & back to Dinner. Mr. Robt. Rutherford came in the Afternoon & went away again.

2. Rid to the Harvest Field in the Neck & back to Dinner.

3. Rid to the Harvest Field in the Neck by the Ferry & Muddy hole Plantations. In the Afternoon Mr. Jno. Smith of Westmoreland came here.

John Smith of Cabin Point, the smallpox inoculator, was going to Warm Springs in Frederick County, apparently for his health, which by fall was so bad that "everyone expected to have the burying of him into whose house he came" (GW to Samuel Washington, 6 Dec. 1771, excerpt, Parke-Bernet Galleries Catalogue, 11 June 1941, Item 578).

4. At home all day with Mr. Smith. In the Afternoon Jno. Custis came.

Jacky probably brought GW the letter that Jonathan Boucher wrote to him on this date, asking for a final decision about the proposed European tour (DLC:GW). GW replied five days later that he thought that Mrs. Washington was so reluctant to part with her son for a long period, and Jacky was so indifferent about the trip, that "it will soon be declared he has no inclination to go" (9 July 1771, DLC:GW). Boucher did not again raise the subject.

5. Mr. Smith set out after breakfast on his journey to the Frederick Sprgs. In the Afternoon I rid to the Harvest Field in the Neck.

6. Writing the forepart of the day. In the afternoon Rid to the Harvest Field at Muddy hole.

7. At Home all day. Mr. Alexr. Ross of Pittsburg and Mr. George Digges dined here & went away in the Afternoon.

Alexander Ross, a Scottish merchant who settled in Pittsburgh in 1763, served as the supplier to the Fort Pitt garrison. When the fort was abandoned by the British army in 1772 Ross bought the buildings. Like GW, he was heavily involved in western lands.

8. Went to a Vestry held at the New Church at Pohick. Doctr. Rumney & Mr. Robt. Harrison came home with me.

After Daniel French's death, responsibility for completing the new church devolved on his executor, George Mason. The work was apparently going well, for the vestrymen today had only a few small changes to request of Mason. Finding that the stone used at the corners of the building's brick walls was "coarse grain'd and rather too soft," they ordered it to "be painted with white Lead and Oyle." They also stipulated "that the rub'd Bricks at the returns of all the Windows ought to be painted as near as possible the same colour with the Arches" and that the dimensions of the altarpiece, which had been incorrectly given in the contract with French, should be "according to the true proportions of the Ionic order" of architecture (Truro Vestry Book, 148–49, DLC).

9. Doctr. Rumney & Mr. Harrison went away after Breakfast. In the Afternoon I rid to my Harvest People.

10. Mr. Jno. Custis returnd to Annapolis. I remaind at home all day writing my Invoices.

These invoices were apparently for goods that GW wished to order from Robert Cary & Co. and other English merchants (see main entry for 20 July 1771).

11. Rid by the Plantation at the Ferry & Mill to my Harvest Field at D. Run. In the Afternn. Messrs. Watson & West came.

12. I set of for Williamsburg & crossing at Laidlers lodgd at Mr. Lawe. Washingtons.

GW was going to attend the House of Burgesses, which had convened 11 July to deal with problems resulting from a great flood that had come down the James, Rappahannock, and Roanoke rivers in late May, causing about 150 deaths and much property damage. The calamity had not affected Mount Vernon or the Custis lands, but many Virginia planters had lost both their recently planted tobacco crop and the harvested tobacco they had stored in public warehouses for shipment to England. Prompt financial relief was needed to save those men from bankruptcy. GW delayed his departure from home, because he apparently knew that the first few days of the session would be devoted to ceremonial and organizational matters and he preferred to use that time to continue supervising his wheat harvest (FREEMAN, 3:273–74). Only 55 of the 118 burgesses were recorded as present at this session (H.B.J., 1770–72, 113–14).

Laidler's ferry landing on the Potomac River was about 14 miles below Port Tobacco, Md. In 1755 a ferry was authorized to cross the Potomac between Lawrence Washington's land in the Chotank neighborhood of Stafford (now King George) County and "the land opposite thereto," in Maryland (HENING, 6:494).

13.   Dined at Leeds Town & reachd Todds Bridge.

Leedstown, founded 1742, was a tobacco port on the Rappahannock River in King George (now Westmoreland) County.

14.   Breakfasted at King Wm. C[our]t Ho[use] Dined at Ruffins and reachd Colo. Bassetts.

15.   Came to Williamsburg abt. 10 Oclock. Dined at Mrs. Campbells—spent the Evening in my own Room.

GW may have arrived too late to attend the House of Burgesses today; during this session the burgesses were sitting at 9:00 A.M. to avoid the midday heat, and this day's meeting was apparently a brief one. The matter of flood relief had been referred 12 July to a committee that was to determine as nearly as possible how much tobacco had been lost in the public warehouses, but it was not yet ready to report (H.B.J., 1770–72, 123–27).

Later this day at the Capitol there was a general meeting of the Virginia association, at which GW was probably present. Responding to complaints from Fairfax and Fauquier counties about unequal enforcement of the current agreements, the associators decided in the future to prohibit the importation of only "Tea, Paper, Glass, and Painters Colours of foreign Manufacture, upon which a Duty is laid for the Purpose of raising a Revenue in America" (*Va. Gaz.*, P&D, 18 July 1771).

GW lodged with Mrs. Campbell.

16.   Dined at the Speakers spent the Evening in my own Room.

17.   Dined at the Treasurers. Supd at Mrs. Campbell's.

18.   Dined and Supped at Mrs. Campbell's.

19.   Dined at Mrs. Campbells & Spent the Evening at Southalls.

The flood relief bill was presented to the burgesses today, and after several amendments were made, it was ordered to be engrossed for a final reading. The bill as amended authorized the issuance of up to £30,000 in treasury notes for payment of planters' claims, which were to be examined and approved by a commission appointed for that purpose. Taxes for redeeming the notes were to be in effect 25 Oct. 1771 to 25 Oct. 1775 (H.B.J., 1770–72, 136–38; HENING, 8:493–503).

20. Dined at Mrs. Dawsons & spent the Evening in my own Room.

The House of Burgesses passed the flood relief bill on its final reading this morning, and having accomplished the main purpose of this session, it was prorogued (H.B.J., 1770–72, 138–40).

GW today dispatched his orders for goods to Robert Cary & Co. and other English merchants. Included in them were many luxuries that he had apparently postponed buying while the nonimportation agreements were in full effect: expensive shoes and boots, fine silk and broadcloth clothing, "a man's very best Bear. Hat," a leather portmanteau and saddle of the very best quality, and two seals made of "Topaz or some other handsome stone . . . w[it]h the Washington Arms neatly engraved thereon" (GW to John Didsbury, 18 July 1771, GW to Thomas Gibson, 18 July 1771, and GW to Cary & Co., 20 July 1771, DLC:GW).

21. Set out early in the Morning for Colo. Bassetts & arrivd there abt. 10 Oclock.

22. Left Colo. Bassetts before Sunrise. Breakfasted at King Wm. Ct. House—dined at Todds bridge & lodgd at Hubbards.

23. Breakfasted at the Caroline Court House & Reachd Fredericksburg before two Oclock & dined and lodgd at Colo. Lewis's.

24. At Fredericksburg all day. Dined & Supped at Mr. Dicks.

25. Dined at Colo. Lewis's & went to the Play.

The American Company of Comedians had been performing in Fredericksburg every Tuesday, Wednesday, and Thursday since late May, when it had come to take advantage of the crowds at the town's annual June fair (*Va. Gaz.*, P&D, 16 May 1771). The plays may have been staged in the county courtroom, a warehouse, or the 44-by-25-foot billiard room of George Weedon's tavern (RANKIN, 160; KING [2], 246–47).

26. Breakfasted at my Mother's. Dined at Dumfries & lodgd at Home.

27. At Home all day.

28. Ditto.   Ditto.

29.   Rid to the Ferry Plantation the Mill—Doeg Run & Muddy hole & returnd to Dinner.

30.   Rid into the Neck and to the Carpenters—also to the Mill Plantation.

CARPENTERS: See "Remarks" entry for 29 July 1771.

31.   Rid to the Ferry Plantation to the Mill—Doeg Run and Muddy hole.

Acct. of the Weather in July

July 1st.   Tolerable cool all day with Clouds. Wind Northwardly in the Morning, & Eastwardly in the Afternoon.

2.   Cloudy all day with the Wind at East, and light Showers in the Afternoon. Cool & pleasant—in the Night a good deal of Rain.

3.   For the most part clear and warm with but little wind and that in the Morning Northerly in the Afternn. Southerly.

4.   Clear, calm, and rather warm in the Afternoon Cloudy but no Rain.

5.   Warm Morning but cooler Afterwards. Wind fresh from the Southwest.

6.   Cool & Cloudy all day with light showers now & then & Wind Southerly.

7.   Clear and tolerably pleasant with but little wind and that Southerly.

8.   Very Warm but clear with the Wind Southerly.

9.   Very Warm with Clouds & a light Shower of Rain.

10.   Cloudy for the most part of the day with a pretty smart Shower & Wind from the Westward.

11.   Very Warm in the forenoon with a good deal of Rain in the Afternoon and Night.

12.   Cloudy, & Misting forenoon. Hot Noon, & Rainy afternoon where I was at Hoes.

13.   Cloudy forenoon & midling pleasant but very Hot afternn.

14.   Still, & very warm in the Forenoon. In the Afternoon much Rain & Wind from the So. West. At Colo. Bassetts.

15.   Something Cooler in the forenoon with Rain. Afternoon Warm.

16.   Clear and Warm. Wind, what little there was, Southerly.

17.   Clear and something Cooler. Wind in the Evening Easterly.

18.   Cooler than Yesterday Wind from the Eastward & fresh.

19.   Warm with appearances of Rain but none fell.

20.   Still Warmer with but little Wind & that at South.

21.   Very Warm the Wind in the same Quarter.

22.   Clear & the Sun very hot but a pleasant breeze from the Westwd.

23.   Clear forenoon with a fresh breeze from the So. West. Afternoon and Night very rainy.

24.   Raining more or less all day sometimes very hard but little wind.

25.   Much such a day as yesterday but not quite so much rain.

26.   Misty Morning. Rainy Evening & cloudy all day.

27.   Clear and warm. Wind Southerly.

28.   Clear and warm forenoon Rainy Afternoon. Wind Southerly.

29.   Clear forenoon & very warm but Cloudy afternoon no Rain however fell here.

30.   Clear and Warm Wind being Southerly.

31.   Just such a day as yesterday.

Remarks & Occurs. in July

July 1.   Began my Wheat Harvest in the Neck. Work'd Ten Cradles 8 of which were my own Negroes. Cut down the 50 Acre Cut upon Carneys Gut next the House.

5.   Finishd the Wheat in the Neck abt. two Hours by Sun in the Afternoon.

6.   Finishd going over my Corn in the Neck the 2d. Time.
     Also Began my Harvest at Muddy Hole this day.

9.   Finish'd Cutting & Securing my Wheat at Muddy hole abt. 4 Oclock in the Afternoon and removd my People to Doeg Run.

12.   Left home for Williamsburg to the Assembly.

18.   Finish'd Cutting and Securg. all my Wheat.

19.   Began to Cut the Meadow at the Mill.

27.   Finishd Curing Do. Weather being very unfavourable.

29.   Three Carpenters belonging to the Estate of Colo. Steptoe (hired of Jas. Hardige Lane at £7 pr. Month) came to work here.

These carpenters were apparently engaged to build a house for GW's miller, but they may have done other construction or repair work. Col. James Steptoe (died c.1757), of Hominy Hall, Westmoreland County, was father of Anne Steptoe Washington, fourth wife of GW's brother Samuel. Steptoe's estate included, besides his Hominy Hall plantation, several hundred acres of land near Mount Vernon. James Hardage Lane (d. 1787), a prominent Loudoun County planter, may have been leasing that Fairfax County land and the laborers on it from Steptoe's executors or their agents (will of James Steptoe, 10 May 1755, Westmoreland County Deeds and Wills, Book 13, 95–98, Vi Microfilm; General Index to Fairfax County Deeds, 1742–97, 119, Vi Microfilm). GW paid Lane £17 6s. 6d. for hire of the carpenters on 24 Dec. 1771 (LEDGER A, 350).

30.   Sowed Turneps at Home House.

31.   Began to Sow Wheat at Muddy hole Plantation.

[August]

Where & how my time is Spent

August 1st.   Rid to Muddy hole the Mill and where the Carpenter's were at Work.

2.   At home all day a writing Letters & Advertisements of Harry who run away the 29th. Ulto.

GW spent £1 16s. to recover this slave, who apparently was soon returned to Mount Vernon (LEDGER A, 340; list of GW's tithables, 10 June 1772, DLC: Toner Collection).

3.   Rid to the Mill—Muddy hole & Neck.

4.   Went to Pohick Church, and came home to Dinner.

Old Pohick Church continued to be used for regular worship services until 15 Feb. 1774, when the vestry officially accepted the new church for use of the parish (Truro Vestry Book, 160, DLC).

5.   At home all day. Colo. Fairfax came here to breakfast & returnd afterwards. Doctr. Craik came to Dinner & went away after it.

6.   Dined at Belvoir and returnd in the Evening. Mrs. Washington & Patcy Custis went with me.

7.   Rid by the Ferry Plantation to the Mill—from thence to Doeg Run & so home by Muddy hole.

8.   Rid into the Neck and from thence to the Mill.

9.   Went to the Mill & returnd from thence to Dinner.

10.   Rid to the Mill Doeg run and Muddy hole.

11.   At home all day. Miss Polly Brazier dined here.

Polly Brazier may be a relation of Capt. Zacharias Brazier, who in 1759 married Elizabeth Fowke Buckner (1727–1797), a widow of Stafford County (agreement between Zacharias Brazier and Elizabeth Buckner, 5 Nov. 1759, Stafford County Deed Book, 1755–64, 241–43, and will of Elizabeth Brazier, 29 June 1795, Prince William County Will Book, 1792–1803, 194–95, Vi Microfilm).

12.   Rid to the Mill by the Plantation at the Ferry.

GW today wrote Robert Cary & Co., requesting that a few goods be added to his last order. The most important article, "and the principal end of my writing," he told the company, was "a pair of French Burr Millstones" for merchant milling. The stones that he was presently using were giving him flour of fine quality, but he wanted to produce superfine flour, which could best be done with buhrstone, noted for its hardness and the many minute cutting edges on its surfaces. In choosing the new millstones, GW instructed, care was to be taken to see that they were "of a good and even quality. I should not Incline to give any extravagent Sum for them on the one hand nor miss of getting a pair of good ones by limiting the price on the other" (DLC:GW; CRAIK [1], 293–94).

13.   Rid to the Mill and returnd home by the Ferry Plantation.

14.   Rid to the Ferry Plantation, Mill, Doeg Run, & Muddy hole.

15.   Rid by the Ferry Plantation to the Mill—from thence into the Neck.

16.   Rid by the Plantation at the Ferry to the Mill, & from thence home.

17.   Rid by Muddy hole to Doeg Run—from thence to the Mill & so home by the Ferry Plantn.

18.   At home all day alone.

19.   Went up to Alexandria to Court, & returnd in the Evening, home.

The court met 19–23 Aug. GW was not recorded as being officially present today, but his name is among the justices who attended on 20, 21, and 23 Aug. (Fairfax County Order Book for 1770–72, 231–74, Vi Microfilm).

20.   Went up to Court again and lodgd in my own House.

GW was to spend little time at his recently completed town house at the corner of Pitt and Cameron streets. After the War of Independence he usually lent it to relatives or rented it.

21.   At Court all day. In the Evening returnd home.

22.   Rid by the Ferry Plantation & Mill to Colo. Fairfax's to see Mrs. Fairfax who was said to be Ill.

Washington's house in Alexandria in an undated sketch by Miss M. I. Stewart. (Alexandria-Washington Lodge No. 22, A.F. & A.M., Alexandria, Va.)

23.   Went up to Court again and returnd home in the Afternoon.

24.   Rid to the Ferry Plantation & Mill before Dinner.

25.   At home all day. Mr. Jno. Smith came here to Dinner on his return from the Springs.

26th.   Mr. Smith went away. After Breakfast I rid to the Ferry Plantn. Mill, Doeg Run and Muddy hole.

27.   Rid to the Mill only before Dinner.

28.   Rid by the Ferry Plantation to the Mill. Miss Manley here.

29.   Went to the Mill, & returnd from thence. Miss Manley went home after Breakfast and Mr. Jno. Johnson who has a nostrum for Fits came here in the Afternoon.

Dr. John Johnson (b. 1745), of Frederick, Md., had for the past few months been sending the Washingtons a special herbal medicine to relieve the seizures that had been plaguing Patsy Custis (Thomas Johnson to GW, 18 June 1770, MnHi). His remedy had proved to be totally ineffective, but Johnson had come to Mount Vernon to prescribe further treatments (GW to Jonathan Boucher, 5 July 1771, WRITINGS, 3:42–48). A nephew many years later characterized Johnson as a person who was "extremely indolent, self-opinionated, and had as little of manhood as he had of his profession" (DELAPLAINE, 351).

30.   Rid to the Mill in the forenoon. Mr. Johnson here all day. In the afternoon Doctr. Rumney came, & stayd all Night.

31.   After Breakfast both Mr. Johnson & Doctr. Rumney went away. I rid to the Mill, and in the afternoon Mr. Lewis Burwell the younger came here.

Lewis Burwell the younger was either Lewis Burwell, Jr., son of Col. Lewis Burwell of Kingsmill, James City County, or Lewis Burwell (1737–1779), lawyer and burgess of Fairfield plantation, Gloucester County, who was also known as Lewis Burwell, Jr. at this time. Lewis Burwell of Fairfield studied law at the Inns of Court in London and represented Gloucester County in the House of Burgesses 1769–74. An avid horseman, he owned the stallion Eclipse, a "Noted High Bred Swift Running Horse" (*Va. Gaz.*, D&N, 8 May 1779).

Acct. of the Weather in August

August 1st.   Clear and very warm with the Wind pretty fresh from the Southwestward.

2.   Clear and warm again with the Wind in the same place. The Afternoon Cloudy with a little thunder & appearances of Rain but none fell here.

3.   Very warm, Wind Southerly & Weather clear.

4.   Still very warm & clear with the Wind Southerly.

5.   Exceeding warm with the Wind still in the same place. Forenoon clear—afternoon Gusty but no Rain fell here tho it thunderd & lightnend.

6.   Very warm with but little Wind. In the Evening a little Rain but not much.

7.   Clear and very warm. Wind Westerly.

8.   Cloudy forenoon with appearances of Rain but none fell. Afternoon clear.

9.   Afternoon Cloudy again with a fine mist for a few Minutes. Very little Wind.

10.   Clear and Cool Wind being Northwesterly.

11th.   Clear and quite Calm. Morning little Cool; Evening Warm.

12.   Some appearance of Rain but none fell. Very warm.

13.   Wind very fresh from abt. SSW with now and then great shews of Rain but very little fell.

14.   Calm, and great appearances of Rain again, but scarce any fell in this Neighbourhood.

15.   Clear in the forenoon and exceeding Hot with Clouds in the Afternoon but no Rain here.

16.   Wind fresh from the Northwest & Cool, tho the Sun was very hot.

17.   Very cool in the Morning & clear all day with the Wind Northerly.

18.   Cool & clear all day. Wind in the same place.

19.   Cool & Clear all day. Wind Northerly.

20.   Evening & Morning very Cool Midday warmer – quite clear.

21.   Quite clear with but little Wind & that at No. or No. East. Morning & Evening Cool – warm midday.

22.   Much warmer than the preceeding days but little Wind & clear.

23d.   Perfectly clear, with very little Wind & warm.

24.   No Wind in the forenoon, or but little, & that Southerly. Afternn. Cloudy with a little Rain & pretty high Wind from the No. West.

25.   Clear and tolerably pleast. with but little Wind and that Westerly.

26.   Clear and calm Morning. Warm Midday. Wind fresh in the Evening from the Southard with some Rain in the Night—but not much.

27.   Morning Cloudy. Afternoon clear with but little Wind.

28.   Clear and Cool in the Morning & Evening but warm in the midday with but little Wind.

29.   Much such a day as yesterday.

30.   Quite clear & pleasant without any Wind. Morning & Evening also Warm.

31.   Wind at Southwest, with Clouds and appearance of Rain but none fell.

Remarks & Occurs. in August

August 1st.   Began to Sow Wheat in the Neck with Wheat steep'd in Brine & allum.

3.   Began to Sow Wheat at the Mill also steepd in Brine with Allum put thereto.
   This day began to sow the Brined Wheat at Muddy hole. Before this the Wheat was not steepd in Brine at this place.
   Note—The Brine was made by the direction's in the Farmers guide, as the common method practiced by Farmers but our Wheat was steepd only 24 hours instead of 35 which he recommends.

GW is steeping wheat in brine and alum in an attempt to prevent the fungus disease called rust. His "Farmers Guide" is *The Farmer's Compleat Guide, through All Articles of His Profession* (London, 1760).

5th.   Began to Sow Wheat at Doeg Run, Steepd in Brine.

8.   Finished Sowing the River Side Cut in the Neck—also the Corn ground at the Mill opposite Mr. Manley's.

10.   Finish'd Sowing all the Corn Ground at the Mill & began to prepare the Fallowd Land there for Sowing.
    Also Raised a House at the Mill for the Miller to live In.

The miller's house, a one-story wooden structure about 24 by 16 feet with a small separate kitchen, was conveniently located within 30 yards of the new mill (GW to Robert Lewis & Sons, 1 Feb. 1785, DLC:GW; Lawrence Lewis's insurance policy, 7 April 1803, Vi).

13.   Began to Sow Wheat at the Ferry Plantation in the Corner next the Ferry Road by the Pine Tree.

17.   Finish'd Sowing Wheat in that Cut next the Gum spring at Muddy hole. [   ] Bushls.
    Also the Second Cut in the Neck that next the Crab tree Branch.

20.   Con McCarty began to Work on the Chimney of the Millers Ho[use] in the Morning, and [   ] Bond abt. 12 Oclock.

McCarty was employed at GW's mill until sometime in October, receiving £9 2s. 6d. for 36½ days of work (LEDGER A, 343). BOND: probably the last name of a helper, but may be a reference to the practice of bonding brick or stone.

22.   Finishd Sowing the Cut of Wheat at the Ferry in which they began.
    The Ground now exceeding dry Corn firing very badly & every discouraging appearance of a scarcity of this Article that can be.

31.   Finish'd Sowing the third Cut of Wheat in the Neck.

[September]

Where & how my time is Spent

Sept. 1st.   At home all day. Mr. Burwell here.

2.   Went up to Alexandria with Mr. Burwell after an early Dinner. Returnd in the Evening with Mr. Piper.

3.   Rid in the Forenoon to the Mill. Mr. Burwell, & Mr. Piper both here.

4.   Mr. Burwell and Mr. Piper both went away after Breakfast. I rid to the Mill.

5.   Rid by the Ferry Plantation to the Mill—from thence to Muddy hole & so home to Dinner. In the Afternoon rid to the Mill again.

6.   At home all the forenoon. In the Afternoon went to Belvoir with Mrs. Washington & P. Custis, & returnd in the Evening.

7.   Rid into the Neck in the Morning early & from thence to the Mill. Mr. Crawford came here in the Aftern.

8.   At home all day. Mr. Crawford went away after breakfast.

9.   Rid to the Mill—from thence to Doeg Run Qr. & by the River Plantation home.

10.   Rid to the Mill in the Forenoon. Mr. Thoms. Triplet dind with me. In the Afternoon set of for Fredericksburg and lodgd at Colo. Harry Lees.

The purpose of this trip was to make final arrangements for Mary Washington, now about 63 years old, to move from the Ferry Farm plantation to a house in Fredericksburg, where she could spend her latter years in comfort, free from the cares of the plantation. GW had previously discussed the matter with her, and in May, at her request and his expense, he had made a down payment of £75 on a house of her choice: a commodious white frame residence on Charles Street near the home of her daughter Betty Lewis (GW to Benjamin Harrison, 21 Mar. 1781, DLC:GW; LEDGER A, 336). Now, in further preparation for his mother's move to town, GW was ready to begin settling her affairs at Ferry Farm and at Little Falls Quarter, a tract of land about two miles farther down the Rappahannock which she had inherited from her father in 1711 (will of Joseph Ball, 25 June 1711, Lancaster County Wills, Book-10, 88, Vi Microfilm).

11th.   Reach'd my Mother's to Dinner after Bating at Peyton's.

12.   Rid all over the Plantn. at the Ho[me] House, & then went to the Quarter and rid all over that & returnd to Dinner Colo. Lewis & my Brothr. Charles being there. In the Afternoon went over to Fredg.

THE PLANTN. AT THE HO[ME] HOUSE: Ferry Farm. At this time it consisted of about 600 acres of land, and by the terms of Augustine Washington's will, it was legally GW's to do with what he wished (*Va. Gaz.*, R, 5 Nov. 1772).

THE QUARTER: the plantation at Little Falls, which apparently contained about 400 acres. During this visit GW agreed to take over the quarter at the beginning of 1772, paying his mother an annual rent for it thereafter. Because the livestock and slaves at both Ferry Farm and the quarter were hers, he further agreed to buy her livestock and to rent her slaves. The price of the livestock and the rents for the land and slaves were to be determined within the next few weeks by Fielding Lewis and Charles Washington (GW to Benjamin Harrison, 21 Mar. 1781, DLC:GW; Mary Washington's account with GW, 14 Sept. 1771–30 Mar. 1775, PHi; Gratz Collection).

13.   Returnd to my Mothers to Breakfast and Surveyd the Fields before Dinner, returnd to Town afterwards.

The survey covered about half of Ferry Farm, extending from the top of the Rappahannock riverbank, where the main house stood, several hundred yards northeast to a fence along a cornfield. GW apparently never platted this survey, but a plat based on his survey notes was drawn in 1932 for GW ATLAS (pl. 9).

14.   Rid with Colo. Lewis to his Mill before Dinner. After it went over to my Mother's & stayd all Night.

GW today advanced his mother £4 12s. 6d. on the money that he was to pay her under their agreement (Mary Washington's account with GW, 14 Sept. 1771–30 Mar. 1775, PHi: Gratz Collection). The exact amount he owed her was not set until 15 Oct., when Fielding Lewis and Charles Washington finished evaluating her property. GW, they determined, was to pay £93 11s. 8d. for her livestock, £30 a year rent for the Little Falls Quarter, and £92 for a year's hire of her slaves: six men and four women, half of whom were at Ferry Farm and half at Little Falls ("Sundrys belonging to Mrs. Mary Washington valued by Chas. Washington & Fielding Lewis," 15 Oct. 1771, ViMtV).

15.   Set of home. Din'd in Dumfries and got up by Sun set.

16.   Rid by the Ferry Plantation to the Mill. Lund Washington returnd from Dr. Craiks this Eveng.

17.   Rid to the Mill—from thence to Doeg Run, and Muddy hole before Dinner. After Dinner Rid into the Neck.

18.   Went up to Court. Dind at Arrells and Lodgd at Mr. Jno. Wests.

The court met 16–19 Sept.; GW attended only the last two days (Fairfax County Order Book for 1770–72, 274–93, Vi Microfilm).
    Richard Arell's tavern in Alexandria was frequently patronized by GW on his visits to the town between 1764 and 1774 and had apparently been the scene of his election ball on 1 Dec. 1768 (LEDGER A, 178, 281; LEDGER B, 80;

Mr. and Mrs. Richard Arell, in a portrait by John Hesselius before 1775. (Mr. and Mrs. Elias Edmonds Gray IV)

Va. Gaz., P, 27 June 1777). Arell (variously spelled) had come to Alexandria from Pennsylvania with his wife, Eleanor, sometime before July 1762 and had been a merchant prior to becoming an innkeeper (BROCKETT, 96; deed of George Mason to Arell, 20–21 July 1762, Fairfax County Deeds, Book E-1, 102–4, Vi Microfilm).

19.   Went to Court again. Dind at Arrells & come home in the Afternoon. Found young Mr. Wormely here.

Ralph Wormeley (1744–1806) of Rosegill, Middlesex County, was the eldest son of Ralph Wormeley (1715–1790) of Rosegill. Young Wormeley had been educated in England at Eton and Cambridge University and earlier this year had been appointed to the governor's council in Williamsburg (VA. EXEC. JLS., 6:412).

20.   Went with Mr. Wormeley to Belvoir on a Morngs. Visit, & returnd to Dinr.

21.   Set out with Mr. Wormeley for the Annapolis Races. Dind at Mr. Willm. Digges's & lodgd at Mr. Ignatis Digges's.

The fall racing at Annapolis was an annual highlight of both the sporting and social seasons for the Chesapeake gentry, being an occasion not only for indulging in "the pleasures of the turf" but for going to dinners, balls, and plays in the city (EDDIS, xxv–xxvi, 54–55). Sponsored by the prestigious Annapolis Jockey Club, the races attracted the finest thoroughbreds in the region to run for purses of up to 100 guineas. This year the jockey club had announced four days of racing to begin at 11:00 A.M. each day from 24 to 27 Sept. and three balls to be held on the nights of 24, 25, and 27 Sept. (*Md. Gaz.*, 12 Sept. 1771).

22.   Dind at Mr. Sam Gallaway's & lodged with Mr. Boucher in Annapolis.

Galloway belonged to the Annapolis Jockey Club, and on 24 Sept. he would race his horse Selim, for which he had paid £1,000 as a yearling in 1760 (*Md. Gaz.*, 26 Sept. 1771).

Jonathan Boucher and Jacky Custis were living in the St. Anne's Parish parsonage on Hanover Street. Jacky had written to GW on 18 Aug., extending an invitation on behalf of Boucher to stay at his house, as it would be "almost impossible to get a Room at any of the ordinaries, the Rooms being preengaged to their [regular] customers" (DLC:GW).

23.   Dined with Mr. Loyd Dulany & Spent the Evening at the Coffee Ho[use].

Lloyd Dulany (1742–1782), son of Daniel Dulany the elder and his third wife, Henrietta Maria Dulany, had recently returned to Annapolis after studying law at the Inns of Court in London. About this time he built a handsome brick house on Conduit Street that reportedly cost him £10,000 (LAND, 294, 296–97).

The Coffeehouse, a popular tavern run by a Mrs. Howard, was on Main (now Church) Street near the State House (*Md. Gaz.*, 12 Sept. 177; RILEY [2]).

Sir Robert Eden, governor of Maryland. From a photograph of a painting, artist unknown. (Maryland Historical Society)

24.   Dined with the Govr. and went to the Play & Ball afterwards.

GW probably attended the races before dinner on this and the following three days. The track adjoined the town on the west, and because of the beautiful autumn weather "there was a prodigious concourse of spectators and considerable sums were depending on the contest of each day" (EDDIS, 54). Gov. Robert Eden's home stood on a small peninsula extending into the Severn River.

The play was performed by the American Company of Comedians, which had begun a run in town on 9 Sept., when a new theater was opened on West Street near St. Anne's Church (EDDIS, 55). The balls were held at the Assembly House on Duke of Gloucester Street. There was a room for dancing in the front of the building, and in a chamber at the back gentlemen gathered to play cards and to drink wine (STEVENS [1], 111). GW recorded losing £13 4s. 3d. "By cards—[at] different times" (LEDGER A, 344).

25.   Dined at Doctr. Stewards and went to the Play and Ball afterwards.

Dr. George Steuart (d. 1784) was a member of the Maryland council and one of the two judges of the proprietary land office who issued land warrants and decided land disputes. A Scotsman, he had been educated at the University of Edinburgh and had immigrated to America in 1721. His wife was Ann Digges Steuart, sister of William Digges of Warburton (COKE, 358–59; RICHARDSON [2], 2:225–26).

26.   Dined at Mr. Ridouts and went to the Play after it.

John Ridout (1732–1797), another member of the council, lived on Duke of Gloucester Street. He was born in England and after studying for six years at Oxford came to Maryland in 1753 as a secretary to Gov. Horatio Sharpe (NORRIS [2], 106–7).

27.   Dined at Mr. Carrolls and went to the Ball.

Charles Carroll of Annapolis lived in a comfortable brick mansion on Spa Creek. His son Charles Carroll of Carrollton also resided there, and GW probably saw both of them on this occasion (ROWLAND [1], 1:93–94).

28.   Dined at Mr. Bouchers and went from thence to the Play and afterwards to the Coffee Ho[use].

29.   Dined with Majr. Jenifer and Suppd at Danl. Dulany Esqrs.

Daniel Dulany the younger (1722–1797), son of Daniel Dulany the elder and his second wife, Rebecca Smith Dulany (c.1696–1737), was one of the most important men in Maryland at this time, being both a councillor and secretary of the colony. Even his antagonist Charles Carroll of Annapolis admitted in 1765 that "He is a man of Great Parts, of Generall Knowledge

Daniel Dulany the younger, an Annapolis attorney and secretary of Maryland. (Mr. and Mrs. R. H. Dulany Randolph)

Rebecca Tasker Dulany, wife of Daniel Dulany the younger. (Mrs. N. Holmes Morison)

indisputably the best Lawer on this Continent, a very entertaining Companion when he pleases" (Charles Carroll of Annapolis to Charles Carroll of Carrollton, 17 April 1761, CARROLL, 10:342–43).

30. Left Annapolis, & Dind and suppd with Mr. Saml. Gallaway.

Acct. of the Weather in Septr.

Septr. 1. Wind fresh from the Eastward. Afternoon Cloudy & Night Raining.

2. Ground now for the first time since the Rains abt. the 25th. July Wet. Very warm and but little Wind.

3. A Breeze from the Northwest but very sultry notwithstanding—quite clear.

4. Still warm & clear—Wind Southerly.

5.   Warm and clear with but little Wind & that Southerly. The Afternoon Showery with some thunder.

6.   Misting more or less all day & somewhat Cool, what Wind there was being westerly.

7.   Very Cloudy in the Morning and raining more or less all day —fine Rain—Wind being about No. East.

8.   Cloudy all day but clear in the Evening with but little Wind but Cool notwithstanding.

9.   Clear and pleasand, rather warm with little Wind.

10.   Warm, with appearances of Rain but none fell here.

11.   Cool Wind fresh from No. West. Afternoon Warmer— Weathr. Clear.

12.   Clear and Warmer. Wind Southerly.

13.   Very warm with but little Wind and that Southerly. Clear.

14.   Very Cloudy & cool. Wind Northerly but not much of it.

15.   Cloudy all day, & cool with the Wind Easterly. In the After- noon and Night Rain.

16.   Raining very close & constant till about 10 Oclock—then clear & calm.

17.   Clear & pleasant all day, Wind Westerly, but neither fresh nor cool.

18.   Clear but cool, very cold wind fresh from the No. West.

19.   A small frost, but to do no Injury Weather still cool and clear, but not so cold.

20.   Clear and pleasant, weather much warmer.

21.   Clear and warm with very little Wind.

22.   Much such a day as yesterday.

23.   Very pleasant with but little Wind & that Southerly.

24.   Warm, clear, and pleasant with but little alteration in the Weather.

25th.   The Weather the same as has been for 3 or 4 days last past.

26.   Very Warm but clear with very little Wind.

27.   Clear and pleasant with the Wind Southerly and warm.

28.   Very warm with but little Wind & that Southerly wt. Clouds.

29.   Wind fresh from the Northwest and very cool.

30.   Still cool & clear—Wind Shifting South Westerly.

Remarks & Occs. in Septr.

Septr. 4.   The Mason's began to work on the Mill Walls.
   Finish'd Sowing the Cut of Corn round the Creek at the Ferry Plantn.

Permanent repairs apparently were being made because of damages that had occurred earlier in the year. The workmen were Michael Clark, Benjamin Mason, Thomas Tayler, William Bacon, and possibly Con McCarty. Clark, Mason, and Tayler were paid 16 Nov., receiving a total of £19 12s. 6d., while Bacon received £15 15s. nine days later (LEDGER A, 343, 345, 347).

10.   Began to Plaister the Millers House.

12.   Agreed with one William Powell to look after my Mothers Quarter on Rappahannock, on the following Terms; to wit—to continue the five hands now on the Plantation, & either to add one more horse to those which are there (amounting to four) or put two good ones there, and take away two of the most indifferent. To allow him 365 lbs. of Porke, the Milk of a Cow, and the Seventh part of all the Corn, Tobo., and Wheat he can make—In consideration of which he is to stay constantly on the Plantn. with

his People furnish himself with bed and other necessaries & to keep no Horse or other Creature [of his own] on the Plantation.

The William Powell whom GW is engaging here as overseer of the Little Falls Quarter may be William Powell (d. 1796), son of the Dumfries merchant William Powell (c.1700–1787). Young Powell later became a lieutenant in the Continental Army and settled in Amherst County (LUCAS, 319–20; BURGESS, 3:1438–39).

GW must have chosen the option of putting two good horses at the quarter, because on 8 Nov. 1771, while at Eltham, he bought four horses costing a total of £30 "for Rappahannock," two of them evidently to go to Little Falls and two to Ferry Farm (LEDGER A, 345).

13.   Agreed with Edwd. Jones to continue overseer at the place my Mother lives at [Ferry Farm] who is also to be constant in his attendance on the People he looks after (five in number) for which he is to be allowd the Seventh of Corn Wheat & Tobo. He also is to have two Horses added to those two he already has.

[October]

Where & how my time is Spent

Octr. [1].   Dined at Upper Marlborough & reachd home in the Afternoon. Mr. Wormley—Mr. Fitzhugh, Mr. Randolph, Mr. Burwell, & Jack Custis came with me. Found Mr. Pendleton here.

Upper Marlboro was a small tobacco town on the western branch of the Patuxent River in Prince George's County, Md., about halfway between Annapolis and Mount Vernon. In 1775 it was described by a visitor as "a very pleasant" place, "containing about a Dozen very neat houses & 3 or 4 stores" (HONYMAN, 4).

Atty. Gen. John Randolph of Williamsburg and Edmund Pendleton (1721–1803) of Caroline County were retained by GW about this time to act with James Mercer of Fredericksburg as attorneys for the Custis estate in a suit that was apparently to be heard in the General Court at Williamsburg between 10 and 15 Oct. The case involved an old claim against the family for payment of a substantial sum of money allegedly owed to descendants of an illegitimate daughter of Daniel Parke (1669–1710), Jacky and Patsy Custis's great-grandfather. That dispute, which had been going on for more than 50 years, would continue for at least a few more years, but the plaintiffs would never obtain a final judgment in their favor (LEDGER A, 345; FREEMAN, 2:281–91, 298–301, 3:225–27, 282, 335).

John Randolph had attended the races in Annapolis with his daughters, traveling there on board the armed schooner *Magdalen* (*Va. Gaz.*, P&D, 17 Sept. 1771).

2.   Mr. Pendleton went away after Breakfast. The other Gentlemen Stayd all day.

3.   The Gentlemen went away after Breakfast & I rid by the Ferry Plantation to the Mill. Doctr. Rumney dind & lodgd here.

4.   Rid to the Mill–Doeg Run, & Muddy hole. Captn. Oliffe dind here, and Mr. Robt. Rutherford Sup'd.

John Oliffe of Norfolk was a sea captain who sailed frequently from Virginia to the West Indies and the British Isles. He married Mrs. Anne Knight at Norfolk in 1769 (LOWER NORFOLK, 4:61).

5.   Went a hunting with Jacky Custis but found nothing. Came home by the Mill. Mr. Rutherford went away after breakfast & Captn. Oliffe dind here.

6.   At home all day. Captn. McCarty & wife Mr. Piper Captn. Oliffe & Polly Brazier dind here. The 3 first Went away after Dinner.

7.   Rid by the Ferry Plantation to the Mill Captn. Oliffe & Polly Brazier here.

8.   Went a hunting in the Neck and Catchd a Dog fox. Then went to the Plantn. there & came home to Dinr.

9.   At home in the Afternoon. Rid to the Mill in the forenoon.

10.   At home all day. Captn. Crawford came here in the Afternoon.

William Crawford had surveyed the lands between the Great and Little Kanawha rivers for the Virginia Regiment, and he was now bringing in his rough field notes from which finished drafts were to be made with GW's help (Crawford to GW, 2 Aug. 1771, DLC:GW). When the two men completed that task several days later, there were 10 surveys covering 61,796 acres, less than a third of the 200,000 acres that, according to the order of the council, had to be included in 20 surveys (VA. EXEC. JLS., 6:438–39). But Crawford reported that few of the tracts could be much "enlarged with rich Land" because the countryside was "generally so Craggy, Steep, and Rocky" that fertile farming areas could be found only in isolated narrow strips along the rivers and creeks (Crawford's surveys, nos. 2–10, dated June 1771, are in DLC:GW; a copy of his first survey, dated June 1771, is at the University of Pittsburgh). Besides the surveys for the Virginia Regiment, Crawford apparently brought GW a personal survey for a 515-acre tract on the Ohio near

Captina Creek (survey, 20 June 1771, DLC:GW) and one for some land about 16 miles from Fort Pitt (Crawford to GW, 2 Aug. 1771, DLC:GW).

11. Still at home all day Plotting & Measuring the Surveys which Captn. Crawford made for the Officers & Soldiers.

12. At home on the same business. Doctr. Craik came in the Afternoon.

13. About the same business. Mr. John West came to Dinner.

14. Ditto—Ditto. Doctr. Craik went away after Breakfast & Mrs. Barnes came. Mr. Manley dind here & Val. Crawford came sick at Night.

Harrison Manley apparently came to Mount Vernon today to ask GW to handle some personal business for him in Williamsburg, where GW was soon to go. GW agreed, undertaking to obtain copies of some legal documents that Manley wanted and to take a sum of money for him to the treasurer of the colony (GW to Manley, 13 Nov. 1771, DLC:GW).

15. At home about this Work. Doctr. Rumney came in the Afternoon.

16. Ditto—Ditto. Mr. West & Doctr. Rumney went away after Dinner.

17. Rid to the Ferry Plantn. & Mill after Breakfast. Captn. Crawford went to Doctr. Craiks after Dinner.

18. Went into the Neck & run some Lines there. Captn. Crawford came in the Afternoon.

19. Rid to Muddy hole Doeg Run & Mill.

20. At home all day. Mr. James Adam dined here.

James Adam brought GW £41 6d. cash, part payment from Robert Adam & Co. for the flour that GW had sold the firm earlier in the year (LEDGER A, 345).

21. Rid to the Mill. Mr. Ross dind here.

Hector Ross brought another £100 from Robert Adam & Co. in payment for flour (LEDGER A, 345).

22.   Rid to the Mill again. Captn. Crawford & his Brothr. returnd home. Mr. Jno. Smith of westmoreld. came in the Aftern.

Before William Crawford left Mount Vernon, GW paid him £41 14s. 4d. on
account of the officers and soldiers of the Virginia Regiment and, on his own
account, "5 half Joes," gold Portuguese coins worth a total of £11 10s.
Virginia currency (LEDGER A, 345).

John Smith of Cabin Point was returning to Frederick County to obtain
permission from the magistrates there to inoculate Samuel Washington and
his family, but he died before he could do so. GW later wrote Samuel it was
fortunate that Smith had not begun inoculating, "for I was morally sure he
could not live to carry you through it. . . . What a madman must he have
been to quit his house and friends in pursuit of so vain a shadow? To per-
sist in it to the last argues something of insanity" (6 Dec. 1771, excerpt,
Parke-Bernet Galleries Catalogue, 11 June 1941, Item 578).

23.   After dinner set of for Williamsburg and lodgd at Mr.
Lawson's. Left Mr. Smith & Mrs. Barnes at Mt. Vn.

GW was going to Williamsburg to give the council a list of 81 members of
the Virginia Regiment who had presented him with claims under the Proclamation of 1754 and to petition the councillors to devise a system for dis-
tributing the 200,000 acres among the claimants (VA. EXEC. JLS., 6:438–39).

24.   Reachd my Mothers to dinner, & lodgd afterwards at Colo.
Lewis's.

25.   At my Mothers all day having lost my Horses. Spent the
Eveng. at Weedons.

26.   At Colo. Lewis's all day—Mr. Wormely & others dining
there.

27.   Continued on to Williamsburg having found my Horses.
Dined at Caroline Ct. House & lodgd at Hubbards.

28.   Breakfasted at Todds bridge, dind at Ruffins, and lodgd at
Colo. Bassetts.

29.   Reach'd Williamsburg before Dinner. And went to the Play
in the Afternoon.

About four weeks before GW arrived in town, Christiana Campbell had
moved again, this time to Waller Street behind the Capitol, and in a newspaper advertisement she had announced that "I shall reserve Rooms for the
Gentlemen who formerly lodged with me" (*Va. Gaz.*, P&D, 3 Oct. 1771). But
for the first time in ten years, GW did not stay with her. He chose, instead,
to lodge with John Carter, a well-established merchant who ran a general

This sketch of George Weedon was made in 1791 by John Trumbull. (Yale University Art Gallery, gift of Mrs. Winchester Bennett)

John Murray, fourth earl of Dunmore and the last colonial governor of Virginia. (Mrs. Charles Murray)

store next door to the Raleigh Tavern and who at this time lived in a house directly across the street from the Raleigh (*Va. Gaz.*, P&D, 6 Feb. 1772). Carter had not advertised rooms for rent, but he, like several merchants and craftsmen in town, was apparently supplementing his income by lodging visitors in his house during public times (GIBBS, 133).

The play was performed by the American Company of Comedians, which had again returned to Williamsburg from Annapolis (RANKIN, 164).

30. Dined at the Speakers and went to the Play in the Afternoon.

31. Dined at the Governors & went to the Play.

John Murray, earl of Dunmore (1732–1809), successor to Lord Botetourt as governor of Virginia, had taken his oath of office before the council 25 Sept. 1771 (VA. EXEC. JLS., 6:430–31). A Scottish peer, he had sat in Parliament for several years and for 11 months before coming to Virginia had been governor of New York.

Acct. of the Weather in October.

Octr. 1st. The Weather clear & pleasant with very little Wind.

2. Clear and pleasant, with but little Wind.

3. Very pleasant forenoon with some Appearances of Rain in the Afternoon.

4. Cloudy forenoon, & now and then Misting–turning Cool.

5. Great Fog & Dew with but little [wind] & that Northerly & Cold.

6. Clear and pleasant not being so cool as yesterday. Wind what little there was of it abt. East.

7. Clear in the forenoon and Warm but cloudy afternoon & very like for Rain with the Wind at So. Wt.

8. Cloudy forenoon and rainy Afternoon with the Wind Southerly.

9. Clear and pleasant till Night then Rain.

10. Raining more or less all day & part of the Night.

11. Clear and Cool.

12. Much such weather as yesterday.

13. Clear and pleasant with but little Wind.

14th. Clear in the forenoon with the Wind Southerly but Cloudy afterwards & Rain.

15. Raining almost all Night & till the Afternoon of this day.

16. Clear with the Wind fresh from the Westward.

17. Clear and Calm in the forenoon a little Windy afterwards but very pleasant notwithstandg.

18. Warm and pleasant with but little Wind.

19. Clear in the forenoon, but lowering afterwards with Rain in the Evening and all Night.

20. Cloudy all day and sometimes Misting with the Wind what little there was at No. East.

21.   Clear, warm, and pleasant with very little Wind.

22.   Clear & very Warm with but little Wind and that Southerly.

23.   Lowering Morning with Rain then clear & Cool Wind fresh from the North West.

24.   Clear and Cool in the forenoon but Warm afterwards.

25.   Clear and pleasant forenoon but lowering afterwards.

26.   Clear and Warm with but little Wind and that Southerly.

27.   Clear and very warm. Wind Southerly.

28.   Clear in the forenoon with slight Rains afterwards & a change of Wind which turnd the Air Cool.

29.   Clear and Cool Wind being at Northwest, and fresh.

30.   Warmer—Wind getting Southerly again. Clear in the forenoon.

31.   Very warm, but clear and pleasant notwithstanding.

[November]

Where & how my time is Spent

Novr. 1st.   Dined at Mrs. Dawson's. Went to the Fireworks in the Afternoon and to the Play at Night.

2.   Dined with the Council and Spent the Evening in my own Room a writing.

GW is probably preparing his petition to the council on behalf of the Virginia Regiment. In it he asked not only that individual allotments be made but that the limit of 20 surveys be removed, each claimant being permitted to survey his own portion of land and the 61,796 acres already surveyed by Crawford being divided only among the claimants who had shared the expense. Such an arrangement, he thought, would have several benefits. By being surveyed in many small plats, the full 200,000 acres could be covered "without taking in so many Mountains and barren Hills as would render the intended Bounty, rather a Charge" (VA. EXEC. JLS., 6:438–39).

"Every man would stand on his own bottom," and a few would not be obliged to bear the whole cost of the initial surveying, "whilst the Major part are standing aloof waiting the Event; if favorable to come in for part of the Prize but to pay nothing for the Ticket in case of a Blank." Claimants would also be spared being "doubly Taxed," not having to pay for both a share of the 20 surveys and an individual survey within one of the 20. In short, GW believed his petition to be "so reasonable, & so consistent with every principle of common justice . . . that . . . it could not possibly be rejected" (GW to George Mercer, 7 Nov. 1771, DLC:GW).

3.   Dined at Anderson's and Supped at Mrs. Dawson's.

4.   Dined with the Council and went to the play afterwards.

Governor Dunmore today presented GW's petition to the council. The councillors promptly decided to continue the limit of 20 surveys but postponed further action on the petition until 6 Nov. (VA. EXEC. JLS., 6:438–39).

5.   Dined at the Treasurers, and Spent the Evening in my own Room.

6.   Dined at Mrs. Dawsons and Spent the Evening at Mrs. Campbells.

On this date GW and James Mercer appeared before the council to argue in favor of the petition presented two days earlier. After hearing them, the councillors met privately to deliberate matters. They reaffirmed the limit of 20 surveys and then proceeded to allot the 200,000 acres: 400 acres to each of 52 private soldiers who had made claims, 500 acres to each of 4 corporals, 600 acres to each of 7 sergeants, 2,500 acres to each of 2 cadets, 6,000 acres to each of 8 subalterns, 9,000 acres to each of 5 captains, and 15,000 acres to each of 3 field officers, including GW. The remaining 30,000 acres, after being used to satisfy the claims of any more private soldiers who might apply, were to "be divided among those who have hitherto born the whole Expense, & who in all Probability must continue to do so till the full Quantity is surveyed" (VA. EXEC. JLS., 6:438–41). The council's answer to the petition did not please GW. In a letter of 7 Nov. to George Mercer, he accused the councillors of "putting the Soldiery upon a worse footing than the meanest Individual in the Community, rather than be thought to give a License to the pillaging of his Majestys, or the Proprietary Lands" (DLC: GW). Nevertheless, he remained determined to pursue the business regardless of the difficulties and expense involved.

Mrs. Campbell's new tavern on Waller Street was the one that Jane Vobe had kept there until recent months. In August, Mrs. Vobe had sold her furniture, and in September she had announced her intention to leave the colony (*Va. Gaz.*, P&D, 25 July and 17 Sept. 1771).

7.   Left Williamsburg on my return home, dined & lodged at Colo. Bassetts.

WILLIAMSBURG, *October* 3, 1771.

I BEG Leave to acquaint the Publick that I have opened TAVERN in the Houfe, behind the Capitol, lately occupied by Mrs. *Vobe*; where thofe Gentlemen who pleafe to favour me with their Cuftom may depend upon genteel Accommodations, and the very beft Entertainment.——⁎⁎ I fhall referve Rooms for the Gentlemen who formerly lodged with me.

CHRISTIANA CAMPBELL.

One of Washington's favorite innkeepers, Mrs. Campbell, announces the opening of her new tavern in Purdie and Dixon's *Virginia Gazette*. (Colonial Williamsburg Photograph)

8.   At Colo. Bassetts all day. Colo. Lewis & Mr. Mercer came here.

On the previous day GW had given Fielding Lewis £200 cash with which to pay the balance due for the house and two lots in Fredericksburg where Mary Ball Washington was to live (LEDGER A, 336, 345). The owner of the property, Michael Robinson, of Spotsylvania County, deeded it to GW on 18 Sept. 1772, but Mrs. Washington apparently moved into the house before spring (CROZIER [2], 294; see main entry for 11 April 1772). Although GW paid the full purchase price of £275 and retained the title to the property, he charged his mother nothing to live there for the nearly 18 years remaining of her life.

9.   Set out in Company with those Gentlemen. Dined at Todds bridge and lodgd at Hubbards.

10.   Dined at Doctr. Todds and reachd Fredericksburg at Night.

George Todd (1711–1790), a physician, operated a tavern from 1750 to 1781 on the stage road in Caroline County at the site of present-day Villboro, Va. (CAMPBELL [1], 411–12, 450). William Todd's ordinary at Todd's Bridge, where GW stopped much more frequently, was about 38 miles south of Dr. Todd's place (see entry for 21 April 1760).

11.   Got home about Dark. And found Mr. Warner Washington his Wife and Child–Mrs. Bushrod & Katy & Nancy Washington– Sally & Nancy Carlyle & Sally Fairfax & Polly Brazier here.

Anne Washington (d. 1777), known as Nancy, was Katy (Catherine) Washington's sister and a niece of Mrs. Bushrod. Reputedly an amiable and attractive young lady, Nancy married Thomas Peyton of Gloucester County in May 1776 and died eight months later (*Va. Gaz.*, D&H, 25 May 1776 and 17 Jan. 1777). Sally Cary Fairfax (b. 1760), eldest child of Bryan Fairfax, visited her aunt and uncle at Belvoir about this time. She died unmarried between 1777 and 1779 (FAIRFAX, 213).

12.   At home all day with the above.

13.   Rid to the Ferry Plantation Mill, Doeg Run and Muddy hole.

14.   Rid to the Mill with the Ladies & back again. Mr. Lawson came in the Afternoon.

15.   Rid to the Ferry Plantation after breakfast Mr. Warnr. Washington his wife & Child, & the two Miss Carlyles—Polly Brazier & Mr. Lawson went away.

16.   Went a hunting but found nothing.

17.   Went to Dinner at Belvoir with Mrs. Bushrod, Mrs. Washington, the two Miss Washington's, & Patcy Custis. Returnd in the Afternn.

18.   Went up to Court. Dined at Arrells & lodged at Mr. John Wests. Sent my Horses home.

The court met 18–21 Nov. GW's name does not appear in the court records for this day, but he was officially present on 19 and 20 Nov. (Fairfax County Order Book for 1770–72, 303–23, Vi Microfilm).

19.   Dined at Arrells and lodgd at my own House. Supped at Arrells also.

20.   Dined at Arrells. Came home in the Afternoon Mr. Magowan with me. Found Mr. Washington his Wife &ca. here as also John Custis.

21.   At home all day. Mr. Danl. Jenifer dined & lodgd here.

Daniel Jenifer (1727–1795) was the son of Dr. Daniel Jenifer of Port Tobacco, Md., and brother of Daniel of St. Thomas Jenifer.

22.   At home again. Mr. Jenefir went away after breakfast as Mr. Washington &ca. did yesterday.

23.   At home all day. Mr. Magowan went away before Dinner. Mr. Campbell came to Dinnr. & Doctr. Craik in the afternoon.

Matthew Campbell probably brought the £60 cash that GW recorded receiving from Robert Adam & Co. on this date (LEDGER A, 341, 347).

24. Doctr. Craik & Mr. Campbell both went away after breakfast.

25. Went a hunting in the Morning with Jacky Custis. Returnd about 12 Oclock & found Colo. Fairfax & Lady here—Mrs. Fanny Ballendine & her Nieces—Miss Sally Fairfax & Mr. R. Adam Mr. Jas. Adam & Mr. Anthy. Ramsay all of whom went away in the Afternoon when Miss Scott came.

Frances Ewell Ballendine was John Ballendine's wife, and the nieces accompanying her are probably daughters of one or more of her brothers: Charles and Bertrand Ewell of Prince William County and Solomon Ewell of Lancaster County (HAYDEN, 334–38). Catherine Scott (b. 1741) was a daughter of Rev. James Scott (d. 1782), rector of Dettingen Parish, Prince William County, and Sarah Brown Scott, a cousin of George Mason of Gunston Hall.

26. Rid to Muddy hole, Doeg Run, Mill and Ferry before dinner.

27. Set off before Sunrise with John Custis for Colo. Masons and went a driving [deer] in his Neck after breakfast—2 deer killed.

28. Went a driving again with Colo. Mason—killed nothing.

29. Went to the Vestry at Pohick Church & reachd home in the Evening. Found Mr. Johnson here.

The Truro Parish vestry today set the parish levy for the year—70 pounds of tobacco per tithable—and appointed various parish officials (Truro Vestry Book, 150–52, DLC).

Dr. John Johnson was continuing to treat Patsy Custis for her epilepsy. He may have been at Mount Vernon earlier in the month also, because on 12 Nov., GW recorded paying him £14 in Maryland currency for his services (LEDGER A, 345). Although Patsy still had not improved in any way under the care of Dr. Johnson, the Washingtons continued to consult him about her health for several more months (Johnson to Martha Washington, 21 Mar. 1772; HAMILTON [1], 4:119, n.2).

30. Went a hunting in the Neck with Mr. Peake—found & killed a Fox. Mr. Johnson still here.

Acct. of the Weather in Novr.

Novr. 1st.   Warm and pleasant—Wind being Southerly.

2.   Very warm in the forenoon & clear, Cloudy afterwards & a good deal of Rain in the Night.

3.   Clear and Cool, wind being fresh from the Northwest.

4.   Clear & pleasant not being so cool as yesterday. Wind however in the same place.

5.   Wind pretty fresh from the Northwest and Cold again.

6.   Less Cool than the day before but the Wind in the same place.

7.   Cloudy & very threatning Wind at No. East in the Afternoon with Rain most part of the Night.

8.   Wind Still Eastwardly with Rain more or less all day. In the Afternoon close hard rain & brisk Wind.

9.   Clear and Cold. Wind fresh from the Northwest.

10.   Clear and pleasant with but little Wind.

11.   Very pleasant and clear with the Wind what little there was of it Southerly.

12.   Very warm, clear and pleasant. Towards Night a little lowering.

13.   Very warm & pleasant with but little Wind.

14.   Clear, warm, and calm in the forenoon. The Afternoon lowering with a very brisk Wind from the Southward.

15.   A good deal of Rain fell last Night. The Wind being very high from the Southward. The day cool with the Wind fresh from the Westward.

16.   Clear Morning and Evening, but Cloudy Midday. Wind pretty fresh from the Southwest and at Night from the Northwest.

17.   Clear, Calm, and pleasant being tolerably warm.

18.   Clear and pleasant but a little Cooler.

19.   Cloudy with the Wind very fresh from the South West. About One Oclock a violent squal of Wind & Rain – clear afterwards.

20.   Clear and Cool Wind Northerly and pretty fresh.

21.   Clear and Cool Wind being again fresh from the Northwest.

22.   Cool and Cloudy, with appearances of Snow but none fell.

23.   Lowering Morning, but clear and pleasant afterwards with the wind Southerly.

24.   Clear & remarkably pleasant with but little Wind and that Southerly.

25.   Exceeding pleasant, being quite clear and Calm.

26.   Pleasant forenoon, but cloudy afternoon with high Wind & Rain from the Southwest in the Night.

27.   Clear, with the Wind fresh from the Northwest.

28.   Wind very fresh from the same point with squally Clouds.

29.   Cloudy & very like for Snow but none fell.

30.   Very Cloudy with some rain but tolerably pleasant afterwards.

Remarks & Occs. in Novr.

Novr. 11th.   Returnd home from Williamsburg.

20.   Began to Plant Cuttings of the Winter Grape in the Inclosure below the Garden.

30.   Left of Planting the ground being two hard froze having planted [   ] Rows beginning to reckon from the side next the Spring.

[December]

Where & how my time is Spent

Decr. 1st.   At home all day. Mr. Johnson still here. Doctr. Rumney came to Dinner & stayd all Night.

2.   Rid to the River Plantation and the Mill. Mr. Johnson went away after breakfast as Did Mr. Rumney.

3.   Rid to Muddy hole, and into the Neck. Mr. Val. Crawford came this aftern.

4.   Went up to the Election & the Ball I had given at Alexa. Mr. Crawford & Jno. P. Custis with me. Stayd all Night.

On 12 Oct. 1771 Governor Dunmore had dissolved the General Assembly, which necessitated new elections to the House of Burgesses (H.B.J., 1770–72, 145). GW and Col. John West were again chosen to represent Fairfax County. GW's election expenses included £4 7s. 8d. to tavern keeper John Lomax (d. 1787) of Alexandria for "getting a Supper" at the ball, £4 1s. 9d. to William Shaw, also of Alexandria, for "Sundries &ca. for the Election & Ball & his own Trouble," 12s. to Harry Piper for his slave Charles playing the fiddle, and £1 9s. 8d. to a Mr. Young for cakes (LEDGER A, 347; LEDGER B, 50).

5.   Came home in the Afternoon and found Miss Mason & Miss Scott who came the day before here.

Miss Mason is probably Ann Eilbeck Mason (1755–1814), eldest daughter of George Mason of Gunston Hall.

6.   At home alone all day. In the afternoon Mr. Phil. Pendleton came.

The purpose of Pendleton's visit was to get the contract for the land that GW had agreed to sell him on 6 June. GW signed it on the following day, witnessed by Lund Washington, Valentine Crawford, and Jacky Custis (CfMMCH).

7.   Went a fox hunting with the above two &ca. Killed a Fox and dined with Doctr. Alexander.

George Dent Alexander had recently attended the College of Philadelphia where he had apparently studied in the college's new medical school but had not qualified for a bachelor or doctor of medicine degree. Despite young Alexander's local family connections, GW did not employ him as a physician, preferring Dr. Rumney's services (GW to John Armstrong, 20 Mar. 1770, from Rokeby Collections, Barrytown, Dutchess County, N.Y., courtesy of Richard Aldrich and others; CARSON [3], 67–75). During the Revolution, Alexander was a surgeon in Col. William Grayson's Additional Continental Regiment, serving from Feb. 1777 until his death in Philadelphia in Jan. 1780 (BURGESS, 1:133–36).

8.   After breakfast Mr. Pendleton & Mr. Crawford went away as Miss Mason & Miss Scott did yesterday.

9.   Went to meet Govr. Eden at Mr. Willm. Digges's where we dined. In the Afternoon the Govr. Mr. Calvert, Majr. Fleming Mr. Boucher, Mr. Geo. Digges and Doctr. Digges came over with me.

Benedict Calvert (c.1724–1788), an illegitimate son of Charles Calvert, fifth Baron Baltimore (1699–1751), lived at Mount Airy (later called Dower House) in Prince George's County, Md., near present-day Rosaryville. Born in England, he was known in his early years as Benedict Swingate, but Lord Baltimore, while refusing to identify Benedict's mother, acknowledged him as his son and provided well for him. Benedict took the Calvert name and at the age of 18 went to Maryland, where in 1745 he was appointed collector of customs at Patuxent and in the following year became a member of the provincial council. In 1748 he married a distant relation, Elizabeth Calvert (1730–1798), daughter of the Charles Calvert who was governor of Maryland 1720–27 (NICKLIN [2], 58, 313–14; W.P.A. [2], 464–65).

Maj. William Fleming of the British army, currently acting commander of the 64th Regiment of Foot stationed at Halifax, Nova Scotia, was visiting the southern provinces for his health. He apparently returned north early the next summer when his regiment was moved to a post near Boston (Thomas Gage to William W. Barrington, 6 Jan. 1769, GAGE PAPERS, 2:493–94; DAVIES, 1:304).

Dr. Joseph Digges, son of William Digges and younger brother of George Digges, had studied at the University of Edinburgh but had not received a degree. During the Revolution he was surgeon to the Charles County, Md., militia 1777–78. In Oct. 1778 the Maryland state council gave him permission to go to Bermuda to recover his health, which had been bad "for some time past" (MD. ARCHIVES, 21:222). He was apparently taken prisoner by the British during the trip; on 1 Nov. 1779, he wrote GW from Teneriffe in the Canary Islands that he had been paroled but had not heard of his being exchanged, "from whence I conclude, that the Family at Warburton either believe me Dead, or have neglected writing me" (DLC:GW). Digges died at Teneriffe a short time later (RAMSBURGH, 131).

10.   The above Gentlemen dined here as did Colo. Fairfax who went away in the Afternoon.

11.   The Govr. and all the Compy. dined at Colo. Fairfaxs & returnd in the Afternoon.

12.   The foregoing Gentlemen still here.

13.   The Governor, and other Gentlemen cross'd over to Mr. Digges on their return home. I dined with them there & came back in the Aftern.

14.   Went a fox hunting with John Parke Custis Lund Washington & Mr. Manley—killed a Fox.

15.   At home all day alone, in the Evening the same.

16.   At home all day. In the Evening Mr. Adam Mr. Belmain, Mr. Campbell & Price Posey came here.

Robert Adam was about to make a voyage to Great Britain, and GW recently had given him several "little Commission's to execute" there (GW to Robert Cary & Co., 22 Nov. 1771, DLC:GW). Adam was to have a gun repaired for GW and was to buy a gold-headed cane with the Washington arms engraved on it, 400 or 500 bookplates also engraved with the Washington arms, and for Jacky, a white agate stone set in a gold socket and engraved with the Custis arms. Also, GW had instructed Adam to try to buy the bounty land rights of two former Virginia Regiment officers who had gone to Britain after the war and, if the opportunity occurred, to engage "a good Kitchen

Washington's familiar bookplate. (Mount Vernon Ladies' Association of the Union)

Gardner" for Mount Vernon. Adam apparently sailed for London a week later aboard his and Thomas Adam's new ship *Martha* (see main entry for 14 Mar. 1771; GW to Robert Cary & Co., 8 Jan. 1772, DLC:GW).

MR. BELMAIN: probably William Balmain (d. 1784), the Alexandria merchant.

17.   Mr. Belmain went away after Breakfast—the others after Dinner.

18.   Went to Doeg Run & carried the Dogs with me who found & run a Deer to the Water.

19.   Rid to the Ferry Plantation, Mill, & Muddy hole.

20.   Rid into the Neck.

21.   Went a hunting in the Neck with Mr. Peake & Mr. Wm. & Thos. Triplet the first two of whom dind with me. Found nothing.

22.   Raining in the Night and most part of this day being tolerably warm. With but little Wind and that Southerly. At home all day alone.

23.   At home all day writing and alone.

24.   At home all day and writing as yesterday. Alone.

25.   Went to Pohick Church with Mrs. Washington and returnd to Dinner.

26.   Went a hunting in the Neck early. Killd a Fox and dined with several others at Mr. Peake's.

27.   Went a hunting again in the Neck found a Fox and lost it. Dined with others at Mr. Thos. Triplets.

28.   Hunted again in the Neck and killed a Fox. Dined at home with the following Person's—the two Mr. Triplets—Mr. Manley, Mr. Peake, young Frans. Adam's and one Stone Street—also Peakes Daughter & Miss Fanny Eldridge.

Francis Adams (1749–1811), only child of Abednego and Mary Peake Adams, inherited Mount Gilead from his father. Humphrey Peake's daughter is probably Ann (Nancy), who later married Francis Adams.

ONE STONE STREET: Humphrey Peake's wife, Mary Stonestreet Peake, had three half brothers living in Maryland: Henry, Richard, and Butler Edelen Stonestreet.

FANNY ELDRIDGE: possibly Mary Peake's niece, Frances Edelen, daughter of Richard and Sarah Stonestreet Edelen of Prince George's County, Md. She was now about 16 years old and apparently a favorite of Humphrey Peake; in his will he bequeathed her a good horse with a saddle and bridle (codicil to will of Humphrey Peake, 10 Sept. 1783 and 11 Nov. 1784, Fairfax County Wills, Book E-1, 91–98, Vi Microfilm; will of Richard Edelen, 17 Jan. 1791, Prince George's County, Md., Wills, No. 1, T, 300, MdAA Microfilm; BRUMBAUGH, 1:59).

29.   At home all day. The two girls above mentioned here.

30.   Went a hunting again with the former Compa. but found nothing. Dined at Mr. Wm. Triplets. Miss Peake &ca. went home.

31.   Went up to Alexandria at the request of Messrs. Montgomerie Wilson and Steward, to settle with them along with Mr. John (as Exr. of Colo. Thoms. Colvil) for the Maryland Tract of Land which they had Purchasd of Mr. Semple. Staid all Night.

John Semple, plagued by many debts and unable to pay off the purchase bond for the Merryland tract that he had bought from Thomas Colvill, had assigned his rights to the land to three merchants: Thomas Montgomerie and Cumberland Wilson of Dumfries and Adam Stewart of Georgetown, Md. The Colvill executors—Frances Colvill, John West, Jr., and GW—had been empowered by the Maryland General Assembly on 23 Nov. 1771 to deed the Merryland tract to Semple, his heirs, or his assignees, provided that the balance due on the original contract was paid by 20 April 1773. If it were not paid, the executors could sell the land at public auction to the highest bidder (MD. ARCHIVES, 63:293–95). The purpose of the meetings on this and subsequent days was to determine exactly what balance was owed for Merryland and to arrange for payment of it by the merchants (see "Remarks" entry for 1 and 4 Jan. 1772).

MR. JOHN: either John West, Jr., or John Semple.

Acct. of the Weather in Decr.

Decr. 1st.   The Wind exceeding hard from the Northwest, & very cold.

2.   Wind variable with Clouds, and at the sametime cold.

3.   The most variable Weather imaginable—sometimes sunshine sometimes snowing—sometimes calm & sometimes the wind very high from the South—the North & Northwest where it contd. all Night.

4.   Wind at Northwest and very cold, with great appearances of Snow, a little of which fell in the Night.

5.   Morning Snowy with the Wind hard from the No. West & cold. Afternoon clear & not so Cold.

6.   Cold & Cloudy with appearances of Snow. Wind variable & in the Afternoon Calm.

7.   Morning Calm, and tolerably pleasant, with great appearances of Snow abt. Noon. Afternoon clear, Calm, & pleast. agn.

8.   Clear and cool threatning bad weather but none fell. Wind North.

9.   Clear and tolerably pleasant being Calm.

10.   Mild, soft and giving with very little or no Wind.

11.   Soft Morning but cloudy & lowering afterwards with the [wind] Westerly & something cooler.

12.   Rain in the Night, and this Morning, but clear warm and pleasant afterwards with but little Wind.

13.   Clear, calm, & pleasant Morning, Wind Southwest & West afterwards and something cooler.

14.   Cool, and more or less Cloudy all day. About Noon it snowd fast—then cleard away and was a tolerable Evening.

15.   Clear, calm, and pleasant till the Evening then lowering.

16.   Clear Calm and pleasant with but little Wind.

17.   Very Calm, & tolerable pleast.

18.   Very white frost. Calm & lowering.

19.   Wind Northerly & cold with Hail & Rain the first part of the day & constant Rain Afterwds.

20.   Clear and very pleasant all day with little or no Wind.

21.   Very white frost. Calm and quite pleasant in the forenoon but lowering afterwards with Rain in the Night.

22d.   Raining in the Night, and most part of this day. At the sametime warm with but little Wind and that at So. West.

23.   The Wind Shifting to Northwest in the Night, blew very hard & cold as it was all this day the ground being very hard froze.

24.   Exceeding hard & frozen with the Wind still high and Cold from the Northwest.

25.   Very raw and Cold with the Wind Northerly.

26.   Clear and Calm morning and tolerable pleasant day.

27.   Clear and calm in the Morning and a remarkable white frost. Evening very lowering.

28.   Raining all the latter part of the Night. The first of the day Cloudy & threatning but the Evening clear and pleasant.

29.   Remarkable clear, calm, & pleasant.

30.   Calm, and tolerably pleasant but lowering especially in the Morning.

31.   Not as pleasant though Cooler Wind getting Northerly.

Remarks & Occurances

Decr. 16.   Finished planting the Grape Cuttings in the Inclosure below the Garden. The first 29 Rows of which Reckoning from the side next the Spring are the winter Grape the other five are the Summer grape of tolerable good taste and ripening in October.

17.   Killed my Porke and distributed the Overseers their Shares.

18.   Agreed to raise Christophr. Shades Wages to £20 pr. Ann.

Shade worked at this rate until 25 Dec. 1773, when his salary was reduced to £18 a year. GW today advanced Shade £4 cash on his wages (LEDGER A, 331; LEDGER B, 39).

Routine Duties and Quiet Pleasures

1772

[January]

Where & how my time is Spent

Jany. 1st.   Upon the same business this day as brought me to Alexandria yesterday. Came home in the Afternoon and found Mr. Ramsay and his daughter here.

2.   At home all day. Mr. Montgomerie Mr. Piper and Mr. Harrison came to dinner & staid all Night.

These gentlemen came to try to resolve the continuing problem of the annuities that Margaret Savage was supposed to receive from her husband, Dr. William Savage (see main entries for 22 Sept. 1769 and 17 April 1770). Harry Piper had replaced Thomas Montgomerie as Mrs. Savage's legal representative in June 1771, but during the previous April her trustees, GW and Bryan Fairfax, had been obliged to settle with Montgomerie for her annuities through 1771, allowing him to receive the money on her behalf. Mr. Piper and the others were now faced with the task of forcing Montgomerie to relinquish those annuities, which he, who was also agent for Dr. Savage, had not sent her. At the same time they had to demand payment of this year's annuity from him (GW to Margaret Savage, 5 Sept. 1771 and 20 Sept. 1772, DLC:GW). When no satisfactory settlement was reached during the next few days, GW and Fairfax directed Robert Hanson Harrison to bring suit against Dr. Savage. Before the end of the month, GW advanced £53 sterling to Mrs. Savage, who was now living apart from her husband in Dublin and was much in want of funds (GW to Margaret Savage, 27 Jan. 1772, DLC:GW).

3.   Still at home with the above Gentlemen. In the afternoon Mr. & Miss Ramsay returnd to Alexandria and Mr. B. Fairfax came.

4.   Went a Hunting with the above Gentlemen. Found both a Bear & Fox but got neither. Went up to Alexandria with these Gentlemen to finish the business with Montgomerie &ca. which was accordg. done.

5.   Returnd home. Mr. Fairfax came with me. A Mr. Willis, & a Rhode Island Captn. dind here. The two latter went away afterwards.

Francis Willis, Jr. (1745–1828), son of John Willis (1719–1769) of Brunswick County, apparently lived in Leesburg at this time (Willis to GW, 16 Aug. 1773 and 17 Oct. 1773, ViMtV). He later moved to Berkeley County and eventually settled in Georgia (see "Remarks" entry for 5 Jan. 1772).

The Rhode Island captain was probably John Howland, master of the sloop *Nelly* of Nantucket, which entered the Potomac River in late Dec. 1771 from Rhode Island with a cargo of British goods, loaf sugar, chocolate, iron and wood ware, and 2,500 pounds of cheese (P.R.O., C.O.5/1350, f. 107).

6. Went a Hunting in the Neck with Mr. Fairfax. Found a fox & run him into a hole near Night, without Killing him. Found Doctr. Rumney & Mr. Magowan here when we returnd.

7. The above Gentlemen continued here all day and Night. Mr. Fairfax & myself rid to my Mill before Dinner.

8th. At home all day. Mr. Fairfax and Doctr. Rumney went away after Breakfast.

9. Mr. Magowan left this after breakfast for Colchester. I rid to the Ferry Doeg Run & Muddy hole & found Mrs. French & Daughter here when I returnd.

Penelope Manley French, sister of Harrison Manley and widow of Daniel French, was still residing with her only child, Elizabeth, at her late husband's home, Rose Hill. Although Mrs. French lived at least until 1799, she never remarried and apparently remained at Rose Hill until her death (will of Daniel French, 20 May 1771, Fairfax County Wills, Book C-1, 134–36, Vi Microfilm; GW to Benjamin T. Dulany, 12 Sept. 1799, NN).

Bryan Fairfax, after a miniature by an unknown artist. (Mrs. Charles Baird, Jr.)

10. Mrs. French & Daughter went away before Dinner. I went to the Ferry Plantn. to run some lines for my fencing &ca.

11. Went a Hunting in the Neck. Found a fox about One Clock and killed it about 3 Oclock. Mr. Magowan returnd from Colchester to Dinner.

12. At home all day. Mr. Magowan went to Mr. Peakes to Dinner & returnd again at Night.

13. Went again to the Ferry Plantation to run some lines for my Fencing. Mr. Magowan went to Mr. T. Triplets to Dinner and returnd.

14. Went to Belvoir with Mrs. Washington, Miss Custis & Mr. Gowan [Magowan] dind and stayed all Night.

15. Dined at Belvoir this day also, and returnd with Mr. Magowan In the Evening.

16. Went to Run some Lines between Mr. Barry & me at the Mill—also to try some of the Lines of Mr. Jno. Wests Land.

17. Went into the Neck to remeasure the Creek field and lay of some Fences. Upon my return to Dinner found one Mr. Hanna here who stayd all Night.

Mr. Hanna is Francis Hanna of Prince William County (DLC: Toner Collection).

18. Mr. Hanna went away after Breakfast as Mr. Magowan also did. I went a Hunting & killd a Fox—was joind by Mr. M. Campbell—Mr. Manley & Mr. Peake who dined here & went away afterwds.

19. At home all day. In the Afternoon Majr. Wagener and Mr. John Barnes with Doctr. Craik came here.

John Barnes, eldest son of Abraham Barnes (d. 1777) of St. Mary's County, Md., had recently gone bankrupt as a tobacco merchant in Port Tobacco, Md. After settling his firm's affairs, he moved to western Maryland, where he eventually developed a prosperous plantation called Montpelier (COPELAND, 110, 160–61).

20. After Breakfast the Majr. went away for Court and Messrs. Lawe. & Jno. Washington with Mrs. Polly Washington came here.

Polly Washington is probably Miss Mary Townshend Washington (see main entry for 10 April 1770).

21. Mr. Barnes and Doctr. Craik went away after Breakfast. The other two Gentlemen & myself rid to my Mill and back before Dinr.

22. At home all day with the two Mr. Washington's.

23. Went up to George Town to convey Deeds to Messrs. Montgomerie Stewart & Wilson for the Marryland Tract of Land wch. was accordingly done Mrs. Colvil being carried up in my Chariot returnd to Mr. Jno. Wests at Night.

As arranged at previous meetings, the three merchants today gave the Colvill executors £816 13s. 7d. in bills of exchange drawn on Glasgow firms (see "Remarks" entry for 1 and 4 Jan. 1772). GW received the bills on behalf of the executors and later this year converted them to Virginia currency (LEDGER B, 21). Although the Merryland tract was not formally deeded to the merchants until this date, they had begun to advertise in the *Maryland Gazette* on 16 Jan. that they would offer it for sale to the public on 28 May "in separate Lots or all together, for Sterling or Current Money." Merryland was eventually sold to several purchasers. However, money was still being collected from the merchants in Nov. 1790, and their obligations to the Colvill estate were not fully discharged until May 1795 (Thomas Montgomerie to GW, 17 Nov. 1790, DLC:GW; LEDGER C, 16).

24. Went from Mr. Wests to Alexanda. and returnd home to Dinner. In the Afternoon Mr. John Byrd and a Mr. Drew came here.

Mr. John Byrd is probably John Carter Byrd (b. 1751), second son of Col. William Byrd III and his first wife, Elizabeth Hill Carter Byrd. Mr. Drew is William or Dolphin Drew, both of whom settled in the Shenandoah Valley. William was appointed clerk of the county court when Berkeley County was organized in 1772 and served in that post until 1785. Dolphin, possibly a brother, practiced as an attorney in Berkeley County from 1772 (NORRIS [1], 224, 235, 295).

25. These Gentlemen went away after breakfast. I contd. at home all day.

26. At home all day alone that is with the Family.

27. At home by ourselves the day being dreadfully bad.

28. Just such a day as the former & at home alone.

29.   With much difficulty rid as far as the Mill the Snow being up to the breast of a Tall Horse everywhere.

30.   At home all day it being almost impracticable to get out.

31.   Still at home for the Causes above.

Acct. of the Weather in Jany.

Jan. 1st.   Lowering with the Wind Westwardly. In the Afternoon it threatned Snow much and at Night began to Rain which contd. till near day.

2.   Clear and pleasant with but little Wind and that Southerly.

3.   Very pleasant forenoon but lowering afterwards with the Wind fresh from the Southward.

4.   A little Rain fell last Night. The Morning calm, and Mild with Clouds; but the Afternoon cold with the Wind hard at No. West.

5.   Clear and cool, with the Wind still at No. West; but neither hard nor cold—tho' the Ground was very close blockd up with frost.

6.   Ground hard froze and Morning lowering without Wind. About 12 Oclock it began to Snow & continued to do so the remainder of the day very fast.

7.   Soft and giving with very little Wind & no Sun. Snow about 3 Inches deep.

8.   Clear, tolerably pleasant & thawing with but little Wind & that Northerly.

9.   Very pleasant Mild Morning, & Clear day. Abt. Noon the Wind blew pretty fresh from the Westward but not Cold—Snow melting.

10th.   Ground froze in the Morning. Till 8 or 9 Oclock it was clear & very pleasant—then cloudy & lowering till abt. two after which it grew clear & very pleast. No wind all day. Snow melted in the Fields.

11.   Lowering Morning, and very Cloudy Afternoon, with but little Wind and that from the Northward. Ground froze in the Morning but thawd afterwards.

12.   Snow fell in the Night and was about an Inch deep this Morning. Misty all day and thawing there being no frost, nor no Wind.

13.   Cloudy forenoon but, tolerably Clear afterwards without any frost. Wind Westwardly but neither Cold nor hard.

14.   Ground froze in the Morning, and thawd in the Afternoon. Wind fresh in the forenoon from the So. West but still afterwds. Clear.

15.   Clear and very pleasant, with but little Wind, and that Easterly. Ground froze in the Morning & thawd afterwards.

16.   Cloudy Morning with the wind pretty fresh from the West-ward—clear afternoon. The Ground froze but not hard in the Morning. Thawd Afterwards.

17.   Very hard frost in the Morng. Ground pretty well thawd in the Evening; which was pleasant—the Morning being cool, the Wind Southerly.

18.   Cloudy in the forenoon, with a little Wind from the South-ward; clear, Calm & pleasant afterwards. The Ground froze in the Morng. but thawd afterwards.

19.   Soft and giving Morning without any Wind. The After-noon Raining with but little wind which contd. through the Night.

20.   No frost, but Cloudy all the forenoon with the wind fresh & Cold from the No. West.

21.   Ground hard froze. Weather clear and very pleasant without any Wind.

22.   A White Frost and ground froze a little. Day a little lowering but very pleasant notwithstanding with the Wind Southerly.

23.   Soft Morning and a White frost. Weather exceeding pleasant as it continued to be through the day without Wind & clear Sky.

24.   Ground Open and Morning Foggy and Warm, with a few drops of rain. Afternoon clear and remarkably pleasant and Calm.

25.   Ground frozen but afterwards thawd. Day clear & a little cool wind being at Northwest Eveng. Calm.

26.   Raw, Cold, and Cloudy all day with the Wind tho not much of it Northerly.

27.   A Snow which began in the Night and was about 5 or 6 Inches deep this Morning kept constantly at it the whole day with the Wind hard & Cold from the Northward.

28.   The Same Snow continued all last Night and all this day with equal violence the Wind being very cold and hard from the Northward—drifting the Snow into high banks.

29.   Fine pleasant Morning without any Wind—but before 11 Oclock it clouded up & threatned Snow all the remaining part of the day—being full 3 feet deep every where already.

30.   Snowd all Night, with a brisk Wind from the Northward. The day cloudy and Misty—now & then Raining till the Afternoon when it grew clear, wind Westerly.

31.   For the most part Cloudy and hazy like with but little Wind & that from the Southward. Warm at least not Cold.

For several days GW had been experiencing what one meteorologist has called "the greatest snowstorm in the history of the middle and lower Potomac Valley" (LUDLUM, 144; BETTS [2], 33; FAIRFAX, 213). Deep snows at Williamsburg delayed the convening of the General Assembly, and the *Virginia Gazette* carried no news from a northern source until 5 Mar.

Remarks & Occurs. in Jany. 72

Jan. 1 & 4.   Settling with the Assignees of Mr. John Semple for the Maryland Tract of Land sold him by Colo. Thoms. Colvil &

fixed the Balle. still due on that Land to £2576.15.2½ [sterling], £1000 of which to be paid upon acknowledgement of Deeds to them at George Town the 23d. Instt. and the Residue in June 1773. An allowance is to be made for any money which it shall appear Mr. Semple has credited Mr. Hough for on Colo. Colvils Acct.

The initial £1,000 to be paid by the three merchants was to cover several protested bills of exchange that John Semple had given in part payment for the Merryland tract. However, sometime before 23 Jan., Semple was credited with £183 6s. 5d. sterling paid in cash to take up part of those bills, and the merchants' initial payment accordingly was reduced to £816 13s. 7d. (LEDGER c, 16). The merchants gave their own bond for the £1,576 15s. 2½d. that was supposed to be paid in June 1773 (GW to John West, Jr., NNebgGW).

5. Told Mr. Willis of Loudoun that he might have my small Tract of Land adjoining Wormeley, Alexander, and others for £250 – provided he took it without measuring; but if I run it out, it should be priced at 25/. pr. Acre let it measure more or less. He also wanted the Plantation Kennedy lives on upon Lease, & would give, if he liked the place upon examining of it, £40 pr. Ann. Rent if he had the liberty of Working 25 hands thereon. To this I told him I would give no definitive answer as I was under promise of giving the preference to another but would write him as soon as I could.

David Kennedy (Kennerly) served as ensign and lieutenant in the French and Indian War and was GW's quartermaster in the Virginia Regiment in 1758. After the war he settled in Frederick County, where he became a militia captain and a justice of the peace (CARTMELL, 89, 135). GW leased a plantation on Bullskin Run to Kennedy 1768-73 for £28 a year (LEDGER A, 248; LEDGER B, 22).

8th. Engaged to advance by, or at the April General Court for the use of Mr. Bryan Fairfax £150, or thereabouts, to discharge the Balle. of his Bond to Doctr. Savage. Also promised, if I could, to take up a Bill of Excha. of about £160 Sterg. with Int[eres]t thereon at the same time; In consideration of which I am to have the liberty of taking any of the Tracts of which he has given me a Mem[orandu]m at the prices there Stipulated in case I like them, or either of them upon examination thereof within [   ] Months from this date. If not he is then to become my Debtor for the money I shall advance on these two Accts.

Receivd 563½ Bushels of Oats from Arlington.

GW paid £150 on Bryan Fairfax's account to Dr. William Savage or his agent Thomas Montgomerie at the Fairfax County court, 20 April 1772, but did not make good Fairfax's bill of exchange, which had been drawn on the merchant John Muir of Alexandria and was held by John Baynes of Maryland (LEDGER B, 5; Fairfax to GW, 15 July 1772, DLC:GW). Nevertheless, Fairfax was grateful for GW's help in discharging his debt to Savage. "I could not have raised the money without your Assistance," he told GW in a letter dated 3 Aug. 1772 (DLC:GW). GW was compensated for the £150 with a tract of land in Fauquier County, which he chose from Fairfax's holdings there during May of this year (see main entries for 27, 29 May and 25 Sept. 1772).

Arlington plantation in Northampton County on the Eastern Shore of Virginia was part of the Custis lands owned by Jacky Custis (MEADE [1], 1:262–63). GW paid £10 13s. 4d. for freight of these oats (LEDGER B, 3).

[February]

Where & how my time is Spent

Feb. 1st.   Attempted to ride as far as the Ferry Plantation to wch. there was a Tract broke but found it so tiresome & disagreeable that I turnd back before I got half way.

2.   At home all day.

3.   At home all day alone.

4.   At home all day alone.

5.   Went to run a line across from the Ferry Plantation to where My Pasture fence strikes the Creek—also to run and measure the Field I am going to Inclose.

6.   Went across the Creek upon the Ice and staked off a fence for the Field on the Creek.

7.   Attempted to ride to the Mill, but the Snow was so deep & crusty, even in the Tract that had been made that I chose to Tye my Horse half way & walk there.

8.   At Home all day.

9.   Ditto—Ditto.

10.   Ditto—Ditto.

11.   Went out to make some further discovery of the Lines of West French & Manley & was much fatiegued by the deepness and toughness of the Snow.

John West, Jr., Penelope French, and Harrison Manley owned land between the Mill and Ferry plantations (see map, 1:240).

12.   Attempted to ride out again but found the Roads so disagreeable and unpleasant that I turnd back before I got to the Ferry Quarter.

13.   Went to the Ferry Plantation to run some Lines there. Returnd before 12 Oclock.

14.   Went out with my Compass agn. & run the Courses of Doegs Creek up to my Mill. Also a line or two of the Wades Land.

15.   At home all day.

16.   Ditto–Ditto.

17.   Rid to the Mill Plantation to See a Negro Man Sick of a Pleurisy.

18.   Rid to the Mill again on the same business as yesterday.

19.   Rid to Muddy hole, Doeg Run & Mill before Dinner.

20.   At home all day.

GW today wrote Robert Cary & Co., that he was "impatiently waiting for" the goods that he had ordered during the summer, especially the millstones of which he was much in need (DLC:GW). Unknown to GW, the ship *Trimley* of London had entered the South Potomac Naval District on the previous day, bringing him and his two stepchildren goods worth £722 17s. 2d. sterling from Cary & Co. On board was a pair of French buhrstones, 4 feet 4 inches in diameter, for which the company had charged him £40 16s. 10d. sterling, including packing and shipping (P.R.O., C.O.5/1350, f.52). All of the goods must have soon arrived at Mount Vernon, and the buhrstones apparently were installed in the mill in time for spring grinding.

21.   Rid to the Ferry Plantation and to the Fishing Landing where a few Fish were catchd in the Sein.

22.   Rid to the Ferry Plantation & Muddy hole, & returnd to Dinner. Mr. Ramsay & Captn. Conway Dind & lodgd here.

During this visit GW gave William Ramsay £25, "advanced on acct of your Son William at the Jersey College" (LEDGER B, 47).

23.　At home. Mr. Ramsay & Captn. Conway stayd all day.

24.　These Gentlemen went away. I rid to the Ferry Plantation and returnd to Dinnr.

25.　Set of for Williamsburg but not being able to cross Accatinck (which was much Swelled by the late Rains) I was obliged to return home again.

The first session of the new Virginia General Assembly, after several prorogations, was scheduled to begin on 6 Feb., but did not obtain a quorum until four days later due to the bad weather and poor roads (H.B.J., 1770–72, 145–53).

26.　Sett off again and reachd Colchester by nine Oclock where I was detain all day by high Winds & low tide.

27.　Crossd early & breakfasted at Dumfries. Got to Fredericksburg in the Afternoon & lodgd at Colo. Lewis's.

28.　Stayd all day in Town with my Brother John &ca. Dined at Colo. Lewis's & Spent the Evening at Captn. Weedon's.

29.　Prosecuted my Journey. Dined at Caroline Ct. House & lodged at Todds Bridge.

The Coleman family tavern at Caroline Court House was now operated by Francis Coleman's widow, Hannah Johnston Coleman (CAMPBELL [1], 413; KING [3], 259).

Acct. of the Weather in Feby.

Feb. 1st.　Snow still so deep that there was no passing from one place to another where there was no tract made. Day for the most part clear, tho' the Sky lookd muddy. Weather Mild & wind what little there was Southerly.

2.　Perfectly Calm and Mild till the Evening, when their Sprung up a little Wind from the Eastward. A little Snow fell in the Morning, the day cloudy and lowering quite thro'.

3.　The Wind which began to rise from the Eastward Yesterday Evening blew very fresh all Night attended with a mixture of

Hail Rain & Snow which made a Sleet. The same Weather contd. through the day the Wind however Shifting Southerly.

4.   The Wind coming on from the No. West & Shifting more Westerly it grew clear and very cold—blowing hard and freezing hard—Rivr. being almost Froze across and the Snow hard enough to bare.

5.   Very severe Frost. River quite froze. Morng. clear & not very cold but the Wind coming out at No. West it became very much so. Clear all day.

6.   Day clear, and morning very hard frozen—first part warm & pleast. latter cool, wind blowg. fresh from the Southward.

7.   Morng. clear, Midday Cloudy & like for Snow but clear afterwards with but little Wind & that Southerly.

8.   Cloudy, Soft and thawing with but very little Wind—that Southerly.

9th.   Raing. and thawing all Night and till 11 or 12 Oclock this day being foggy & Calm. About 12 the Wind came out hard & cold from the No. Wt. & froze.

10.   Clear and Cold—Morning being hard froze with the Wind at No. West. In the Afternoon it got Southerly but still kept cool.

11.   A Cold & fresh Southerly Wind blew all day. Clouds for the most part with appearances of falling Weather.

12.   Wind & Weather both variable. In the Morning the Wind was Northerly Raw & Cloudy—in the Afternoon Southerly & clear—at least not very Cloudy.

13.   Calm and pleasant in the Morning and till the Afternoon when the Weather Clouded and the Wind blowing pretty fresh from the So. and So. Et. grew raw & Cold.

14.   Calm Warm and pleasant. Snow Dissolving a good deal.

15.   Very variable both in Wind & Weather. In the Morning early it haild fast—then hail & Rain Mixd after that constant Rain

till abt. Noon then clear Warm & pleasant. Wind in the Morning at No. East–then fresh from the So. Et. & south from thence to South West & died away becomg. quite Calm.

16. The Wind shifting to Northwest abt. 9 Oclock last Night blew hard & grew exceeding Cold as it contd. to be all this day. Wind fresh from the same Quarter.

17. A Cold and Sharp Southerly Wind blowing all day the Snow and Earth thawd but little.

18. Thawing pretty considerably to day Wind continuing at So. and Warm being also clear.

19. Warm and Hazy, with now and then a little Rain. Wind Southerly and thawing fast.

20. Fresh Southerly Wind with some heavy Showers in the fore-noon–Snow melting exceedg. fast Ground in the old fields being almost bear.

21. Calm, clear, and very warm in the forenoon. But Cloudy a little in the Afternoon & Wind Easterly.

Jonathan Boucher today wrote GW from Maryland and began with an observation about the weather: "I congratulate You, & the World with Us, on our Restoration to a temperate Zone; for, in Truth, We have had a kind of a Greenland Winter" (DLC:GW).

22. Wind very fresh all the forepart of the day from the Southward Melting all the Snow in the Fields & drying the Ground fast.

23. The latter part of the Night and this Morning raining with Lightning and Thunder. Raing. more or less all day.

24. Raining in the Morning & Cloudy and lowering all day. In the Evening misting which afterwards turnd to Rain a good deal of which fell in the Night.

25. Raining fast the first part of the Morning–afterwds. clear, when the Wind blew violently hard at No. West.

26. Continued blowing violently hard all Night and the whole day through at least till the Evening but not remarkably Cold tho the Wind was at No. Wt.

27. Calm and exceeding pleast. Ground this Morning and yesterday's pretty hard froze.

28. Very white frost & fresh Southerly Wind with Clouds & now & then a slight sprinkle of Rain. Ground not froze.

29. Wind at No. West and pretty Cool but no frost—also Cloudy till the Evening.

[March]

Where & how my time is Spent

Mar. 1st. Reachd Colo. Bassetts from Todds Bridge by 12 Oclock. Stayd there the remainder of the day.

GW crossed the Pamunkey River at Ruffin's ferry (LEDGER B, 3).

2. Set out for Williamsburg and got in about 12 Oclock. Dined at the Speakers and supd at the Treasurers.

Because the House of Burgesses met only briefly this morning, GW probably did not renew his burgess oaths until the next day (H.B.J., 1770–72, 204). This session of the assembly had already met for three weeks and was to continue for another six.

GW lodged with Edward Charlton, whose two-story frame house stood almost directly across Duke of Gloucester Street from the Raleigh Tavern (WILLIAMSBURG, 17). A wigmaker in Williamsburg for many years, Charlton had not advertised himself as a tavern keeper and was apparently renting private rooms in his house only during public times. His brother, Richard Charlton, had operated a regular Williamsburg tavern during the late 1760s, but there is no indication that his tavern was in business at this time (see main entry for 4 May 1768). Edward Charlton's wife, Jane Hunter Charlton, was a milliner who often furnished Mrs. Washington and Patsy Custis with various goods.

3. Dined and Supd at the Governors.

GW today was reappointed to the standing committees of privileges and elections, propositions and grievances, and religion, and was one of a committee of three appointed to review a petition for financial relief from John Robinson, a disabled veteran of the Virginia Regiment (H.B.J., 1770–72, 204).

4. Dined at the Attorneys and Spent the Evening at the Governors.

In the House of Burgesses today GW reported committee approval of John Robinson's claim; he should be allowed £5 "for his present Relief" plus an annuity of £6 for life. The house promptly agreed to this proposal, and GW was ordered to take the resolution to the council for its concurrence, which it gave on 11 Mar. Later in today's proceedings a petition for relief was received from a second disabled veteran, Philip Hand. A new committee, again including GW, was appointed to consider his claim (H.B.J., 1770–72, 209–10, 234).

5. Dined at Mrs. Dawson's and Spent the Evening in my own Room.

6. Dined and Spent the Evening at the Treasurer's.

7. Took an early Dinner at Mrs. Dawson's and went up to Colo. Bassetts with him in the Afternoon.

8. At Colo. Bassetts all day.

9. Returnd to Williamsburg by 12 Oclock and Dined at the Club at Mrs. Campbells.

10. Dined and Spent the Evening at the Palace.

11. Dined and Spent the Evening at the Club at Mrs. Campbells.

Earlier in this session of the burgesses, the house had ordered its committee on propositions and grievances to prepare a bill empowering two planters to erect gates on public roads that crossed their property to public ferries. Today the committee was further instructed to include GW, Burwell Bassett, and Joseph Cabell in the bill. GW was to be permitted to "Keep a Gate or Gates, on his Land, across the Road leading to *Posey's* Ferry, on *Potowmack* River," while Bassett was to be allowed the same privilege on the road to the Brick House ferry on York River and Cabell on the road to his ferry on the James (H.B.J., 1770–72, 198, 235).

12. Dined at the Club and went to the Play.

The play was presented by David Douglass's American Company, which came to Williamsburg for the spring season, from the convening of the General Assembly in early February through the April session of the General Court (RANKIN, 165).

13. Dined at the Club and Spent the Evening at Southalls.

The House of Burgesses today referred a bill for docking the entail on some land owned by John Hancock of Princess Anne County to a special committee of five members, of which GW was one (H.B.J., 1770–72, 241–42).

14.   Dined at the Club & Spent the Evening there also.

15.   Dined at the Speakers & Spent the Evening at my own lodgings.

16.   Dined at the Club, & spent the Evening there also.

17.   Dined at the Club and went to the Play in the Afternoon.

18.   Dined at the Club and Spent the Evening at the Burgesses Ball in the Capitol.

On this day the burgesses received a petition from several "Inhabitants and Freeholders of the County of *Frederick*," requesting passage of an act for improving "the Navigation of the River *Potowmack* from Tide-Water to Fort *Cumberland*." Such improvement, the petitioners argued, "would be productive of great Advantage, not only to those who are settled upon the adjacent Lands, but to the whole Colony, by introducing a most extensive Trade." Financing could be obtained from any of three sources: public tax money, private venture capital, or public subscription of private capital. According to usual procedure, the petition was referred for study to the committee on propositions and grievances. Other business before the house today included a report from the committee on John Hancock's bill that the bill's allegations were true (H.B.J., 1770–72, 252–53).

The burgesses' ball was briefly noted the following day in Purdie and Dixon's *Virginia Gazette:* "Last Night there was a Ball and elegant Entertainment at the Capitol, given by the gentlemen of the Honourable the House of Burgesses to his Excellency the Governour and the People of Rank in this City."

19.   Dined at Mrs. Dawsons & went to the Play in the Evening.

20.   Dined at Mrs. Amblers and Spent the Evening at Southalls.

Mary Cary Ambler had a town house in Williamsburg, where GW apparently dined with her on this day, but her principal residence was at her plantation about seven miles away on Jamestown Island.

21.   Dined at the Club & Spent the Evening there also.

The burgesses today passed an act to divide Frederick County into three counties: the northernmost portion to be called Berkeley County, the central portion Frederick County, and the southernmost portion Dunmore County. By this act, which the council approved two days later, GW's Bullskin Run lands became part of Berkeley County (H.B.J., 1770–72, 262, 268; HENING, 8:597–99).

22.   Went over to Colo. Warner Lewis's in Gloucester. Dined & Lodged there.

GW crossed the York River on the ferry running between Yorktown and Gloucester (Tindall's) Point (LEDGER B, 4).

23. Returnd to Williamsburg before 10 Oclock and dined at the Club & Spent the Evening at the same.

24. Dined at the Club & Spent the Evening at Mr. Andersons.

25. Dined at Mr. Lewis Burwells and went to the Play.

26. Dined at the Club and went to the Play.

GW is here attending the local premiere of the "new Comedy . . . *A Word to the Wise,*" by Hugh Kelly (1739–1777). It was received, reported Purdie and Dixon's *Virginia Gazette* a week later, "with the warmest Marks of Approbation." The newspaper went on to comment: "If the comick Writers would pursue Mr. Kelly's Plan, and present us only with moral Plays, the Stage would become (what it ought to be) a School of Politeness and Virtue."

27. Dined at the Club and Spent the Evening in my own Room.

28. Dined at the Club and Spent the Evening at Mrs. Campbells.

29. Dined at Mrs. Dawsons and Spent the Evening at My Own Lodgings.

30. Dined and Spent the Eveng. at Mrs. Campbells.

In the House of Burgesses today John Hancock's bill was passed (H.B.J., 1770–72, 280, 289).

31. Dined at Mrs. Campbells & spent the Evening there also.

Acct. of the Weather in March

Mar. 1st. Ground pretty hard froze. Morning Calm & pleasant. Cool & Windy afterwards Wind fresh from the Northward.

2. Pretty Cool all day – Wind being abt. No. Et. & Cloudy in the Afternoon.

3. Cloudy & Snowing in the forenoon & raw & cold all day.

4.   Morning clear and tolerably pleasant but raw and Cold in the Afternoon & raining in the Night.

5.   Wind blew very fresh and cold from the Northwest.

6.   Hard frost and unpleasant with Clouds.

7.   Tolerably pleasant—Wind getting Southerly.

8.   Clear, Warm, and very pleasant with but little Wind.

9.   The Rain which began to fall in the Night continued till abt. 9 Oclock when it ceased & cleard. away warm.

10.   Tolerably pleasant in the Forenoon but lowering & like for Snow in the Afternoon.

11.   Cold & raw in the forenoon Snowing in the afternoon.

12.   Clear Morning but very hard frost ground being blocked up close. In the Night Snow again.

13.   Snow about an Inch deep but soon Melted. The day Clear & cool especially in the Evening.

14.   Hard frozen Morning & Cold all day but clear.

15.   Very raw and Cold with the Wind Northerly and clear.

16.·   Wind fresh & raw in the forepart of the day from the So. West—afterwards still & pleasant.

17.   Hard frost and very Cold, Wind at No. West again.

18.   Lowering Morning, and Snowy day.

19.   Cloudy & disagreeable in the Morning. Raining in the Afternoon & Misty Evening.

20.   Snow several Inches deep this morning & continued Snowing, & Melting as it fell till 2 or 3 Oclock in the afternoon.

21.   Clear & Windy from the No. West & cool for the Season.

22. Wind very fresh from the same & clear but cold.

23. White Frost but clear till the Afternoon—then lowering a little.

24. Tolerably pleasant & at the same time clear & mild.

25. Raining more or less all the Afternoon.

26. Clear and Cool Wind Northerly.

27. Tolerably pleasant in the Forenoon but raw & cold afterwards.

28. Pleasant forenoon but very Wet & Rainy afterwds.

29. Wind very fresh from the westward with Cool Clouds.

30. Wind from the same Quarter and Cool but clear.

31. Forepart clear but a little Cool—latter part Cloudy & like for Rain.

[April]

Where & how my time is Spent

Apl. 1. Dined and Spent the Evening at Mrs. Campbells.

2. Dined and Spent the Evening at Mrs. Campbells.

On this day GW was appointed to a committee of three to consider a proposed amendment to the act regarding deer hunting and the control of hounds. Today also a report was submitted from the committee on Philip Hand's claim to which GW had been appointed on 4 Mar. Hand's petition, the committee found, was reasonable, and the house promptly approved giving him £6 for "his present Relief" and an annuity of £5 for life (H.B.J., 1770–72, 290–91).

3. Dined at Mrs. Campbells and went to the Play—then to Mrs. Campbells again.

On this day GW was appointed to two committees, one to write a Potomac navigation bill and one to amend the colony's flour inspection regulations.

Some previous thought must have been given to the second matter; a short time later today the flour inspection committee presented a bill to amend the current inspection act (H.B.J., 1770–72, 292–93). Designed "to prevent frauds, which may be committed by millers, bakers, and others, employed" in Virginia's growing flour export trade, this bill, as passed a week later, placed several new restrictions on mill owners. All flour for export must be "genuine and unmixed with any other grain, and . . . all of the same fineness, and faithfully packed in good casks, made of seasoned timber, and, when delivered, well and securely nailed." The casks were to be branded with the first letter of the mill owner's Christian name and his full surname or with the name of his mill and conveyed with an invoice "to the place of exportation" in a vehicle or vessel "sufficiently covered and secured from the weather." There the contents of each cask were to be examined by an official inspector, and if they were "found to be good and merchantable," he was to "stamp or brand" the cask's head with a "V" for Virginia, the first letter of county's name, his own name, and the quantity and grade of the flour (HENING, 8:143–44, 511–14).

Other business before the burgesses today included a favorable report on the deer-hunting amendment by the committee to which it had been referred and passage of the bill allowing GW and others to erect gates on public roads leading to ferries. The gate bill, however, was not approved by the council and it did not become law (H.B.J., 1770–72, 293–94, 298).

4.   Took a Cold dinner at Mr. Southalls & came up to Eltham in the Afternoon.

5.   Went to see Mrs. Dandridge betwn. Breakfast and Dinner.

6.   Returnd to Williamsburg. Dined at Mrs. Campbells — went to the Concert & then to Mrs. Campbells again.

Today Thomson Mason, burgess for Stafford County, presented the Potomac navigation bill to the house on behalf of the committee. The bill, which authorized a public subscription to finance the project, was received, read, and ordered to be engrossed for final action (H.B.J., 1770–72, 297; HENING, 8:570–79). Later this day the burgesses passed a public road act which included a provision authorizing the county courts of Fairfax, Loudoun, Berkeley, and Frederick to impose special levies on their inhabitants for the next three years, to finance repair of the public roads leading from Alexandria and Colchester to the Shenandoah Valley. These roads, it was noted in the act, had been "rendered almost impassible" by "the great number of waggons which use the same," and the normal method of maintaining them entirely by local laboring tithables had proved to be "insufficient" (H.B.J., 1770–72, 299; HENING, 8:549–51).

7.   Dined at Mrs. Campbells and went to the Play then to Mrs. Campbells again.

On this day the burgesses referred the flour inspection bill for further work to four of the six members on the committee that had prepared it. GW was one of the four (H.B.J., 1770–72, 302).

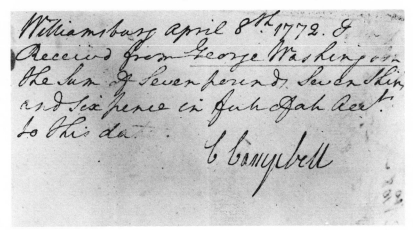

Washington pays a bill owed to Mrs. Christiana Campbell for service at her tavern. (Colonial Williamsburg Photograph)

8.　Dined at Mrs. Campbells and Spent the Evening at my lodgings.

GW today paid Jane Charlton £1 12s. 3d. for goods supplied Patsy Custis and Mrs. Washington and £11 for his "Board . . . since the 1st. of March" (LEDGER B, 4).

In the House of Burgesses today three bills in which GW had some interest were passed and sent to the council: the deer-hunting bill, the Potomac navigation bill, and a bill to improve Alexandria's wharf and marshy lots. All three were soon approved by the councillors (H.B.J., 1770–72, 304–5, 310–13).

9.　Took an early Dinner at Southalls and set of for Eltham on my return home.

Also on this day the flour inspection bill was reported with several amendments from its committee. The amendments were promptly accepted by the house, and on the following day the bill was passed by the burgesses and approved by the council (H.B.J., 1770–72, 311, 313).

GW left Williamsburg two days before Governor Dunmore prorogued the General Assembly (H.B.J., 1770–72, 317). Before GW left, he finished paying his personal accounts in town: £5 12s. 6d. for various play tickets for himself and others during his stay, £2 12s. 6d. for his and his servant's expenses at the Raleigh Tavern, and 5s. to a blacksmith for shoeing his horses. He also received from Jane Charlton, acting on behalf of her husband Edward, £240 Virginia currency for a £200 sterling bill of exchange GW had held as a Colvill executor since 23 Jan. Earlier in his stay he had converted two other bills of exchange for the Colvill estate at the same rate but through another merchant (LEDGER B, 4, 5).

10.   With Colo. Bassett & Lady & there 3 daughters set of for Mount Vernon. Dined at Todds Bridge and lodged at Hubbards.

Two of the Bassett daughters, Elizabeth and Anna Maria, had visited Mount Vernon with their parents three years earlier. The third, and youngest, daughter, Frances Bassett (b. 1767), later married George Augustine Washington, eldest son of GW's brother Charles.

GW again crossed the Pamunkey River at Ruffin's ferry (LEDGER B, 5).

11.   Breakfasted at Hubbards and dined at Colo. Lewis's in Fredericksburg where Colo. Bassett &ca. lodged. I lodged at my Mothers.

During this stay in Fredericksburg, GW left £8 cash with his mother for his brother Charles, who was to use the money to buy corn for Ferry Farm. On the following day GW recorded paying 1s. 6d. for "ferriages at Hunters," indicating that he did not cross the Rappahannock River until then and that his mother was no longer at Ferry Farm but was ensconced in the house on Charles Street (LEDGER B, 5, 48).

12.   Dined in Dumfries and reachd home in the Afternoon where I found Mrs. Barnes, Miss Carlyle, Miss Alexander Miss Hunter, Colo. Carlyle & Son & Daughter Nancy.

Miss Alexander is probably Mary Ann Alexander, daughter of Gerard and Mary Dent Alexander. The Alexanders' other daughter, Nancy, was by this time married to Fielding Lewis, Jr. (will of Gerard Alexander, 9 Aug. 1760, Fairfax County Wills, Book B-1, 327–29, Vi Microfilm).

John Carlyle's only son was George William Carlyle (1765–1781). During the Revolution he was a cadet in Lee's Legion and was killed at the Battle of Eutaw Springs in 1781.

13.   All the above went away but Mrs. Barnes & Miss Hunter. About 12 Oclock Colo. Bassett & Family arrived.

14.   At home all day.

15.   Walk'd to the Fishing Landing at Poseys between breakfast & dinner with Colo. Bassett.

16.   At home all day.

17.   Rid with Colo. Bassett to my Mill from thence to Poseys & home to Dinner.

18.   Walkd with Colo. Bassett to the Fishing Landing at the Ferry between Breakfast & Dinner. Captn. Posey dined here. J. P. Custis came here.

Jacky Custis was returning from Jonathan Boucher's new home, Mount Lubentia, in Prince George's County, Md. Boucher had moved there from Annapolis the previous December to become rector of Queen Anne Parish, taking three of his students with him: Jacky, Overton Carr of Louisa County, Va., and Charles Calvert (1756–1777), son of Benedict Calvert of Mount Airy. Mount Lubentia was rented from the Magruder family of Maryland, a fact that inspired Boucher's students to dub it "Castle Magruder" (BOUCHER [1], 75; W.P.A. [2], 474–75).

19.   At home all day. Mr. Campbell dined here.

20.   Went up to Court, Colo. Bassett & Jno. Custis with me. Returnd in the Afternoon—Mr. Tilghman & Mr. Hanson with us.

The April court met only this day (Fairfax County Order Book for 1772–74, 25–26, Vi Microfilm). While GW was in Alexandria, he clubbed at Arell's tavern (LEDGER B, 5).

James Tilghman, Jr. (1748–1796), was the third son of James Tilghman (1716–1793), who moved from Talbot County, Md., in the 1760s to practice law in Philadelphia. James Jr. was living in Alexandria at this time, but later settled in Talbot County, Md., where he practiced law (see JOHNSTON [1], 369, 374; TILGHMAN [2], 1:8).

Mr. Hanson is probably young Samuel Hanson or his brother Thomas Hawkins Hanson, sons of Samuel Hanson of Green Hill, Charles County, Md.

21.   Walkd to the Fishery at Poseys between Breakfast & dinnr. Mrs. Fairfax dined here & returnd in the Afternoon.

22.   Rid to the Mill and Fishery with the Ladies & Gentlemen. Mr. Tilghman & Mr. Hanson went away.

23.   Dined at Belvoir with Colo. Bassett & Lady & Daughter, Mrs. Washington & Patcy. Returnd in the Evening. J. P. Custis dind also.

24.   Rid to Muddy hole Doeg Run and Mill with Colo. Bassett before Dinner. Mr. Mitchell & Mr. Ball who came yesterday went away.

Mr. Ball may be Burgess Ball of Lancaster County, Va., and Mr. Mitchell one of Ball's second cousins: William, Robert, or Richard Mitchell (HAYDEN, 62, 111–12).

25.   Went a Hunting with Colo. Bassett. Found nothing.

26.   Colo. Bassett & Mrs. Bassett, Mrs. Washington & Self went to Pohick Church & returnd to Dinr.

27. At home all day writing to send to Williamsburg by Colo. Bassett.

Bassett was to settle several financial matters for GW in the Williamsburg area (GW Memorandum, 27 April 1772, NjMoNP).

28. Colo. Bassett & Family set of home. I rid to the Mill and Fishing Landing at the Ferry.

29. Rid to the Mill and Fishing Landing again. Doctr. Rumney dined here.

30. Went to the Fishing Landing at the Ferry again.

GW today lent £2 10s. to John Posey, who was "going to Maryl[an]d" (LEDGER A, 256).

Acct. of the Weather in April

Apl. 1. Raw, Cold, & Cloudy Morning. Close and constant Rain afterwards.

2. Raining a kind of fine Rain more or less all day with the wind at East—cold & disagreeable.

3. Cloudy, Cold, & unpleasant all day. Wind Northerly.

4. Wind still in the same quarter. Cloudy & equally disagreeable with now and then a Sprinkle of Rain.

5. Clear, Calm, and tolerably pleasant but not very warm.

6. Rain Early this Morning and Cloudy till about 12 Oclock then clear and tolerably pleasant.

7. Clear and tolerably pleast. in the Forenoon. In the afternn. appearances of Rain and Wind Easterly.

8. Tolerably pleasant in the Morning but before 11 Oclock began to Rain and raind more or less all day—with thunder & lightning in the Evening.

9. Very Cold and very Windy from the Northwest with flying Clouds & sometimes a sprinkle of Rain.

10.   A little Cool and Windy from the westward but tolerably pleasant notwithstanding.

11.   Warm, Calm, & pleasant in the forenoon, brisk wind from the Southward with Clouds & some Rain in the Afternoon.

12.   Clear and Cool wind being Northerly.

13.   Clear and Warm in the forenoon–but very windy in the Afternoon.

14.   Clear but Cool with the Wind high from the Westward.

15.   Clear, Calm, & Warm in the Forenoon, but Cloudy afterwds. with the Wind variable.

16.   Lowering and Misting all day with but little Wind & Warm in the forenoon but Cooler afterwds. with the Wind Easterly.

17.   Clear, & Cool in the forenoon wind at Northwest–Warmer afterwards.

18.   Clear and tolerably pleasant with but little in the fore-noon–lowering afterwards.

19.   Raining more or less all day with the Wind at East.

20.   Clear but the Wind very hard at No. West and Cold.

21.   Tolerably pleasant and Moderately warm with but little Wind and that Southerly.

22.   Calm and Warm in the Morning. Wind very fresh from the Southwest in the Afternoon.

23.   Quite calm and pleast. but a little cool.

24.   Very cool with squaly Clouds & Snow with wind from the Northwest.

25.   Cool, and Calm in the Morning but windy afterwards from the Northwest.

26.   Clear Calm and Warm.

27.   Tolerably warm and pleasant but a little windy from the Southwest.

28.   Clear and Calm, and very Warm.

29.   Clear, Calm and very warm again.

30.   Not quite so warm as yesterday but pleasant, clear & Calm— very smoky.

[May]

Where & how my time is Spent

May 1st.   Went a Hunting with Mr. Jno. Custis. Found nothing. Returnd to Dinner.

2.   At home all day. Mr. Foxcraft Mr. Hoops and Mr. Ramsay came here to Dinner and stayd all Night.

Two of GW's visitors were from the postal service. After 1764 British America was divided between a southern postal district, from the Carolinas to the West Indies, and a northern postal district, from Virginia to Canada. John Foxcroft, who shared direction of the northern postal district with Benjamin Franklin, was in direct charge of that district 1764–74 while Franklin was in England. John's brother Thomas Foxcroft became postmaster of Philadelphia in 1766. This Mr. Foxcroft was probably John, who often traveled to Virginia on postal business. William Ramsay was postmaster at Alexandria at this time (see HARRISON [4]; KONWISER; SMITH [1]; LABAREE [3]).

Mr. Hoops was David Hoops, probably traveling from his home in Philadelphia to Hanover County where a married sister lived (GLAZEBROOK, 2:xiii). He was a son of Adam Hoops (1709–1771), of Philadelphia, with whom GW had dealt when he was a commissary for the British troops during the 1758 campaign against Fort Duquesne (GW to John Forbes, 30 Dec. 1758, DLC:GW).

3.   Mr. Foxcraft and Mr. Hoops went away after breakfast and Mr. Ramsay after dinner. I continued at home all day.

4.   Rid to the Mill and Ferry Plantations, and to the Fishery at the Ferry. J. P. Custis returnd to Mr. Bouchers, and Mr. Ballendine came in the afternoon.

John Ballendine, now out of Fairfax County's debtor's prison (see main entry for 16 April 1770), had been encouraged by Virginia's recent Potomac navigation act and was rounding up support for a trip to England to study canal building there. He came to Mount Vernon today to ask for GW's support and for letters of introduction to leading men in Maryland, including Governor Eden, who might be persuaded to back him. GW obliged, but he warned his Maryland friends that although "Mr. Ballendine has a natural genius to things of this sort . . . I cannot help adding, that his Principles have been loose; whether from a natural depravity, or distress'd circumstances, I shall not undertake to determine" (GW to Jonathan Boucher, 5 May 1772, CSmH).

5. Mr. Ballendine Went away abt. 11 Oclock. At home all day.

6. Rid to the Mill, Doeg Run, and Ferry before Dinner. In the Afternoon Doctr. Rumney and Mr. James Adam came here & lodged.

James Adam's visit today and Matthew Campbell's calls during the next four days must have concerned GW's current business with Robert Adam & Co.: the sale of 929,700 herring and 10,894 shad for a total price of £184 17s. and the purchase of three slaves for £185 (LEDGER B, 42).

7. Mr. Adam went away in the Morning early. Rid with the Doctr. to the Fishery at Poseys who came back to Dinner with Mr. Campbell & went away in the Afternoon.

8. Rid into the Neck, and to Muddy hole.

9. Rid to Doeg Run Mill and Ferry. Mr. Campbell lodged here.

10th. Went to Pohick Church & returnd home to Dinner. Mr. Campbell Dined here.

11. Rid to the Ferry Plantatn. & Mill. Old Mr. Wm. Bayly dined here.

William Baily, Bailey, or Bayly (d. 1782), an original settler of Colchester in the late 1750s, had established a tavern there and later became the proprietor of the Colchester tobacco warehouse (SPROUSE [3], 173). Baily came to Mount Vernon today to discuss the rental of GW's bateau (LEDGER B, 28, 64).

12. Went up to Alexandria with Mrs. Washington & Miss Custis to see Captn. Woods Ship Launched. Returnd in the afternoon.

13. Rid to Muddy hole, Doeg Run, Mill and Ferry Plantations before Dinner.

14.   Dined at Belvoir, and returnd in the Afternoon. Found Colo. Mason here.

15.   At home all day. Colo. Mason & Captn. McCarty dined here, the former went away after Dinner the latter stayed all Night.

16.   Went to Mr. Barnes's on Business of Mrs. Barnes & returnd to Dinner. Captn. McCarty went away after breakfast.

17.   At home all day without Company.

18.   Went up to Court and stayed all Night. In the Evening Mr. Peale & J. P. Custis came to Mount Vernon.

The court met 18–19 May; GW attended both days (Fairfax County Order Book for 1772–74, 27–34, Vi Microfilm).

Charles Willson Peale (1741–1827), a resident of Annapolis, came to Mount Vernon with a letter of introduction from Jonathan Boucher. Peale had forsaken his saddlery business, to which he had been apprenticed as a youth, to take up painting. He visited John Singleton Copley in Boston in 1765 and studied painting with Benjamin West in London 1767–69. He was now making his living painting miniatures, and on occasion larger portraits, of gentry and merchants in Pennsylvania, Maryland, and Virginia.

19.   Mrs. Barnes came up to Alexandria. I returnd home in the Afternoon, & found Colo. Blackburn & Lady, Miss Scott Miss Brown, & Doctr. Brown here who came before Dinner—also found Mr. Peale & J. P. Custis.

Col. Thomas Blackburn (c.1740–1807), a Prince William County justice, lived at Rippon Lodge near Dumfries. His wife was Christian Scott Blackburn (b. 1745), younger sister of Miss Catherine Scott. Dr. William Brown (c.1752–c.1792) had graduated from the University of Edinburgh during the previous year and had begun to practice medicine in Alexandria. He would soon marry Catherine Scott. Miss Brown is probably Dr. Brown's sister Frances Brown (d. 1823), who would later marry Charles Alexander of Fairfax County (HAYDEN, 165, 177–78, 601–3).

20.   Colo. Blackburn & the Compa. with him went away after Breakfast. I sat to have my Picture drawn.

On 21 May, GW wrote to Jonathan Boucher: "Inclinations having yielded to Importunity, I am now contrary to all expectations under the hands of Mr. Peale; but in so grave— so sullen a mood—and now and then under the influence of Morpheus, when some critical strokes are making, that I fancy the skill of this Gentleman's Pencil, will be put to it, in describing to the World what manner of man I am" (WRITINGS, 3:83–84).

Charles Willson Peale visited Mount Vernon to make portraits of the Washington family, including these miniatures of Jacky and Patsy Custis. (Mount Vernon Ladies' Association of the Union)

21. Captn. Posey who came here the 19th. went up to Alexandria this day. I set again to take the Drapery.

Peale's practice was to sketch the painting out in one neutral color, show the sketch to the subject for his approval, and then paint the portrait, thus demanding a minimum of time and patience of the subject. On this day Peale had GW wear the "Drapery" (clothing) chosen for the painting, which was GW's colonel's uniform from his service in the Virginia Regiment (SELLERS, 1:106; MORGAN [1], 24; see frontis., vol. 1).

22. Set for Mr. Peale to finish my Face. In the Afternoon Rid with him to my Mill. I returnd home by the Ferry Plantation.

23. Rid into the Neck, and to Muddy hole before Dinner.

24. Set out after Dinner for Loud[ou]n &ca. Reachd Mr. Fairfax's and lodged there.

Peale remained at Mount Vernon to paint miniatures of Patsy and Jacky Custis. Jacky also paid Peale for a miniature of his mother, Martha Washington, probably for Jacky's own use (LEDGER B, 50; CUSTIS ACCOUNT BOOK, 30 May 1772).

25. Got to Leesburg to Dinner & Stayed all Night.

26.   At Leesburg all day.

27.   Set out with Mr. Bryan Fairfax to view some of his Lands on Goose Creek and Little River. Lodged at Mr. Charles Wests.

GW was inspecting Fairfax's lands in Loudoun and Fauquier counties in order to choose a tract as compensation for the £150 that he had previously paid on Fairfax's account (see "Remarks" entry for 8 Jan. 1772).

28.   Surveyed one of Mr. Fairfax's Tracts on Little Rivr. Dined at one Jon. Jacksons a Tenant of his and loged again at Mr. Chs. Wests.

Charles West today signed an agreement to sell GW 484 acres of land on Dogue Creek for 25s. an acre, a total price of £605 (NjMoNP; LEDGER B, 59). GW had tried to purchase the eastern part of the tract in 1769, because its boundary on that side came within a few rods of the place where his merchant mill was soon to be built and because there was good timber on the land suitable for use in construction of the mill, but no deal was made at that time (GW to West, 6 June 1769, DLC:GW).

29.   Went up to Mr. Robt. Ashbys dined and lodged there. After dinner went to view some more of Mr. Fairfaxs Land on Goose Ck. & Chattens R.

GW took a 600-acre tract on Chattins Run as his compensation from Bryan Fairfax. Located in Fauquier County near Rectorstown, this land had been inherited by Fairfax from his younger brother William, a lieutenant in the British army who died at Quebec in 1759. The patent for the tract was sent to GW in August (Fairfax to GW, 3 Aug. 1772, DLC:GW).

30.   Set out early. Viewd some Land belonging to Jesse Ball & one Kinner. Stopd a little while among my Tenants under the Ridge. Dined at Snickers's and lodged at Mr. Warnr. Washingtons.

31.   At Mr. Washingtons all day.

Acct. of the Weather in May

May 1st.   Very Smoaky and a little lowering with but little Wind and tolerably Warm.

2.   Very smoaky and hazy all day—warm in the Afternoon and perfectly Calm.

3.   A little Rain, with the Wind fresh from the No. East in the Morning and very cool—clear afterwards.

4.   Tolerably calm in the Morning but Windy and cool afterwards with Rain in the Afternoon & Night.

5.   Tolerably calm and pleast. wind Southerly.

6.   Wind very fresh from the Southward with Clouds & a little Rain in the Morning.

7.   Clear and tolerable warm with the wind very fresh from the Southward.

8.   Wind Easterly with Clouds & much appearance of Rain about Noon but very little fell.

9.   Still Cloudy with appearances of Rain but none fell. Wind high from So. West.

10.   Cool, Wind being pretty fresh from the Northwest.

11th.   Rather Cool & lowering with the Wind varying from South to East.

12.   Very warm — there being but little Wind and that Southerly. Day clear.

13.   Cooler than yesterday with some appearances of Rain but none fell.

14.   Clear, and tolerably pleasant with but little Wind and that Southerly.

15.   A little Cool but clear & not unpleasant.

16.   Very Warm, and but little Wind, that Southerly.

17.   Warm and clear in the forenoon. In the Afternoon & first part of the Night a fine Rain from the So. Wt.

18.   Lowering forenoon & Warm. Wind from the Westward afterwards but not Cold.

19.   Clear and somewhat cooler than yesterday — but pleasant notwithstanding.

20.   Clear and warm in the forenoon with but little wind. In the Afternoon a heavy Shower of Rain with Wind from the No. West which turnd the Air very Cool.

21.   Clear, and Cool all day—with the Wind Westerly.

22.   Still cool and clear the Wind in the same place.

23.   Lowering Morning. Wind Southerly & day warm. With Rain in the Afternoon.

24.   Very warm and Sultry especially in the Afternoon with but little wind.

25.   Wind shifting to the No. West this day was a little cool in the forepart but pleast. notwithstanding.

26.   Tolerable warm with but little Wind.

27.   Pleasant but rather warm.

28.   Much such a day as yesterday, with but little Wind.

29.   Warm in the forenoon with Clouds and appearances of Rain in the Afternoon but none fell.

30.   Very warm with Thunder and Rain. (Fred[eric]k).

31.   Very Warm again with Rain abt. 2 Oclock.

[June]

Where & how my time is Spent

June 1st.   Went with Mr. Wr. Washington & Mr. Willis to my Brother Saml. where we dined and stayed all Night.

2.   Went to Run off the Land Captn. Kennedy lives on also my smaller Tract by Mr. Keiths. Accomplished the former but not the latter. Got to Mr. Wr. Washingtons to Dinnr. & met my Br. Jno. & Wife there.

3.   Stayed at Mr. Washingtons all day.

4. Set of on my return home. Dined at the Widow Evans's & lodged at Mr. Edward Paynes.

Two widows named Evans lived in Loudoun County about this time: Mary Evans (died c.1789), widow of John Evans (d. 1770), and Sarah Evans, widow of Price Evans (d. 1770), formerly of Pennsylvania (KING [6], 11–12, 53).

5. Met the Vestry at our New Church & came home in the Afternoon where I found Captn. Posey—who had been since I w[en]t.

The vestrymen today dealt with matters relating to the building of the new church. George Mason, who was overseeing the construction, was directed to have three flights of stone steps put at the front door instead of the one flight previously specified. The churchwardens, George William Fairfax and Edward Payne, were ordered to have the roof painted, to arrange for the building of a brick vestry house nearby, to engage workmen to carve ornaments on the altarpiece, and to have the religious inscriptions on the altarpiece gilded with gold leaf donated by GW and George William Fairfax. The vestrymen also decided that 12 pews in the church should be sold at the laying of the next parish levy on 20 Nov. (Truro Vestry Book, 153, DLC).

6. At home all day. Posey & Mr. Robt. Alexander dined here. The latter went away afterwds.

7. Went to Pohick Church and Return'd to Dinner. J[ohn] P[arke] C[ustis] came.

8. Rid to the Ferry Plantan. and Mill.

GW today gave John Posey £50 in cash and a horse and saddle worth £10 for a deed to the six-acre strip of land where Posey's house and ferry were located (LEDGER B, 50; deed of John Posey to GW, 8 June 1772, PPRF). Although the legal dispute between Posey and John West, Jr., over ownership of this land apparently remained unresolved in the courts, GW's purchase of Posey's rights cleared the way for a settlement of another kind. He now had only to conclude his deal with West on acceptable terms to gain undisputed possession of the strip (see main entry for 22 Sept. 1772).

9. Went into the Neck in the forenoon. Found Mr. Chichester & Wife–Miss Molly McCarty, and Mr. Phil. Pendleton here. The first went away.

Molly McCarty is probably Mary McCarty (d. 1786), a daughter of Capt. Daniel McCarty and a younger sister of Mrs. Sarah McCarty Chichester, who appears here.

10th. Rid to the Ferry Plantation & Mill. Mr. Pendleton went away after Dinner.

11.   Went into the Neck & run Round Johnson's Plantatin. also run some Lines across the Neck.

Susannah (Suckey) and Hannah Johnston were now renting from GW the Clifton's Neck plantation that their parents, Samuel Johnston (d. 1769) and Hannah Johnston (d. 1771), had previously rented (LEDGER A, 200, 308; LEDGER B, 46; will of Hannah Johnston, 8 July 1771, Fairfax County Wills, Book C-1, 123–24, Vi Microfilm).

12.   Rid over Muddy hole Wheat Field—also that at Doeg Run. Dr. Rumney came in the Ev[ening].

Rumney brought Patsy Custis eight musk capsules to be used for relief of her epileptic seizures (receipt from William Rumney, 24 June 1772, ViHi: Custis Papers).

13.   At home all day. Doctr. Rumney Dined here & returnd in the Afternoon. J. P. Custis returnd to Mr. Bouchers.

14.   Made a Visit to Lord Fairfax at Belvoir. Mr. Byrd & Mr. Willis came home with me.

15.   Mr. Willis went away early. Mr. Tilghman, & a Mr. Andrews came to Dinner & stayd all Night as did Mr. Magowan at Night.

16.   The Gentlemen went away. I went up to Court & returnd at Night. Mr. Magowan came home with me.

The court met 15–18 June. GW was not recorded by the court clerk as one of the justices present today (Fairfax County Order Book for 1772–74, 61–89, Vi Microfilm).

17.   Rid to the Ferry Plantation & back again from thence.

18.   At home all day.

19.   At home all day. Mr. Magowan went away after Breakfast.

20.   At home all day. In the Afternoon Mr. Byrd—Mr. Andrews & Mr. Wagener came here.

21.   Mr. Andrews & Mr. Wagener went away. Mr. Byrd & I went to Pohick Church & returnd to Dinner.

22.   Lord Fairfax, Colo. Fairfax & Mrs. Fairfax dined here & returnd afterwards.

23.   Rid to the Ferry Plantation & into Muddy hole Corn Field.

24.   At home all day. In the Afternoon Mr. Tilghman came here & stayed all Night.

25.   Rid as far as the Mill and turnd back on Acct. of Rain. In the Afternoon my Brothr. Jno. & Wife & Son Corbin came here on there way from Fred[eric]k.

Corbin Washington (1765–c.1799) was the youngest of John and Hannah Washington's four known children (WAYLAND [1], 113, 318, 330).

26.   At home all day with my Brother &ca.

27th.   Rid with my Brother to Muddy hole, Doeg Run & Mill. Found Mr. Byrd (who went from here on thursday last) & Mr. Tilghman here, who Stayed all Night.

28.   With the above went after Dinner in my Whale Boat to the Spring at Johnson's Place.

In a letter dated 5 Mar., Jonathan Boucher told GW that Governor Eden of Maryland "has got You a very handsome . . . Whale Boat, for £20, which, I fancy is by this Time at Mount [Vernon]" (DLC:GW). On 22 May, Boucher invited GW to visit him in Maryland, and added: "Shou'd . . . your Whale Boat be arriv'd, perhaps You may be tempted to try her" (DLC:GW). Since GW paid 18s. for "Freight of my Whale Boat from Patux[ent]" on 17 June, this excursion may have been his first in it (LEDGER B, 50).

29.   At home all day.

30.   My Brother & Family Set of home – Mr. Tilghman also after Breakfast. I rid with Mr. Byrd in the Forenoon to my Meadow at Doeg Run and to the Mill and in the Afternn. went to Sound the Depth of the sevl. Fishing Shores from Poseys up to Gilbt. Simpson's.

Gilbert Simpson (d. 1773) leased land in Clifton's Neck, first from William Clifton, and then from GW after his purchase of the land in 1760 (LEDGER A, 113, 137, 209).

Acct. of the Weather in June

June 1st.   But little Wind. Weather very hot & Sultry, with appearances (only) of Rain.

2.   Very hot and Sultry in the forenoon, with a good deal of Rain & Wind in the afternoon (in Frederick) but not much at Mt. Vernon.

3.   Misting & Raining more or less all day (in Frederick) with the Wind fresh & Cool from the Eastward.

4.   Flying Clouds, with the Wind very fresh & Cool from the Eastward.

5.   Very Cold in the Morning & Cool all day, with the Wind high from the same point.

6.   Very Cloudy & Misting, now & then all day, from the Eastward from whence the Wind blew fresh & Cool. No Rain.

7.   Clear and grown warmer with the Wind Southerly.

8.   Warm in the forepart of the day, but cool afterwds.

9.   Cool in the forenoon with the Wind Easterly — warmr. afterwards.

10.   Tolerably warm again with but little Wind and that Southerly.

11.   Cloudy Morning. Clear Noon & Warm Sun with a small Shower or two of Rain in the Afternoon & good d[ea]l Wind.

12.   Clear and Cool Wind Westwardly.

13.   Clear and something Warmer Wind southerly.

14.   Clear and but little Wind — very warm.

15.   Very hot, with but little Wind in the forenoon — pretty fresh afterwards from the South.

16.   Very Warm in the Morning but cooler afterwards wind getting to the Westward.

17.   Tolerably Cool.

18.   Warmer again Wind Southerly tho but little of it.

19. Clear & not very warm—but little Wind & that Southerly.

20. Warm and lowering—afterwards misting with a good appearance of Rain wch. went off.

21. Wind pretty fresh from the No. West and cool in the forenoon—warmer afterwds.

22. Warm again, & cloudy in the forenoon—with a fine moderate Rain for an hour or more abt. 1 or two Oclock from the Eastward.

23. Wind Southerly and warm with flying Clouds & showers about—but none here.

24. Clear and Cool. Wind fresh from the Westward. Weather Clear.

25. Misting in the forepart of the day. Towards Night a close & constant Rain.

26. Misting more or less all the Forenoon, the Afternoon clear & Windy from the Westward.

27. Clear—Wind Westerly, & pretty fresh but warm notwithstanding.

28. Warm and a little lowering with scarce any Wind, & that Southerly.

29. Clear and warm with but little Wind & that from the same Quarter.

30. Lowering all the forepart of the day but clear afterwds. with but little Wind from the So.

[July]

Where & how my time is Spent

July 1st. At home all day with Mr. Byrd.

2. Mr. Byrd went over to Belvoir. I continued at home all day.

3. Rid to the Ferry Plantation Muddy hole & Doeg Run.

4. After Dinner Rid to Muddy hole to my Harvest People.

5. At home all day alone.

6. In the Afternoon Rid to my Mill where Messrs. Wm. Shaw and Adam Lynn had been Inspecting my Flour.

William Shaw (died c.1774), an Alexandria cooper, had been appointed an inspector of flour by the Fairfax County court 18 Dec. 1769, and Adam Lynn (died c.1785) of Alexandria had received his appointment as inspector from the justices 2 Feb. 1770 (Fairfax County Order Book for 1768–72, 278, 287, and Fairfax County Order Book for 1772–74, 312, Vi-Microfilm). By law, inspectors could charge mill owners a 3d. inspection fee for each barrel of flour weighing 220 pounds net or less and 6d. for each barrel over 220 pounds (HENING, 8:143–44). On 17 June 1771 GW had credited Shaw with £3 2s. 1½d. for inspecting 497 barrels, half the lower legal rate, and today credited him with £1 14s. 1½d. for 273 barrels, again half the lower legal rate. Although Lynn may have received the other half of the inspection fees, no cash payments to him for that purpose are recorded in GW's ledger (LEDGER A, 341; LEDGER B, 58).

7. Went up with Mrs. Washington and Patcy Custis to see Mr. Adams New Store. Returnd before Dinr.

GW did much business with Robert Adam & Co.'s store during the next 2½ years, and there is some evidence that he obtained "better terms than common" in return for his patronage (LEDGER B, 42, 133; GW to Matthew Campbell, 7 Aug. 1772, DLC:GW).

8. Rid to the Harvest field at the Mill—Doeg Run and Muddy hole.

9. Rid to Muddy hole, & into the Neck before Dinner and to the Mill &ca. after Dinner. J. P. Custis came.

10. At home all the forenoon. In the Afternoon Rid to the Mill &ca. Mr. Benjn. Dulany & Mr. Tilghman came in the Evening.

Benjamin Tasker Dulany (c.1752–1816), younger son of Daniel Dulany the younger and Rebecca Tasker Dulany, had been a student with Jacky Custis at Boucher's school in Annapolis. Dulany became a frequent visitor at Mount Vernon during this period, for he was courting Elizabeth French, whom he married in 1773.

11. At home all day with those Gentlemen.

12.   Mr. B. Dulany &ca. went up to Church in Alexa. and re-turnd again in the Afternoon.

The new church in Alexandria was still not finished, but the Fairfax vestry agreed with John Carlyle during this year to complete work on it for £220 (see main entry for 31 July 1768; POWELL, 87).

13.   Mr. Dulany Mr. Tilghman & J. P. Custis went to Belvoir.

14.   The above Gentlemen returnd to Dinner. I rid to the Ferry & Mill Plantn. In the Afternn. we went on board of Captn. Jordan. Mr. Geo. Digges returnd with us.

15.   At home all day. Mr. Tilghman went away in the Morning early—the other Gentlemen in the afternoon.

16.   Went up in the Afternoon with Mrs. Washington, J. P. Custis, Miss Custis, & Milly Posey to a Ball in Alexandria. Lodgd at my House in Town.

17.   Came home to Dinner. Mr. Byrd returnd in the Afternoon.

18.   At home all day except Riding to the Ferry Plantn. Mr. Byrd here.

19.   Went with Mr. Byrd & J. P. Custis to Pohick Church & Dined at Belvoir. Returnd in the Evening.

20.   Colo. Fairfax & Lady, Mr. W. Washington Lady & 3 Children; Mrs. B. Fairfax, Miss Carlyle, Mr. Norton, Mr. Prentis, Mr. Whiting & Mr. Jno. Lewis Dined here & in the afternoon Colo. Lewis came.

Mr. Norton is John Hatley Norton (1745–1797) of Yorktown, who, after his father's return to London in 1767, became the Virginia agent for John Norton & Sons of London (PRICE, 401–2). Mr. Prentis is Joseph Prentis (1754–1809) of Williamsburg, a ward of Norton's father-in-law, Robert Carter Nicholas. Both Norton and Prentis had been invited by George William Fairfax to accompany him this summer to Warm Springs, "not so much for the recovery as for the Establishment of his [Norton's] Health" (Robert Carter Nicholas to John Norton, 4 Aug. 1772, MASON [1], 263).

21.   Colo. Fairfax & the two Mrs. Fairfax's—Miss Carlyle, Mr. Norton & Mr. Prentis went away after Breakfast.

22.   At home all day with the Company that remaind yesterday. Mr. Jenifer Adams Dined here.

Daniel Jenifer Adams (b. 1751), only son of Josias and Ann Jenifer Adams of Charles County, Md., had been taken into a trading partnership with GW, John Carlyle, and Samuel Brodie. Flour from GW's and Carlyle's mills was to be shipped to the West Indies on board the brig *Fairfax,* captained by Brodie. Adams was to be the supercargo, or agent, who would accompany the flour and decide on which island and at what price it should be sold (FREEMAN, 3:295, 307, 345; see "Remarks" entry for 24 July 1772).

23.   Dined (with the above Compa.) at Belvoir & lodged there.

24.   Dined at Belvoir this day also, & returnd in the Evening with Colo. Lewis, Mr. Jno. Lewis, Mr. Byrd & Mr. Whiting.

25.   Went a fishing and dined at the Fish House at the Ferry Plantation.

26.   Mr. W. Washington & Wife, & Mr. Norton & Mr. Prentis dined and Lodged here as did C[aptain] Posey.

27.   The above four went away after Breakfast. As did Mr. Byrd also, along with them in order to set of home the next day.

28.   Colo. Lewis & Son, and Mr. Whiting went away after Breakfast. So did J. P. Custis to Mr. Boucher's.

29.   Rid to the Mill Plantation the Mill, and Doeg Run—also to the Meadow at the Mill. Mrs. Cox came here. Captn. Posey & Daughter went over to Mary[lan]d.

Mrs. Cox may be Elizabeth Cox (d. 1792), wife of Presley Cox of Fairfax County. She was at Mount Vernon "making and altering Gowns for Mrs. Washington [and] Miss Custis" (LEDGER B, 55).

30.   Rid into the Neck.

31.   At home all day. Mr. Hy. Peake dined here. Mrs. Cox went away after Dinner.

Acct. of the Weather in July

July 1st.   Lowering kind of a forenoon but clear afterwards with the Wind Southerly.

2.   Wind tolerably fresh from the Southwest in the forenoon, and very Sultry. In the Afternoon a pleasant Shower, but not much of it.

3. Very hot and Sultry with the Wind Southerly.

4. Very hot with a little Wind from the Southward. In the Afternoon a little, & but a little Rain.

5. Again very hot—Wind in the same Quarter. In the Afternoon a very pretty Rain.

6. Still warm and Sultry, Wind being Southerly.

7. Wind pretty fresh from the Southward—but Warm & Sultry Notwithstanding—appearances of Rain in the Evening but none fell.

8. Very Warm, with appearances of Rain but none fell. Wind Southerly.

9. Wind Easterly & Weather cooler than the preceeding days.

10. Cool & pleasant with the Wind still Easterly.

11. Much such a day as yesterday wind being in the same place.

12. Still tolerably Cool—Wind Southerly however.

13. Wind fresh from the Southward but pretty warm notwithstandg.

14. Lowering Morning with a little Rain (& but little) abt. Noon. No Wind. In the Night a little more Rain.

15. Lowering Morning, with little or no Wind. Clear afternoon & very warm.

16. Clear & Warm in the forenoon—a fine Shower betwn. two and five Oclock in the Afternoon.

17. Clear & pleasant, but tolerably warm.

18. Lowering all day with the Wind very fresh from the So. West.

19. Clear & pleasant with but little Wind.

20.   Much such a day as yesterday with but little wind.

21.   Wind tolerably fresh in the forenoon & pleasant but Calm, & very warm afterwards.

22.   Clear and tolerably pleasant with but little Wind & that Northerly.

23d.   Lowering all the forenoon with some Rain which fell moderately, but in no quantity. Afternoon clear.

24.   Clear in the forenoon, with some appearances of Rain but none fell here. But little Wind & that from the So. West.

25.   Clear but Warm, with little wind from the Southward.

26.   Much such a day as yesterday, except there being a little more Wind from the Westward.

27.   Warm with but little Wind and that from the Southward.

28.   Clear, Calm, and exceeding Hot.

29.   Clear, & very Warm, Wind Southerly but very little of it.

30.   Very Warm, notwithstanding the Wind blew fresh from the So. West. In the Afternoon a moderate Rain for upwards of two hours.

31.   Cool, Wind blewing fresh from the Northwest which dryed the Ground fast.

Remarks & Occurs. in July

July 3d.   Began my Wheat Harvest at Muddy hole & Doeg Run in the following Manner. Viz.—At Doeg Run with the two Davy's & two Sons of Brummit as Cradlers, & the Wheat being rather green no regular assortment of Cradlers was allotted to them as yet.

At Muddy hole, Palmer (who did not work himself, but only acted as an Instructer) and Six of the youngest Cradlers began.

Brummit may be William Brummitt, who lived close enough to GW to have made occasional use of the blacksmith at Mount Vernon (LEDGER B, 76).

6.   Began in the Neck with Mike & Tom and three white Men. But as hands were Shifted from place to place there were sometimes more, & sometimes less in each Field.

10.   Finished the Harvest at Muddy hole & carried the hands from thence to the Ferry Plantation.

11.   Finished at Doeg Run, from whence some hands went into the Neck, and the Rest to the Mill.

18.   Compleated my Harvest in the Neck—The Ferry Plantation, & every where else. Began to Sow Wheat in the Neck.

22d.   Began to cut my Meadow at the Mill & finished it the 30th.

23.   Began to Ditch the Swamp at the Ferry.

24.   Captn. Brodie Saild for the West Indies with my Flour on Board 273 Barls.

27.   Began to Sow Wheat at Muddy hole; also at Doeg Run.

30.   Finished Sowing one Cut in the Neck—that is the uppermost but one on the Creek 67 [bushels].

31.   Began to Sow Wheat at the Mill.

[August]

Where & how my time is Spent

Augt. 1.   Rid to the Ferry Plantn., Mill, Doeg Run, and Muddy hole.

2.   Went to Pohick Church and Dined with Mrs. Washington & Patcy Custis at Captn. McCartys. Came home in the Afternn.

3.   At home all day alone.

4.   Rid to the Ferry Plantation and returnd from thence.

5.   At home all day alone.

6. Rid to the Ferry Plantation Mill Doeg Run and Muddy hole.

7. At home all day writing & Posting my Books.

8. Ditto–Ditto.

9. At home all day alone.

10. Rid to the Ferry Plantation to the Mill & where my Ditchers were at Work there. In the Evening Doctr. Rumney, Mr. Kirkpatrick, Mr. Balmain & Mr. Cox came here.

Mr. Cox may be Presley Cox (d. 1783).

11. Went with those Gentlemn. a Fishing and Dined undr. the Bank at Colo. Fairfax's near his White Ho[use]. Found Mrs. Cox here when we returnd.

In 1758 George William Fairfax obtained the position of collector of the customs for the South Potomac River Naval District (VA. EXEC. JLS., 6:100). The fishing party was dining near the customshouse, which was painted white to be clearly seen by ship captains, and thus referred to locally as Fairfax's White House.

12. After Breakfast the Gentlemen went away. Mrs. Cox continued, & I rid to my Ditchers at the Mill.

13. Went into the Neck and run round and divided the New Plantn. I intend to make there into three fields.

14. Rid to the Ditchers at the Ferry and Mill. Mrs. Cox went away about 12 Oclock.

15. At home all day alone.

16. At home this day also. In the afternoon Captn. Posey & his Daughter returnd.

17. Went up to Alexandria to Court. Stayd all Night. Dind with Mr. Adam.

The court met 17–21 Aug., and GW attended each day (Fairfax County Order Book for 1772–74, 89–118, Vi Microfilm).

18. In Town all day and Night. Din'd & Supd at Arrells.

19.   Ditto. Ditto. Dined at Arrells. Suppd no where.

20.   Still in Town. Dined at Arrells & went to the Ball in the Afternoon.

On this day Robert Hanson Harrison and William Ellzey brought suit for GW against John and William Barry to force a division of the 193-acre tract on Dogue Creek, part of which GW had bought 18 Dec. 1770. GW excused himself from the bench while the case was being heard. The court ruled in his favor and ordered county surveyor George West to divide the land fairly between the two parties before the court met in September. The surveying and other costs were to be equally shared by GW and the Barrys. Five justices were appointed to supervise the division: Sampson Darrell, Daniel McCarty, George Mason, John West, and John West, Jr., but only three were required to be present (Fairfax County Order Book for 1772–74, 114–15, Vi Microfilm).

21.   Dined at Arrells again & returnd home after Dinr.

22.   Rid to the Plantations at the Ferry, Mill, Doeg Run, & Muddy hole—also to the Mill & Ditchers there.

23d.   At home all day alone.

24.   Went a Hunting, and into the Neck, but found nothing; came home by 12 Oclock.

25.   At home all day a writing.

26.   At home this day also.

27.   Went with Mrs. Washington and Miss Custis to Mr. William Digges's and Dind there—only Betcy & Jenny Digges at home. Returnd in the Afternoon.

JENNY DIGGES: Jane Digges (c.1754–1826) was apparently the youngest of William and Ann Digges's many children (BOWIE, 255; RAMSBURGH, 130–31).

28.   Surveyd Mr. John West's Land in my Neck at his request.

29.   Rid to Muddy hole, Dogue Run and to the Ditchers at the Mill.

30.   At home all day. Mr. Willm. Digges Dined here.

31.   At home all day alone. In the Evening Mr. Custis came.

Acct. of the Weather in Augt.

Augt. 1. Cool—wind still Westerly.

2. Clear & pleasant, but rather Cool. Wind hanging still to the Westward.

3. Cool yet—Wind Eastwardly & Weather Clear.

4. Still Cool with the Wind Easterly.

5. Warmer, Wind getting Southerly.

6. Clear, Calm and Warm.

7. Very Warm in the forenoon. Wind pretty fresh in the Afternoon from the Southward.

8. Exceeding warm in the forenoon. Cooler afterwards the Wind rising from the Southwd.

9. Still Warm, with great appearances of Rain about two Oclock & all the Afternn. but only a few drops fell.

10. Great appearances of Rain all this day also with the Wind fresh from Southward—but none fell.

11. Wind very high all day from the Southwest & for the most part clear.

12. Cooler than the preceeding days. Wind Northerly and weather quite clear.

13. Warmer than Yesterday but not hot. Wind Southerly & Weather clear.

14. But little Wind and very Warm.

15. Clear and Warm with the Wind fresh from the Southward.

16. Very warm—in the Evening great appearances of Rain but none fell here.

17.   Still very Warm—in the Afternoon a very fine Rain all around but very little here.

18.   Cloudy with little Showers about none here. Wind Westerly & not warm.

19.   Wind Westerly with appearances of Clouds but no rain here.

20.   Clear and pleasant with but little Wind and that Westerly.

21.   Clear and pleasant again with but little Wind.

22d.   Quite clear with very little Wind & something Warmer than the preceeding days.

23.   Clear with the Wind Southerly & rather Warm.

24.   Cloudy a little and something Cooler.

25.   Cloudy with fine Rain till towards 2 Oclock—then close & constant for an hour or two which wet the Ground thoroughly.

26.   Clear with but little [wind] & warm.

27.   Wind fresh all the Forenoon from the Southward. In the afternoon frequent Showers of Rain—some of them pretty heavy.

28.   Clear and pleasant in the forenoon being neither warm nor Cool. In the afternoon Clouds but no Rain.

29.   Very little Wind and pretty warm in the forenoon.

30.   Clear, and pleasant the Wind at East but not fresh.

31.   Wind at So. & pretty fresh Weather clear.

Remarks & Occurs. in Augt.

Augt. 3d.   Finished Sowing the Cut next the Tumbling Dam at Doeg Run with Wheat 43 Bls.
    The same day began to Sow Wheat at the Ferry Plantn.

4. Finished Sowing the uppermost Cut with wheat in the Neck —
the Cut next Abn. Adams's 64 Bls.

10. Dennis Curran, Cook Jack, Schomberg Arlington, Peter &
London began to Work on my Mill Race, Scouring it out.

11. Finished the third Cut in the Neck with Wheat 65½ Bushls.

12. Also finished the Cut at Doeg Run about Jno. Gists Houses
53 Bushels.

14. Sowed all the Ground at the Ferry on this side the Swamp
68½ Bushels put therein.

17. Finishd Sowing the large Cut with Wheat at Muddy hole,
70 Bushls. & began to Sow the Small Field adjoining.

19. Finishd that also and Sowd 14 Bushls. of Wheat in it.
   Finishd the third Cut with wheat at Doeg Run; to wit that next
Marshalls Plantn. and Sowd 43 Bush. therein.

20. Finishd my fourth & last Cut in the Neck 74½ Bushels
which makes the whole amount sowed there upon 210 Acres, 271
Bushls.

29. Finishd sowing the 4th. & last Cut with Wheat at Doeg Run
Qr. 50 Bushls. which makes in all Sowed thereupon abt. 150 Acres
189 Bushels.

[September]

Where & how my time is Spent

Septr. 1st. Rid to the Ferry & from thence to the Mill. In the
Afternoon Doctr. Rumney came & lodgd all Night.

2. Rid to the Ditchers at the Mill the Doctr. going away after
Breakfast.

3. Rid to the Ditchers again.

4. Set out with Mrs. Washington & Miss Custis (attended by
Mr. Custis) on a Visit to Mr. Boucher &ca. Breakfasted at Mr.

Wm. Digges's (the Horses & carriage being got over the day before) and dined at Mr. Bouchers with Govr. Eden and Mr. Calvert & his two Daughters.

In June, Jonathan Boucher had married Eleanor Addison (1739–1784) of Oxon Hill, niece of his benefactor Rev. Henry Addison. The Washingtons had intended to pay their respects to the newlyweds earlier in the summer but had been prevented by "Harvest, Company, and one thing or another" (GW to Boucher, 18 Aug. 1772, DLC:GW). Benedict Calvert's two eldest daughters were Elizabeth (Betsey) Calvert (born c.1752) and Eleanor (Nelly) Calvert (1754–1811). Unknown to the Washingtons or the Bouchers, Jacky Custis was at this time courting Nelly Calvert. When their romance did become known several months later, Boucher was shocked: "Never . . . had I the most distant Suspicion of any such Thing's being in Agitation," he wrote GW. "You will remember, I always thought, that He was enamoured of Miss Betsey [Calvert]; tho' even in that, I suspected not, that there was any Likelihood of its be coming so serious, without my first knowing more of it" (8 April 1773, DLC:GW).

5. Dined at the same place & in the said Company. Mr. Calvert & Daughters went away in the Afternoon.

6. Went to Church with Govr. Eden in his Phaeton.

St. Barnabas Church, located several miles southeast of Mount Lubentia, was the parish church for Jonathan Boucher's parish of Queen Anne.

7. Dined at Mr. Calverts (going with the Govr. in his Phaeton & calling at Mr. Sprigs). Mr. Igns. Digges & Family dind here also—we lodgd—they retd.

Osborne Sprigg, Jr., son of Osborne Sprigg (1707–1750) and Rachel Belt Sprigg, lived less than two miles northwest of Boucher's house in Prince George's County.

8. At Mr. Calverts all day and Night. The Govr. returnd to Annapolis this Morning.

9. Mr. Boucher who came to this place with us returnd home early this Morning. We dined at Mr. Igns. Digges with a good deal of Compa. among whom Mr. Calverts D[aughte]rs he himself going to Annapolis.

10. At Mr. Digges's all day. Miss Calverts came, & returnd in the afternoon.

11. Returnd home by the way of Mr. William Digges's where we Dined & where my Boats met us.

12. Rid to Muddy hole, Doeg Run, Mill & Ferry Plantations—
also to the Ditchers in my Mill Race.

13. At home all day; In the Afternoon Mr. Willis came & lodgd.

14. Set out for Fredericksburg about 7 Oclock; Dined & Fed my
Horses at Peytons on Acquia & reachd Fredericksburg abt. Dusk.
Lodgd at my Mothers.

GW's purpose in going to Fredericksburg at this time was to meet with other
veteran officers of the French and Indian War "to consider of a proper
method to obtain the Lands granted" by the king's Proclamation of 1763
(resolutions of veteran officers, 15 Sept. 1772, MoSW).

15. Rid to my two Plantations on the River & returnd to Mr.
Lewis's to Dinner. Spent the Eveng. at Weedons.

GW was preparing to advertise Ferry Farm in the *Virginia Gazette* "To
be SOLD, RENTED, *or* EXCHANGED, *for back lands in any of the northern counties*" of Virginia (5 Nov. 1772). Fielding Lewis agreed to act as GW's
Fredericksburg agent in this business.
  Weedon's tavern was probably the scene of today's meeting of the veteran
officers. Fourteen officers, including GW, were present and agreed to organize
in order to push their claims. Each man was to be assessed £3 for every thousand acres claimed, and five officers living in the Fredericksburg neighborhood were appointed to disburse the collected money for surveying and other
expenses (resolutions of veteran officers, 15 Sept. 1772, MoSW).

To be **SOLD**, **RENTED**, *or* **EXCHANGED**, *for*
back Lands, in any of the northern Counties in this
Colony,

A TRACT of fix Hundred ACRES, including about two Hundred of
cleared Land on the north Side of *Rappahannock* River, oppofite to
the lower End of *Fredericksburg*. On this Tract (a little above the Road)
is one of the moft agreeable Situations for a Houfe that is to be found
upon the whole River, having a clear and diftinct View of almoft every
Houfe in the Town, and every Veffel that paffes to and from it. Long
Credit (if defired) will be given, the Purchafer paying Intereft from the
Sale; and an indifputable Title will be made. For farther Particulars
inquire of Colonel *Lewis* in *Fredericksburg*, or of the Subfcriber in *Fairfax.*
                                    GEORGE WASHINGTON.

Sale of Washington's Ferry Farm near Fredericksburg is announced in Purdie and Dixon's *Virginia Gazette*, 5 Nov. 1772. (Colonial Williamsburg
Photograph)

16.   Dined at my Brother Chas. & spent the Evening at Colo. Lewis's.

GW today recorded paying his mother £30 cash in the presence of brother Charles (LEDGER B, 45).

17.   Set of on my return home. Dined at Dumfries & reachd home abt. Dusk. Found Mrs. French & her Daughter & Miss Molly Manly here.

18.   Went upon the Survey & Division of Wades Land between Barry & me. Colo. West, Mr. Jno. West, Captn. McCarty, & Captn. Darrel Commrs. came home with me as did Val. Crawford Mr. Geo. West & Chs. West.

As ordered by the court on 20 Aug., George West divided the disputed tract on Dogue Creek, allotting 75 acres to GW and 118 acres to William Barry (GW's list of quitrent lands for 1772, DLC:GW). GW received less land, probably because he received riparian rights on the creek as part of his share of the property. Almost 11 years later GW bought the 118 acres from William Barry and his wife, Sarah, for £150 Virginia currency (deed of William and Sarah Barry to GW, 16 June 1783, ViMtV).

19.   Went on the same business again to day. Mrs. French &ca. went away after Breakfast. Colo. West Jno. West came home with me to Dinnr. & went afterwds.

20.   At home all day — Weather clear and Warm with but little Wind.

21.   Went up to Court at Alexa. Dined at Arrels, & supped at Arrels. Lodged at my own House.

The court met 21–24 Sept., and GW was present the first three days (Fairfax County Order Book for 1772–74, 118–31, Vi Microfilm).

22.   In Alexandria Still. Dined and Supped at Arrels.

GW today paid John West, Jr., £436 9s. for the land near Mount Vernon that West had previously agreed to sell to him (see main entry for 29 April 1769). Two separate tracts were specified in the deeds: the undisputed section which GW had been renting from West since 18 Sept. 1770, said here to contain 196 acres, and the six-acre strip over which West and John Posey had been contending. Having bought Posey's rights to the strip 8 June 1772, GW with this purchase effectively ended the dispute between the two men and established his own unchallengeable right to that land (LEDGER B, 41; West's deed to GW, 21 Sept. 1772, MoSW; excerpt from West's deed to GW, 22 Sept. 1772, American Art Assoc. Catalogue, 21–22 Jan. 1926, Item 295).

23.   In Alexandria till the Afternoon. Dined at Arrels & came home with Colo. Fairfax & Val. Crawford.

24.   Went with Colo. Fairfax to Survey Charles Wests land — wch. I finished a little before Night. Mr. Bryan Fairfax came here.

GW and Fairfax were surveying the 484 acres of land on Dogue Creek that West had previously promised to sell to GW (see main entry for 28 May 1772). This tract extended west from the creek into Belvoir Neck, and because GW was primarily interested in the eastern part next to his mill, he agreed to sell Fairfax 72 acres of the land in the neck at the same rate he was to buy it from West: 25s. an acre, a total price of £90 (LEDGER B, 63, 66). West deeded the full 484 acres to GW on 28 Oct. 1772, and within the next few months GW gave a deed to Fairfax for his 72 acres (deed of Charles West to GW, ViMtV; General Index to Fairfax County Deeds for 1742–97, 218, Vi Microfilm).

25.   Rid with Mr. Bryan Fairfax to look at some Land of his on Pohick. Tom Gist came this aftern.

Bryan Fairfax was showing GW this 463½-acre tract on the South Run of Pohick Creek with the hope that GW would pay off his £160 bill of exchange in return for it, but GW declined to accept the deal (Fairfax to GW, 3 Aug. and 2 Dec. 1772, DLC:GW; see "Remarks" entry for 8 Jan. 1772). Fairfax later sold the tract to Alexander Henderson of nearby Colchester for £166 (deed of Fairfax to Henderson, 16–17 April 1773, Fairfax County Deeds, Book K-1, 433–54, Vi Microfilm).

Christopher Gist had a brother Thomas and a son Thomas. This Tom Gist is probably the son, who lived in southwest Pennsylvania on the main route to the Ohio country (BAILEY [5], 154).

26.   Went and resurveyed Wests Land—some mistake happening the first time. Mr. Gist & Mr. Vale. Crawford both went away this Morning.

27.   Set of for Pohick Church and got almost there when word was brought that Mr. Massey was Sick. Returnd & found Nanny Peake & Biddy Fleming here who went away after Dinner.

Bridget Fleming was an unmarried daughter of Thomas Fleming of Alexandria (will of Thomas Fleming, 7 April 1786, Fairfax County Wills, Book E-1, 160, Vi Microfilm).

28.   At home all the forenoon. In the Afternoon Rid to the Ferry Plantn. the Mill and Dogue Run.

29.   Rid to Muddy hole Doeg Run & Mill and to the Ditchers on the Race. In the Afternoon Prior Theobald came here and lodged.

30. Went to Colo. Fairfax's & Dined. Returnd in the Eveng. Mr. Fitzhugh – Mr. Brown & Mr. Burwell came here in the Afternoon.

Mr. Fitzhugh could be almost any of the many Mr. Fitzhughs living in Stafford or King George counties. Mr. Brown may be one of Dr. William Brown's brothers. Mr. Burwell is probably one of the two younger Lewis Burwells. Colonel Burwell who came the next day is Robert Burwell, and John Fitzhugh is probably John Fitzhugh of Marmion, but may be John Fitzhugh (1727–1809) of Bell Air, Stafford County.

Acct. of the Weather in Septr.

Septr. 1st.   Wind at No. Et. & Weather Cloudy but no Rain fell.

2.   Clear, & Wind fresh from the No. West. Warm notwithstanding.

3.   Clear & Warm, wind in the same place as yesterday.

4.   Very Sultry Morning with great appearances of Rain which fell in the Afternoon for abt. an [   ].

5.   The Air somewhat Coold, the Wind getting Northwardly.

6.   Cool & pleasant – Wind still Northwardly.

7.   Warmer a good deal but pleasant. Weather clear.

8.   Rather Warmer than yesterday, but clear with the Wind Southerly.

9.   Very Warm and Sultry all day and Night.

10.   Cloudy & Warm all the day; in the Night a good deal of Rain.

11.   Frequent Shower's about Noon. In the afternoon the Wind got to Northwest and blew fresh.

12.   Wind fresh from the Northwest all day and Cool.

13.   Clear and Cool tho there was but little Wind and that Southerly.

14. Lowering for the most part of the day with but little wind moderately warm.

15. Clear and but little Wind—very warm.

16. Misting & sometins Raining with but little Wind & Warm.

17. Clear forenoon and Warm with Showers in the Afternoon.

18. Clear and very pleasant. At the sametime Warm with a little Wind from the Southd.

19. Very pleasant being much such a day as yesterday.

20. Pleasant but warm with little Wind and that Southerly.

21. Very Warm with the Wind Southerly.

22. Misting in the Morning & for most part of the day, with a very heavy Rain & high wind in the Afternoon. Much Rain fell in the Night.

23. Clear and Cool. Wind at No. West—but not very fresh.

24. Much such a day as yesterday.

25th. Still cool with the Wind Westerly and fresh.

26. Same kind of day as yesterday.

27. Very Cloudy & like for Rain all the forenoon with the Wind Northerly. In the Afternoon Misting.

28. Misting more or less all day with but little [wind] and not Cold.

29. Clear, and Warm, and without any wind.

30. Much Such a day as Yesterdy.

Remarks & Occurs. in Septr.

Septr. 1st. Finish'd Ditching at the Ferry Plantation—200 Rod in the whole.

2. Finishd Sowing Wheat at Muddy hole Plantation 123½ Bushls. in the whole.

Finishd Sowing Wheat at the Ferry Plantation also 84 Bushls. on the other side the Swamp next Mrs. French's making in all 152½ Bushl. Sowed there.

3. Sent Adam & Jupiter from Muddy hole to work on the Mill Race. Also Bath & Robin from Dogue Run there.

4. Began to Sow Wheat at the Home House.

9. Finishd Sowing Wheat at the Mill Plantation 89 Bushl.

10. Compleated Sowing my Wheat at the Home House 66½ Bush. which makes in all this year

At Ho[me] House	66½ Bushls.
In the Neck	271
Muddy hole	123½
Ferry Plantn.	152½
Doeg Run	189
Mill	89
In all	891½ Bushls.

17. This day agreed with my Overseer Powell, at the lower Plantation on Rappah. [Little Falls Quarter] to continue another year on the same lay as the last provided the Number of hands are not Increased — but, if I should add a hand or two more, & let him (as I am to do at any rate) choose 5 of the best Horses at that Quarter & the upper one [Ferry Farm] he is in that case to receive only the 8th. of what Corn, Wheat, & Tobo. he makes on the Plantation.

29. Danl. Minor and Joshua Key came here to work.

Joshua Kay was a boat builder who during the next two years repaired GW's fishing boats and ferryboat. He also built a boat with a 29-foot keel for GW (LEDGER B, 74).

[October]

Where & how my time is Spent

Octr. 1st. At home all day with the Gentn. that came yesterday Afternoon — Colo. Burwell & Mr. Jno. Fitzhugh & Colo. Fairfax came to Dinner. Colo. Burwell & Mr. Jno. Fitzhugh Stayd all Night. The other Gentn. went away after Dinner.

2.   Colo. Burwell & Mr. Fitzhugh went away after Dinner.

3.   I rid to Muddy hole Doeg Run &ca. before Dinner, in the Afternoon went into the Neck.

4.   Set of for the Annapolis Races. Dined and lodged at Mr. Boucher's.

Jacky Custis accompanied GW on this trip to the races (LEDGER B, 60).

5.   Reachd Annapolis. Dined at the Coffee House with the Jocky Club & lodgd at the Govrs. after going to the Play.

6.   Dined at Majr. Jenifers—went to the Ball and Suppd at the Govrs.

The four days of racing began this morning at 11:00. The *Maryland Gazette* expected "good Sport, as a great Number of Horses are already come from the Northward and Southward, to start for the different Purses." GW lost £1 6d. on this year's races (LEDGER B, 60). The ball was held at the Assembly House, "Tickets for Gentlemen [priced] at a Dollar each (without which they cannot possibly be admitted)" (*Md. Gaz.*, 1 Oct. 1772).

Daniel of St. Thomas Jenifer in a portrait by John Hesselius. (National Portrait Gallery, Smithsonian Institution, Washington, D.C.)

7.   Dined at the Govrs. and went to the Play afterwards.

The plays attended by GW this week were part of the fall season of David Douglass's American Company, which opened in Annapolis 1 Sept. (RANKIN, 166–67).

8.   Dined at Colo. Loyds and went to the Play. From thence early to my Lodgings.

Edward Lloyd (1744–1793), of Wye House, Talbot County, Md., was the son of Edward Lloyd (d. 1770) and Anne Rousby Lloyd. He was a member of the Maryland General Assembly with a handsome town house in Annapolis. He was married to Elizabeth Tayloe, daughter of John Tayloe of Mount Airy in Richmond County, Va.

9.   Dined at Mr. Ridouts. Went to the Play & to the Govrs. to Supper.

Playing at the theater today were a new comedy, *The West Indian,* and a new comic opera, *The Padlock* (*Md. Gaz.,* 8 Oct. 1772; RANKIN, 132, 164).

10th.   Dined with Mr. Carroll of Carrollton & set out for Mr. Bouchers which place I arrivd at abt. 8 Oclock.

11.   Got home to a late Dinner. Jno. Parke Custis came with me found Mrs. Barnes there.

12.   Rid to the Ferry, Mill, Doeg Run & Muddy hole Plantns. before Dinner & went into the Neck to run some lines afterwds.

13.   Went up to Alexandria & returnd home to Dinner. C[aptain] Posey came.

14.   Went into the Neck to lay of some Fencing &ca. Posey went away.

GW today paid Posey £11 11s. 3d. for his right to 3,000 acres of land under the Proclamation of 1763 (LEDGER B, 61).

15.   Rid to the Mill &ca.

16.   At home all day. Mr. Piper & Mr. Adam came to Dinner and went away afterwards. Captn. McCarty his wife & Son came after Dinnr. & stayd the Night.

Capt. Daniel McCarty and his wife, Sinah Ball McCarty, had one son, Daniel McCarty (1759–1801), who married a daughter of George Mason.

17.   They went away after Breakfast. I rid out in the Afternoon to the Mill & Doeg Run.

18. Dined at Belvoir & returnd.

19. Went up to Court at Alexa. Returnd in the Afternoon.

The court was in session 19–20 Oct., but GW was not recorded among the justices present (Fairfax County Order Book for 1772–74, 131–39, Vi Microfilm).

20. Rid to the Ferry, Mill, Doeg Run & Muddy hole Plantns.

21st. Set of for Williamsburg. Dined at Colchester & lodgd in Dumfries. Mrs. Washington Mr. & Miss Custis with me.

22. Reachd Fredericksburg to Dinner. Lodgd at Colo. Lewis's.

23. Dined at Caroline Court House and reachd Hubbards in the Afternoon. Founderd two of my Horses.

24. Reachd Todds Bridge to Breakfast & Colo. Bassets in the Evening.
   Captn. Crawford came there to Dinner.

25. Assisting Crawford with his Surveys.

William Crawford had returned from the Ohio country with 13 surveys totaling 127,899 acres out of the 200,000 acres of bounty land promised in 1754 by Governor Dinwiddie to soldiers and officers of the Virginia Regiment. Crawford and GW were now preparing to enter the surveys and have patents issued to the various officers and men, or to their survivors (receipt for surveys from Thomas Everard, 13 Nov. 1772, ICHi).

26. About the same business day also.

27. On the same business.

28. Still employed in the same Work.

29. Ditto—Ditto.

30. Ditto—Ditto.

31. Went a fox hunting & killed a Fox in Compa. with sevl. others.

Acct. of the Weather in Octr.

Octr. 1.   Clear, Calm & pleasant being warm.

2.   Very pleasant & warm without any Wind.

3.   Such a day as yesterday but rather Warmer.

4.   Very lowering with Mists now and then but no Rain.

5.   Misting, & sometimes Raining in the forenoon with the wind Eastwardly.

6.   Much such a day as yesterday. Misting more or less all day—wind in the same place.

7.   Misting & sometimes Raining pretty smartly.

8.   Clear & pleasant. Wind Westerly but neither cold nor very fresh.

9.   Very pleasant without much wind—that however Westerly.

10.   Very pleasant again with but little wind.

11.   Cloudy & lowering with the wind westerly but no Rain.

12.   Very foggy Morning but clear afterwards.

13th.   Clear & very warm with but little Wind & that Southerly.

14.   Much such a day as yesterday.

15.   Clear, Calm & pleasant with but little Wind.

16.   Very pleasant & clear with but very little Wind.

17.   Just such a day as Yesterday.

18.   Such a day as yesterday. Wind a little fresher from the Southward.

19. Warm & pleasant with but little Wind. In the Eveng. a black Cloud with thunder & Lightning but little Rain.

20. Warm & pleasant in the Afternoon another black Cloud with Thunder—Lightning & Rain—which cleard away with a high No. West Wind.

21. Clear with the Wind high from the No. West all day.

22. Calm and pleasant being moderately Cool.

23. Clear, calm, and very Warm.

24. Exceeding warm with very little Wind and that Southerly.

25. Still Warm, but Cloudy with Rain at Night and the Wind Easterly.

26. Wind fresh from the same point with more or less Rain all day.

27. Much such a day as the preceeding one.

28. Not much unlike yesterday. Wind in the same Quarter & now & then Raining.

29. Still lowering with the Wind Easterly.

30. Wind high from the Westward with squally Clouds & now & then Rain.

31. Clear, & pleasant with but little Wind & that Southerly.

Remarks & Occurs. in Octr.

Octr. 7. Finished getting and Securing my Fodder at the Ferry Plantn.

8. Turnd the Water into My Mill Race this day finishing cleansing it out.

10. Finishd Securing my Fodder at the Mill.

12. Finished Do. at Muddy hole & Doeg Run.

13. Also finishd Do. in the Neck.

[November]

Where & how my time is Spent

Novr. 1st.   At Colo. Bassetts all day.

2.   Went to Williamsburg in Company with Captn. Crawford. Dined at Southalls & went to Mr. Baylor's Ball in the Evening.

In town GW lodged with Edward Charlton, while the rest of the family remained at Eltham (LEDGER B, 62; CUSTIS ACCOUNT BOOK). John Baylor (1750–1808) was the eldest son of Col. John Baylor (1705–1772), of Newmarket, Caroline County (CAMPBELL [1], 218; MEADE [1], 2:464–65).

3.   Breakfasted, Dined & Suppd at the Governors.

4.   Dined at the Speakers and Supped at Mrs. Vobes.

Jane Vobe had changed her mind about leaving Williamsburg, and by February of this year had opened a tavern called the King's Arms, across the street from the Raleigh, in the house where John Carter had been living (*Va. Gaz.*, P&D, 6 Feb. 1772). She remained in business there until about 1785.

In the council today was presented a petition that GW had prepared on behalf of himself and veterans of the Virginia Regiment, renewing his arguments for allowing the veterans more than 20 surveys for their 200,000 acres and asking the councillors "to direct in what manner Patents ought to issue for the Lands already surveyed." The latter business was postponed until 6 Nov., but the request for more surveys was rejected without further consideration (VA. EXEC. JLS., 6:510, petition of GW and Virginia Regiment to Lord Dunmore and Virginia council, Oct. 1772, PPRF).

5.   Dined with the Council. Spent the Evening in my own Room.

6.   Took a Cold Cut at Southalls & went up to Colo. Bassetts.

On this day GW appeared before the council and presented a plan that he had devised for apportioning the 127,899 acres of veterans' bounty lands already surveyed. Although the council had set the quantity of each claimant's land the previous year, there remained the more complex problem of giving everyone equal quality of land. The council accepted GW's solution to the problem and authorized issuance of patents according to his plan. But before the council rose, GW promised that if objections about the equity of distribution were raised at a meeting of veterans scheduled for Fredericksburg on 23 Nov. or "any Reasonable time after," he would "give up all *his* Interest" in the 20,147 acres allotted as his share "and submit to such Regulations" as the council might think proper (va. exec. jls., 6:513–14; freeman, 3:298–300).

7.   Busy with Captn. Crawford all day.

GW today paid Crawford £31 15s., the balance due to him from the veterans of the Virginia Regiment (ledger b, 36, 61).

8.   At Colo. Bassetts all day.

9.   Ditto – Ditto.

10.   Rid up with Mr. Hill to Rockahock, & Plantations, in New Kent; & returnd, after Dining with Mrs. Chamberlayne, to Colo. Bassetts at Night. Mr. Custis went with me.

James Hill of King William County had become steward of the Custis estates on 17 Mar. of this year, succeeding Joseph Valentine, who had died 7 Dec. 1771 (agreement of GW with Hill, 17 Mar. 1772, MH). Although Hill was now living on some of the Custis land near Williamsburg, he retained his own plantation of about 640 acres in King William (William Dandridge to GW, 21 Dec. 1771, DLC:GW; lee [3], 327).

11.   Went with Mr. Custis over to Claibornes & returnd to Dinnr.

12.   Went to Williamsburg with Mrs. Washington Mr. & Miss Custis lodged at Mrs. Amblers also dined there & spent the evening at Mrs. Vobes.

Although GW and Jacky stayed this night in Mrs. Ambler's house, they apparently lodged at Edward Charlton's place for the remainder of their visit, leaving the ladies to continue lodging with Mrs. Ambler (ledger b, 62; custis account book; receipt from Edward Charlton, Nov. 1772, ViHi: Custis Papers).

13th.   Dined at Mrs. Dawsons & went to a Ball at the Apollo [Room, Raleigh Tavern] in the Evening.

14.   Dined with Mrs. Ambler & Spent the Evening at the Coffee House.

On 23 Jan. 1772 an anonymous advertisement appeared in Purdie and Dixon's *Virginia Gazette*, informing the public that "private lodgings may be had for seven or eight Gentlemen, during the Assembly, at the Coffee-

Washington's trips to Williamsburg included many visits to the Raleigh Tavern. (Colonial Williamsburg Photograph)

house, near the Capitol." This coffeehouse is probably the one "in the main Street" that Mrs. Campbell had briefly occupied before moving to Waller Street and possibly the one that Richard Charlton had operated as a tavern during the late 1760s (*Va. Gaz.*, P&D, 16 May 1771; see main entries for 4 May 1768 and 2 May 1771). In the fall of 1774 John Webb of Halifax, N.C., advertised "For SALE That valuable and well situated Lot in *Williamsburg* where the Coffeehouse is now kept," but it apparently was not sold until 1777 or later (*Va. Gaz.*, P&D, 13 Oct. 1774 and P, 26 Sept. 1777).

15. Dined and Spent the Evening at the Speakers.

16. Dined at Mrs. Amblers & Spent the Evening there also after setting a while with Colo. Bassett at Mrs. Dawsons.

Among the expenses that GW recorded in his ledger under this date were 7s. 6d. for "seeing Wax work" and 11s. 6d. for a "Puppit Shew" (LEDGER B, 61).

17. Rid to the Plantations under Mr. Hill near Town & dined at Southalls.

18. In my own Room setling Mr. Hills Accts. all Dinner time — but spent the Evening at Anderson's.

19. Dined at Mrs. Dawson's and Spent the Evening in my own Room a writing.

20. Set out about two Clock for Colo. Bassetts.

GW was obliged to leave Williamsburg today in order to be present in Fredericksburg for the meeting of the Virginia Regiment, scheduled three days later. He left with some reluctance, because he had not been able to finish his personal business in Williamsburg "by reason of the late coming in of the merchants" (GW to Charles M. Thruston, 12 Mar. 1773, DLC:GW; *Va. Gaz.*, P&D, 12 Nov. 1772).

21.   Left Colo. Bassetts on my return home. Dined at King William Court House and lodged at Mr. Hubbards.

22.   Breakfasted at Hubbards, and reachd Fredericksburg about 4 Oclock. Lodgd at Colo. Lewis's.

23.   At Fredericksburg—attending the Intended meeting of Officers at Captn. Weedens.

Besides GW, six officers were present or represented at this meeting. Learning of GW's recent actions on behalf of the veterans, they warmly thanked him for his efforts and approved his distribution of the surveyed lands as an equitable one. He should, they recommended, be excused from his offer to sacrifice his own bounty lands in case of a redivision (resolves and statement of officers of the Virginia Regiment, 23 Nov. 1772, H. Bartholomew Cox). The council considered this recommendation on 9 Dec. and agreed that if no complaints were received by June, GW would be released from his promise (VA. EXEC. JLS., 6:516; FREEMAN, 3:302–3).

24.   On the same business all day and at the same place.

25.   Still in Fredericksburg.

26.   Rid over the River to my Plantation's & examind the Land at the upper place.

All of the "tillable & Pasture Land" of the Ferry Farm had now been let by Fielding Lewis to James Hunter, Sr., and William Fitzhugh, both of whom had quarters adjoining the Ferry Farm (GW to Hugh Mercer, 11 April 1774, DLC:GW).

27.   Set of from Fredericksburg & reachd Colo. Henry Lees where we lodged.

GW today recorded paying his mother £15 cash in the presence of his sister Betty (LEDGER B, 45, 62).

28.   Stayed at Colo. Lees all day.

29.   Reachd home to Dinner.

30.   At home all day—writing.

Acct. of the Weather in Novr.

Novr. 1.   Clear, very Warm, & but little wind—that Southerly.

2.   Clear & warm in the forenoon with Rain in the Afternoon, after which clear & Cool.

3.   Clear & pleasant, being somewhat cool Wind Westerly.

4.   Rather Warmer than Yesterday with some appearances of Rain.

5.   Very Cool Wind fresh from the Westward & clear.

6.   Clear, but not so cool as yesterday. Evening a little lowerg.

7.   Lowering all day, with a little Rain now and then.

8.   Still lowering in the forenoon & warm—clear afterwards.

9.   Clear and pleasant with but little Wind & that Southerly.

10.   Clear and Pleasant with but little Wind & that Southerly.

11.   Wind Easterly & pretty fresh in the forenoon but calm & warm also clear in the forenoon.

12.   Clear & warm in the forenoon but cool, cloudy & a good deal of Rain afterwards with high So. Westerly Winds.

13.   A little Rain, with flying Clouds & high Wind from the Westward.

14th.   Clear & somewhat Cool Wind still pretty fresh from the same quarter.

15.   Cold & raw wind getting to the Northwest.

16.   Very Cold, with appearances of falling Weather, wind at Northwest.

17.   Wind fresh from the same Point and very cold but clear.

18.   Very hard frost, but pleasant afterwards, with the Wind moderate, & more Southerly.

19.   Very pleasant with but little Wind & that Southerly.

20.   Pleasant forenoon & clear after the fog broke away which was very heavy.

21.   Foggy Morning, but clear and pleasant afterwards.

22.   Cloudy, with Rain more or less all day.

23.   Much such a day as yesterday Wind being at No. Et. all day.

24.   Weather as the day before but the Rain rather more constt.

25.   Still Raining more or less Wind in the same Quarter.

26.   Clear Morning but Cloudy and unsettled afterwards.

27.   Clear and very pleasant with but little Wind.

28.   Remarkably pleasant & Calm in the forenoon – but lowering before Sunset, with the Wind spring[ing] up fresh from South, & Shifting more Easterly. In the Night blew a mere hurricane & was attended by a good deal of Rain.

29.   Clear after the Morning with the Wind high – from the South & West.

30.   Windy and Cold.

[December]

Where & how my time is Spent

Decr. 1st.   At home all day a Writing to Williamsburg.

Most of GW's two days of writing was in regard to the bounty lands, including his final reports sent to the council in Williamsburg.

2.   At home all day. Messrs. Dulany & Tilghman came at Dinner time, & stayd all Night.

3.   Went a Fox hunting, found one in Mr. G. Alexanders Pocoson & killd it after 3 hours chase. In the Afternoon Mr. B. Fairfax and Mr. Wagener came here.

4.   Went a hunting again but found nothing. Mr. Wagener & Messrs. Tilghman & Dulany went home in the Afternoon.

5.   Went a hunting with Mr. Fairfax. Found a Fox between Edd. William's & Johnsons which we lost after a Chase of two hours.

Edward Williams became GW's tenant in 1760 when GW bought the Clifton's Neck land. Williams was still there in 1786, when he was listed for tax purposes as having 12 whites and no blacks (LEDGER A, 113; LEDGER B, 19; HEADS OF FAMILIES, VA., 17).

6.   Mr. Fairfax went away after breakfast, & Mr. Jno. Fitzhugh of Marmion came in the Afternoon.

JNO. FITZHUGH OF MARMION: possibly the son of William Fitzhugh (1725–1791) of Marmion in the old Chotank neighborhood. Another John Fitzhugh, son of Maj. John Fitzhugh (d. 1733) of Marmion, had died earlier in the year.

7.   Mr. Fitzhugh went away abt. 12 Oclock. I rid to the Ferry Plantation before Dinner.

8.   Rid over Muddy hole, Doeg Run, & Mill Plantations before Dinner. In the Eveng. my Brothrs. Jno. & Chas. & Mr. Jno. Smith came.

John Smith is probably John Smith (1750–1836), son of John Smith of Cabin Point. By this time the elder Smith's lands, Fleets Bay plantation in Northumberland County and a large tract in Gloucester County, had been sold to satisfy the enormous debts of his estate, and in 1773 young John, with his brother Edward Smith (1752–1826), moved to Frederick County, settling near Winchester (*Va. Gaz.*, P&D, 6 Aug. 1772; TYLER [2], 95–100).

9.   Went into the Neck abt. 11 Oclock a fox hunting. Touchd the Drag where we found the last but did not move the Fox.

10.   At home all day.

11.   My Brothr. Jno. set of homewards Mr. Smith to Frederick. I accompanied him as far as Alexa. from whence I returnd in the Afternoon—Mr. Dulany—Doctr. Brown & Mr. Brown with me.

12.   Doctr. Brown went away abt. 12 Oclock & Mr. Brown after Dinner.

13.   My Brother Chas. returnd home very Early this Morning and Mr. Dulany went up to Alexa. after Breakfast.

14.   Went into the Neck on foot crossing the Creek with a Gun. Captn. McCarty & his Bro. Thadeus, & a Dutch Minister Dined here.

Thaddeus McCarty (c.1737–1812), of Loudoun County, was the youngest of the three sons of Dennis and Sarah Ball McCarty of Cedar Grove, and hence a brother of GW's neighbor Capt. Daniel McCarty. Thaddeus married Sarah Elizabeth Richardson in 1768.

15.   Went a Hunting & found two Foxes both of which were killd, but only one got, the Dogs running out of hearg. with the 2d.; found these Foxes on the Hills by Isaac Gates's.

The Isaac Gates family lived southwest of Mount Vernon. Gates occasionally used the services of GW's blacksmith and weavers, paying for them with chickens and eggs. In 1782 he was listed for tax purposes as having six whites and no blacks (DIARIES, 2:89, n.1; LEDGER A, 87; HEADS OF FAMILIES, VA., 18).

16.   Mr. Val. Crawford who came yesterday went away this day. At home all day.

17.   Govr. Eden & Mr. Custis came here to Dinner & Mr. Geo. Digges after Dinner.

18.   Mr. Boucher, his Wife & Sister came to Dinner.

The sister may be Mrs. Boucher's sister Ann Addison, but GW probably means Boucher's unmarried sister Jane, who lived in her brother's household (BOUCHER [1], 91, 200).

19.   Mr. William Digges & his four Daughters came as also a Mr. B. Buckner who bot. Flour of me.

William Digges's will written in 1780 mentions four daughters: Theresa, Ann, Jane, and Elizabeth. Two other daughters are known: Susannah who died young and Mary who died single (BOWIE, 255; RAMSBURGH, 130–31). Baldwin Mathews Buckner (d. 1778) and his brother John Buckner (d. 1790), both of Gloucester County, were in partnership in the West Indies trade. Their younger brother Mordecai Buckner of Spotsylvania County, had served under GW in the Virginia Regiment (LEDGER B, 65; BUCKNERS, 154–58).

20.   All the above Company here all day.

21.   The whole went over to Mr. Digges's. Mrs. Washington, myself &ca. went with them & stayd all Night.

Today William Shaw inspected 300 barrels of flour for GW and was credited with £1 17s. 6d. in fees (LEDGER B, 58).

22.   Returnd home early in the Morning, & went up to Alexa. to Court. Came back in the Aftern.

The court met 21–22 Dec., but GW was not recorded present. On the previous day the justices had registered GW's brand for his flour, "G: WASHINGTON," in accordance with the act passed during the last session of the assembly (Fairfax County Order Book for 1772–74, 158–65, Vi Microfilm; see main entry for 3 April 1772).

23.   Went a Hunting but found nothing. In the Evening Colo. Fairfax came.

On this day Baldwin Buckner, on behalf of himself and his brother John, contracted with GW to buy 300 barrels of "Superfine Flour & Cask" for £300 13s., to be paid the following April at the meeting of merchants in Williamsburg (LEDGER B, 65).

24.   At home all day. After breakfast Mr. Buckner went away as Colo. Fairfax did after Dinr.

25.   Went to Pohick Church and returnd to Dinner. Found Mr. Tilghman here.

26th.   At home all day with Mr. Tilghman.

27.   At home all day. Mr. Tilghman went away after Breakfast.

28.   Went out a hunting. Found a fox back of Captn. Darrells & killd it. Doctr. Rumney & a Lieutt. Winslow Dind here the former stayd all Night.

29.   Doctr. Rumney stayd all day & Night. To Dinner Came Mr. Wren, Mr. Carr, & Mr. Addison the former of whom went away.

Mr. Wren is probably James Wren (d. 1808) of Fairfax County, who supplied the building plans for Pohick Church (SLAUGHTER [1], 70). Mr. Carr is probably either Overton Carr or his father, John Carr (1706–1778), of Bear Castle, Louisa County. Mr. Addison may be Rev. Henry Addison or any one of the three sons of his brother John Addison (1713–1764) of Oxon Hill: Thomas, John, or Anthony Addison.

30. Went a Hunting but found nothing. Messrs. Addison & Carr dining here—as did Mr. Manley.

31. Mr. Magowan came here Yesterday in the Afternoon & this day with Messrs. Carr & Addison went up after Dinner to Alexa.

Acct. of the Weather in Dec.

Decr. 1st. Cloudy & like for Falling weather; being also Cold.

2. Clear in the forenoon but Cloudy & cold afterwards.

3. Clear & calm in the forenoon but Wind fresh from the Northward abt. Midday—which died away in the Afternoon.

4. Clear and Calm in the Morning, but Winday afterwards from the Northwest.

5. Calm & Cold Morning, & very Cold day. Wind hard from the Northwest.

6. Very like for Snow in the Morning with the Wind at South. Afternoon clear but still Cold.

7. Clear and pleasant with but little Wind & that Southerly.

8. Clear & warm with the Wind in the same Quarter.

9. The forenoon quite calm, warm & pleasant. Afternoon a little more Windy from the Southward.

10. Much such a day as yesterday being very pleasant.

11. Very pleasant, but somewhat Cooler. Wind Northwardly.

12. Clear, Calm, & very pleasant.

13. Wind pretty fresh from the Southwest & very lowering.

14. Clear and very pleasant, with little or no wind & that Southerly.

15. Tolerably, but a little Cloudy in the forenoon & calm, wind fresh from the Eastward in the Afternoon with Rain all Nig[ht].

16. Raining in the forenoon but clear afterwards & pleasant.

17. Very pleasant, being Mild and little Wind.

18. Wind Eastwardly & Raining more or less all day.

19. Misting Raining, & Foggy all day with but little Wind.

20. Much such a day as yesterday, but not quite so wet & bad.

21. Exceeding pleasant with but little Wind from the Southwd. & Clear.

22. Wind Southerly and pleasant, being clear.

23. Wind pretty fresh from the Northwest but not Cold.

24. But little Wind, & that Easterly with Rain more or less all Day.

25. Moderate, & tolerably clear in the forenoon. Afternoon Lowering with a good deal of Rain in the Night.

26. More or less Rain all day with the Wind Easterly.

27. Raining this day also with variable Winds which sometimes was pretty fresh from the No. West.

28. Calm and very pleasant Morning. Wind pretty fresh from the So. West afterwards.

29. Clear, Calm, & pleasant all day with but little Wind.

30. Calm and pleasant in the Morning. A good deal of Wind from the Westward afterwards.

31. Calm, Clear, & pleasant all day.

The Loss of Patsy Custis

1773

The following is the opinion of the late Lord Chanceller Camb-den, and Chanceller York, on Titles derivd by the Kings Subjects from the Indians or Natives.

"In respect to such places as have been, or shall be acquired by Treaty or Grant from any of the Indian Princes, or Governments, your Majestys Letters Patents *are not necessary, the Property of the Soil, vesting in the Grantee by the Indian Grants,* Subject only to your Majestys Right of Sovereignty over the Settlements, and over the Inhabitants as English Subjects *who carry with them, your Majestys Laws wherever they form Colonies, and receive your Majestys Protection, by Virtue of your Royal Chartres.*"

OPINION OF THE LATE LORD CHANCELLOR CAMBDEN: In 1757 the East India Company had requested an opinion from Charles Pratt, first Earl Camden, and Charles Yorke, two prominent English jurists, on the validity of land grants acquired in India from native rulers. The Camden-Yorke opinion, up-holding the validity of such grants, was clearly intended to apply only to company grants in India. In 1772, however, the opinion was resurrected by agents of the Vandalia Company and bowdlerized versions, such as the one quoted here by GW, were widely circulated in America to give substance to the claims of land speculators that purchases from Indian tribes were valid without sanction from the crown (LIVERMORE, 106–7; ABERNETHY, 116).

Sales of the Pews in Alexandria Church – to whom – &ca.

Nos.	Purchasers	Price
4	. Mr. Townsd. Dade	£28.
5	. Colo. G. Washington	36.10
13	. Mr. Robt. Adam	30.
14	. Mr. Robt. Alexander	30.10
15	. Mr. Dalton	20.
18	. Mr. Thos. Fleming	21.5
19	. Colo. Carlyle	30.
20	. Mr. Wm. Ramsay	33.
28	. Messrs. Jno. Muir &ca.	36.5
29	. Mr. Jno. West Junr.	33.
		£298.10
	Average price	£29.17

The new church at Alexandria was formally presented to the Fairfax vestry on 27 Feb. 1773 (POWELL, 87). By that date GW had paid the £36 10s. for his pew, and all of the pews were ready for use. But he was disturbed to learn that some of the vestrymen were proposing to refund the purchasers' money and reclaim the pews as the common property of the parish, paying for them by a general tax on the parishioners. Such action, GW wrote to vestryman John Dalton on 15 Feb. 1773, would be "repugnant . . . to every Idea I entertain of justice . . . and the right of reclaiming the Pews by the Vestry . . . I most clearly deny; therefore, as a Parishioner who is to be sadled with the extra charge of the Subscription Money I protest agt. the Measure. As a Subscriber who meant to lay the foundn. of a Family Pew in the New Church I shall think myself Injurd" (DLC:GW). According to the vestry book, GW was not officially sold a pew in the church until April 1785 (FREEMAN, 6:3, n.11).

The Camden-Yorke opinion and the list of pews in the church in Alexandria are written in the front inside cover of GW's 1773 almanac.

TOWNSD. DADE: There were at least five Townshend Dades living at this time and their genealogies appear to be hopelessly confused and contradictory. This is probably Townshend Dade (d. 1781), the father of Rev. Townshend Dade (b. 1744), minister of Fairfax Parish from 1765 to 1778.

[January]

Where & how my time is Spent

Jany. 1st.   Dined at Belvoir and returnd in the Afternoon. Found Mr. Grafton Dulany, Mr. Ben. Gallaway, Mr. Sam Hanson & Mr. Magowan and Doctr. Rumney here.

Grafton Dulany, son of Mary Grafton and Walter Dulany, the commissary general for Maryland, was a student at Jonathan Boucher's school in Annapolis. He became a Loyalist in the Revolution and served with the Maryland Loyalist Battalion in Florida, where he died in 1778 (LAND, 325). Benjamin Galloway, son of Samuel Galloway of Tulip Hill, Anne Arundel County, Md., lived at Hagerstown, Md. Samuel Hanson, son of Samuel Hanson of Green Hill (b. 1719) and Ann Hawkins Hanson, usually called himself Samuel Hanson of Samuel, in order to distingush himself from several cousins of the same name. He may have been a student at Boucher's school with Jacky Custis and Grafton Dulany.

2.   Doctr. Rumney went away after Breakfast. Lord Sterling & Captn. Foy with Colo. Fairfax came to Dinner. The latter went away afterwards. The other Gentlemen stayd.

Capt. Edward Foy was secretary to Lord Dunmore. William Alexander (1726–1783) of New Jersey called himself Lord Stirling, although his claim to a Scottish earldom was disallowed by the House of Commons. He had served as aide and secretary to Gov. William Shirley of Massachusetts during the French and Indian War, and in the coming Revolution he was to serve throughout the war as a major general in the Continental Army. Stirling was a man of wealth and social prominence, but for several years he had overextended himself and was currently attempting to solve his financial difficulties by holding a lottery. It was to promote this "Delaware Lottery" that he visited Mount Vernon. He put 60 tickets into GW's hands, 6 of which GW kept himself, 12 were given to Walter Magowan to sell, and 42 were sent, by Stirling's instructions, to James Cocke, mayor of Williamsburg (LEDGER B, 83). The venture, however, was a failure, and Stirling eventually refunded the money to those who had bought tickets. George William Fairfax had written GW earlier to make arrangements for Stirling's and Foy's visit (GW to Fairfax, 19 Jan. 1773, DLC:GW).

3. In the Afternoon Mr. Ben Dulany came here. The other Gentlemen continued all day here.

4. Lord Sterling & Captn. Foy set out after Breakfast for the Northward thro Alexa. to which place I accompanied them. The two Dulanys & Mr. Hanson allso went away after Breakfast.

5. Mr. Gallaway went away. Mr. Magowan & I went a Hunting. Found a fox on Ackatinck just by Lawson Parkers and lost it. In the Afternoon Mr. Dulany came.

Lawson Parker was listed as head of a household of six whites in Fairfax County in 1782 (HEADS OF FAMILIES, VA., 18). His wife, Mrs. Dorcas (or Dorchas) Parker, sometimes acted as a midwife to GW's slaves (LEDGER B, 91, 149, 156).

6. The 4 Mr. Digges's came to Dinner also Colo. Fairfax, Colo. Burwell Messrs. Tilghman, Brown, Piper, Adam, Muir, Herbert, Peake, and Doctr. Rumney all of whom stay'd all Night except Mr. Peake.

The four Mr. Diggeses were probably Ignatius Digges of Melwood, William Digges of Warburton, and William's two sons, George and Dr. Joseph Digges. Mr. Brown may be Bennett Browne (Brown), who had business dealings with James Tilghman, Jr., of Alexandria (LEDGER B, 79). There was a merchant of this name in Urbanna, near the Rappahannock River (*Va. Gaz.*, P&D, 9 June 1775). William Herbert (1743–1818), merchant of Alexandria, emigrated from Ireland to Virginia c.1770. Herbert married Sarah Carlyle, eldest daughter of John Carlyle by his first wife, Sarah Fairfax Carlyle.

The large host of dinner and house guests who descended upon Mount Vernon this day may have been celebrating Twelfth Night and Twelfth Day.

7. All the above Company went away before Dinner except Doctr. Rumney & Mr. Magowan who both went afterwards.

8. I rid to Muddy hole, & into the Neck before Dinner. Captn. McCarty Dined here, & Mr. Magowan lodged.

9.   Mr. Magowan returnd to Maryland. I went a Hunting. Found a Fox near Timber Landing & lost it near Mrs. French's.

Penelope French's home, Rose Hill, was on the Fairfax Rolling Road, or Back Road, between the upper reaches of Dogue Run and Pike Branch (STETSON [1], 102).

10.   At home all day. Mr. Geo. Digges Messrs. David & Chas. Steuart—Mr. Danl. Carrol Junr. & Mr. Richmond dind & lodged here.

Charles Steuart (1750–1802) and David Steuart (1751–1814) were sons of Dr. George Steuart, of Annapolis, and Ann Digges Steuart. Charles later married Benedict Calvert's oldest daughter, Elizabeth. Daniel Carroll, Jr. (d. 1790), was the son of Commissioner Daniel Carroll (1730–1796) of Rock Creek, in Frederick County, Md., and his wife, Elizabeth Carroll of Dudding-ton. In 1776 he married Elizabeth Digges (1753–1845), daughter of William Digges of Warburton.

Mr. Richmond is probably Christopher Richmond of Maryland, who in 1785 was a member of the Potomac Company. He was also at that time audi-tor of Maryland.

11.   Went a Hunting with the above Gentlemen. Found a Fox by Gilbt. Simpsons & killd him by Mrs. Frenchs. Mr. P. Pendleton & Mr. M. Campbell dined & lodgd here the others went away.

Philip Pendleton either no longer wanted or could not afford the parcel of land near Bullskin Run that GW had agreed to sell him 6 June 1771, be-cause about this time he transferred his right to buy it to GW's brother Samuel (LEDGER B, 22, 36). Pendleton had not paid any part of the purchase price or the interest due, and Samuel would prove to be too impoverished to pay. Reluctant to press his brother on the matter, GW eventually allowed Samuel to keep the land and wrote off the debt (GW to David Stuart, 21 Sept. 1794, PHi: Dreer Collection).

12.   At home all day, Mr. Peake dind here, who with Mr. Camp-bell went away afterwards.

13.   Went into the Neck in the forenoon to lay of a Fence at Hallerys.

HALLERYS: GW probably means Samuel Halley (Haley), who had married John Sheridine's (d. 1768) widow, Barberry. Halley and his wife still lived in Clifton's Neck on the land her father-in-law, John Sheridine of Charles County, Md., rented from GW.

14.   Mr. Pendleton went away after Breakfast. I rid up to Alex-andria. Dind with Mr. Robt. Adam & returnd.

15.   Rid to the Ferry, Mill, & Mill Plantation before Dinner writing afterwards.

16.   Rid into the Neck, to the Mill and Muddy hole.

17.   At home all day alone. Mrs. Barnes went up to Alexandria.

18.   At home all day alone.

19.   At home all day alone.

20.   At home all day alone.

21.   Ditto. Ditto. In the Afternoon Doctr. Rumney came & stayd all Night.

22.   At Home all day, Doctr. Rumney continuing here.

23.   Doctr. Rumney went away after Breakfast. I went by the Mill to Doeg Run Plantation to lay of a fence there. Returnd to Dinner—Abedo. Adams here.

24.   At home all day alone.

25.   Went a hunting, & found a Fox upon the Hills by Edd. Wathings which run near 4 hours & was either killd or treed—but the wind blewing fresh we were thrown out & coud only judge from Circumstances. Came home to Dinner & found Doctr. Rumney here who stayd all Night.

Edward Wathing (Wathen) made shoes at various times for GW's slaves and in return had work done at GW's blacksmith shop (LEDGER B, 77).

26.   Doctr. Rumney continued here all day. In the forenoon I rid to the Mill & returnd to Dinnr.

27.   At home all day Doctr. Rumney continuing here this day also.

28.   After breakfast Doctr. Rumney returning home I rid to Muddy hole Doeg Run, Mill, & Ferry Plantations.

29.   At home all day alone.

30. Went a Fox hunting with Lund Washington. Took the drag of a Fox by Isaac Gates, & carrd. it tolerably well to the old Glebe then touchd now & then upon a Cold Scent till we came into Colo. Fairfax's Neck where we found about half after three upon the Hills just above Accotinck Creek. After running till quite Dark took of the Dogs & came home.

The old glebe was located on the Colchester-Alexandria road, along a branch of Accotink Creek. The 300-acre tract was bought from John Heryford in 1734 as a glebe for Truro Parish and in 1737 the vestry contracted for the building of a mansion house on the land. In 1752, however, the vestry sold this land and instead bought an adjoining tract of 176 acres from Rev. Charles Green to use as its new glebe (SLAUGHTER [1], 12, 29; Fairfax County Deeds, Book C-1, 362–63, Vi Microfilm).

Fairfax's Neck, or Belvoir Neck, was the neck of land between Dogue and Accotink creeks, where Belvoir was located.

31. At home all day alone.

Account of the Weathr. in Jan.

Jany. [1.] Calm, clear, & exceeding pleasant.

2. Calm & very pleasant in the Forenoon with Wind, Clouds, & Rain from the Southward & Eastward in the Afternoon.

3. Clear with the Wind pretty fresh first from the Southwest, & then from the Northwest. But neither Cold nor frosty.

4. A little Cool, but not frozen in the Morning. Clear, calm & pleasant afterwards.

5. Ground not frozen. Morning Cloudy & Calm—clear and Windy, but not cold afterwds.

6. Remarkable White frost, but Calm, clear and pleasant afterwards till the Evening when it clouded up & began to Rain.

7. Misty Morning but clear afterwards, with the Wind fresh from the South.

8. No Frost. Calm in the Forenoon Windy from the Westward afterwds. clear all day.

9. Very white frost & ground pretty hard froze. Wind after 10 Oclock fresh from the Southward.

10th. Lowering Morning. Clear Midday & Raining in the Evening with but little Wind & that Southerly.

11. Ground a little frozen. Clear & Calm day.

12. Wind fresh from the So. Wt. in the forenoon. Then shifting to the No. West blew hard but moderated towards Night. Clear all D[ay].

13. Lowering Morning & very like for Snow—ground hard froze. Afterwards clear. Wind South.

14. Raining more or less all day. Wind Easterly. Ground froze.

15. Ground froze—day clear & Cold. Wind very hard from the No. West.

16. Ground very hard froze—but calm and moderate after the Morning.

17. Wind Shifting to the No. West in the Night it turnd exceeding cold froze the ground very hard & shut up the Creeks. Thawd very little all day.

18. Very piercing. The River allmost froze over but opend with the Wind wch. contd. Northerly thawd none.

19. More moderate; the Wind getting Southerly but thawd little—lowering in the Evening.

20. A Sleet till the Afternoon, with the wind (tho not much of it) at No. East. After that thawing and foggy—quite Calm.

21. A little Snow in the Night—ground about an Inch thick in the Morning. Variable Weather in the forenoon but clear afterwards with the Wind No. of West but neitr, hard nor cold.

22. Ground hard froze, fore part of the day Cold, Wind at No. West. Latter part calm, clear and more moderate.

23. Ground very hard froze again and day variable – sometimes threatning snow – then promising to be fair and warm. Wind for the Most part Easterly but not much of it.

24. Ground very hard frozen. But little wind all day & that Easterly; with Rain now and then all the Afternoon. Evening moderate.

25. Ground froze again, but afterwards thawd – notwithstanding the Wind blew fresh from No. West till the Eveng. – clear all day.

26. Wind Southerly, & day moderate, but cloudy and lowering.

27. Raining very slow, and moderately all the forenoon, and ceasd about Noon. No wind all day, and Warm. No frost in the Morning it beginning to Rain in the Night.

28. No Frost. Very warm all day. Wind blew very fresh from the Southward which veer'd round to the Northwest before Morning & turnd very cold.

29. Exceeding cold – ground very hard froze & the Wind blowing very hard from the Northwest till the Evening when it lulld.

30. Ground very hard froze & thin Ice almost over the whole River. Day moderate with but little Wind & that Southerly.

31. Wind Southerly, all day & towards the Evening fresh. Cloudy more or less all the day.

[February]

Where, how, or with whom, my time is Spent

Feby. 1. At home all day. In the Afternoon Mr. Bryan Fairfax came here & Stayd all Night – as did three Travellers going to Maryland.

2. Mr. Fairfax & I went out with the hounds. Touchd upon the Drag of the Run[nin]g Fox upon the Hills just above Wathings but it being cold, as the day also was, we took the Dogs of and came home.

3.   Went out again and touchd upon a Fox upon the Hills by Gates's & found another in Colo. Fairfax's Neck abt. 2 Oclock which was killd after an hours chace. This Fox was found upon the Hills.

4.   At home all day with Mr. Fairfax.

5.   Mr. Fairfax went away. I continued in the House all day a Writing.

6.   Rid into the Neck, and taking the Hounds with me, after being at the Plantns. found a fox between the two which was killd in 3/4 of an hour.

7.   At home all day alone.

8.   Doctr. Rumney came to Dinr. and stayd all Night. I contd. at home all day.

9th.   Doctr. Rumney continued all day, & Night. After an early Dinner I set of to Mr. Robt. Alexanders upon Fox hunting Party & in the Afternoon, Young Mr. Danl. Dulany Revd. Mr. Montgomerie, Mr. Tilghman & Jno. Custis came here & stayd all [night].

This Daniel Dulany (1750–1824) was called Daniel Jr. or Daniel III and was the son of Daniel Dulany the younger (1722–1797) and Rebecca Tasker Dulany of Hunting Ridge near Baltimore. He was educated in England and returned to Maryland about 1770, where he began to practice law in his father's Annapolis office. Having strong Loyalist feelings, Dulany left Maryland for England on 17 July 1775. There he remained for the rest of his life, except for a brief visit to America in 1785. His property in Maryland was confiscated (LAND, 192, 309–65).

John Montgomery was at this time minister at St. Anne's, sometimes called Middle Neck, Parish in Anne Arundel County, Md. During the Revolution he and his wife, Margaret Dulany Montgomery, daughter of Walter and Mary Grafton Dulany, fled to England.

This whole party of young people was undoubtedly on its way to Benjamin Dulany's wedding, which took place on 10 Feb. at the bride's home, Rose Hill, near Mount Vernon. A newspaper announced the marriage of "Benjamin Dulany, Esquire, of Maryland, to Miss FRENCH, of Fairfax county, with a fortune of twenty thousand pounds" (*Va. Gaz.*, R, 11 Mar. 1773).

10.   Found a Fox in Mr. Phil. Alexanders Island which was lost after a chase of 7 hour's.

Philip Alexander (d. 1790) lived on an island in the Potomac River which was part of the 904 acres left him by his father, Gerard Alexander (Fairfax County Wills, Book B-1, 327, Vi Microfilm). The island, just north of Four Mile Run, contained 302 acres (STETSON [1], facing p. 10). Commonly called Alexander's Island, it had earlier been known as Holmes Island.

11.   Found a fox in the same place again which was killd at the end of 6 hours after wch. I came home & found Mr. Dulany & Mr. Custis here.

12.   At home all day Mr. Dulany continuing here.

13.   Still at home. Mr. Dulany & Mr. Custis went to Mrs. Frenchs after Breakfast.

The two young men undoubtedly went to visit young Daniel Dulany's brother Ben and his new bride.

14.   At home all day alone.

15.   Went up to Court, & returnd again in the Afternoon.

The Fairfax court met on 15 and 16 Feb. and GW attended both days, although he arrived late on the second day (Fairfax County Order Book for 1772–74, 166–71, Vi Microfilm).

16.   Went up again this day also and returnd in the Afternoon.

17.   Went to Colo. Fairfax's to Dinner and returnd again in the afternoon.

18.   At home alone all day except one William Thompson's coming abt. a Lott of Land in Fauquier.

From 1772 to 1775 William Thompson rented 115 acres of land in Fauquier County from GW for £4 a year (LEDGER B, 73). This may be the man who visited Mount Vernon with Charles Washington on 17 Feb. 1771.

19th.   Rid to the Ferry, Mill, Doeg Run & Muddy hole Plantations before Dinner; at home alone afterwards.

20.   Rid in the Forenoon to the Mill & Mill Plantation. Mr. Thomas Hite, & Mr. Wm. Shaw dind here, & went away after it.

Thomas Hite (1750–1779) son of Jacob Hite (d. 1778) and his first wife, Catherine O'Bannion Hite, lived in Berkeley County, Va. He was a justice of the county and a member of the House of Burgesses and later the House of Delegates until his death. In 1776 Hite was one of the trustees for the new town of Warm Springs in Berkeley County. He was married to his stepsister, Frances Madison Beale (DU BELLET, 4:336–50; *Tyler's Mag.*, 3:49–50). In 1770 GW had been involved in a legal dispute with Hite (William Grayson to GW, 23 Sept. 1770, PHi: Gratz Collection).

Shaw had inspected 200 barrels of flour for GW on 16 Jan. and 137 on 10 Feb. for fees totaling £2 2s. 11½d. (LEDGER B, 58).

21. At home all day. Mr. Hoops & a Mr. Warton calld here but would not stay dinner–taking a Cut before it.

MR. WARTON: probably a member of the prominent Wharton family of Philadelphia.
A CUT: a lunch or snack.

22. At home all day alone.

23. At home this day also alone.

24. Rid to the Ferry–Mill–Mill Plantn. Doeg Run & Muddy hole. In the Afternoon Mr. Bryan Fairfax & Mr. Robt. Alexander came here.

25. Went a hunting with those Gentlemen, & being joind by the two Mr. Triplets, Mr. Manley, & Mr. Peake all came here to Dinner & Mr. Thos. Triplet stayd all Night. Found a Fox in this Neck but did not kill it.

26. Went a Hunting again with the above Company. Found a Fox in Colo. Fairfax's Neck with part of the Dogs but believe it was not killd. Found Mr. Tilghman here upon our return at Night.

27. Mr. Fairfax–Mr. Tilghman & Mr. Alexander went away after Breakfast. I contind. at home all day alone.

28. At home all day. About Noon Mr. Francis Willis–Mr. Warnr. Washington & my Brothr. Saml. came here.

Acct. of the Weather in Feby.

Feby. 1. Wind shifting in the Night to the No. West blew fresh & turnd Cold especially towards Night.

2.   Ground very hard froze, & River quite shut up. Day somewhat more moderate Wind not blowing hard but coming still from the same Point.

3.   Ground very hard froze which thawd but little being Cloudy & like for falling weather all day—with the wind what little there was of it Southerly.

4.   Raining more or less all day. Calm all the forenoon. In the Afternoon the wind came out from the No. & No. East.

5.   Cloudy Morning with some Snow which had slightly coverd the Ground. More or less Cloudy till the Evening with the Wind at No. West—but not hard.

6.   Ground froze in the Morning, but thawd afterwards, being Warm, Calm & pleasant.

7.   Ground not froze—day warm & Pleasant till the Evening when the wind coming out from the No. Wt. blew violently, & turnd Cold.

8.   Ground very hard froze. Forepart of the day cold & high Wind from the No. Wt. Latter part Calm, & more moderate.

9.   Ground froze—but wind getting Southerly it presently turnd warm & thawing.

10.   Ground not froze. The day very pleasant till the Evening when the Wind shifted to the No. West & began to freeze.

11.   Ground froze again, but the Wind soon getting Southerly it turnd very pleasant.

12.   Open Morning, & abt. 9 Oclock perfectly calm. Soon after wch. the Wind came out hard from the No. West and Shifted to the Southwest.

13.   Ground hard froze—day Cold. Wind at No. West and fresh.

14.   Cold Morning, but more moderate afterwards—being Calm & clear. Grd. hard froze.

15.   Wind, what little there was of it Southerly—day pleasant but ground froze notwithstanding.

16.   Very pleasant, clear, & but little Wind which blew from the Southward.

17.   Ground a little froze, but soon thawd. Wind however pretty fresh from the No. Wt. in the forenoon but calm afterwards & lowering.

18.   Snow about 2 Inches Deep, or more, with the Wind pretty cool from the Northward. Afternoon Calm.

19.   Clear and Cool, tho the wind was Southerly—blowing pretty fresh.

20.   Clear but not very warm. Wind fresh from the So. West and weather variable. Snow for the most part gone.

21.   Wind coming out hard from the No. West in the Night it froze exceedingly & the day very cold Wind continuing fresh from the same Point.

22.   Last Night colder by odds than any this year—froze over the River, & every thing in the Cellars; day continuing very Cold—wind still at No. West but not fresh.

23.   Weather somewhat more moderate—but still Cold, Wind continuing at No. West & North.

24.   Quite calm, clear, and pleasant; Ground which had been froze exceeding hard thawd a little at Top.

25.   Day quite Calm, & Cloudy, yet thawing a little—ground being very hard froze in the Morning.

26.   A thick fog, or Mist, which continued without Wind & being Cold till the Evening when it set in to Raining.

27.   A Good deal of Rain fell in the Night. Morning Misting and day Cloudy—with the Wind at No. West but neither hard nor Cold. Afternoon quite clear & perfectly Calm.

28. Clear, & remarkably pleasant with the Wind fresh from the Southwest.

[March]

Where, how, or with whom my time is Spent.

March 1st.   At home all day—in Company with Mr. Willis, Mr. Warner Washington & my Bro. Saml.

2.   Set of for Williamsburg abt. 8 Oclock. Dined at Portobacco & Lodged at Laidlers.

Governor Dunmore had summoned the General Assembly to meet in Williamsburg beginning 4 Mar. to deal with problems resulting from a flood of bogus money that had been loosed on the colony by a counterfeiting ring in Pittsylvania County (H.B.J., 1773–76, 6–7; FREEMAN, 3:309–11).

3.   Breakfasted at Port Royal, & Supped and Lodged at Todds Bridge.

In Port Royal, GW patronized the tavern run by William Buckner (LEDGER B, 82; CAMPBELL [1], 219, 413).

4.   Dined at Doncastles, and got to Williamsburg abt. half an hour by Sun. Lodgd at Mr. Charltons, spending the Eveng. in my own Room alone.

In Dec. 1775 Thomas Doncastle described his tavern as "the noted and well accustomed TAVERN in *James City* County, about 15 Miles from *Williamsburg,* on the main Road from said City to *New Kent* Courthouse, *Ruffin's* Ferry, and the *Brickhouse* Ferry" (*Va. Gaz.,* D&H, 30 Dec. 1775). GW today used Ruffin's ferry to cross the Pamunkey River (LEDGER B, 82).

5.   Dined at the Speakers & Spent the Evening there also.

In the House of Burgesses today, GW was appointed to the standing committee of privileges and elections (H.B.J., 1773–76, 10).

6.   Dined at the Treasurers & Spent the Evening at Mrs. Campbell's.

7.   Dined at the Governors and Spent the Evening at Mrs. Campbells.

GW and Governor Dunmore were planning a trip sometime in the summer to inspect western lands in the Ohio Valley (FREEMAN, 3:317). The House of Burgesses did not meet today, Sunday (H.B.J., 1773–76, 13).

8. Dined, and Spent the Evening at Mrs. Campbells.

9. Dined at the Attorneys and Spent the Evening in my own Room Writing.

10th. Dined at Mrs. Campbells and Spent the Evening there also.

11. Dined and Spent the Evening in the Club Room at Mrs. Campbells.

12. Did the same.

After passing an act authorizing new treasury notes to replace the colony's current compromised ones, the House of Burgesses today turned its attention to what it perceived as increasing British encroachments upon both English liberty and colonial rights (H.B.J., 1773–76, 26–28). A group of younger burgesses, including Thomas Jefferson, Patrick Henry, and Richard Henry Lee, proposed that the house create a committee of correspondence, whose "first measure would be to propose a meeting of deputies from every colony at some central place," as Jefferson later recalled (JEFFERSON [2], 1:8). Sitting as a committee of the whole house, the burgesses drafted a resolution authorizing and appointing an 11-member committee of correspondence and then passed it in open session without dissent (H.B.J., 1773–76, 28). GW was not a member of the committee of correspondence.

13. Dined no where but reachd Colo. Bassetts in the Afternoon on my return home.

On this Saturday the burgesses passed an act making it a felony to counterfeit paper money of other British colonies, but the General Assembly did not finish its business until the following Monday, when it was prorogued by the governor (H.B.J., 1773–76, 31–36; HENING, 8:651–52).

14. Set off about 10 Oclock. Dind at King William Court House and lodgd at Todds Bridge..

15. Breakfasted at Port Royal about 12 Oclock, and lodgd at Mr. Lawe. Washingtons.

16. Breakfasted in Port Tobacco & reachd home abt. 4 Oclock in the Afternoon.

17. At home all day alone.

18. Ditto–Ditto. Except Riding to Muddy hole & the Plantation in the Neck & to sheridines Point where my People were clearing a fishing Landing.

19.   Went a hunting. Found a Fox by Muddy hole Plantation and killd it after a chase of two hours & 3 Quarters.

20.   Rid to the Ferry, Mill & Doeg Run Plantations—also to the Mill.

21.   At Home all day alone.

22.   At Home this day also—alone.

23.   Went over to Mr. Wm. Digges's to Dinner, to Meet Govr. Eden who with Mr. Calvert Mr. Digges, Mr. Geo. Digges & Mr. Custis returnd with me. Found Mr. Loyd Dulany here.

GW wrote James Tilghman, Jr., in Alexandria, "I expect Govr. Eden, and some Gentlemen from Maryland here this afternoon. If you are disengaged, I should be glad if you would come down & stay with us a day or two, or as long as they remain" (23 Mar. 1773, NjMoNP).

24.   At home with those Gentlemen til the Evening when we went to Mr. Digges's again. Mr. Ben. Dulany also Dind with us.

25.   At Mr. Digges's all day.

26.   Ditto—Ditto.

27.   Returnd home to Breakfast. Mr. Loyd Dulany, and Mr. Geo. Digges with me, at home all the remaining part of the Day.

28th.   Went with Mr. Dulany, and Mr. Digges, &ca. to Dine with Mr. Benj. Dulany at Mrs. Frenchs. Returnd again in the Afternoon.

29.   Went a hunting with those Gentlemen. Found a Fox by Thos. Baileys & had it killd by Cur Dogs in half an hour. Retd. to Dinner Mr. Manley with us.

Thomas Bailey had worked on GW's millrace in 1770. He also bought corn from GW and had some work done at the Mount Vernon blacksmith shop (LEDGER A, 130).

30.   Went a hunting again. Found Nothing. Colo. Fairfax & Mr. Lan. Lee—also Mr. Herbert & Mr. Miller Dined here, the last two stayd all Night.

Lancelot Lee was George William Fairfax's nephew, the son of his sister Ann Fairfax Washington Lee by her second husband, George Lee of Mount Pleasant, Westmoreland County. MR. MILLER: William Milnor, a Philadelphia merchant who had business connections with William Herbert and was interested in buying fish from GW.

31.   Mr. Herbert & Mr. Milner, also Mr. Digges went away before Breakfast—Mr. Dulany continuing.

Acct. of the Weather in Mar.

March 1st.   Snowing all the forenoon—Wind being at No. East, which shifting to the No. West blew hard and dispeld the Clouds.

2.   Ground a little froze. Day clear & pleasant with but little Wind & that Southerly.

3.   A little Raw in the morning, & Cool, tho' the Wind continued in the same place. Afternoon Muddy & like for falling weather.

4.   Wind fresh from the Northward & Snowing till about 10 Oclock. Afterwards clear, & more moderate, Morning being very Cold & disagreeable.

5.   Wind Westerly, Clear, & tolerably pleasant—but Cool.

6.   Lowering and like for falling Weather all day. In the Night Rain.

7.   Close & heavy Morning—but no Rain. Afternoon clear & pleasant with but little wind.

8.   Clear and very pleasant Morning—but somewhat Cooler in the Afternoon Wind Westerly.

9.   Lowering Morning & Rainy day. Wind Easterly but not Cold.

10th.   Heavy & Cloudy all day, & sometimes a little Rain.

11.   Clear and turnd a little Cooler—Wind Westerly.

12.   Very pleasant, being Calm clear & warm especially in the Morning.

13. Raw & Cool with the Wind Easterly and cloudy withal.

14. Raining & Snowing till abt. 10 Oclock a good deal of the former having fallen in the Night. Wind Northerly and Cold.

15. Cloudy & Raw in the forenoon with the Wind still Northerly which shifting Southerly it became warm clear & pleasant.

16. More or less Cloudy all day with the Wind about So. Et. and South.

17th. A good deal of Rain fell last Night. This day variable with some Rain. At length the Wind came to No. Wt. & blew hard.

18. Clear & somewhat Cool. Wind blowing hard at No. West till the Evening when it turnd Calm.

19. Very pleasant—calm & clear in the forenoon—a little Wind from the Southward in the Afternn.

20. Lowering all day and sometimes Raining—with the Wind Southerly, warm, and growing.

21. Wind at North East and Raining more or less all day—in the Evening fast as it had done the Night before.

22. Raining all the forenoon with the Wind fresh from the No. West. Afternoon clear with less Wind thoh. from the same point.

23. Clear and pleasant with very little Wind, and that Southerly.

24. Calm, and Clear in the forenoon—lowering afterwards with the Wind at No. East and pretty fresh.

25th. The Wind having shifted in the Night to No. and No. Westerly, their came on a Most violent Storm, attended with much rain, which did inconceivable damage by the freshes—Many Houses Trees &ca. being blown down. This Storm of Wind & Rain continued with little abatement all this day likewise.

26. Raining ceasd, but the Wind continued to blow very hard at No. West, till Night.

27.   Wind still at No. West, but not much of it. Weather Clear and pleasant.

28.   But little Wind and that Southerly. Weather clear & very Warm.

29.   Clear, Calm, and very Warm.

30.   Lowering all day with some Rain about Noon—the Wind being pretty fresh from the Southward.

31.   Clear and pleasant with very little Wind.

[April]

Where, how, or with whom my time is Spent

April 1st.   Rid to my Mill, and Plantations on this side the Creek. Mr. Dulany went away after Breakfast & Colo. Frans. Thornton & his Son came to Dinner & stayd all Night.

Col. Francis Thornton was probably Francis Thornton (d. 1784) of Society Hill, King George County. He was a justice of the peace, colonel of the county militia, and a well-known breeder of horses. He had married Sarah Fitzhugh in 1747 and had two sons, John and William.

2.   They with myself &ca. went up to Alexandria to the Genl. Muster & returnd in the Afternoon. One old Wilper came here to Dinner.

John David Woelpper (Wilper), born in Germany, was living in or near Philadelphia at this time. Now about 64 years old, he was asking GW for advice regarding a land grant for his service as a sergeant in GW's Virginia Regiment during the French and Indian War. GW went out of his way to help Woelpper, and the old sergeant returned the favor by giving GW advice on bringing Germans to America to be settled on GW's Ohio Valley lands (see GW to William Milnor, 23 Jan. 1775, DLC:GW; Woelpper to GW, 23 Mar. 1774, DLC:GW).

3.   Colo. Thornton & Son went away after Breakfast. Mr. Custis also returnd to Maryld.

Jacky Custis probably carried with him a letter which GW wrote to Benedict Calvert on this date. Having just been apprised that Jacky had contracted a secret engagement to Calvert's daughter Eleanor (Nelly), GW wrote Calvert his feelings on the matter: "I am now set down to write to you on a Subject of Importance, & of no small embarrassment to me. My Son in Law [stepson] & Ward, Mr. Custis, has, as I have been informd, paid his Addresses to your Second Daughter, & having made some progress in her Affections required her in Marriage." He then expressed his approval of Nelly, but added firmly that Jacky was too young and inexperienced for marriage and needed to complete his education. "Delivering my Sentiments thus, will not, I hope, lead you into a belief that I am desirous of breaking of the Match—to postpone it, is all I have in view; for I shall recommend it to the young Gentleman with the warmth that becomes a Man of honour (notwithstanding he did not vouchsafe to consult either his Mother, or me, on the occasion) to consider himself as much engaged to your Daughter as if the indissoluble Knot was tied; and as the surest means of effecting this, to stick close to his Studies (in which I flatter myself you will join me) by which he will, in a great measure, avoid those little Flirtations with other Girls which may, by dividing the Attention, contribute not a little to divide the Affection" (DLC:GW).

4.   Mrs. Fairfax and Polly Brazier Dined here, as did Majr. Wagener. The latter stayd all Night. Mr. Jno. Baylor came in the Afternoon.

5.   At home all day, Majr. Wagener contd. till the Afternoon— Mr. Baylor all day & Night. Mr. Campbell and Captn. ⟨   ⟩ of the Brig Nancy Dind here.

BRIG NANCY: This brig was probably from the West Indies, and seems to have been tied up at GW's dock for at least five days. On 8 April GW bought a parrot for 6s., probably from the captain of the *Nancy* (LEDGER B, 88). The brigantine *Nancy,* Capt. John Cox, master, which sold a barrel of flour to Lund Washington on 12 May may have been the same vessel (LEDGER B, 140).

6.   Mr. Baylor went away after Breakfast. The Captn. Dined here again & Mr. Campbell lodgd all Night.

7th.   Mr. Herbert, Doctr. Rumney & the Captn. Dined here the Doctr. staying all Night. I went into the Neck this day.

8.   The Doctr. went away after Breakfast. The Captn. Dind here.

9.   At home all day. The Capt. Dined here—otherwise alone.

10.   At home all day alone. Mr. Custis came in the afternoon.

John Parke Custis was probably returning from the Calvert home of Mount Airy with Benedict Calvert's reply (8 April 1773, DLC:GW) to GW's letter (3 April 1773, DLC:GW) regarding Custis's betrothal to Calvert's daughter Nelly. Calvert agreed with GW that the match, which met with his approval, should be postponed while Custis studied at King's College in New York City.

11.   Went to Pohick Church with Mrs. Washington & Mr. Custis & returnd to Dinner.

12.   Set of for Annapolis with Mr. Custis. Dined & lodgd at Mr. Bouchers with Govr. Eden & others.

Jonathan Boucher had written to GW 8 April: "I am told, You have Business to our Provincial Court, the next week; I hope to see You either agoing, or returning. The Govr., Mr. Calvert, the chief Justice, & Mr. Dulany dine here on Monday: shou'd You set out on that Day, You know, You can be here in Time to Dinner" (DLC:GW). GW's business at the Maryland court was to submit a proved account against Daniel Jenifer Adams for £106 14s. 6d. Virginia currency. Adams, who had taken some of GW's flour to the West Indies to be sold (see main entry for 22 July 1772), had perpetrated what GW feared was a swindle, and GW was afraid he would be able to get no money from Adams for his cargo (for further information, see letters of GW to Robert McMichan, 12 Jan. 1773, 12 Feb. 1773, Feb. 1773, and 14 June 1773, DLC:GW).

   GW's visit to Jonathan Boucher's home is his last contact with Boucher recorded in the diaries. In the fall of 1774 Boucher, coming under increasing attack for his personal resistance to the rising activism of local Whigs, moved to The Lodge, a plantation near Oxon Hill, across the Potomac from Alexandria (BOUCHER [1], 93; *Va. Gaz.*, Pi, 1 June 1775). On 6 Aug. 1775, a month before he and his wife sailed for England, Boucher wrote GW a long letter regarding GW's apparent lack of sympathy toward his sufferings, which concluded: "You are no longer worthy of my friendship: a man of honour can no longer without dishonour be connected with you. With your cause I renounce you" (BOUCHER [1], 141). In 1797, however, Boucher published a collection of sermons on the Revolution and included a long dedication to GW in which he wrote: "I was once your neighbour and your friend: the unhappy dispute . . . broke off our personal connexion: but I never was more than your political enemy; and every sentiment even of political animosity has, on my part, long ago subsided" (BOUCHER [2]). GW replied 15 Aug. 1798 in a friendly letter that closed "With very great respect" (DLC:GW).

13.   Got to Annapolis. Dind & lodgd at the Governors – where I also Supped.

14.   Dined and Suppd at Mr. Loyd Dulany's. Lodgd at the Govrs.

15.   Dined at Colo. Sharpes and returnd to Annapolis. Supd & Lodgd at the Governors.

Horatio Sharpe (1718–1790), former governor of Maryland, had retired in 1769 to his summer home on the Whitehall River in Anne Arundel County, seven miles from Annapolis. Sharpe had been governor during the French and Indian War and had been active in strengthening the frontier forts. He had been replaced in 1769 by Robert Eden, brother-in-law of the proprietor of Maryland.

16.   Dined and Supped at Mr. Danl. Dulany's. Lodgd at the Govrs.

17.   Left Annapolis. Dined & lodgd at Mr. Calverts.

18.   Reachd home to Dinner after passing through Piscataway Town.

19.   At home all day alone except Mr. Smith (manager of Messrs. Herberts &ca. fishery) who stays here.

Mr. Smith may be Edward Smith (1752–1826). According to Toner, Smith— who first appeared at Mount Vernon on 7 July 1770—was a clerk for Herbert & Co., the firm which contracted for the catch from one of GW's fisheries (DLC: Toner Collection). Herbert & Co. probably rented one of the fisheries on Clifton's Neck (*Md. Gaz.*, 9 Sept. 1773).

20.   Dined at Belvoir with Mrs. Washington & Patcy Custis. Returnd in the Afternoon & found Mr. Tilghman, Mr. Harrison, Mr. Robt. Adam & his Nephew as also David Arrell. All of whom Stayd all Night.

Mr. Harrison is either Robert Hanson Harrison or Richard Harrison, a merchant (see main entry for 14 Oct. 1773). Robert Adam's nephew must have been his brother John's son Robert (Fairfax County Wills, Book E-1, 315–17, Vi Microfilm).

David Arell (d. 1792), son of Richard and Eleanor Arell, was a lawyer in Alexandria. During the Revolution he became a captain in the 3d Virginia Regiment.

21.   Mr. Adam & Nephew went away after breakfast. The rest stayd to Dinner & all Night. Mr. Robt. Brent came to Dinner & stayd the Evening.

Robert Brent (c.1730–1780), the son of George and Catherine Trimmingham Brent, lived at Woodstock on Aquia Creek in Stafford County and owned the quarry at Aquia. Brent had undoubtedly come to see GW about the estate of Brent's aunt Elizabeth Clifton. Mrs. Clifton had appointed GW one of her executors, but GW was showing some reluctance to serve in an active capacity. Brent, another of the executors, wrote GW in Feb. 1774, urging him to accept the office. He added that he did not feel it would be a troublesome business, for Mrs. Ann Slaughter, who was Mrs. Clifton's only daughter and heiress, would probably continue to live apart from her husband, and in that case "the trust may be said in some measure to have ceas'd, as it does on her becoming a Widow" (DLC:GW).

22.   All went away before breakfast. I rid into the Neck after it.

23.   Rid to Doeg Run & Mill. Mr. W. Washington & Lady came to Dinner & stayd the Night.

24.   Lord Fairfax & Colo. Fairfax—Mr. Calvert, his Lady & two Daughters, & Mr. Geo. Digges & sister Teresa dind here. The two first went away—the others contd.

25.   At home all day with the above Company.

26.   Went with Mr. Calvert &ca. to the Fishing Landing at the Ferry. Found Doctr. Digges Mr. Tilghman & Mr. Fitzgerald here upon our return who Dind & stayd all Night.

John Fitzgerald (d. 1800), a native of Ireland, came to America in 1769 and settled in Alexandria as a partner of Valentine Peers (Piers) in a mercantile business. During the Revolution he served as aide-de-camp to GW. After the Revolution, Fitzgerald was mayor of Alexandria, collector of customs, and served as a director and later as president of the Potomac Company. He later married Jane Digges, daughter of William Digges of Warburton.

27.   At home all day with the above Company. Mrs. Calvert Mrs. Washington & my wife went to hear Mrs. Masons Funeral Serm.

Ann Eilbeck Mason (Mrs. George Mason) in a copy of a John Hesselius portrait. (Mr. S. Cooper Dawson, Jr.)

This funeral sermon was for Ann Eilbeck Mason, wife of Col. George Mason of Gunston Hall. She had died on 9 Mar., following a long illness, and was buried at Gunston Hall. This memorial service was preached at Pohick Church by James Scott, rector of Dettingen Parish (MASON [2], 1:481).

28.   Mr. Calverts Family, Mr. Washingtons, & the other Company all went away after Breakfast. I contd. at home all day.

29.   Rid into the Neck, & from thence went to Sheridines Point attempting to clear it for the Sein.

30.   Went to the Point again and made one or two pretty good Hauls.

Acct. of the Weather in April

April 1st.   Warm and pleasant in the forenoon—but Cloudy & Cold in the Afternoon, Wind blowing fresh from the No. West.

2.   Clear and Cool, Wind blowing fresh from the same quarter.

3.   Much such a day as yesterday Wind from the same place but not quite so fresh.

4.   Clear, Calm, and pleasant in the forenoon. In the Afternoon wind fresh from the No. Wt. and turning Cool.

5.   Wind at No. West all day—fresh and Cool.

6.   Clear, Calm, and pleasant. Wind what there was of it came from the Southward.

7.   Clear but the Wind pretty fresh from the Southward & Warm.

8.   Wind tho not much of it from the same quarter. Warm and Smoaky.

9.   Very warm and Smoaky with but little Wind & that Southerly.

10th.   Just such a day as the preceeding one. What little Wind there is coming from the same Quarter.

11. Clear, Wind coming from the No. West blew hard, & turnd Cold.

12. Calm, clear, & pleasant, growing warm again.

13. Much a day as the preceeding one.

14. Lowering Morning & rainy afternoon with the Wind fresh from the No. East – all day.

15. Raining & drisling forenoon but clear afternoon – Wind getting to the South East.

16. Clear and pleasant with the Wind Westerly.

17. Lowering forenoon with the Wind at No. East. Afternoon Rainy & Cool.

18. Wind very fresh and Cool all day, from the No. East.

19. Much such a day as yesterday with the Wind fresh & a little Rain now & then.

20. Cool in the Morning but warm afterwards – wind getting to the Southward.

21. Clear and very warm with but little Wind and that Southerly.

22. Clear and warm, Wind in the same place and but little of it.

23. Again Warm and Clear with little or no Wind from the Southward.

24. Calm & warm in the forenoon, but Cool in the Evening Wind springing up fresh from the Eastward.

25. Rather Cool with Easterly winds. Clear but Smoaky.

26. Clear, Calm, and pretty warm in the forenoon – but Cool in the Evening, Wind fresh from the Eastward.

27. Cold & raw all day, Wind fresh from the Eastward and like for Rain – but none fell.

28. Cold, raw, and Misting in the forenoon—but warm afterwards—Clouds dispersg.

29th. Clear and tolerably warm in the forenoon but cool, the wind blowing a little fresh from the Eastward in the Afternoon.

30. Wind still Easterly, and Weather much the same as yesterday.

[May]

Where—how or with Whom my time is Spent

May 1st. Went to the different Fishing Landings on both sides the River as high as broad Creek & found that few Fish had been catchd.

This was a bad year for the herring and shad fisheries. The catch during May was much smaller than that of 1772 or 1774 (LEDGER B, 42). Broad Creek enters the Potomac in Prince George's County, Md., four miles above Piscataway Creek.

2. Went to Belvoir and dined. Returnd in the Afternoon.

One of the Mason children made this pencil drawing of the family home, Gunston Hall, ca.1830–40. (Board of Regents of Gunston Hall)

3.   Went by the Church to Colo. Mason's where I dind and returnd in the Afternoon. F[oun]d Mr. Ramsay here who stayd all
Night.

4.   Went with Mr. Ramsays to the fishing Landings at the Ferry
& Sheridines point.

5.   Mr. Ramsay went away before Dinner. I rid to Muddy hole,
Dogue Run—Mill & Ferry Plantations. Found Mr. Hall & Mr.
Adam's here, who dind & went away afterwards.

6.   At home all day. Mrs. Fairfax & Mrs. Washington came &
went before Dinner. Mr. Tilghman came to Dinr. & stayd all
Night.

7th.   Mr. Tilghman & Captn. Mathis dind here—both of which
went away afterwds.

8.   Mr. Custis, set of for Mr. Calverts on his way to New York. I
rid to the Plantations in the Neck.

Jacky Custis was on his way to enroll at King's College, now Columbia University. GW had been dissatisfied with his young stepson's progress under
Jonathan Boucher and his desire to settle Jacky in college was further
strengthened by the young man's engagement to Nelly Calvert. GW's first
choice was the College of Philadelphia but Boucher persuaded him to enroll
his stepson in King's College where Dr. Myles Cooper, president of the college, had introduced extensive reforms in curriculum and discipline. Although GW planned to leave for New York on 10 May to place Jacky in
school, young Custis left two days early to spend some time at his fiancee's
home in Maryland.

9.   At home all day. Messrs. Ramsay, Rumney, & Herbert dind
here—the last of whom went away. The others stayd all Night.

10.   Those two Gentlemen stayd to Dinner, after which I set out
on my Journey for New York. Lodgd at Mr. Calverts.

11.   Breakfasted at Mr. Igns. Digges. Dind at the Coffee Ho. in
Annapolis & lodgd at the Govrs.

12.   Dined, Supped & lodgd at the Governors.

13.   After Breakfast & abt. 8 Oclock set out for Rockhall where
we arrivd in two hours & 25 Minutes. Dind on Board the Annapolis at Chester Town & Supped & lodgd at Mr. Ringolds.

ROCKHALL: The route GW took from Annapolis to Philadelphia crossed the Chesapeake Bay by packet or ferryboat from Annapolis to Rock Hall in Kent County, on the Eastern Shore of Maryland. Another traveler who took the same route a year later in bad weather needed 4½ hours to make the same 25-mile crossing (FITHIAN, 130).

The *Annapolis* was owned and commanded by Capt. Thomas Eden, Gov. Robert Eden's brother. Thomas Eden's mercantile firm, T. Eden & Co., was engaged in the tobacco trade between Maryland and England (EDEN, 155, 164). Governor Eden was accompanying GW and Jacky Custis to Philadelphia, where he had a horse entered in the races.

Chestertown, Kent County, Md., was on the Chester River. Although it was officially named New Town, the names Chester or Chestertown were more commonly used at this time and the name was officially changed in 1780 to Chestertown. The town had been a port of entry for Cecil, Kent, and Queen Anne's counties on the Eastern Shore since 1708, and was a flourishing place during the eighteenth century, rivaling Annapolis in importance.

Thomas Ringgold (c. 1744–1776), a merchant, lived with his wife, Mary Galloway Ringgold, in Chestertown (CLARK [2], 82; BEIRNE, 79).

14.   Stopd at George Town, on Sasafras, & dind & lodgd at Mr. Dl. Heaths.

Georgetown, Kent County, Md., is on the Sassafras River about 16 miles northeast of Chestertown. Daniel Charles Heath was the son of James Paul and Rebecca Dulany Heath, a sister of Daniel Dulany the younger (MC-GRATH, 299; LAND, 191–92, 219, 354).

15.   Dined at Newcastle & lodgd at Wilmington.

New Castle and Wilmington, both in New Castle County, one of the Three Lower Counties on Delaware. Dr. Robert Honyman in 1775 described Wilmington as "a large place, at least as large as Fredericksburgh [Va.], but much better built, the houses being all of Brick, & very neat" (HONYMAN, 11). New Castle, on the Delaware River at the confluence of Brandywine Creek and Christina (Christiana) River (Creek), was the capital of the Three Lower Counties until 1777. A British officer described it in that year as "small, and its Buildings mean & scattered" (SERLE, 257).

16.   Breakfasted at Chester & Dined at Govr. Penns in Philadelphia.

Richard Penn (1735–1811) was the second son of Richard and Hannah Lardner Penn and the grandson of William Penn. He was appointed lieutenant governor of Pennsylvania in 1771 to replace his brother John, who returned to England. Richard served until Aug. 1773, when John returned to America and reclaimed the lieutenant governorship, thereby beginning a bitter feud between the two brothers. Richard returned to England in 1775. The governor's house, later owned by Robert Morris, was occupied by GW during his presidency.

17.   Dined again at Govr. Penns & spent the Evening at the Jocky Club.

The Jockey Club was formed in 1766 to promote racing and the breeding of good horses. Many prominent men in Philadelphia were members, including Governor Penn, president of the club, and John Cadwalader, vice-president (JACKSON, 116–17). The meeting on this evening was held at Michael Duff's tavern on Second Street, and among the visitors attending were GW, Jacky Custis, Lord Stirling, and Gov. Robert Eden of Maryland (JACKSON, facing p. 118).

18.   Dined with sevl. Gentlemen at our own lodgings and went to the Assembly in the Evening.

OUR OWN LODGINGS: GW lodged at the same place both on his way to New York and on his return (see main entry for 2 June 1773). On 3 June he paid 10s. "By Board at Mrs. Greydon" (Cash Memoranda, DLC:GW). Rachel Marks Graydon, widow of Alexander Graydon, for many years ran a fashionable boardinghouse in Philadelphia. At the time of GW's visit she was probably still at the famous old house known as the Slate House on Second Street at Norris's Alley. The house had had a long history and several famous occupants before it became a boardinghouse. In later years Mrs. Graydon moved to a larger house on Front Street (GRAYDON, 62–63).

The Philadelphia Assemblies, or subscription balls, begun in the winter of 1748–49, are the oldest series of society balls in the country. The directors of the assembly laid down strict rules governing the dances, the refreshments, and the behavior of the participants. For those who did not wish to dance, there were other entertainments, such as cards (BALCH [1], 14, 39–42).

19.   Dined at the Govrs. and spent the Evening at Mr. Allans.

MR. ALLANS: probably William Allen (1704–1780), Philadelphia merchant and chief justice of Pennsylvania 1750–74. Allen had held a number of other important posts in the provincial government. His son James (1742–1778) mentions in his diary that "Governor Eden & Coll. Washington are in Town came to the races. . . . I asked Gov. Eden & Coll. Washington to dinner but they are engaged during their stay" (ALLEN, 180).

20.   Dined with Mr. Cadwalader & went to the Ball.

John Cadwalader (1742–1786) was the son of Dr. Thomas Cadwalader and Hannah Lambert Cadwalader. He and his brother Lambert were Philadelphia businessmen.

On 18, 19, and 20 May an important series of races was run in Philadelphia, which GW and Jacky Custis almost surely attended, although there is no mention of it in the diaries. The races were run under the auspices of the Jockey Club and were among the most important social events of the year in Philadelphia. Governor Eden had entered his bay horse, Why-Not, in the Jockey Club Purse, the first and richest of the races, but the race was won by Israel Waters's horse, King Herod (*Pa. Chronicle*, 24 May 1773; HARRISON [3], 2:117–18).

21.   Dined with Mr. Merideth & Spent the Evening at Mr. Mease's.

Mr. Meredith is either Reese Meredith (1705–1777) or his son Samuel Meredith (1741–1817). Both were Philadelphia merchants. Samuel was at the meeting of the Jockey Club GW had attended a few nights before (JACKSON, facing p. 118). During the Revolution he served as a brigadier general of Pennsylvania militia, and he was a member of the Continental Congress 1786–88. GW later appointed him first treasurer of the United States.

Mr. Mease is probably either Matthew or James Mease, both members of the Jockey Club, who had met GW at the meeting 17 May (JACKSON, facing p. 118). James was GW's host at dinner during the latter's stay in Philadelphia the following year (see 21 Sept. 1774). He became a commissary of the Continental Army in 1776 and clothier general in 1777 (LMCC, 1:205, n. 6).

22.   Dined at Mr. Morris's & Spent the Evening at the Club.

Mr. Morris could be either Robert or Gouverneur Morris, both of whom were members of the Philadelphia Jockey Club (JACKSON, 117). The club which GW visited after dinner may have been the Jockey Club.

23.   Set out for New York with Lord Sterling, Majr. Bayard & Mr. Custis after Breakfasting with Govr. Penn. Dind with Govr. Franklin at Burlington & lodgd at Trenton.

Major Bayard is probably Maj. Robert Bayard, a member of the Jockey Club (JACKSON, 118). Lord Stirling had been a guest at the 17 May meeting of the Jockey Club (JACKSON, facing p. 118).

William Franklin (1731–1813), son of Benjamin Franklin, became the last royal governor of New Jersey in 1763. His championship of the rights of the crown led to an estrangement between father and son. During the Revolution he was held prisoner for two years by the Americans and went to England shortly after his exchange.

24.   Breakfasted at Princeton. Dined at Bound Brooke & reachd Lord Sterlings at Basking Ridge in the Afternoon.

Lord Stirling's new home on the outskirts of Basking Ridge, N.J., was seven miles southwest of Morristown. The still unfinished house and grounds were designed in imitation of a large British estate, complete with deer park. The enormous expenses involved in building this country seat were partially responsible for Lord Stirling's financial straits (see 2 Jan. 1773).

25.   Din'd and Lodg'd at Lord Sterling's. Drank Tea at Mr. Kimbles.

Peter Kemble (1704–1789), president of the royal council of New Jersey, lived near Morristown.

26.   Din'd at Elizabeth Town, & reachd New York in the Evening wch. I spent at Hull's Tavern. Lodg'd at a Mr. Farmers.

Hull's tavern, run by Robert Hull, was located "in the Broadway" (*N.Y. Gazette & Weekly Mercury*, 8 Nov. 1773). In 1774, according to John Adams, Hull's tavern was at "the Sign [of] the Bunch of Grapes" (ADAMS [1], 2:102).

27. Din'd at the Entertainment given by the Citicens of New York to Genl. Gage.

Gen. Thomas Gage (1721–1787) had been for ten years commander in chief of British troops in North America with headquarters at New York. He was at this time relinquishing his post and returning to England for a brief visit. He returned to America a short time later as the last royal governor of Massachusetts. GW had known Gage during the French wars, when Gage served as lieutenant colonel of the 44th Foot in the ill-starred Braddock expedition. The entertainment GW attended was a farewell from the merchants of New York to General Gage, held at Hull's tavern (*Rivington's N.Y. Gazetteer,* 3 June 1773).

28. Dined with Mr. James Dillancey & went to the Play & Hulls Tavern in the Evening.

MR. JAMES DILLANCEY: James De Lancey (1732–1800), eldest son of Lt. Gov. James De Lancey (1703–1760) of New York, was a merchant and landowner. He was also the owner of New York's largest racing stable, and GW had met him 17 May at the meeting of the Philadelphia Jockey Club, of which De Lancey was a member (JACKSON, facing p. 118). Although at first a supporter of the colonial position, he later became a Loyalist and fled to England with his family.

The plays GW saw this evening were *Hamlet* and a new farce by William O'Brien called *Cross Purposes,* performed for the first time. The playhouse was a large, red, wooden building on the north side of John Street (MONAGHAN, 123; DAY, 3:127).

29. Dined with Majr. Bayard & Spent the Evening with the Old Club at Hulls.

THE OLD CLUB AT HULLS: In the mid-eighteenth century, "most public houses of any reputation or following had their own loosely knit groups of customers, who met weekly to dine, drink, play cards or discuss, and from them developed an amazing number of social clubs of a more carefully organized type" (BRIDENBAUGH, 22).

30. Dined with Genl. Gage & spent the Evening in my own Room writing.

GW wrote to Rev. Myles Cooper, president of King's College, concerning financial arrangements for Jacky's stay at the college. He sent Cooper bills of exchange for £100 for Jacky's use and asked him to establish credit for him with recommended merchants. However, GW added, if Jacky was too extravagant he hoped Cooper would "by your friendly admonitions . . . check the progress of it" (GW to Cooper, 31 May 1773, PHi: Gratz Collection). GW had evidently discussed arrangements for young Custis's room and board with Cooper earlier, for on 5 July 1773 Jacky wrote reassuringly to his anxious mother: "I beleive I may say without vanity that I am look'd upon in a particular Light by them all [the faculty]. There is as much Distinction made between me, & the other Students as can be expected. I dine with them [the professors] (A liberty that is not allow'd any but myself) associate & pertake of all their recreations & their Attention to my Education keeps pace with their other good offices. . . . I have a large parlour with two Studies or closets, each large enough to contain a bed, trunk, & couple of chairs, one I sleep in, & the other Joe [his servant] calls his" (DLC:GW).

31.   Set out on my return home. Dind with Captn. Kennedy near New Ark & lodgd at Amboy.

Capt. Archibald Kennedy (d. 1794) lived on an estate called Pavonia between Newark and Powles Hook. He had been a captain in the British navy, until he lost his command after refusing to take stamped paper aboard his ship in Boston harbor for safekeeping during the Stamp Act controversy. Kennedy was suspected of being a Loyalist during the Revolution and much of his property was destroyed. In 1790 he went to England and two years later, upon the death of a cousin, became the eleventh earl of Cassillis.
   Amboy is Perth Amboy, N.J.

Acct. of the Weather in May

May 1st.   Cool, & clear, Wind being pretty fresh all day from the No. West.

2.   Wind So. West, & West, & Cool especially in the Evening.

3.   Wind much in the same place & very cool in the Morning.

4.   Wind Easterly all day with some appearances of Rain very little of which fell altho it thunderd more or less all the Afternoon.

5.   Wind at No. West, and Cool, till the Afternoon when it grew warm again.

6.   Calm & warm all day. Very Smoaky as it hath been for a Month pass'd.

7.   Warm and clear (except smoak). Wind pretty fresh from the Eastward.

8.   Wind Easterly in the Morning and pretty fresh—also Cool. Afternoon Calm—clear & Warm.

9.   Warm, & Clear, all day. Calm in the forenoon. Wind fresh from the So. East afterwards.

10th.   Clear and Warm all the day. Wind at So. East.

11.   Clear & Warm again. Wind continuing in the same place.

12.   It began about 9 or 10 Oclock to Rain from the Southward & contd. more or less so all day.

13.   Now & then Raining. Wind from the same Quarter & fresh.

14.   Cloudy & somewhat Cool wind Shifting more Westerly.

15.   Windy & Cloudy all day being also Cool.

16.   Little or no Wind, & that being Southerly it grew warm again.

17.   Again warm Wind Southerly & clear. In the Afternoon Thunder Lightning & Rain.

18.   Clear & pleasant being at the same time a little warm.

19.   Clear and pleasant the Wind Westerly.

20.   Still clear & midling Cool wind fresh from the west.

21.   A little Rain in the Morning but clear & pleasant afterwards.

22.   Raining in the forenoon but clear afterwards then Raing. in the Night.

23.   Cloudy in the forenoon but clear & warm afterwards with but little Wind.

24.   Clear & tolerably with but little wind.

25.   Clear in the forenoon, cloudy afterwards & Cool. Wind Easterly.

26.   Misting till about 9 or 10 oclock then clear and warm there being but little Wind and that Southerly.

27.   Cool Wind Westerly and Weather clear.

28.   Much such a day as yesterday—in all respects.

29.   Clear and pleasant being rather Cool wind still Westerly especially towards the Evening.

30.   Very warm—there being but little Wind.

31st.   Very warm notwithstanding the Wind blew tolerably fresh from the Southward.

[June]

Where, how, or with whom my time is Spent

June 1st.   Breakfasted at Brunswick on the Banks of the Rariton, din'd at Princeton and lodgd at Bristol.

BRUNSWICK: New Brunswick, N.J., on the Raritan River.

While at Princeton, GW "paid Doctr [John] Weatherspoon Presidt of Princeton College £48.16.0 Jersey" currency, equal to £39 9d. Virginia currency, for the schooling of William Ramsay, Jr., eldest son of William Ramsay of Alexandria (LEDGER B, 47).

On this same visit, GW looked up his two nephews, George and Charles Lewis, sons of Betty and Fielding Lewis, who were enrolled at the college. He gave his nephews and the Ramsay boy each a present of one pistole for pocket money (Cash Memoranda, DLC:GW).

Bristol, Pa., is 20 miles northeast of Philadelphia and 3 miles northeast of the Neshaminy Creek.

2.   Got to Philadelphia by Nine Oclock to my old lodging. Dind at my lodgings & spent the Evening there.

3.   Rid to the Meadows along the River before breakfast. Abt. 11 Oclock left Phila. Dind at the Sorrel Horse 13 Miles from it & lodgd at the Ship Tavern 34 [miles] off.

GW probably rode along the Schuylkill River. This area was popular for drives and outings because of the scenic meadows and large estates on both sides of the river. The Sorrel Horse Tavern was just east of Radnor Meeting House in Radnor Township. Michael Stadleman, whose family kept several taverns in the area, bought the building about 1765 and called it the Horse and Groom. The name was shortly afterwards changed to the Sorrel Horse (BARKER [2], 218).

The Ship Tavern was built by an Irishman, Thomas Parke (c.1704–1758), and seems to have been run after his death by his wife, Jane Edge Parke. It was one mile west of Downingtown on the Lancaster Road. Later, the sign was moved to a building in West Whiteland Township, east of Downingtown (LANDIS, 42 [1918], 24–25).

4. Breakfasted at the Sign of the Bull 13 Miles from the Ship. Dind at Lancaster 19 Miles further & lodgd at Wrights Ferry 10 Miles from Lancaster.

Wright's ferry, now called Wrightsville, is on the south bank of the Susquehanna River in York County. The ferry crossed from Columbia, in Lancaster County.

5. Breakfasted in York Town. Dind at the Sign of the Buck 14 Miles from Yk. wch. is 12 Miles from Wrights Ferry & lodgd at Suttons 15 M. from the Buck.

YORK TOWN: York, Pa. Sutton's was probably a tavern called the Black Horse in Harford County, Md., near the Baltimore County line. A village called Blackhorse now occupies the site.

6. Breakfasted at Slades 10 Miles from Suttons & dind and lodgd at Baltimore Town.

Slade's tavern was probably located on My Lady's Manor in Baltimore County, Md., a few miles east of the present town of Cockeysville.

7. Breakfasted at the Widow Ramsays 15 Miles from Baltimore & lodgd at Mr. Calverts.

The Widow Ramsay's, known as "Stevens" during the Revolution (MD. RED BOOKS, 134), was about 16 miles south of Baltimore at the junction of the Baltimore road with a road leading to the Carroll estate, Doughoregan Manor (W.P.A. [2], 461).

8. Reach'd home to Dinner about two Oclock. Mr. Buckner came here in the Evening & lodgd.

In Dec. 1772 GW had sold the firm of Baldwin & John Buckner, of Gloucester, 300 barrels of superfine flour, for which he received a bond to secure payment the following April in Williamsburg. Fielding Lewis was delegated to collect some debts for GW in Williamsburg at that time but was unable to collect from the Buckner brothers. The money was finally paid in June by Richard Robinson (LEDGER B, 65; GW to Lewis, 20 April 1773, PHi: Gratz Collection; GW's account with Lewis, 20 April 1773, NjMoNP).

9. Went up to Alexandria wth. him & returnd in the Afternn.

10. At home all day alone.

11. Mr. Buckner & Mr. Robinson dind here—also Captn. Harper & a Mr. Large. After Dinner Miss Reed, Miss Nelly Calvert, Doctr. Rumney & Mr. Campbell came all of them staying the Night.

Mr. Robinson is probably Richard Robinson, who paid GW the £616 13s. which had come due in April from Baldwin & John Buckner's bond. GW recorded the payment in June 1773 (LEDGER B, 65).

John Harper (1728–1804), a Quaker from Philadelphia, carried a letter of introduction from Reese Meredith of that city. Harper and his partner, William Hartshorne, were considering moving their mercantile firm to Alexandria (5 May 1773, DLC:GW). The partnership was dissolved in 1775, and Harper became a prosperous shipping merchant in Alexandria.

Mr. Large is probably Ebenezer Large, a Philadelphia merchant.

Miss Mary Read, evidently a sort of retainer in Benedict Calvert's family, was left in his will a legacy "for Services in my family" (Prince George's County, Md., Wills, No. 1, T, 258–62, MdAA Microfilm).

12. Captn. Harper Mr. Large & Mr. Campbell went away after Breakfast, Mr. Buckner & Mr. Robinson after Dinner.

13. Went up with Miss Reed &ca. to Alexa. Church. Returnd to Dinner with Mr. Willis. Doctr. Rumney wt. away.

GW was apparently attending worship service at the new church for the first time.

14. At home all day Mr. Willis continuing here.

15. Still at home being here Mr. Willis. In the forenoon Mr. Tilghman came.

16. Mr. Willis went away after Breakfast. Mr. Robinson & Mr. Buckner came to Dinner & stayd all Night.

17. All of the Company here Rid to the Mill. To Dinner came Lame Jno. Washington & Miss Terrett.

Lame John Washington (d. 1787) of Leedstown, King George County, was crippled in both legs. He was a son of Robert Washington (d. 1765) and grandson of John Washington (b. 1671) and Mary Townshend Washington of Stafford County. His second wife, Constantia Terrett Washington, was a daughter of GW's neighbor, William Henry Terrett. The Miss Terrett who came with him to Mount Vernon was probably his wife's younger sister Susanna.

18.   Every one but Miss Reed & Miss Nelly Calvert went away after Breakfast. In the Afternoon my Bror. Jno. his wife, Daughter Jane & young Child came here.

The two children who came on this visit were Jane Washington (1759–1791), who later married GW's nephew William Augustine Washington (1757–1810), and her brother, another William Augustine Washington (1767–1785), who died unmarried.

19.   At home all day. About five oclock poor Patcy Custis Died Suddenly.

GW wrote to Burwell Bassett 20 June that "yesterday removed the Sweet Innocent Girl into a more happy, & peaceful abode than any she has met with in the afflicted Path she hitherto has trod. She rose from Dinner about four Oclock, in better health and spirits than she appeared to have been in for some time; soon after which she was siezd with one of her usual Fits, & expired in it, in less than two Minutes without uttering a Word, a groan, or scarce a Sigh. This Sudden, and unexpected blow, I scarce need add has almost reduced my poor Wife to the lowest ebb of Misery" (20 June 1773, NNMM).

20.   Colo. Fairfax & Lady as also Mr. Massey dind here—Patcy Custis being buried—the first went away. Mr. Massey stayd.

Patsy was laid to rest in the family vault, about 200 yards south of the main house. Rev. Lee Massey read the funeral service, and GW paid him £2 6s. 3d., about normal compensation (LEDGER B, 90; JONES [1], 99–100). The coffin, which had been bought from James Connell of Alexandria, was draped with a black pall belonging to GW (LEDGER B, 90; Robert Adam to GW, 16 Sept. 1773; HAMILTON [1], 4:261).

21.   Mr. Massey went away after Breakfast. I continued at home all day.

22.   My Brother, his Wife, Miss Reed & Nelly Calvert Dind at Belvoir & returnd in the Afternn. I contd. at home all day.

23.   My Brother & Family also Mrs. Reed went away early. I contd. at home all day.

24.   Mr. Digges & Mrs. Tracy came here to Dinner also Mr. Hoops & his Wife the latter of whom went away afterwards as did Mr. Digges. Miss Calvert came in the Afternoon.

MRS. TRACY: GW means Miss Tracy Digges; see main entry for 26 June. David Hoop's wife was his bride of seven months, Mildred Syme Hoops, daughter of Col. John Syme (1728–1805), of Hanover County, who was a half brother of Patrick Henry. Hoops lived in Louisa County until the death

Patsy Custis was buried in the old family vault. (Mount Vernon Ladies' Association of the Union)

of his wife (c.1778), when he removed to Sussex County, N.J. During this visit GW paid Hoops £40 Virginia currency for a phaeton (GLAZEBROOK, 2:64–76; LEDGER B, 90).

25.   Walkd into the Neck.

26.   Rid to Muddy hole Ferry &ca. after Miss Digges went away in the Morning.

27. The two Miss Calverts went up to Church. Mr. Calvert came over to Dinner & stayd all Night as did Mr. Tilghman from Alexa.

28. Mr. Calvert & his Daughters & Mr. Tilghman all went away in the Morning Early.

29. Went with Mrs. Washington & dind at Belvoir. Returnd in the Afternoon.

30. At home all day. Doctr. Rumney Dind & lodgd here, as did Doctr. Craik & another Person with him.

Acct. of the Weather in June

June 1st. Cloudy & tolerably pleasant in the forenoon, Wind being fresh from the southward. Afternoon exceeding hot being clear & still.

2. Very warm again, notwithstanding the wind blew fresh from the Southward.

3. Again Warm after the Sun Broke out which happend about 9 Oclock.

4. Foggy, Misty, & tolerably Cool till abt. 10 Oclock—then Warm & Clear. In the Night a good deal of Rain.

5. Close & sultry, with Rain about Midday, & but little Wind till the Evening.

6. Very Cool Wind being fresh from the No. West, & Cloudy.

7. Grown Warm again, Wind getting Southerly.

8. Much such a day as yesterday, there being but little Wd.

9. But little Wind, but Rain at different times through the day with thunder.

10th. Warm and pleasant with some Clouds.

11. Cloudy & exceeding Cold Wind fresh from the No. West, & Snowing.

SNOWING: "Memorandum—Be it remembered that on the eleventh day of June in the year one thousand seven hundred and seventy three It rain'd Hail'd snow'd and was very Cold" (Fairfax County Order Book for 1772–74, inside front, Vi Microfilm).

12.   Equally Cold with the preceeding day Wind in the same place and as fresh.

13.   Clear & moderately warm again, there being but little Wind and that Southerly.

14.   Wind fresh from the Eastward and Cool.

15.   Wind in the same place, with the Weather equally Cool. Some Rain in the Morning.

16.   Growing warm again Wind Southerly, & but little of it.

17.   Clear, Calm, and exceeding Hot.

18.   Again very hot with appearances of Rain but none fell here. Wind from the southward.

19.   Again very warm, & clear, wind being Southerly.

20.   Still very warm with thunder and appearances of Rain but none fell here.

21.   Warm again with a shower of Rain in the Afternoon wch. Cool'd the Air.

22d.   Very Cool—Wind being fresh from the No. West.

23.   Pleasant enough—Wind being pretty fresh from the So. West.

24.   But little Wind, and very Warm.

25.   Very little Wind again and exceeding Hot. In the Afternn. Rain, but none here with thunder.

26.   Again warm with a little Rain in the afternoon & Very high Wind.

27.   Appearances of Rain but little or none fell. Still warm but not so hot as it had been.

28.   Cloudy & like for Rain in the forenoon but clear afterwards.

29.   Exceeding Warm with but little Wind & that Southerly.

30.   Again very warm but not so hot as yesterday there being more Wind.

[July]

Where, how, or with [whom] my time is Spent

July 1st.   Doctr. Craik & his Companion went away before Breakfast; & Doctr. Rumney after Dinner. Miss Molly Manley came in the Afternn. & stayd all Night. Rid with Mrs. Washington to the Ferry Plantn.

2.   At home all day alone.

3.   Rid into the Neck & by Muddy hole. Miss Molly Manley went home in the Afternoon.

4.   At home all day. Mrs. Peake & her daughter dind here.

Mrs. Peake's daughter is probably the younger girl Elizabeth Peake (c.1763–c.1783).

5.   Rid with Mrs. Washington to Muddy hole, Doeg Run, & Mill Plantations.

6.   At home all day. Mr. Peake dined here.

7.   Rid to Muddy hole Doeg Run and the Mill. Mrs. Barnes & Molly McCarty came.

Mary (Molly) McCarty was Mrs. Sarah Barnes's granddaughter.

8.   At home all day. Colo. Fairfax & Mrs. Fairfax came in the Aftern. to take leave of us & returnd again. Doctr. Craik also came & stayd all Night.

The inheritance of an estate in England necessitated George William Fairfax's presence there for an indefinite period. GW was to take over the management of his affairs during his absence, with the help of Francis Willis, Jr., and Craven Peyton. On this day GW was given Fairfax's power of attorney (see power of attorney to Craven Peyton, 14 Jan. 1774, NjMoNP). On 5 Aug., Fairfax wrote GW that their ship was still at Yorktown, where it had been delayed by sickness among the crew. He added, "Knowing that a House & Furniture, suffers much, by being uninhabited, I have directed Mr. Willis if any offers should be made to Rent the whole, to take your Advise, or the House with what Land may be wanted seperate. If neither should offer, would it not be the best way to addvertise the Furniture?" (CSmH). GW retained his power of attorney and continued to supervise the Fairfax properties until the Revolution, when he wrote Fairfax that he could no longer continue to do so (26 July 1775, DLC:GW).

9. Doctr. Craik went away in the Morning Early—Miss Molly McCarty in the Afternoon. Mrs. Washington & self went to Belvoir to see them take Shipping. Mr. Robt. Adams and Mr. Mattw. Campbell dined here.

10. Mr. Calvert his Lady & two Daughters, & Mr. Geo. Digges & Sisters Nancy & Jenny came over early in the Morning & stayd all day.

11. Old Mr. Digges came over in the Forenoon—also Mr. Willis & Polly Brazier. Willis returnd in the Afternoon.

12. Mr. Digges's, & Miss Digges; as also Mr. & Mrs. Calvert went this forenoon the two Miss Calverts rem[ainin]g.

13. At home all day alone.

14. Rid with the two Miss Calverts & Mrs. Washington to the New Church at Pohick.

Construction of the new church was now nearing completion. A stone baptismal font and step costing £7 5s. were being made, and the pews were either ready or almost ready for the congregation. Although GW had been in Williamsburg 20 Nov. 1772, the day that the pews were auctioned, he had engaged to buy one next to the communion table for £16. Lund Washington, probably acting for GW in that transaction, had bought the adjoining pew for £13 10s. (Truro Vestry Book, 20 Nov. 1772, 156, and 4 June 1773, 157, DLC).

15. Rid to Muddy hole, Doeg Run, & Mill Plantations.

16. At home all day. Mr. Tilghman came.

17. Went down to Colo. Fairfax's White House to haul the Sein. Returnd to Dinner.

18. Mr. Tilghman returnd to Alexa., Miss Calverts, Mrs. Washington & self went to Pohick Church. In the afternoon Mr. B. Fairfax came.

19. Mrs. Washington and the two Miss Calverts went to Alexa.

20. I went up to Alexandria and returnd in the Eveng.

21. Rid into the Neck and to Muddy hole Plantation.

22. Rid to the Meadow at the Mill—to the Mill, & Ferry Plantations. Mrs. Barnes went away yesterday Bag & Baggage.

23. At home all day.

24. Mr. Calvert came here to Breakfast after wch. Mrs. Washington the two Miss Calverts & my self went over with him to Mr. Digges & dind. Nelly Calvert returnd with Mrs. Washington & myself in the Afternoon. Doctr. Rumney came here in the Eveng.

25. Went up to Alexandria Church & returnd to Dinner.

26. At home all day.

27. Ditto—Ditto.

28. Ditto—Ditto—Mr. Tilghman came here in the forenoon— as did Miss Sally Carlyle & Sister.

29. Colo. Carlyle & Son & Mr. Piper dind here & went away again in the afternoon with his Daughters.

HIS DAUGHTERS: Col. Carlyle's daughters.

30th. Mr. Tilghman returnd home. Mrs. Washington Miss Nelly Calvert & myself went to Mount Airy (Mr. Calverts) to Dinner.

31. At Mount Airy all day.

Acct. of the Weather in July

July 1st.   Clear & Warm—Wind howevr. fresh from the East-ward.

2.   Very Warm. Clear & still in the forenoon—Wind pretty fresh from the Eastward afterwards.

3.   Again very warm—being just such a day as yesterday.

4.   Very warm in the forenoon some appearances of a Settled Rain in the Evening but none fell.

5.   Very warm and calm in the forenoon. Wind pretty fresh from the Southward in the Aftern.

6.   Clear & Warm in the forenoon. No Wind—fresh breeze in the Afternoon from the Southwd.

7.   Again very warm in the forenn. Good Breeze in the After-noon from the Southward.

8.   Same kind of Weather and Wind as yesterday.

9.   Very warm and like yesterday in all respects.

10.   Again very warm & clear with the Wind Southerly & fresh in the Afternoon.

11.   Same as yesterday with some appearances of Rain but none fell here.

12.   Very Warm. Wind Southerly. In the Afternoon a Refreshing shower or two for a few Minutes.

13.   Very warm with some appearances of Rain again but none fell here.

14.   Very warm with great appearances of Rain in the forenoon. In the afternoon a little fell.

15.   Wind in the Afternoon fresh from the So. West & great prospect of Rain but none fell here.

16.   Wind fresh from the No. West & tolerably cool.

17.   Grown more warm with but little Wind.

18.   Turnd very hot again, Wind getting Southerly.

19.   Very warm. In the Evening Rain but very little of it here.

20.   Exceeding close and warm with Rain again in the Afternoon but little or none here.

21.   Still warm, and again Showers but little or none here.

22.   Cool Wind at Northwest all day. And quite clear.

23.   Turning rather warmer but still Cool.

24th.   Warm with but little wind, & that Northwest[er]ly.

25.   Very warm with some appearances of Rain but none fell.

26.   More appearances of Rain but none fell here. Weather Warm.

27.   Still very warm with Clouds & thunder but no Rain here.

28.   Appearances of Rain but none fell here. Weather Warm & Wind southerly.

29.   Great appearances of Rain again but none fell here. Weather warm.

30.   Morning very warm, close & still—but somewhat cooler afterwards. Wind freshing up.

31.   Warm—close and still in the forenoon. More Wind and Cooler afterwards.

[August]

Where—how or with whom my time is Spent

Augt. 1st.   At Mr. Calverts all day.

2. Dined at Mr. Igns. Digges's & returnd to Mr. Calverts in the afternoon.

3. Dined at Mr. Willm. Digges's & got home in the afternoon.

4. At home all day. Captn. Posey here—he came on Sunday last.

Posey's visit lasted for a week and was for the purpose of extracting more money from GW. His nerve failed, however, and it was not until he was on his way back to Maryland that he wrote GW the purpose of his visit: "You have grant'd me many Favours since I have been Acquaint'd with you. I am now Reduc'd Very Low and advanc'd in years. I have noe Person in the world to Apply to for Assistance and Really am not Able to work. Pray would you be kind Enough to Let me have the Some [of] About £50 Maryland Currancy. I think with that some I could fix myself for Life, and not to want again. . . . I want'd to mention'd this affaire to you when I was at your house but I could not have the Face to Doe" (9 Aug., DLC:GW) . GW did not let Posey have the £50 but continued to supply him with small amounts of money from time to time. His ledger records £4 "By Charity to Captn. Posey" on 15 Oct. 1773 and, in April 1774, £12 (LEDGER B, 93, 106) .

5. Rid to Muddy hole, Doeg Run, Mill, & Ferry Plantations.

6. At home all day. Captn. Posey went to Captn. McCarty's.

7. At home all day, alone.

8. Went up to Alexa. Church & returnd to Dinner. Captn. Posey & Son Price here. The last of whom went away after Dinner.

9. Mrs. Brown came here in the Afternoon & stayd all Night.

Mrs. Brown is Catherine Scott Brown, wife of Dr. William Brown of Alexandria.

10. Mr. George Digges & Sister's Teresa & Betcy came to Dinnr. & stayd all Night.

11. Mrs. Brown went away after Breakfast.

[12.] Mr. Digges & Sisters went away after Breakfast. I continued at home all day.

13. At home all day. Price Posey came to Dinner: & stayd all Night.

14. Very warm. Rid to an intended meeting of Vestry at the New Church. Dind at Captn. McCartys.

Washington's pew is still preserved at Christ Church, in Alexandria. The tower is an early nineteenth-century addition. (Virginia Historical Society)

There was no meeting on this day and the next meeting was not held until 22 Nov.

15.   At home all day alone.

16.   Went up to Alexandria being Court day. Returnd in the Afternoon. Found Majr. Jenifer & Colo. Mason here.

GW did not appear as a justice at this brief court meeting (Fairfax County Order Book for 1772–74, 262–63, Vi Microfilm). However, he did apparently meet with several people to receive and pay out money on behalf of the Colvill estate (LEDGER B, 91).

17.   At home all day—the above Gentlemen remaining here.

18.   After breakfast Colo. Mason & the Major left this. I continued at home all day. Mr. Craven Peyton came in the Afternoon and stayd all Night.

Major Jenifer was on his way home to Maryland and carried with him a letter from GW to Benedict Calvert, requesting Calvert to buy him an artisan in Annapolis (for Calvert's reply, see Calvert to GW, 25 Aug. 1773, DLC:GW).

   Craven Peyton (d. 1781), the son of Valentine Peyton, was a justice of Loudoun County and a vestryman and churchwarden of Shelburne Parish. Peyton was a collector of rents for some of George William Fairfax's lands and in late 1773 and early 1774 had some surveying done on Fairfax's lands in Berkeley and Fauquier counties (account of Craven Peyton with Fairfax, 16 Sept. 1773, 26 April 1774, ViMtV).

19.   Mr. Peyton went away after Breakfast. I continued at home all day.

20.   Rid with Mrs. Washington to Muddy hole, Mill Plantn. & Mill before Dinner. At home afterwards alone.

21.   At home all day. In the Afternoon a Mr. Lambkin came & stayed all Night.

Mr. Lambkin is probably George Lambkin or Lamkin of Fairfax County, who signed a bond of copartnership with Opie Lindsay, 21 Oct. 1771, to build a mill on Wolf Run in Fairfax County near the Prince William County line (Fairfax County Deeds, Book K-1, 36–40, Vi Microfilm). He is also probably the George Lambkin who was a justice for Fauquier County when it was formed in 1759 and was granted a license in 1761 to keep an ordinary in or near Warrenton (*Va. Gaz.*, R, Mar. 1768; GROOME [1], 188). Lambkin had owned a mill on Goose Creek in Loudoun County which he sold to Daniel Jenifer (1727–1795) in 1771 (MOFFETT, 37–38).

22.   Went up to Church at Alexa. and returnd to Dinner. Found Doctr. Craik here who stayed all Night.

23.   At home all day. In the Afternoon came David Allan, & James Whitelaw, two Scotchmen empowerd by a Number of Familys about Glasgow to look out Land for two hundred Familys who had a Mind to settle in America.

Although there had been a large emigration from Scotland for a number of years, after 1763 it greatly increased, and between 1763 and 1775 about 25,000 Scots immigrated to America. North Carolina received the largest number of them, most of whom were Highlanders, and only a small number Lowlanders (MERRENS, 57). David Allen and James Whiteland were commissioners sent by the Glasgow-based American Company of Farmers to find a large tract of land, 16,000–20,000 acres in size, upon which to settle the

200 Lowland families waiting in Scotland. Although they promised to view GW's Ohio lands, they were concerned that the frontier area would be too far from markets or landing places (WYLIE, 322–23).

24. The above person's prosecuted their journey towards Carolina in pursuit of this scheme purposing also to view the Lands on Ohio, & to see Mine there before they returnd with their Report to Scotland. I rid to the Ferry Doeg Run and Mill Plantations.

GW had decided to lease his 20,000 acres of bounty land on the Ohio and Great Kanawha rivers (*Pa. Gaz.*, 22 Sept. 1773, supp.; see 6 Nov. and 23 Nov. 1772). He felt that these lands, leased to tenants who would settle and develop them for their own use, would prosper more than lands placed under the management of an overseer. Nothing ever came of this scheme. Perhaps, as one prospective tenant claimed, GW's terms were unrealistic (Richard Thompson to GW, 30 Sept. 1773, DLC:GW).

25. At home all day. Alone.

26. Went over (to dinner) to Mr. Digges's to meet Govr. Eden &ca. Kept there all Night by Rain.

27. Govr. Eden, Captn. Ellis, Mr. Danl. Dulany & Mr. George Digges—as also Miss Nelly Calvert, Miss Tracy Digges & Mrs. Jenny Digges came over with me to Dinr. Also came Mr. Ben. Dulany & Mr. Tilghman—all of whom stayd all Night.

CAPTN. ELLIS: John Joiner Ellis joined the 18th Regiment of Foot (Royal Irish) in America 21 Jan. 1773. Although Ellis was listed in a 1774 army list as holding the rank of lieutenant in the regiment, he may, like many other British officers, have held a higher rank in the army or for the duration of his service in America (BRITISH FIELD OFFICERS, 72).

Eden, Ellis, and the Dulanys were on their way to Williamsburg. Purdie and Dixon's *Virginia Gazette* for 9 Sept. 1773 reported that "Sunday last his Excellency Robert Eden, Esquire, Governour of Maryland, arrived in this City [Williamsburg] in Order to qualify to his new Commission before the Commander in Chief of this Colony, agreeable to Instructions from the Government, which having performed he sat out upon his Return on Wednesday Morning. He was accompanied by Captain Ellis of the Royal Irish, and Daniel Dulany, and Benjamin Dulany, Esquires." Upon the death of the sixth Baron Baltimore in 1771, the Maryland proprietorship had devolved upon Henry Harford, illegitimate son of Lord Baltimore. By an order in council dated 5 Mar. 1773, the proprietary lieutenant governor was required, upon this change of proprietorship, to take an oath to uphold the acts of trade and navigation and give security thereof. This oath was to be administered by the governor of Virginia (MD. ARCHIVES, 63:423–25).

28. Mr. Tilghman went away after Breakfast & Mr. Digges & his Sisters in the Afternoon.

29.   Govr. Eden, & the other Gentn. went away after breakfast. I continued at home all day.

30.   Rid to the Mill & Mill Plantation – Muddy hole & into the Neck.

31.   At home all day.

Acct. of the Weather in Augt.

Augt. 1st.   Weather clear and Warm, Wind Southerly.

2.   Warm forenoon – a little Rain in the Afternoon.

3.   Still Warm. Forenoon a little Cloudy with some Rain. Afternoon clear.

4.   A Great deal of Rain fell this day and Night ground being thoroughly wet.

5.   Clear with but little Wind & pleasant.

6.   Flying Clouds with the Wind pretty fresh from the Southwest. Afternoon Cloudy – with a little Rain in the Evening. Weather pleasant.

7.   Warm.

8.   Very warm with Clouds in the Afternoon but no Rain.

9.   Cloudy forenoon with appearances of Rain, but none fell.

10.   Very warm with no wind in the forenoon.

11.   Fine showers at different periods through the day being gentle & general in appearance.

12th.   Warm, with little or no Wind throughout the day.

13.   Again warm with the Wind pretty fresh from the Southwd. with Clouds & much appeare. of Rain in the Afternoon but none fell here.

14.   Very warm with great Rain to the No. West. None or very little fell here.

15.   Still warm & clear.

16.   Rather Cooler but pleasant notwithstanding.

17.   Clear and pretty warm with but little Wind, and that Southerly. Pretty Shower of Rain.

18.   Calm still, & clear and very warm especially in the afternoon.

19.   Wind at No. West & somewhat Cool in the Forenoon Warmer afterwards.

20.   Very warm with some appearances of Rain but none fell here.

21.   Clear with but little Wind and that Southerly. Also warm.

22.   Clear and pretty warm, especially in the Afternoon. But little Wind and that Southerly.

23.   Tolerably Cool Wind Northwardly with some appearances of Rain but little of which fell here.

24.   Clear and Cool, especially in the forenoon. Wind being fresh from the Northwest.

25.   Cool in the forenoon, but warmer afterwards; Wind Easterly.

26.   Wind fresh from the Eastward all day. About Noon it set in to Raining & continued to do so more or less all day.

27.   Clear and cool; Wind very fresh from the Northwest all day.

28.   Warm again, with very little Wind and that Southerly.

29.   Quite calm all day—also clear, warm, and growing.

30.   Calm, Clear, and tolerably warm for the Season being.

31st. Wind fresh all day from the Southward with fine Rain now and then but not enough to wet any thing.

[September]

Where—how or with whom my time is Spent

Septr. 1. Went with Mrs. Washington and Nelly Calvert to Mr. Digges's. Din'd & returnd in the Aftern.

2. Rid to Belvoir, Mill, & Mill Plantation. Found Mr. Magowan here upon my return.

3. At home all day.

4. Went with Mr. Magowan &ca. to the Barbicue at Accatinck.

5. Went up with him and Miss Nelly Calvert to Alexa. Church. Returnd to Dinner.

6. At home all day. Mr. Wilper came to Dinner and stayd all Night.

7. At home all day alone except Mr. Magowan & Nelly Calvert.

8. Mrs. Craig, Mrs. McCarty, Mrs. Chichester & Miss Nancy McCarty came here to Dinner & stayd all Night.

MRS. CRAIG: GW probably means Mariamne Ewell Craik, a cousin of Mrs. McCarty. GW and others sometimes spelled Craik's name "Craig."

9. The Company that came Yesterday went away after breakfast except Nancy McCarty. Mrs. Stewart of Annap[oli]s & her Son & Daughter, as also Mr. Geo. Digges & his Sisters Teresa & Nancy came to Dinnr. & returnd. Mr. B. Brown also came to Dinr. & stayd the Night.

MRS. STEWART: Ann Digges Steuart, wife of Dr. George Steuart and sister of William Digges of Warburton.

10. Mr. Brown, as also Mr. Magowan went away after Breakfast. I continued at home all day.

11. At home all day alone.

12.   Govr. Eden, Captn. Ellis, Mr. Dulany, Mr. Lee & Mr. Fendal came to Dinner & stayd all Night as did Mr. F. Willis Junr.

MR. FENDAL: probably Philip Richard Fendall of Maryland. Mr. Lee is presumably a relative of Fendall's wife, Sarah Lettice Lee.

Francis Willis, Jr., was at Mount Vernon to seek GW's advice on the rental of Belvoir. George William Fairfax had left no instructions with Willis regarding either the number of years or the amount for which he would rent his house. During today's visit Willis and GW decided that they would no nothing about leasing the house or selling the furniture until they heard from Fairfax (NEILL, 137).

13.   All the Gentlemen except Mr. Fendal & Mr. Lee went away after breakfast. Mr. Herbert & Mr. Miller came to Dinner & stayd all Night. In the Evening Mr. Tilghman also came.

MR. MILLER: GW probably means William Milnor. He confused the name earlier (see 30 Mar. 1773).

14.   All the Gentlemen went away after breakfast.

15.   I rid to Muddy hole Doeg Run & Mill Plantations.

16.   Rid into the Neck to the Plantations there. In the Aftern. Mr. Robt. Harrison came here.

17.   At home all day. In the Afternoon Mr. Harrison went away.

GW paid Harrison on this day £5 for sundry legal opinions (LEDGER B, 93).

18.   Went to a Barbicue of my own giving at Accotinck. Mr. Robt. Alexander & his Bror. George came home with me.

19.   The two Mr. Alexanders went away after breakfast. My Brother Sam—his Wife & Two children came to Dinner.

Samuel Washington's wife is Anne Steptoe Washington, and the two children are probably Thornton and Ferdinand Washington, although George Steptoe Washington, who was born to Samuel and Anne sometime during the early 1770s, may have been one of them (WAYLAND [1], 139, 143).

20.   I went up to Court, & returnd in the Afternoon. Colo. Mason, & Mr. Fendal came with me.

The Fairfax court met only one day this month, and GW's name does not appear on the list of attending justices. George Mason, who returned from Alexandria with him, had several cases that were being heard at this meeting (Fairfax County Order Book for 1772–74, 263–68, Vi Microfilm).

21.   Colo. Mason & Mr. Fendal went away after Breakfast. I contind. at home all day. Mr. Robt. Hooe dind & lodgd here.

Robert Townsend Hooe of Charles County, Md., was a partner in an Alexandria firm called Hooe, Stone & Co. until 1773, when it became Jenifer & Hooe. A few years later it became known as Hooe & Harrison (*Pa. Mag.*, 61:64). Hooe was a member of the Charles County committee of correspondence and a lieutenant colonel of the Charles County militia. In 1780 he became mayor of Alexandria. After the Revolution he was a member of the Fairfax County court and of the Fairfax vestry.

22.   My Brother and my self rid to my Mill & returnd to Dinner.

23.   At home all day.

24.   Ditto. Ditto.

25.   Still at home all day writing.

26.   I set of for Annapolis Races. Dined at Rollins's & got into Annapolis between five & Six Oclock. Spent the Evening & lodged at the Governors.

Most of the Rollins (Rawlins, Rawlings) families of Maryland lived in the South River and West River neighborhoods of Anne Arundel County, Md. For their presence on GW's probable route, see COLLES, 178, 180. One old Rawlins house, which served as a tavern for much of the colonial period, was owned by Ann Gassaway Rawlins and inherited by her son Gassaway Rawlins, who owned it until 1810 (RICHARDSON [1], 115–16).

27.   Dined at the Govrs. and went to the Play in the Evening.

Five days of racing began this day with a three-horse sweepstakes. As usual, all races began at 11:00 A.M.

28.   Again Dined at the Govrs. and went to the Play & Ball in the Evening.

Tuesday's race was for the Jockey Club purse of 100 guineas, limited to horses of club members. The play was given by the American Company, which played through September in Annapolis. The ball was announced in the newspaper: "Assemblies as usual, on Tuesday and Friday" (*Md. Gaz.*, 9 Sept. 1773).

29.   Dined at Mr. Sprigs & went to the Play in the Evening.

Today's race was run in three heats of three miles each, for a purse of £50.
    Richard Sprigg (1739–1798), only son of Thomas and Elizabeth Galloway Sprigg, was born at West River Farm (later known as Cedar Park) in Anne

Arundel County, Md. (KELLY [1], 41). In 1765 Sprigg married Margaret Caile (d. 1796) of Dorchester County, Md., and shortly afterwards moved to a new house designed for him by his friend William Buckland. This home, Strawberry Hill, was built on a promontory overlooking Annapolis and the Chesapeake Bay and the site is now a part of the United States Naval Academy grounds. Sprigg became a leading citizen of the town, a steward of the Jockey Club, and one of the founders of St. John's College (TILGHMAN [1], 89).

30th.   Dined at Mr. Ridouts & spent the Afternoon & Evening at Mr. Jenifers.

GW may mean Maj. Daniel of St. Thomas Jenifer rather than his brother Daniel Jenifer. During the years that Maj. Daniel of St. Thomas Jenifer served on the governor's council in Maryland, he lived at Stepney, a few miles south of Annapolis in the South River country of Anne Arundel County, Md.

Acct. of the Weather in Septr.

Septr. 1.   Wind fresh all day from the Southward with small Showers of Rain.

2.   Wind Northwardly in the Morning & a little Cool but calm afterwards & Warm.

3.   Clear and Warm in the forenoon with but little Wind. Evening Cloudy & like for Rain very little fell however.

4.   Great appearances again for a Settled Rain but it went of again without any.

5.   Clear and Cool. Wind pretty fresh from the No. West.

6.   Again clear and cool wind being in the same place but not so fresh.

7.   Clear and much warmer than yesterday. But little wind & that Southerly.

8.   Clear, calm, and warm.

9.   Clear, Calm and still again also warm.

10.   Much such a day as the one preceeding there being very little Wind & Warm.

11.   Clear and Warm with but little Wind, and that Southerly.

12.   Very Warm without any Wind all day.

13.   Misty kind of a Morning with the Wind at No. East but no rain all day—in the Night a sml. Showr.

14.   Another Misty Morning, with great appearances of Rain all day—only a little fell however.

15.   Clear and Cool Wind still at No. East & fresh.

16.   Clear and warmer. With but little wind and that East.

17.   Quite Calm, clear, & warm Morning being foggey.

18.   Again Foggy; & somewhat Cloudy. Day very close & Warm.

19.   Some, but not much, Rain fell in the Night. Day for the most part Cloudy with the wind at East.

20.   Clear and warm with the Wind Southerly.

21.   Also clear and warm—wind in the same place.

22d.   Warm—Wind blowing pretty fresh from the So. West.

23.   Still Warm & Clear—Wind Blowing very fresh from the So. West.

24.   Foggy Morning & a little Wind from the East. Forenoon Raining but clear afterwards.

25.   Clear with a little Wind from the Eastward—a little in the Night.

26.   Clear and very warm with but little Wind.

27.   Clear & very warm with but little Wind and that Southerly.

28.   Still Clear and very warm Wind fresh from the Southwd.

29.   Very Warm with the Wind fresh from the Southward. In the Evening it began to Rain.

30.   Raining more or less all day with the Wind at No. Et.

[October]

Where—how or with whom my time is Spent

Octr. 1st.   Still at Annapolis. Dined with Mr. Ogle. Spent the Evening at the Governors.

Benjamin Ogle (1746–1808) was elected governor of Maryland in 1798. He was the son of Samuel Ogle (d. 1752) who served three times as governor of Maryland in the colonial period. In the Monday sweepstakes, Ogle's horse came in second out of three.

2.   Set of on my return home. Dined at Marlborough & lodged at home. Mr. Custis coming with me.

The town of Upper Marlboro was frequently called Marlboro.
    Jacky Custis, who had left King's College to return home for a holiday, evidently met GW in Annapolis. He carried with him highly laudatory letters from Dr. Cooper and from John Vardill, one of his tutors. Vardill wrote that Jacky "has discover'd a remarkable purity of Morals . . . [and] has with such constancy devoted himself to his Studies, as to give us the surest ground to expect that he will hereafter attain to that excellence which his natural powers render him capable of" (20 Sept. 1773, DLC:GW). Dr. Cooper wrote GW that Jacky's "Assiduity hath been equal to his Rectitude of principle; and it is hoped his Improvements in Learning have not been inferior to either" (20 Sept. 1773, DLC:GW).

3.   At home all day. Alone.

4.   At home all day. Mr. Thos. Triplet came here.

5.   Went a hunting in the Neck with Mr. Custis & Lund Washington. Found a Fox & after runng. it two hours & half lost it.

6.   At home all day.

7.   At home all day. In the Afternoon Mr. Richd. Thompson came and stayed all Night.

Richard Thompson was interested in leasing some of the Ohio lands that GW was advertising for sale but considered the terms unrealistic. In a letter of 30 Sept. 1773 to GW, Thompson laid down what he considered to be appropriate terms and informed GW of his intention to visit him soon to discuss the matter.

8.   I continued at home all day. After Breakfast Mr. Thompson went away.

9.   At home all day. Mr. Tilghman & Mr. [Herbert] Came here & stayd all Night.

10.   Mr. Herbert went away before Breakfast. Mr. Tilghman went with Mrs. Washington and I to Pohick Church & returnd with us.

11.   Mr. Tilghman went away after Breakfast. I rid to Muddy hole—Doeg Run Mill & Mill Qr. & Ferry.

12.   At home all day. In the Afternoon Mr. Bell of Maryland came & stayd all Night.

13.   Mr. Beal went away after Breakfast. I continued at home all day. In the Afternoon Mr. Willis & my Brother Charles came. As also Mr. Baker Surgeon Dentist.

Mr. Baker is Dr. John Baker (d. 1796), a Williamsburg surgeon dentist. Baker, who had a medical degree, was a native of England but had practiced in several countries before coming to America before 1767. One of the first qualified dentists to practice in the colonies, he settled in Williamsburg in 1772 but moved to Philadelphia during the Revolution. GW had consulted him as early as April 1772 for help in solving what were to become his perennial dental problems and used his services on other occasions, both in Williamsburg and later in Philadelphia (FAGGART, 551). Baker made short trips throughout the colonies, offering his services to the residents of the principal cities. On this trip to Mount Vernon, he stayed several days and charged GW £5 (LEDGER B, 93).

14.   At home all day. In the Afternoon Mr. Harrison the Lawyer & Mr. Harrison the Merchant came.

Richard Harrison (d. 1841), Maryland merchant, may have been of the same family as Robert Hanson Harrison. He was by 1775 a partner in the firm of Hooe & Harrison. Early in the Revolution he was sent to Martinique as commercial agent for Virginia to further trade between that island and Virginia. In Cadiz, 1780–86, he acted as unofficial consul for the United States. Later he settled in Alexandria as a merchant. After refusing an appointment by GW as consul to the port of Cadiz, he served as auditor of the

U.S. Treasury 1791–1836. Some time after this visit, Harrison married Nancy Craik, daughter of GW's old friend Dr. James Craik.

15. Mr. Richd. Harrison went away before Breakfast. The others continued all day. At home.

16. Mr. Robt. Harrison & Mr. Baker both went away after Breakfast. I remaind at home all day. Captn. Bronaugh Dined here, as also did Mrs. Blackburn & Mrs. Brown.

William Bronaugh (1730–c.1800), son of Col. Jeremiah Bronaugh, was at this time a member of the vestry of Shelburne Parish, Loudoun County. He later became a trustee of the new town of Middleburg in Fauquier County. He had served as a lieutenant with GW in the Fort Necessity campaign and later was promoted to captain. Bronaugh was entitled to 6,000 acres of land under the Proclamation of 1754, and it may have been in regard to this that he was visiting GW. In June 1774 GW bought 2,000 acres of Bronaugh's land on the Great Kanawha River for £50 (LEDGER B, 114).
Mrs. Christian Scott Blackburn and Mrs. Catherine Scott Brown were sisters.

17. At home all day. Captn. Conway Breakfasting here from the Madeiras. Mr. Willis & my Brother went up to Church.

Capt. Thomas Conway commanded the 40-ton sloop *Molly*, which had been built earlier in the year in Norfolk. The owner of the vessel was Richard Conway of Alexandria, who may have been an elder brother of Thomas. During the previous summer GW had shipped 80 barrels of superfine flour on board the *Molly* to Lamar, Hill, Bisset & Co. in the Madeira Islands, to be exchanged for wine (GW to Thomas Newton, Jr., 10 July 1773, DLC: GW). The *Molly* returned to the Potomac 13 Oct. with a cargo that included four pipes of Madeira wine and two boxes of citrons for GW (P.R.O., C.O.5/1352, f. 133; LEDGER B, 92).

18. At home again the whole day. Mr. Willis & my Bror. go[in]g up to Court & returng. at Night.

19. Mr. Willis & my Brother set of home—as Mrs. Washington Mr. Custis & myself did for Wmsburg.—dining at Colchester & lodging at Colo. Blackburns.

20. Dined at Acquia & lodged at Colo. Lewis's in Fred[ericksbur]g.

21. Rid to my Plantation at the little Falls. Dind & Supd at Colo. Lewis's.

22.   Dined at Caroline Ct. House and lodged at Hubbards.

23.   Breakfasted at Todds Bridge and reachd Colo. Bassett in the Afternoon.

24.   At Colo. Bassetts all [day].

25.   Ditto. Ditto.

26.   Went to Williamsburg. Dined at the Raleigh & supped at the Coffee House.

27.   Dined at the Govrs. & spent the Evening in my own Room.

28.   Dined at the Speakers and Spend the Evening in my own Room.

29.   Dined at Mrs. Dawsons & Spent the Evening in my Room.

30.   Returnd to Colo. Bassetts.

31.   At Colo. Bassetts all day.

Acct. of the Weather in Octr.

Octr. 1st.   Raining more or less all day—with the Wind fresh from the No. Et.

2.   Raining in the Morning with fine mists through the day.

3.   Clear, Wind at So. West & Warm.

4.   Still Clear with but little Wind and that at the same point.

5.   Still clear and Warm wind from the same Quarter.

6.   Raining all the forenoon with the Wind Easterly & pretty fresh.

7.   Lowering most part of the day. Wind Northerly.

8.   Very like for Rain all the forenoon but Clear afterwds. Wind at East—but not much of it.

9.   Cloudy & threatning forenoon but clear afterwards. Wind Easterly.

10.   Clear and pleasant – but little Wind & that rather Southerly.

11.   Foggy Morning, but clear afterwards and warm wind Southerly.

12.   Clear and Calm, as also warm there being but little wind & that Southerly.

13.   Again Clear & Calm, wind what little there is of it Southerly.

14.   Much such a day as yesterday there being but little Wind Southerly. Weather Clear.

15.   Clear Calm and pleasant but rather too warm.

16.   Cooler, Wind at No. & No. East & somewhat Cloudy but no Rain.

17.   Clear & pleasant, with very little Wind.

18.   But little Wind – that Southerly with some Rain in the Nig[ht].

19.   Wind fresh from the Westward all the forepart of the day & somewhat Cooler.

20.   Clear with but little Wind, & that getting Southerly again.

21.   Lowering for most part of the day with a little Rain in the Evening.

22.   Cloudy, lowering Morning & very warm all day but no Rain.

23.   Wind fresh from the Southward, with much appearance of Rain, but none fell.

24.   A Good deal of Rain fell last Night.

25.   Clear and Warm with but little Wind.

26.   Still clear and Warm with but little Wind.

27. Clear and Warm with but little Wind & that Southerly.

28. Again clear warm and pleasant.

29. Wind Northerly, and somewhat Cooler.

30. Wind still Northerly but pleasant, & rather Warm than otherwise.

31. Pleasant with but little [wind] & that westerly.

[November]

Where, how, or with whom my time is Spent

Novr. 1. Went to Willmsburg. after Dinner. Spent the Evening in my own Room.

2. Dined at the Attorney's, and Spent the Evening in my own Room.

3. Dined at Mrs. Dawson's & Spent the Evening in my own Room.

4. Dined at the Speakers & Spent the Evening at Southalls.

5. Took an Early Dinner & came up to Colo. Bassetts afterwards.

6. At Colo. Bassetts all day.

7. Dined at Mrs. Dangerfields & returnd to Colo. Bassetts in the Afternoon.

8. Went over to see Mr. Blacks Land in King & Queen & King William. Dined at Colo. B. Moores & returnd to Colo. Bassetts in the Evg.

During the forced sales held to settle the Robinson affair, William Black acquired some lands of John Robinson's estate. Black also won some of Bernard Moore's land in the raffle held 14 Dec. 1769, for which GW was a manager. Black was now selling out, and in Dec. 1773 GW, on behalf of Jacky Custis, bought some of these lands in the Pamunkey River valley to add to the Custis estates.

Miss Lucy Harrison, of Berkeley, made this watercolor of Westover ca.1825–30. (Virginia Historical Society)

9. At Colo. Bassetts all day.

10. Ditto. Ditto.

11. Went to Westover with Colo. Bassett & Mr. Custis. Dind at New Kent Court House in our way there.

The plantation of Westover is about 25 miles due west of Williamsburg and overlooks the James River in Charles City County. Built c.1730 for William Byrd II (1674–1744), Westover was inherited by Col. William Byrd III, who was residing there in 1773 with his second wife, Mary Willing Byrd (d. 1814) of Philadelphia, whom he married in 1761.

12th. Dined at Westover. Riding to Colo. Harrisons Mills in the forenoon.

The home plantation of Benjamin Harrison (d. 1791), named Berkeley, was immediately to the west of Westover. In 1773 Harrison was a burgess for Charles City County; later he became a signer of the Declaration of Independence and governor of Virginia (1781–84). Harrison married Burwell Bassett's sister Elizabeth (1730–1792), who on 9 Feb. of this year had given birth at Berkeley to William Henry Harrison (d. 1841), ninth president of the United States (see WATERMAN, 163–68; HARRISON [5]).

Benjamin Harrison as a young man, in a miniature attributed to Henry Benbridge. (Virginia Historical Society)

13.   Rid with Colo. Byrd to see Shirly. Dined at Berkley & Returnd to Westover at Night.

The Shirley plantation, about six miles up the river from Westover and overlooking the confluence of the James and Appomattox rivers, was the home of Charles Carter (1732–1806), son of Elizabeth Hill Carter Cocke (d. 1769) and her first husband, John Carter (1690–1742/43) of Corotoman, Lancaster County (WATERMAN, 358). Since Carter shared with GW a keen interest in experimental farming, this visit was probably agricultural in nature.

14.   Returnd to Colo. Bassetts to Dinner.

15.   Went a Fox hunting. Found but did not kill. Returnd to Dinner.

16.   Went with Mrs. Washington & Mr. Custis, to Mr. Burbidges to see Mr. Bat. Dandridge. Stayed all Night.

Julius Burbidge's daughter Mary married Bartholomew (Bat) Dandridge (1737–1785), of New Kent County, a brother of Martha Washington.

17.   After Dinner returned to Colo. Bassetts.

18.   Went to my Plantation in King William, & with Mr. Custis over Blacks Land calld Woromonroke.

GW and Jacky Custis were inspecting land won from Moore by Black in the raffle. It was part of GW's purchase for the Custis estate and was thereafter called the Romankoke plantation.

19.   Came to Williamsburg with Colo. Bassett. Spent the Eveng. at the Coffee House.

Berkeley, on the James River, in a watercolor by Miss Lucy Harrison, ca.1825–30. (Virginia Historical Society)

20. Dined at Mrs. Dawson's & Spent the Evening at the Coffee House.

21. Dined at the Speakers & Spent the Evening in my own Room.

22. Dined at Mr. Southalls & spent the Evening at the Coffee House.

23. Dined with Lord Dunmore at his Farm & spent the Evening at Anderson's.

Dunmore had two estates, apparently continguous, totaling 579 acres, about six miles from Williamsburg in York County. One, called the Old Farm, Dunmore purchased from Robert ("Councillor") Carter in 1772 (petitions of Lord Dunmore to the commission on losses of American Loyalists, 1784, P.R.O., A.O.13/28; MORTON [1], 201). The other, called Porto Bello, had just been purchased by Dunmore two weeks before this visit (*Va. Gaz.*, R, 4 Nov. 1773). A description of Porto Bello made in 1769 presented "its situation beautiful, the land good, fine meadows, plenty of fish, no end to oysters, close at the door; and the orchard accounted one of the finest on the continent" (*Va. Gaz.*, R, 30 Nov. 1769).

24. Dined at the Speakers & Spent the Evening at the Coffee House.

25. Dined at Southalls and spent the Evening again at the Coffee House.

26. Dined at Southalls and spent the Evening in my own Room.

27. Dined at Southalls and came up to Colo. Bassetts in the Afternoon.

28. At Colo. Bassetts all day.

29. Went to Williamsburg again & Dined at Southalls. Spendg. the Evening at the Coffee House.

30. Again Dined at Southalls. Spent the Evening at Anderson's.

Acct. of the Weather in Novr.

Novr. 1st. Very pleasant—rather warm Wind being Southerly.

2. A good deal of Rain fell last Night. Wind Northerly today & a little Cooler.

3. Pleasant, and somewhat warmer than yesterday. Wind getting Southerly again.

4. Warm and pleasant in the forenoon—but cloudy with Rain in the Afternoon.

5. A good deal of Rain fell in the Night. Squally forenoon but clear & cooler afterwards.

6. Clear & pleasant but somewhat Cool.

7. Cool—wind being Northerly & clear.

8. But little wind in the forepart of the day. In the Afternoon it got to So. East & much rain fell.

9. Continued Rain all most the whole day & Night.

10. Wind fresh from the No. West & Cold. Clear after the Morning.

11. Clear and pleasant but a little Cool.

12. Cold & lowering forenoon but pleasanter afterwards.

13. Again Cold and lowering (like for Snow) in the forenoon, but pleasanter afterwards, Wind Shifting to the No. West.

14. Clear and Cold in the Morning. Ground hard froze with Ice. Afternoon pleasant.

15. Remarkable white frost but clear and pleasant all day.

16. A white Frost & pleasant, afternoon somewhat lowering — but clear Evening.

17. Very pleasant with but little Wind & that Southerly.

18. Very pleasant with but little Wind.

19. Raw & Cold. Wind Northerly & great appearances of Snow but none fell.

20. Clear & Cool, but pleast. notwithstanding wind Northerly.

21. Clear forenoon but cool wind rather variable but not much of it. Afternoon a little lowering.

22. Clear warm and pleast. with but little Wind.

23. Again clear & warm with but little wind.

24. Pleasant and clear. In the Night the wind changed & grew cool.

25. Cool but still tolerably pleasant being clear & but little wind.

26. Raw & Cold threatning bad weather but none fell.

27. Clear, Warm, & pleasant again with but little Wind. In the Evening Cloudy, with some appearances of Rain.

28. Raw & Cold, with flying Clouds in the forenoon but clear afterwards.

29. Clear but rather Cool — Wind being at No. West.

30. Pleasant and clear.

[December]

Where, how, or with whom my time [is] Spent.

Decr. 1st.   Dined at Mrs. Dawsons & spent the Evening in my own Room.

2.   Dined at Southalls, & Spent the Evening at Mrs. Campbells.

On 29 July 1773, Mrs. Campbell's tavern on Waller Street had been put up for auction by Nathaniel Walthoe's executor. Mrs. Campbell had bought it and two lots on six months' credit and got the deed in Jan. 1774 (*Va. Gaz.*, P&D, 20 May 1773; York County Deed Book, 1769–77, 385–86, Vi Microfilm). During the next few years the local Freemasons habitually held balls at her tavern, and she apparently prospered until 1780 when the capital was moved to Richmond (MASONS, 152). She was still on Waller Street three years later but was no longer open for business and her house, a traveler said "had a cold, poverty struck appearance" (MACAULAY, 187–88). She eventually moved to Fredericksburg, where she died in 1792 and was buried in the Masonic cemetery (JETT, 24–25).

3.   Dined at the Treasurers & Spent the Evening in My own Room.

4.   Din'd at Southalls & reachd Colo. Bassetts in the Afternoon.

5.   At Colo. Bassetts all day.

6.   Set out on my return home. Dined at King Wm. Court Ho. & lodged at Hubbards.

7.   Breakfasted at Caroline Ct. House & reachd Fredg. abt. 4 Oclock. Lodgd at Colo. Lewis's.

8.   Breakfasted with my Mother & lodgd at Dumfries.

9.   Breakfasted at Dumfries & reachd home to Dinner. Found Doctr. Rumney & Mrs. Barnes here the former going after Dinner.

10.   At home all day alone. Mr. Custis comg. in the Aftn.

11.   At home all day. In the Afternoon Mr. Wm. Brown & his Sister, & my Brothr. John came.

Probably Dr. William Brown and his sister Frances, who later married Charles Alexander of Fairfax County. Brother John came to borrow money.

On 13 Dec GW recorded that £400 belonging to Jacky Custis was lent to John A. Washington on interest (LEDGER B, 96).

12. At home all day the above Company here. Mrs. Washington & Miss Brown going to Ch[urc]h & returng. to Dinner.

13. At home all day—the above Compa[ny] Continuing.

14. My Brother Mr. Brown & his Sister went away after breakfast.

15. I rid out and joind the Dogs in hunting a Fox but did not kill it.

16. Rid to the Ferry & Mill Plantns. as also to the Mill.

17. Rid to Muddy hole, & into the Neck. Mr. George Mason Dined here.

During much of GW's lifetime there were three George Masons living within eight miles of Mount Vernon. Col. George Mason of Gunston Hall, who appears regularly in the diaries as "Col. Mason," had a son named George Mason (1753–1769), who lived near his father in Mason's Neck at Lexington. This George was called George Mason of Lexington, and sometimes George Mason, Jr. A third George Mason, first cousin of Col. George Mason of Gunston Hall, lived near Pohick Creek, where in 1782 he owned one tithable slave (HEADS OF FAMILIES, VA., 18). This George was called George Mason of Pohick and, to distinguish him from his elder cousin and neighbor Col. George Mason, was also sometimes called George Mason, Jr. (COPELAND, 88).

18. At home all day alone.

19. At home all day, alone. After Dinner Mrs. Barnes went to Mrs. French's.

20. Went up to Alexandria to Court. Returnd in the Eveng.

There is no record in the Fairfax County Order Book for 1772–74 of a session on this day or any other day in December.

21st. At home all day alone.

22. Went out after Breakfast with the Dogs. Dragd a fox for an hour or two, but never found. Returnd to Dinner & found Mrs. Slaughter here.

Anne Clifton Slaughter (d. 1798), only child of William and Elizabeth Brent Clifton (d. 1773) of Clifton's Neck, was married to Thomas Slaughter. She borrowed £6 from GW on this day—the loan was not repaid until 1788 (LEDGER B, 98).

23.   At home all day. In the Afternoon Doctr. Craik came.

24.   At home all day. Doctr. Craik continuing here.

On this date Dr. Craik paid GW £10 12s. 6d. for flour bought in November. He also paid an old balance of £4 1s. 3d. from a previous year (LEDGER B, 44, 98).

25.   At home all day. After breakfast the Doctr. went off homewards.

26.   At home all day. Mr. Ben Dulany, & Mr. Peale dined here.

27.   Went out in the Forenoon with the Dogs. Traild a Fox but did not find. Mr. Cato Moore dined here & in the Afternn. Mr. Geo. Digges & Mr. Custis came.

Cato Moore later served in the Revolution as a lieutenant in Grayson's Additional Regiment 1777–79. After the Revolution, Moore, along with GW's brother John Augustine, became one of 11 founding trustees of the new town of Charles Town, Berkeley County, Va. (now Jefferson County, W.Va.), which was laid out on land owned by GW's brother Charles. In 1795 Moore was sheriff of Berkeley County (BERG, 48; HEITMAN [1], 298; HENING, 12:371; VSP, 7:463).

28.   At home all day Mr. Digges & Custis continuing here.

It was probably during this week at Mount Vernon that Benjamin Dulany, George Digges, Jacky Custis, and Charles Willson Peale participated in an event which Peale later related: "One afternoon several young gentlemen, visiters at Mount Vernon, and myself were engaged in pitching the bar, one of the athletic sports common in those days, when suddenly the colonel appeared among us. He requested to be shown the pegs that marked the bounds of our efforts; then, smiling, and without putting off his coat, held out his hand for the missile. No sooner . . . did the heavy iron bar feel the grasp of his mighty hand than it lost the power of gravitation, and whizzed through the air, striking the ground far, very far, beyond our utmost limits. We were indeed amazed, as we stood around, all stripped to the buff, with shirt sleeves rolled up, and having thought ourselves very clever fellows, while the colonel, on retiring, pleasantly observed, 'When you beat my pitch, young gentlemen, I'll try again'" (CUSTIS, 519).

29.   Went out with the Dogs. Found a Fox but did not kill it.

30. Mr. Digges & Mr. Custis went up to Alexa. returng. in the After.

31st. Went out with Mr. Digges & Mr. Custis a huntg. Found a Fox but did not kill it.

Acct. of the Weather in Decr.

Decr. 1st. Clear Warm and pleast. with but little Wind, and that Southerly.

2. Also Warm and pleasant a little lowering in the Eveng.

3. Clear Warm and pleasant again. With but little Wind & that from the Southward.

4. Much such Weather as yesterday in all respects.

5. Clear, and tolerably pleast. but rather Cooler. Wind being fresh from the Westward.

6. Warm and lowering – Wind being fresh from the So. West.

7. A good deal of Rain fell in the Night, & the Wind getting to No. West it turnd cold.

8. Cold but pleasant notwithstanding it being clear and but little Wind.

9. Cold, & Raw in the forenoon, the Wind being at No. West.

10. Clear and very pleasant with little or no Wind.

11. Clear but the Wind fresh from the No. West it grew Cold.

12. Clear, Calm and exceeding pleasant.

13th. Also clear Warm & pleasant. Wind being So. Westerly.

14. Calm, warm, & very foggy all day.

15. Just such a day as yesterday in all respects.

16. Still Foggy & still, all day there not being Wind enough to dispel it. Also Warm.

17. Foggy & cloudy in the forenoon. Afternoon clear & pleasant.

18. Lowering Morning. Afterwards Rain, then Snow, after which a mixture of both. Wind Northerly.

19. Clear (except flying [clouds]) & very cold, Wind being at No. West & very fresh. Ground coverd abt. an Inch deep with Snow.

20. Wind in the same place & blowing hard. Weather very cold & clear.

21. Much more moderate than yesterday there being but little Wind & quite clear.

22. Wind in the forenoon fresh from the So. West wch. shifted round to the Northwd. & grew cold.

23. A Snow near Six Inches Deep fell in the Night—also Snowing more or less till near noon, after which clear & Warm.

24. Clear warm and pleast. in the forenoon. Afternoon Lowering. Not much Wind forenoon foggy.

25. Raining more or less all day with the Wind fresh from the Southward. Snow intirely dissolv'd.

26. Last Night there fell Snow enough to cover the ground abt. an Inch, which was again dissolvd this day. It being but Cool, & Windy tho clear.

27. Cloudy & threatning Snow all the forenoon. In the afternoon it Snowd on & off till Night then haild & was very bad Weather being also Windy from the Northward.

28. Cold with fine Snow on & off all day. Wind fresh from the No. Ward. The Snow about 4 Inches deep.

29.   Clear & moderate in the forenoon, Wind Southerly tho the River was quite shut up in the Morning opening afterwards. Afternoon Cold Wind getting to No. Wt.

30.   Wind at No. West & the River quite shut up again. However it opend and was more moderate the wind dying away.

31.   Little or no Wind & quite Warm and pleasant.

A Restless Nation Stirs

1774

[January]

Where, how, or with whom, my time is Spent

Jan 1st. Fox hunting with Mr. George Digges, Mr. Robt. Alexr. & Peake who all dind here, together with Mr. Jas. Cleveland. In the Afternoon all went home but Mr. Alexander.

2. At home all day. Mr. Alexander went home after Breakfast. Mr. Benjn. Dulany Mr. Peale & Mr. Cox came here to Dinner, & stayd all Night.

3. Mr. Dulany & Mr. Cox went away after Breakfast as also did Mr. Custis to Maryland. Mr. Peale stayed, Captn. Jno. Ashby came in the Afternn. & stayd all Night.

Jacky was now in the midst of preparations for his wedding to Nelly Calvert, to be held the following month. On this day GW advanced him £24 "to provide your Wedding Cloaths" (CUSTIS ACCOUNT BOOK).

4. Captn. Ashby went away and Mr. Grafton Dulany—Mr. Anthy. Addison—Mr. Saml. Hanson & Mr. Fitzgerald came to dinnr. & stayd all N.

Anthony Addison was the youngest son of John Addison (1713–1764), of Oxon Hill, Md.

5. All the above Gentlemen stayd here this day & Night also, except Mr. Fitzgerald who went away after Dinner.

6. Mr. Fitzgerald came down again this day in the Afternoon together with Mr. Herbert and a Mr. Stewart from Philadelphia— the whole staying all Night.

Mr. Stewart may be Andrew Stewart, who, in a mercantile partnership with William Herbert, purchased commercial property on the corner of Water and Princess streets in Alexandria later this year (Fairfax County Deeds, Book M-1, 1–4, Vi Microfilm).

7. Mr. Peale & all the other Gentlemen went away after Breakfast. Mr. Robt. Adam came to Dinner & stayd all Night.

8. Rid with Mr. Adam (who dind here & went away in the afternoon to my Mill). Mrs. Slaughter & Mesr. Peake also dind here.

9. At home all day. In the Evening Captn. Posey came here.

10. At home all day. A Mr. Young recommended by Mr. Adams came here and dind—going away afterwards.

MR. YOUNG: GW was facing a deadline for establishing his rights to the Kanawha land in the Ohio Valley that he received under Governor Dinwiddie's 1754 Proclamation. Having been unable to attract settlers either from the colonies or from Ireland, Scotland, or Germany, GW was now planning at least to "seat" the lands within the three-year period provided by law. This "seating" involved making minimal improvements on the land that had been granted and surveyed, including constructing buildings and clearing and planting at least one out of every 500 acres (HENING, 3:313–14). For this job GW was buying white servants and hiring carpenters. George Young had been recommended to GW by Robert Adam of Alexandria to be the leader of GW's Kanawha expedition (12 Jan. 1774, DLC:GW).

11. Rid into the Neck. Captn. Posey still here.

12. Rid to the Mill—Mill Plantn. Dogue Run & Muddy hole before Dinner. A Rope Maker one Paterson Dind here.

Thomas Patterson was one of eight artisans with whom GW contracted for repairs to his brig *Anne and Elizabeth* (see main entry for 28 Mar. 1774).

13. Dind here no body but Captn. Posey. I walked out with my Gun. In the Afternoon Mr. Geo. Young came here to live.

GW hired Young at £25 for one year to accompany the Kanawha expedition (LEDGER B, 107).

14. Captain Posey went away to Maryland after Breakfast. Mr. Craven Peyton came to Dinr. & went away afterwards.

Craven Peyton came to Mount Vernon to receive a power of attorney from GW "for all & singular the purposes within mentioned as also for the further purposes of acknowledging Leases for Land Let & terms agreed on by the said Geo. Wm. Fairfax Esqr. in the Counties of Culpeper and Fauquier as also for conveying Sundrie pieces of Land sold by the said George Wm. Fairfax to Majr. Angus McDonald & Mr. Philip Bush both of the County of Fredk." (power of attorney to Peyton, 14 Jan. 1774, NjMoNP).

15. Went out a hunting, & killd a dog fox wch. was found in Hell hole, after a chase of 3 hours. At home afterwards alone.

16. At home all day alone.

17. Went up to Alexa. to Court. Dind at Arrels. Suppd at Mrs. Hawkins & came home afterwards.

Mary Hawkins, a widow with five children, ran a tavern in Alexandria until her death in 1777.

18. At home all day. Mr. Custis came from Maryland yesterday & Hanson Posey came this Eveng.

19. Mr. Custis & I went into the Neck a Hunting. Found two Fox's but killd neither. Doctr. Rumney came to Dinr. & stayd all Nt.

20. At home all day. Doctr. Rumney continuing here. Miss Sally Carlyle & her Sister Nancy & Miss Betcy Ramsay & Miss Jenny Dalton all came to Dinnr. & stayed all Night.

Jenny Dalton was a daughter of John Dalton, merchant of Alexandria.

21. Doctr. Rumney went away after Breakfast. Mr. Custis & I went a hunting in the Neck & after run[nin]g a Fox 3 hours lost it.

22. At home all day. Miss Carlyle & the other Girls went away after Dinner—and Mr. Young to Bladensburg before it.

George Young, who had been working for Dr. David Ross, merchant of Bladensburg, was now probably returning to his old employer to move his effects to Mount Vernon.

23. At home all day. In the Evening Mr. Robt. Rutherford came.

24. At home all day. Mrs. Blackburn her Son & Miss Ellzey as also Mrs. Brown, came to Dinner & Doctr. Brown in the Afternoon as also did Valene. Crawford.

Christian Scott Blackburn (b. 1745) was the wife of Col. Thomas Blackburn of Rippon Lodge. Her son here is probably her elder son, Richard Scott Blackburn (d. 1804–5), whose daughter Jane Charlotte Blackburn was later mistress of Mount Vernon as the wife of GW's grandnephew John Augustine Washington (d. 1832). Miss Ellzey is probably a daughter of Thomasin Ellzey and his wife Alice, a sister of Col. Thomas Blackburn of Rippon Lodge.

25.   Mrs. Blackburn & those that came with her as also the Doctr. went away after Dinner.

The main diary entries for 25–31 Jan. and the weather entries for 9–15 and 25–31 Jan. were inadvertently dated December by GW.

26.   Mr. Rutherford went away after Breakfast. I contd. at home all day.

27.   At home all day alone, except Mr. Valentine Crawfords being here.

Valentine Crawford was GW's first choice to lead the Kanawha expedition (see main entry for 11 Feb. 1774).

28.   At home all day. Majr. Chas. Smith & Andw. Wagener came here to dinner. The last went away after it—the other stayd all Night.

Smith and Andrew Wagener (Wagoner, Wagner), both veterans of the 1754 campaign against the French, were probably at Mount Vernon to discuss their shares of the bounty land promised to all such veterans (GW to Charles Mynn Thruston, 12 Mar. 1773, DLC:GW). Wagener had made no effort heretofore to cooperate with GW in obtaining the grant for the veterans. On this visit GW presented Wagener with a bill of £9 5s. 3d. for his share of the expenses already incurred (bill, GW to Andrew Wagener, 25 Jan. 1774, excerpt, Paul C. Richards, Autographs, Catalogue No. 46, 1969, Item 14).

29.   At home all day. Majr. Smith went away after Breakfast.

30.   At home all day. Mr. Bryan Fairfax came to dinner and stay'd all Night.

30[31].   At home all day—Mr. Fairfax continuing here. Mr. Custis returnd to Mr. Calverts by way of George Town.

On this day GW advanced Jacky £37, "given you when you went over to be married" (CUSTIS ACCOUNT BOOK).

Acct. of the Weather in Jany.

Jan. 1st.   A little Rain fell in the Night. The day remarkably pleasant. Wind in the Afternn. at So. West.

2.   Quite calm in the forenoon also clear & exceeding pleasant and Warm.

3.   Calm for the most of the day, clear in the forenoon, but very cloudy afterwards with a good deal of Rain in the Night. Wind Southerly.

4.   Somewhat Cloudy with but little wind in the forenoon. In the Afternoon it got Northerly but did not blow much.

5.   It Began raining in the Night, & continued to do so the whole day without intermission the wind being at East.

6.   Tolerably clear in the Morning but Cloudy & lowering afterwards. In the Night a good deal of Rain fell.

7.   A little Cloudy. The Wind fresh from the No. West.

8.   Still lowering. Wind Southerly & raw. Towards Night a little Snow just sufficient to cover the Ground fell—the Wind blowing hard at No. West.

9th.   Wind blowing hard all day at No. West. And very cold.

10.   Exceeding Cold. Wind in the same place & harder than Yesterday. Much Ice.

11.   Still a good deal of Ice upon the Flats. Wind at So. West, fresh & Cold all day—at Night shifted to No. West again & grew very cold.

12.   River almost close froze—day cold, Wind fresh at No. West.

13.   River entirely close in the Morning, but free from Ice afterwards except upon the Flats. Day cloudy with but little wind.

14.   Ground lightly cover'd with Snow. Day foggy—Misty, & thawing with little or no Wind.

15.   Foggy & warm Morning, with little or no Wind. Afterwards Windy from the No. West & turning Cold. Ice almost gone out of the River.

16th.   Very Cold all day & not very Windy—but Northerly.

17.   Tolerably pleasant. But little Wind & clear.

18. Wind fresh from the No. West and very Cold all day. Clear.

19. Cold & hard frozen Morning but clear and not much wind from the Southward. Thawd but little.

20. Little or no Wind, and more moderate than yesterday—but sometimes threatning falling Weather being lowerg. all day.

21. Wind Southerly in the Morning, but about Noon it Shifted to the Northwest, blew hard & turnd exceeding Cold.

22. Very cold Morning. River quite Shut up in the Morning early; but opend into holes afterwards, & before Night broke much away. Not much Wind but that Northerly. Very cold & Cloudy.

23. Was also very cold. Wind still Northerly.

24. Raw cold & Cloudy all day, Wind still at No. West & fresh.

25. Tolerably pleasant—being clear with little or no Wind.

26. Clear and pleasant but little Wind and that Southerly.

27. Wind blowing fresh and cold all day from the No. West & freezing very hard. With Clouds.

28. Snowing till the Afternoon but not fast—ground coverd abt. 2 Inches. Very cold River quite shut up. Wind Northerly.

29. Wind in the same place & Cold. In the Afternoon abt. an Inch more Snow.

30. A kind of a Sleet after the Morning continued all day with the Wind abt. No. Et.

31. Clear and not so cold as yesterday. A great deal of Rain fell in the Night.

[February]

Where, how, or with whom my time is Spent

Feby. 1st.   At home all day. Mr. Fairfax went away after Breakfast. In & abt. Dinner time Nancy Carlyle came.

2.   I still continued home–alone except Mr. Crawford.

3.   Set out after an early Dinner (with Lund Washington) for Mr. Calverts, to Mr. Custis's Wedding who was this Eveng. married to Miss Nelly Calvert.

On 15 Dec. 1773 GW had written to Rev. Myles Cooper, president of King's College, N.Y., that his hopes of Jacky's continuing his education were "at an end; & at length, I have yielded, contrary to my judgment, & much against my wishes, to his quitting College; in order that he may enter soon into a new scene of Life, which I think he would be much fitter for some years hence, than now; but having his own inclination, the desires of his mother & the acquiescence of almost all his relatives, to encounter, I did not care, as he is the last of the family, to push my opposition too far; & therefore have submitted to a Kind of necessity" (DLC:GW).

4.   At Mr. Calverts all day. With much other company.

5.   Returnd home to a late Dinner. Found Mr. Gist here who came the day I left home. Also found Doctr. Rumney & Val. Crawford here.

6.   At home all day. Mr. Gist went away after Breakfast.

7.   Went with Mrs. Washington and Nancy Carlyle by the New Church to Captn. McCartys. Dind there & came home in the Afternoon. Doctr. Rumney went away after Breakfast.

8.   Rid into the Neck to the Plantation's there. And to the fishing Landing–where my Carpenters were at Work. Came home by Muddy hole. Mrs. Slaughter dind here & went away afterwards.

9th.   At home all day. In the Afternoon Mr. Matthew Campbell & Captn. Crawford came.

10th.   At home all day. After Breakfast Mr. Campbell went away and in the Afternoon Mr. Hugh Stephenson came.

Hugh Stephenson, a son of GW's old friend Richard Stephenson of Frederick County and a half brother to Valentine and William Crawford, lived in the Shenandoah Valley until the Revolution. In response to a request by the Continental Congress in June 1775, Virginia raised two companies of riflemen, most of whom came from the Valley and the frontier. The two companies, led by Capt. Daniel Morgan and Capt. Hugh Stephenson, marched to Cambridge and participated in the siege of Boston. A year later (June 1776) Stephenson, now a colonel, was put in command of a combined Virginia-Maryland rifle regiment in the Continental service and died that summer during the New York campaign (BERG, 120, 132; HEITMAN [1], 381).

11.   At home all day. Mr. Thos. Rutherford came here to dinner & Mr. Resin Bell in the afternn.

Rutherford is probably Robert Rutherford's brother Thomas, of Berkeley (later Jefferson) County (see GREENE [3], 375–82). Rezin Beall (1723–1809), whose name is variously spelled, was a descendant of Thomas Beall the immigrant and lived on Little Paint Branch, one mile north of Beltsville in northern Prince George's County, Md. (BEALL, 112–13). From 16 Aug. to 1 Dec. 1776 Beall served as a brigadier general with Maryland troops in the campaign in the Jerseys (HEITMAN [1], 79; BERG, 42, 67, 108).

Beall had brought a note from Jonathan Boucher recommending him for the job Valentine Crawford had just accepted from GW (see 27 Jan. 1774). On 15 Feb., GW explained to Boucher: "Before Mr. Beall deliver'd me your Letter of the 10th . . . (under a supposition of his willingness to undertake my business on the Ohio) I had conditionally agreed with Mr. Vale. Crawford for this purpose; who you must know, had Imbark'd in a Courting Scheme (in this neighbourhood) and, as I conceiv'd the task of pleasing a Master & Mistress, equal to that of two Masters, I made a point of his settling this business somehow or other with the Lady before he undertook mine; and this he did unfavourably to his wishes, the very day Mr. Beall came here & was at liberty for me" (NN; see main entry for 27 Jan. 1774).

12.   After dinner the two Crawfords & Mr. Stephenson set out for Wmsburg. & Mr. Rutherford and Mr. Beall for their respective homes.

Valentine Crawford and Hugh Stephenson were carrying a letter from GW to Governor Dunmore, dated 11 Feb., attesting to their satisfactory military service in the early 1760s, by which they hoped to qualify for western bounty land under the royal Proclamation of 1763 (ViW). Thomas Rutherford was carrying a letter from GW dated this day recommending him as an assistant surveyor (PPiU).

13.   At home all day alone.

14.   Again at home all day. To Dinner came Master Geo. Carlyle—who went away afterwards with his Sister Nancy. In the Afternoon Captn. Bullet & his Brother Cuthbert came & stayed all Night.

Capt. Thomas Bullitt, who had been surveying land in the Ohio Valley for Governor Dunmore and others, was now reporting to GW on his trip and on land he had chosen for GW. Thomas's brother Cuthbert Bullitt (d. 1791) was an attorney living in Prince William County. In 1788 Cuthbert Bullitt was elected by the General Assembly an additional judge of the Virginia General Court (vsp, 4:537). Another Bullitt brother, Benjamin, had been killed while serving with GW in the Virginia Regiment (HARRISON [6], 24:212).

15.   These Gentlemen went away. I went to a Vestry at the New Church & returnd in the Aftern.

The main business for the Truro vestry at this meeting was recorded in the vestry book: "George Mason Esqr. Executor of Daniel French dec[ease]d, Undertaker [contractor for the construction] of the Church near Pohick, having finished the said Church tender the same to this Vestry . . . and the said Vestry being of Opinion that the said Church is finished . . . do receive the same . . . the said George Mason undertaking to finish the Horse Blocks and Benches under the Trees" (Truro Vestry Book, 160, DLC).

16.   At home all day alone—being engaged in writing.

17.   Went a Hunting. Found a dog fox in this Neck and killed him after treeing 3 times and running about 2 hours.

One of the Mason children drew this sketch of Pohick Church, ca.1830–40. (Board of Regents of Gunston Hall)

18.   At home all day alone Writing. In the Aftn. Mr. Jas. Lawson came.

This is probably James Lawson of Glasgow, who had come to Virginia to settle the accounts of the financially troubled Occoquan ironworks, which his brother-in-law John Semple had taken over from John Ballendine in the early 1760s (SKAGGS, 63:28, n.15; *Va. Gaz.*, P&D, 13 June 1771). Lawson was now planning to sail for Scotland "to settle all his Business in Glasgow, and return here with his Wife and family to spend the rest of his Life" (Alexander Hamilton to James Brown & Co., 27 June 1774; MACMASTER, 61:166).

19.   Went a Hunting in the Neck see three Foxs but killd none. Mr. Lawson went away after Breakfast.

20.   At home all day. Mr. Willm. Brent & Mr. Notley Rozer came to Dinner & stayd all Night.

At least two William Brents lived along the Potomac at this time. One was William Brent of Charles County, Md.; the other was William Brent (1733–1782), of Richland, near Aquia Creek in Stafford County, Va., who married Eleanor Carroll (d. 1804), daughter of Daniel Carroll of Upper Marlboro, Md. (BRENT, 123). Notley Rozer was a son of Henry and Eleanor Neale Rozer, of Piscataway Parish, Prince George's County, Md. (BOWIE, 572).

21.   A Wm. Stevens came here in the Evening, & stayd all Night. I continued at home all day.

GW hired William Stevens to accompany the expedition of workers GW was sending west to seat his Kanawha lands (GW to William Stevens, 6 Mar. 1775, DLC:GW; LEDGER B, 103).

22.   At home all day. Stevens went away Early. Miss Digges Miss Betcy Digges, & Mrs. Slaughter Dind here & went away afterwards.

23.   At home all day. Mr. Robt. Adam came to dinner and Mr. B. Fairfax and Captn. Crawford came after Dinner—the whole staying all Night.

24.   Went a huntg. in the Morning and from thence to the Vestry. Mr. Adams going away—upon my return found Doctr. Craik, Val. Crawford & Mr. Thos. Gist.

Meeting again "at the new Church near Pohick," the Truro vestry assigned pews, first to those (including GW) who bought pews at auction in the fall of 1772. Other pews were then assigned: the "Upper Pew . . . adjoining the South Wall . . . to the Use of the magistrates and Strangers, and the Pew opposite thereto to the use of their Wives, and the two Pews next below

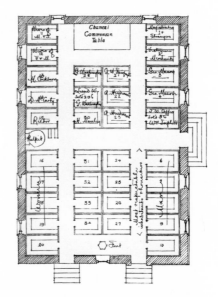

A twentieth-century floor plan of Pohick Church as visualized by architect Glenn Brown and published in Philip Slaughter, *History of Truro Parish*, Philadelphia, 1908. (University of Virginia Library)

them . . . to the Vestrymen and Merchants and their Wives." The "eight Pews below and adjoining the Cross Isle of the Church [were] assigned to the Use of the most respectable Inhabitants and House Keepers of the Parish, the Men to sit in the four Pews next the South Wall, and the Women in the other four next the North Wall" (Truro Vestry Book, 161–62, DLC).

The vestry also ordered "that the new Church . . . be furnished with a Cushion for the Pulpit and Cloths for the Desks & Communion Table of Crimson Velvet with Gold Firing, and that Colo. George Washington be requested to import the same" (Truro Vestry Book, 162, DLC). This was the last vestry meeting GW is recorded as having attended, although he remained a vestryman until he resigned the position in 1784 (GW to Daniel McCarty, 22 Feb. 1784, DLC:GW).

25.   At home all day. Mr. Fairfax & Doctr. Craik went away after Breakfast. Hancock Lee came to Dinr. & went away after it.

Hancock Lee (1740–1819), of Greenview, Fauquier County, did much exploring and surveying in the Ohio Valley and later settled in Kentucky (LEE [1], 268, 355–56; WEAKS, 420, 436). Lee, newly commissioned as a surveyor, was preparing to accompany Capt. William Crawford on a surveying trip down the Ohio River (MASON [2], 1:448).

Although GW was not present, the Truro Parish vestry met again on this day to finish details regarding the new church. Among the business was an order "that William Bernard Sears gild the Ornaments within the Tabernacle Frames the Palm Branch and Drapery on the Front of the Pulpit (also the Eggs on the Cornice of the small Frames if the Gold will hold out) . . . to be done with the Gold Leaf given to the Parish by Colo. George Washington" (Truro Vestry Book, 164, DLC).

26. At home all day. Captn. Crawford and Mr. Gist went away after Breakfast.

27. At home all day alone.

28. Mr. Tayler, Mr. Wagener & one Mordaica Red came to Breakfast & went away afterwards.

MR. TAYLER: possibly Hancock Taylor, who accompanied his first cousin, Hancock Lee, on a surveying trip into Kentucky in the spring of 1774. During that trip Taylor was killed by Indians (*Va. Gaz.*, P&D, 15 Sept. 1774). Mordecai Redd, of Frederick County, later bought a piece of land in Frederick County from the estate of George Carter, for which GW was a trustee (see main entry for 10 Mar. 1769).

Acct. of the Weather in Feby.

Feby. 1st. Tolerably warm, and thawing all day. Wind Southerly.

2. Still warm and thawing with little or no Wind. Ice upon the River beginning to Break & move about.

3. Raining very close and constant all the Morning with the Wind fresh from the So. West. Ice a good deal dispersd. In the Evening clear & Wind at No. West.

4. Clear, but rather cold, wind Westerly & pretty fresh. Ground froze in the Morng. but thawing afterwards.

5. Cloudy & a good deal like Snow with little or no wind.

6. Clear with the Wind pretty fresh from the No. West in the Forenoon, but calm, & not cold afterwards.

7. Pleasant Morning, being clear and Calm. Afterwds. windy from the westward, & Cold with appearances of Snow.

8. Clear Calm & pleasant again in the Morning. Wind Southerly afterwards and tolerably fresh. Afternoon a little Muddy.

9th. Wind shifting to the No. West it turnd very cold & freez'd exceeding hard before Night.

10.   Not so Cold as yesterday. Wind getting more westerly.

11.   But little Wind, and that for the most part Easterly. After-noon very lowering.

12.   Last Night fell a good deal of Rain. Forenoon Cloudy and afternoon Raining Wind being Easterly.

13.   The forenoon of this day Cloudy & afternoon Rainy.

14.   Snow this morning abt. 3 Inches deep & weather very Cold —Wind being at No. Wt.

15.   Clear & Cold with but little Wind, & Northerly. River quite Shut up again.

16.   Clear, with but little [wind] & that Inclining to the South-ward. Weather moderating.

17.   Clear and pleasant—but little Wind and that southerly. Ice breaking fast.

18.   Remarkably fine, with little or no Wind in the Morng. After Noon Raing. Wind at No. Et.

19.   Pleasant and Warm in the Morning—after much Rain. Afternoon windy from the No. West but not Cold.

20.   Ground not froze—day clear, calm, & very pleasant.

21.   Morning lowering, but clear Calm & pleasant afterwards.

22.   Very white frost, & ground a litle froze—but clear and pleas-ant with but little Wind.

23.   Clear calm and exceeding pleasant. Ground little or noth-ing froze.

24.   Again exceeding pleasant being Calm & clear without any frost.

25.   Very pleasant, but somewhat Cooler, ground froze & Wind at No. West but neither hard nor Cold.

26.   Clear, with very little Wind, and exceeding pleasant—being warm.

27th.   Lowering in the Morning but clear afterwards being also warm & pleasant.

28.   Clear, Wind blowing pretty fresh from the No. West and turning some what cooler—but not Cold.

[March]

Where, how, or with whom my time is Spent

March 1.   Mr. & Mrs. Calvert & Miss Calvert with Mr. Custis & his Wife & Mr. George Digges came to Dinner.

On 20 Feb., Jacky Custis had written to GW: "All the [Calvert] family . . . expect to see you on Tuesday 1st. of March, if the Weather permits" (DLC: GW).

2.   Walkd with Mr. Calvert &ca. to my Mill & Back. Mr. Muir, Mr. Piper, & Mr. Adams came to Dinner & stayd all Night.

3.   Miss Carlyle, Miss Ramsay, Mr. Dulany Doctr. Rumney, & Messrs. Herbert, Brown, Fitzgerald, Harrison Campbell and Alexr. Steward came to Dinner & Stayd all Night—as did Vale. Crawford. Piper Adam & Muir went away after Dinner.

Valentine Crawford was on his way to Baltimore with a request from GW to a sea captain, William McGachen, to buy some white servants for Crawford to take with him on the Kanawha expedition (13 Mar. 1774, DLC:GW).

4.   All except Mr. Calverts Family Mr. Digges, Dulany & Doctr. Rumney went away after Dinner.

5.   Mr. Dulany & Doctr. Rumney went away after Dinner.

6.   The rest of the Company remaining.

7.   Mr. Calvert, Lady, & daughter with Mr. Geo. Digges went away after breakfast.

8.   I set of for Berkley &ca. & to Meet Mr. James Mercer at Bull run, on a div[isio]n of that Land between him and his Brothers. Dined at Moss's & lodgd at Leesburg.

GW was a court-appointed trustee for James Mercer's brother George, who was in England.

GW took the main road from Alexandria to Leesburg. Later that same year Nicholas Cresswell, in taking the same route, found the road to be "very bad, cut to pieces with the waggons." Cresswell stopped halfway between Alexandria and Leesburg at "Mosses Ordinary, Loudoun County," which he found to be the only "public House" between those two towns (CRESSWELL, 47–48). In 1759 John Moss had been licensed by the Loudoun County court to keep an ordinary in Leesburg (WILLIAMS [1], 105). By 1774 Moss had probably moved to the ordinary that had earlier been run by James and Richard Coleman, on Sugar Land Run, about halfway between Alexandria and Leesburg. This southernmost section of Loudoun County was added to Fairfax County in 1798 (HARRISON [1], 326–29).

9. Dined at Snickers's & lodgd at Fairfield.

10. Went by my Tenants on Bullskin to my Brothers at Harewood.

11. At Harewood all day.

12. Returnd by my Tenants on Bullskin to Fairfield.

13. At Fairfield all day with others.

14. Set of for my Tenants in Fauquier, and lodged at one Lewis Lemarts a Tenants.

Lewis Lemart (Lamart) began leasing one of GW's lots on the Fauquier-Loudoun County border in Dec. 1772 at £7 per year for 150 acres. The lease was renewed annually, at the same rental, until 1786 (LEDGER B, 68).

15. At Lewis Lemarts till the Afternoon with my Tenants & making Leases. Rid to Cap. Ashby's in the Afternoon.

16. Viewed my Land on Chattins Run & Goose Creek, & came to Mr. Thos. Wests to Dinner to meet Mr. Mercer.

Charles West's son Thomas was now assisting his father at the family ordinary.

17. Looking over & running some Lines of Mercers Bullrun Tract. Returnd & lodgd at Wests again.

In checking some boundaries of the Mercer land that he would be responsible for selling in the fall, GW found that a mill had been built by a local settler inside a supposed Mercer line. GW sided with the mill owner (GW to James Mercer, 28 Mar. 1774, NNebgGW).

18. On the same business again. Returnd to Mr. Wests at Night.

19. At Wests (my Horses being lost) till One Oclock then (after they were found) rid down to Mr. Edd. Paynes & lodgd there.

20. Got home to Breakfast.

21. At home all day. Alone.

22. At home all day. In the afternoon Mr. Thos. Addison came & stayed all Night. Also Mrs. Barnes.

In 1767 Thomas Addison (d. 1774) of Oxon Hill, eldest son of John Addison (1713–1764), married Rebecca Dulany, daughter of Walter Dulany (d. 1773) of Annapolis.

23. At home all day. Doctr. Rumney came to Dinner.

24. At home all day Doctr. Rumney continuing here. As did Mr. Valentine Crawford who came last Night.

Crawford returned from Baltimore with four servants indentured for three years, four convict servants, and a married couple indentured for four years, at a total price of £110 sterling (William McGachen to GW, 13 Mar. 1774, DLC:GW). GW apparently sent most of these servants on the Kanawha expedition that left Mount Vernon on 31 Mar.

25. At home all day. Doctr. Rumney went away after Dinner.

26. At home all day. Doctr. Craik came here to Dinner and stayd all Night.

27. Went to Pohick Church and returnd to Dinner.

28. Doctr. Craik went away after Breakfast. I went up to Alexandria to the Sale of the Anne & Elizabeth which I bought myself at the price of £175. Returnd home in the Afternoon.

This purchase was in consequence of the voyage of John Carlyle's brigantine the *Fairfax* to the West Indies in the summer of 1772, carrying a cargo of herring and flour which GW had placed in the care of Daniel Jenifer Adams (see main entry for 22 July 1772). After selling the cargo, Adams bought the *Fairfax* from the captain, renamed it the *Anne and Elizabeth* (in honor, apparently, of his sisters), and proceeded to sail and trade about the West Indies and along the Atlantic coast without ever paying GW for the cargo. It was not until the fall of 1773 that GW was, by court order, finally able to get the brig to Alexandria, "within Thirty days after her arrival at which place if Mr. Daniel Jenifer Adams did not pay my demand agreeably to the terms of the Bottomry Bond I am to dispose of the Vessell" (GW to Thomas Pollock, 29 Nov. 1773, DLC:GW). GW later recorded that "after laying a Month agreeable to the terms of the Bond and being Advertized for Sale during that time . . . I was compelled to buy it in myself . . . much against my Inclination, as I had no desire of being concernd in Shipping." GW renamed the brig the *Farmer* and sent it off to the West Indies in May with another cargo of herring and flour (GW to Robert McMickan, 10 May 1774, DLC:GW; LEDGER B, 57, 99, 117). GW alternately called this craft a brig and a brigantine, although by this time these were two distinct types of vessels. Both were two-masted, square-rigged vessels, but the brigantine differed from the brig in not carrying a square mainsail.

29th.   At home all day alone.

30.   Walk in the Evening over my three Plantations in the Neck.

On this day GW revised and completed his instructions to Valentine Crawford for the party setting out to seat GW's Kanawha River lands. The instructions, which are quite detailed, include the following directions: "that as much Ground as possible may be got in order for Corn, & planted therewith, I would have you delay building & Tenting till the Season is too late for Planting. . . . It will be essentially necessary to have all the work done upon any one Tract appraisd before you move to the next Tract" (DLC:GW). The appraisal, usually by local county court justices, was to satisfy the land law requiring improvements within the three-year limit (HENING, 3:312–13).

31.   Mr. George Johnston dind here. I rid as [far as] the Gumsp[rin]g with my People and Vale. Crawford who were moving to the Ohio.

George Johnston, Jr. (1750–1777), a son of George Johnston (d. 1766), attorney of Fairfax County, in 1775 was made a captain in the 2d Virginia Regiment. In Jan. 1777, with the rank of lieutenant colonel, he became an aide-de-camp to GW, serving until his death in the fall of 1777.

Before Crawford could get his "People" to GW's lands, Dunmore's War broke out between settlers and Indians along the Ohio frontier. Less than two months after leaving Mount Vernon, Crawford gave up in the face of the hostilities and sold the servants to frontier buyers, including two to himself (Crawford to GW, 27 July 1774, DLC:GW).

Acct. of the Weather, in Mar.

March 1.   Rather raw & Cold in the forenoon–pleasant afterwards and clear.

2.   Warm in the forepart of the day with Rain and the Wind at So. West. Afterwards Cooler.

3.   Clear with the Wind at No. West but neither Cold nor hard.

4.   Pleasant & Clear in the forenoon with the Wind Southerly. Afternoon lowering.

5.   Raining constantly all day with the Wind pretty fresh from the No. East.

6.   Drizling, & Cloudy all the forenoon. Afternoon clear & pleasant.

7.   Clear, wind very hard, and tolerably cold from the No. West all day.

8.   Very pleasant in the forenoon with but little wind. After-noon lowering & wind at N. E.

9.   Rain last Night. Wind high & Cool from the No. West all day but moderating towards Night.

10.   Wind abt. So. West & tolerably fresh, but pleasant notwith-standing being also clear.

11.   Very pleasant & Warm with but little wind & that South-erly.

12th.   Wind fresh & Cool from the No. West in the Morning. Shifting to the No. Et. in the Afternoon & raw.

13.   Clear and pleasant with but little Wind.

14.   Lowering Morning & Rainy Afternoon. Slow Rain.

15.   Pretty cool in the Morning but moderate & pleasant after-wards.

16.   Clear in the forenoon & warm all day with but little Wind. Afternoon lowering.

17.   Clear in the forenoon, but cloudy & lowering afterwards with a good deal of Rain in the Night.

18.   Misting and very much like Rain all day but none fell. Wind at No. Et.

19.   Snowing in the forenoon with a Mixture of Rain and Misting afterwards. Wind No. Et.

20.   Misting, and Raining, more or less all day. Wind in the same Quarter.

21.   Misting with Rain in the forenoon. Clouds dispersg. afterwards—Wind west[erl]y.

22.   Clear—Wind pretty fresh from the Westward and Cool.

23.   Clear Wind still pretty fresh from the Westward & Cool.

24.   Pretty smart frost—ground being hard.

25.   Lowering but no Rain, Wind Southerly.

26.   Wind at No. West and fresh also Cool.

27.   Forenoon a good deal like Rain, but none fell. Afterwards clear. Wind Southerly and rather Raw.

28.   Clear and Warm. Wind still Southerly, & fresh.

29.   Clear. Wind Southerly.

30.   Moderate Rain, from Morning till Evening. Wind Northerly. Evening clear.

31.   Clear and Cool Wind being at No. West but not very hard.

[April]

Where, how, or with whom my time is Spent.

April 1st.   At home all day. Price Posey dined here.

2.   At home all day. Mr. Robt. Adam dined here.

3. At home all day. Mr. Hooe & Mr. Robt. Harrison dined and lodged here.

4. The above Gentlemen went away early in the morning & Mrs. Washington and myself went & dined at Mr. Digges's with Mr. & Mrs. Custis on their way to Mr. Calverts.

5. Tuesday, at home all day. Captn. Posey came in the Evening.

6. At home all day.

For the past several weeks GW had been corresponding with Dr. Hugh Mercer of Fredericksburg, who wished to buy the Ferry Farm. On this day Dr. Mercer accepted GW's price, promising to pay the £2,000 Virginia currency in five annual payments, plus interest (Mercer to GW, 6 April 1774, DLC:GW).

7. At home all day. Captn. Posey went away after Dinner as Mrs. Barnes also did to her own habitation.

8. At home all day alone.

9. At home all day. Colo. Bassett, Mrs. Bassett, with Billy & Fanny came here to Dinner. Mr. Robt. Adam also dind here.

10. Went with Colo. Bassett &ca. to Pohick Church. Returnd to Dinner. Doctr. Brown dind here.

11. At home all day. Mr. Milner & a Mr. Marle dined here.

William Milnor, merchant of Philadelphia, had come to Mount Vernon to buy fish taken from GW's fishing grounds along the Potomac (LEDGER B, 123). Milnor also rented a new fish house, which GW had built for him at Johnston's fishery, on the Clifton's Neck land (GW to William Milnor, 16 Dec. 1773, DLC:GW). MR. MARLE: may be Richard Marley, merchant of Philadelphia.

12. Rid with Colo. Bassett &ca. to the Fishing Landing at Posey.

The fishermen were taking some shad but mostly herring, worth over £100 sterling, most of which was sold to Milnor on credit (LEDGER B, 123).

13. Rowed to the different Fishing Landings as high as Broad Creek. Met & brot. Mr. Custis & his wife home with us.

14.   Went a hunting. Killd a bitch Fox with three young ones almost hair'd. Doctr. Rumney dind here & stayed all Night.

15.   Rid with Mrs. Bassett &ca. to the fishing Landing at Johnson's. Mr. Digges & his three daughters Teresa Betcy & Jenny dind here. Doctr. Rumney went away.

16.   Rid with Mrs. Bassett &ca. to the Mill & Fishing Landing at Posey's. Colo. Richd. Lee dind & Lodgd.

17.   Attempted to go to Alexa. Church but broke the Poll of the Chariot & returnd. Colo. Lee went away after Breakfast.

18.   Went with Colo. Bassett &ca. to Alexa. Returnd in the Afternoon. Mr. Magowan came home with us.

19.   Went with Colo. Bassett, Mrs. Bassett &ca. to Mr. Digges's & dined.

20.   Rid to the Fishing Landg. at Johnson's. Mr. Herbert & Mr. Stewart came home with us to Dinner. Mrs. Brown dined here & in the Aftern. Colo. Mason, Doctr. Brown, Mr. Jno. Cook, & my Brother John came.

John Travers Cook (1755–1823), of Stafford County, married Mary Thomson Mason, daughter of George Mason of Gunston Hall.

21.   At home all day. Mr. Herbert, Mr. Stewart, Colo. Mason, & Doctr. Brown & Wife went away before Dinner. Mr. Warnr. Washington & Captn. Nourse came to it.

22.   Went with the above Compy. to the Fishing Landing at Johnsons.

23.   All the foregoing Company except Colo. Bassett & Family went away after Breakfast. I rid with him to the Fish[er]y at Posey.

24.   Mr. Tilghman & Mr. Stewart came here to Dinner. The first stayed all Night the other returnd.

On 7 April 1774 James Tilghman, Jr., had written to GW, mentioning "the agreeable Prospect that I have of shortly seeing all my Friends in Virginia, I shall leave Philadelphia in a Week, and in one week more hope to pay a Visit to Mount Vernon" (DLC:GW).

25.   Colo. Bassett & family went away after Breakfast and Mr. Tilghman after Dinner. Mr. Adam dind here. Mr. Lanphire came to W[or]k.

MR. LANPHIRE: Going Lanphier (1727–1813), a house joiner and carpenter from Alexandria, had first done interior carpentry for GW in 1758, when the Mount Vernon mansion house was "raised" from 1½ to 2½ stories (LEDGER A, 58). GW had now hired Lanphier to work on extending both ends of the house, which would add a downstairs library and upstairs master bedroom on the south end and a two-story room on the north end later referred to as the Banquet Hall. The south end, built first, was not completed until after GW had left Mount Vernon to serve in the Revolution. On 10 Dec. 1775 Lund Washington wrote to GW that the south addition was almost done, adding, "we have been trying to Cure the [new] Chimney from smokeg. & I am in hopes [I] have done it, after doing & undoing twenty times" (ViMtV). Because of his service in the Revolutionary War, GW did not see the south end or the unfinished north end until the fall of 1781.

26.   At home all day alone.

27.   Mr. & Mrs. Cox & Mr. Robt. Adam Dined here. The latter went away afterwards. The other two stayed.

28.   At home all day. Mr. Robt. Adam Dined here.

29.   At home all day. Mrs. French Miss Molly Manley and Mr. Thos. Addison dind here and went away afterwards.

30.   At home all day alone.

Acct. of the Weather in Aprl.

April 1st.   Clear & pleasant Forenoon with but little Wind. Lowerg. afterwards.

2.   Raining a little in the forenoon with the Wind Easterly wch. ceasd in the afternoon Wind getting more Westerly.

3.   Clear and tolerably pleasant but a little cool.

4.   Clear but cool, wind pretty fresh from the South West.

5.   Warm and pleasant with but little Wind & that Southerly.

6.   Cool again with the Wind at No. East & pretty fresh.

7.   Wind in the same quarter & fresh. Also Cool.

8.   Raw and Cold. Wind at No. Et. and like for Rain.

9.   Raining a little in the forenoon—but clear afterwds. & Cool. Wind westwardly.

10.   Cool in the forenoon with the Wind at No. West—Warmr. afterwards & Calm.

11.   Tolerably pleasant & clear all day with not much Wind.

12th.   Wind Westwardly & Cool. Weather clear.

13.   A little Cool. Wind pretty fresh from the So. East. Clear.

14.   Warm with but little Wind & that Southerly. Lowering with much appearances of Rain but little fell.

15.   Clear, calm, & pleasant in the forenoon. Cool afterwards with the Wind fresh from the West, & No. West.

16.   Clear & calm in the Morning. Wind pretty fresh from the Westward afterwards.

17.   Wind very fresh from the Southwest all day & in the Evening like to Rain but none fell.

18.   Clear all day & Warm with but little Wind & that Southerly.

19.   Clear & Warm. Wind pretty fresh from the So. East.

20.   Clear and very warm with but little Wind & that Southerly.

21.   Again very warm with very little Wind.

22.   Very Warm—with little or no Wind. In the Afternoon Thunder, with appearances of Rain, but none fell.

23.   A little Cool in the Morning, but warm afterwards with but little Wind.

24.   Clear and warm, with but very little wind. That Southerly.

25. Much such a day as yesterday being clear, still and warm.

26. Clear & warm all day with very little Wind and that Southerly.

27. Very warm with but little wind and that Southerly again.

28. Lowering in the Morning with the Wind abt. No. Et.
In the Afternoon moderate Rain which con[tinue]d through the Night.

29. Warm in the forepart of the day with Showers. Cool in the Afternoon with the Wind blowing violently hard from the Northwest which again moderating it set in to Raining & Raind all Night.

30. Very cold. Wind blowing exceeding hard at No. West all day.

[May]

Where, how, or with whom my time is Spent

May 1st. At home all day. Alone.

2. Rid in the forenoon with Mrs. Washington to Belvoir.

3. At home all day. Mr. Adam dined and lodged here.

4. At home all day alone.

5. Set off for Mr. Calverts. Dined and lodged there.

6. After dinner returnd home. Mr. & Mrs. Custis & Miss Calvert came home with us. Found Mr. Tilghman here.

7. Went with the above Company to a Boat Race & Barbicue at Johnson's Ferry. Returnd at Night with Mr. Milner.

In 1745 a ferry was authorized to cross the Potomac from the land of William Clifton to the Maryland shore (HENING, 5:364). GW's 1760 purchase of the Clifton's Neck land included Clifton's home, which, after Clifton moved out in 1761, GW rented to Samuel Johnston (Johnson). Near the house was the ferry, which was now called Johnston's ferry. It was often used by GW in trips northward, and GW described it in 1773 as being "upon the most direct Road leading from *Annapolis* . . . to *Williamsburg*" (*Va. Gaz.*, P&D, 29 July 1773). A boat race held in 1774 on the Rappahannock River involved two long boats, each with a captain and five or six Negro hands, who rowed a mile out "round a Boat lying at Anchor" and then back to shore. Among the spectators, who picnicked on the shore and in boats in the river, small bets were made (FITHIAN, 198, 202). GW ordered 48 bottles of claret "for the Boat Race at Johnsons Ferry" from William Herbert, who later assumed the cost (LEDGER B, 122).

8.   Mr. Tilghman, & Mr. Milner went away after Breakfast. We (that is the rest) went to Pohick Church.

9.   At home all day alone.

10.   Miss Calvert, Miss Custis & Mr. Custis went over to Maryland. I contd. at home all day. Major Wagener and Mr. Thoms. Triplet dind here.

MISS CUSTIS: GW obviously meant Mrs. John Parke Custis.

11.   At home all day alone.

12.   Set of with Mrs. Washington for Williamsburg. Dined at Dumfries & lodgd at Colo. Lewis's in Fredericksburg.

13.   At Fredg. all day. Dined at Colo. Lewis's & spent the Evening at Weedens.

On 11 April 1774 GW wrote to Dr. Hugh Mercer: "I will bring down my title papers [for the Ferry Farm] & leave them with you, as I go to the Assembly" (DLC:GW). The sale by GW of his boyhood home to Hugh Mercer was concluded, probably on this day; but within a year the Revolution broke out, and in Jan. 1776 Mercer was appointed brigadier general in the Continental Army. He was with GW's army from the New York campaign in 1776 to the Battle of Princeton, where he was mortally wounded. Mercer's brother-in-law George Weedon, as executor of the estate, offered to pay GW in the current (1778) much-inflated currency. "After animadverting a little upon the subject," GW authorized Lund Washington to accept the payment (GW to Lund Washington, 17 Aug. 1779, DLC:GW).

14.   Dined at Roys Ord[inar]y & lodgd at Tods Bridge.

During the previous year John Hoomes had built a new tavern on the main road, "a little above the Bowling Green," and it was now being kept by Wiley Roy (*Va. Gaz.*, R, 2 Dec. 1773, and P, 6 Dec. 1776).

15.   Breakfasted at Ruffins Ferry and dined and lodgd at Colo. Bassetts.

16.   Came to Wmsburg., dind at the Governors & spent the Evening at Mrs. Campbells.

The current session of the House of Burgesses opened on 4 May and achieved a quorum the next day. During this week, GW and John West received petitions from William Ramsay, Robert Adam, John Carlyle, and John Dalton, four of the leading merchants and town fathers of Alexandria, requesting certain acts to be passed in this session. One would lower the duty on rum. A second was for "the inlargement of our Town . . . as this place is in a very thriving condition." A third act would standardize the quality and packing of "the Herring fishery which you well know, is become very considerable." Finally, the two Fairfax County burgesses were advised they would also receive "a petition for a more effectual method to prevent the raising of Hogs and suffering them to run at large, also Goats and Geese" (16 May 1774, DLC:GW).

17.   Dined at the Speakers & Spent the Evening at Southalls.

18.   Dined at the Club at Mrs. Campbells and Spent the Evening at Southalls.

19.   Dined & Spent the Evening at Mrs. Campbells.

20.   Dined at Mrs. Campbells & Spent the afternoon at my own lodgings.

21st.   Dined at the Speakers & went up to Colo. Bassetts in the afternoon.

During this week, news reached Williamsburg of the passage of an act by the British Parliament closing the port of Boston on 1 June until it paid reparations for the tea destroyed in the Boston Tea Party the previous December.

22.   At Colo. Bassetts all day.

23.   Came to Williamsburg with Mrs. Washington. Dined at the Attorneys, & spent the Evening there.

While the Washingtons were dining at the home of John Randolph, a handful of younger burgesses, led by Thomas Jefferson, Patrick Henry, and Richard Henry Lee, "cooked up a resolution," as Jefferson later recalled, "for appointing the 1st day of June, on which the [Boston] port-bill was to commence, for a day of fasting, humiliation, and prayer." To introduce the resolution, the young burgesses "agreed to wait the next morning on Mr.

[Robert Carter] Nicholas, whose grave and religious character was more in unison with the tone of our resolution. . . . He moved it the same day [24 May]; the 1st of June was proposed; and it passed without opposition" (BERGH, 1:9–10).

24. Dined at the Speakers & Spent the Evening at Mrs. Campbells.

25. Dined and spent the Eveng. at the Governor's.

26. Rid out with the Govr. to his Farm and Breakfasted with him there. Dined at Mrs. Dawson's, & spent the Evening at my lodgings.

Today's House of Burgesses session did not begin until 11:00 A.M., giving GW ample time to return the few miles from Governor Dunmore's farm. When the governor returned to town this day he proceeded to dissolve the assembly, ostensibly because of the resolution for a fast day. GW later discussed Dunmore's action in a letter to George William Fairfax: "this Dissolution was as sudden as unexpected for there were other resolves of a much more spirited nature ready to be offerd to the House wch. would have been unanimously adopted respecting the Boston Port Bill as it is call'd but were withheld till the Important business of the Country could be gone through. As the case stands the assembly sat In 22 day's for nothing—not a Bill being [passed]" (10 June 1774, WRITINGS, 3:223).

The expiration of two laws in particular would lead to major consequences in the colony. One was the law setting the schedule of fees for the colony's court system (HENING, 8:515), which had expired the previous month, thus closing the courts to civil cases. The other was the colony's basic militia act (HENING, 7:93–106), which had come up for renewal in the spring 1773 assembly but had been caught in a conflict between the burgesses and the council when Governor Dunmore had prorogued the assembly on 15 Mar. The militia act had thus expired on 20 July 1773.

27. Dined at the Treasurers and went to the Ball given by the House of Burgesses to Lady Dunmore.

For this date the *Virginia Gazette* had some political news: "This Day, at ten o'Clock, the Honourable Members of the late House of Burgesses met, by Agreement, at the long Room in the Raleigh Tavern, in this City, called the Apollo," where an "Agreement was unanimously entered into by that patriotick Assembly, in Support of the constitutional Liberties of AMERICA, against the late oppressive Act of the British Parliament respecting the Town of Boston, which, in the End, must affect all the other Colonies" (*Va. Gaz.*, P&D, 26 May 1774).

The meeting agreed to boycott tea and other goods of the East India Company. They then directed their committee of correspondence to write to other colonies "on the expediency of appointing deputies from the several colonies of British America, to meet in general congress" (H.B.J., 1773–76, xiv). GW joined the other burgesses and a number of local leaders in signing the statement.

The "Ball and Entertainment at the Capitol" was given "to welcome Lady DUNMORE and the rest of our Governour's Family to Virginia" (*Va. Gaz.*, P&D, 26 May 1774).

28. Dined at Mrs. Campbells & Spent the Evening at my Lodgings.

29. Went to Church in the fore, & afternoon. Dined at Mrs. Dawsons & spent the Eveng. at my Lodgings.

On this Sunday afternoon letters from Boston to the Virginia committee of correspondence arrived in Williamsburg asking for a nonimport and nonexport association by all of the colonies, to reopen the port of Boston.

30. Dined at Mr. Southalls. Spent the Evening in my own Room.

Peyton Randolph called together the 25 burgesses who remained in town to discuss what action Virginia should take on the circular letters from Boston. The meeting agreed that Virginia should act in concert as much as possible with the other colonies and voted to call a meeting of the burgesses in 90 days to decide on steps to be taken. The group then agreed to send the news of their decisions "through the Hands of our Friends in *Philadelphia* to our Friends in *Boston*" (H.B.J., 1773–76, 139–40).

GW commented that "the Ministry may rely on it that Americans will never be tax'd without their own consent that the cause of Boston . . . is and ever will be considerd as the cause of America (not that we approve their conduct in destroyg. the Tea) and that we shall not suffer ourselves to be sacrificed by piece meals though god only knows what is to be become of us" (GW to George William Fairfax, 10 June 1774, WRITINGS, 3:224).

31. Dined at Mr. Charltons & spent the Evening in my Room.

Although by law only the governor could summon the burgesses into session, the members remaining in Williamsburg today called for a convention of all their colleagues on 1 Aug. (Peyton Randolph et al. to members of the late House of Burgesses, 31 May 1774, DLC:GW; see also JEFFERSON [1], 1: 105–12; FREEMAN, 3:348–66).

Acct. of the Weather in May

May 1st. Cool, Wind blowing fresh all day from the Northwest. Also clear.

2. Clear and rather Cool. Wind still Northerly.

3.   Warm in the Morning. Sultry about Noon and exceeding Cold before Night Wind blowing very hard at No. West.

4.   Very Cold all day with spits of Snow and the Wind blowing hard at No. West.

A severe frost this day killed half of GW's 1,000 acres of wheat, "as it hath also done our fruit, and the foliage of all most all the Forest Trees" (GW to Robert McMickan, 10 May 1774, DLC:GW). Later he wrote to his agent Robert Cary in London that the crop had been equal to his best prospects before the frost.

5.   Ground Froze, & Ice, killing most things in the Garden the Leaves &ca. Wind at So. West & less Cool blowing pretty fresh however.

6.   Wind pretty fresh from the So. East, and Cool, though more moderate.

7.   Calm and pleasant in the forenoon, but a little Windy from the Eastward in the Afternoon.

8.   A little lowering and warm in the forenoon. Cooler afterwards.

9.   Lowering most part of the day with not much wind.

10th.   Clear and tolerably pleasant with but little Wind.

11.   Much such a day as yesterday.

12.   Lowering in the forenoon with Rain more or less all the Afternoon. Wind Easterly.

13.   Misting all day, with but little Wind and that Easterly.

14.   Again Misting in the Morning with Showers in the Afternoon accompanied in some places with violent Hail.

15.   Lowering all the forenoon & clear about Noon with but little Wind.

16.   Clear and Cool, wind abt. No. West & pretty fresh.

17.   Still Cool, Wind being in the same place.

18.   Clear and rather incling. to turn warm—there being but little Wind.

19.   Warm with but little Wind and that Southerly.

20.   Very warm, with a Thunder Shower in the Afternoon.

21st.   Very warm in the forenoon with a Thunder Shower in the Afternoon.

22.   A little Cloudy & still warm.

23.   Clear and pleasant with the Wind pretty fresh at So. West.

24.   Warm and clear.

25.   Warm, with thunder, & some Rain at Night.

26.   Warm with Rain about Noon & after it.

27.   Clear and something Cooler.

28.   Clear and warm with but little Wind & that Southerly.

29.   Clear and pleasant but somewhat Warm.

30.   Much such a day as yesterday but the wind pretty fresh from the So. West.

31.   Much such a day as yesterday.

[June]

Where, how, or with whom my time is Spent

June 1st.   Went to Church & fasted all day.

This service was pursuant to the resolution passed on 24 May for a day of fasting, humiliation, and prayer to symbolize Virginia's solidarity with the people of Boston, and many of the Virginia parishes joined in the observance. In this service at Bruton Parish Church, Rev. Thomas Price, chaplain of the House of Burgesses, preached on the destruction of the city of Sodom, taking for his text the answer to Abraham's question to the Lord:

"Wilt thou also destroy the righteous with the wicked?" And he answered, "I will not destroy *it* for ten's sake" (GEN., 18:23, 32; see also VAN SCHREEVEN, 1:103).

2.   Dined at Mr. Charlton's & came up to Colo. Bassets in the Afternoon.

3.   At Colo. Bassetts all day in Compa. with Mr. Dandridge &ca.

Probably Bartholomew Dandridge and his family.

4.   Went up by Water with Mr. & Mrs. Bassett, Mrs. Dandridge & Mrs. Washington to the L[an]d bot. of Black in King & Queen. Returnd to Colo. Bassetts to Dinr.

Douglas Southall Freeman gave the price paid to Black for these lands as £3,679 and attributed the figure given by Fitzpatrick of £6,375 to a typographical error (FREEMAN, 3:336; DIARIES, 2:129). The figures in GW's ledgers show a payment of £3,679 sterling (entered also in Virginia currency as £4,875) and also a subsequent payment of £500 (Virginia currency), which totals £5,375 in Virginia currency (LEDGER B, 96). Hence Freeman gave only the first of two payments, and that in sterling, while Fitzpatrick figured the total of the two payments in Virginia currency but somehow gave it as £6,375 rather than £5,375, the price actually paid in Virginia currency.

5.   At Colo. Bassetts all day.

6.   Set [out] with him for Williamsburg. Dined at Richd. Charltons & Supped at Anderson's.

7.   Dined at Mrs. Dawson's and Spent the Evening at the Raleigh.

8.   Dined at the Raleigh, and Spent the Evening at Andersons.

9.   Dined at the Raleigh and spent the Evening there also.

10.   Dined at the Raleigh, & went to the Fire works.

Fireworks were occasionally used to celebrate a public event, as in the "elegant set of fireworks . . . displayed in this city [Williamsburg] on the arrival of . . . Lady Dunmore" (*Va. Gaz.*, R, 10 Mar. 1774; CARSON [2], 200–203). They may also have been to commemorate the second anniversary of the burning of the British revenue cutter *Gaspee*.

11.   Dined at Mrs. Dawsons & went up to Colo. Bassetts in the Afternoon.

12.   At Colo. Bassetts all day.

13.   Returned with him to Will[iamsbur]g. Dined at the Raleigh and Spent the Evening at Andersons.

14.   Dined with the Council at Southalls and spent the Evening at Anderson's.

15.   Dined at Mrs. Dawson's & Spent the Evening at the Capitol at a Meeting of the Society for promoting useful Kn[owledge].

The Philosophical Society for the Advancement of Useful Knowledge was formed in May 1773 in Williamsburg (BEAR, 122). This 1774 meeting, held "at the Capitol . . . at four o'Clock in the Afternoon," was the first attended by GW, and he paid his dues of £1 (*Va. Gaz.,* P&D, 9 June 1774; LEDGER B, 115). At this meeting the society voted a "pecuniary Reward, and Medal" to John Hobday, a local Virginian, "for his Model of a very ingenious and useful Machine for threshing out Wheat" (*Va. Gaz.,* P&D, 16 June 1774). The society's first president, the botanist John Clayton (1694–c. 1773), of Gloucester County, having died, the amateur astronomer John Page (1743–1808), of Rosewell, was elected president (BERKELEY [1], 168). With the outbreak of the Revolution no more meetings were held, although as president Page remained active on behalf of the society into the 1780s (*Va. Gaz.,* P, 16 May 1777; Page to Thomas Jefferson, 28 April 1785, JEFFERSON [1], 8:119–20).

16.   Dined at the Governors & Spent the Evening at Anderson's.

17.   Dined at Anderson's and Spent the Evening there.

18.   Dined at Mrs. Dawson's and came up to Colo. Bassetts in the afternoon.

19.   At Colo. Bassetts all day.

20.   Set of from thence on my return home. Dined at Todds bridge & lodged at Hubbards.

21.   Breakfasted at the Bolling green. Dind & lodged at Colo. Lewis's in Fredericksburg.

22.   Reachd home to a late Dinner, after Breakfasting at Aquia.

GW breakfasted at the old Peyton's ordinary on Aquia Creek, run since Mar. 1773 by Charles Tyler (*Va. Gaz.,* R, 25 Mar. 1773).

23.   At home all day. Alone.

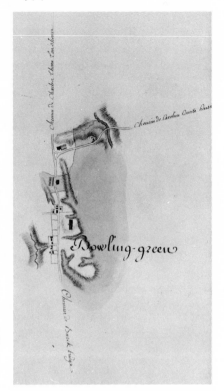

An artist with General Rochambeau's army made this plan of Bowling Green, Va., in 1782. (Map Division, Library of Congress)

24. Rid up to Alexandria and returnd in the Afternoon.

25. At home all day alone.

26. Went up to Church at Alexa. Returnd to Dinner.

27. At home all day. Mr. Custis came here to dinner.

28. I rid to the Plantation's in the Neck and to the Muddy hole. Found Doctr. Rumney here upon my return who stayed all Night.

29. At home all day alone.

30. At home all day alone except Mr. Peake coming here in the Afternoon.

Acct. of the Weather in June

June 1st.   Very hot & clear with but little Wind.

2.   Also very hot. Wind from the Southward but not fresh.

3.   Clear & tolerably pleast. with but little Wind.

4.   Clear. Wind Northerly but not much of it.

5.   Clear in the forenoon but not warm. Lowering in the Afternoon but no Rain. Wind Easterly.

6.   Wind in the same Quarter & Cool for the Season.

7.   Wind more Southerly & warmer. With some appearances of Rain.

8.   Wind Southerly & exceeding warm. Clear withal.

9.   Very warm with wind Southerly.

10.   Again warm with the Wind in the same place and some appearances of Rain.

11.   Very warm Wind Southerly in the forenoon & Easterly afterwards.

12.   Clear, with the Wind pretty fresh from the South west, & pleasant.

13.   Wind blew very hard ,at So. West in the Night. Morng. lowering. Fine Rains abt. Mid day.

14.   Cloudy in the forenoon, but clear afterwards.

15.   Warm & clear wind at So. West.

16.   Clear in the forenoon with a little Rain in the Afternoon.

17.   Clear and tolerably pleasant—being a little warm.

18.   Warm the wind being at Southwest.

19.   Clear and pretty Cool. Wind chiefly Eastwardly.

20.   Lowering & Showery most part of the day.

21.   Clear and tolerably pleasant. Wind Northwardly.

22.   Tolerably cool in the forenoon, but warm afterwds. Wind Southerly.

23.   Exceeding Warm. Two or three very fine showers in the Afternoon.

24.   Clear and pleasant. Wind rather Westerly.

25.   Warm, with some appearances of Rain but none fell here.

26.   Tolerably pleasant. Wind pretty fresh from the Northd.

27.   Warm with little or no Wind, & that Southerly.

28.   Exceeding Warm, wind being Southerly with great appearances of Rain—but none fell here.

29.   Very Warm again. Wind blowing fresh from the Southward.

30.   Again warm with little or no Wind & that in the same Quarter. A little Rain in the Night.

[July]

Where, how, or with whom my time is Spent

July 1st.   Rid to Dogue Run, Mill, Mill Plantation & the Ferry at Posey's, before Dinner.

2.   At home all day. Mr. Wm. Waite dind here.

William Waite (died c.1787), of Fauquier County, was a stonemason who owned his own quarry. On this day GW made his first payment to Waite for an order of over 700 feet of stone (LEDGER B, 111).

3.   Went to Pohick Church & returnd home to Dinner.

In anticipation of the upcoming burgesses election, GW wrote Bryan Fairfax 4 July: "I entreated several gentlemen at our church yesterday to press Colonel [George] Mason to take a poll. . . . And therefore I again express my wish, that either you or Colonel Mason would offer. I can be of little assistance to either, because I early laid it down as a maxim not to propose myself, and solicit for a second" (WRITINGS, 3:227–28).

4. At home all day. Mr. & Mrs. Custis came here from Maryland.

5. Went up to Alexandria to a Meeting of the Inhabitts. of this County. Dined at Arrells & lodgd at my own Ho[use].

The date for the convention in Williamsburg had been set as late as 1 Aug., so that each burgess might "have an Opportunity of collecting the Sense of their respective Counties" (see main entry for 31 May 1774), and it was for this purpose that GW attended this Fairfax County meeting of inhabitants, probably held at the courthouse.

6. Dined at Doctr. Brown's & returnd home in the Eveng.

The meeting of inhabitants, held yesterday, chose a committee to draft resolutions to instruct their two burgesses, who would represent them in the August convention, on nonimportation, nonexportation, aid to Boston, a continental congress to give the 13 colonies one voice, and general views on English liberty and American rights. GW was chosen chairman of the committee, which was probably meeting in Alexandria on this day.

7. At home all day.

8. At home all day alone.

9. At home all day. Ditto.

10. At home all day—Ditto.

11. At home all day. Doctr. Rumney came here, Dined & stayed all Night.

12th. Rid to Muddy hole, Dogue Run & Mill Plantation. Mr. Digges, Doctr. Digges & Miss Tracy Dind & went away in the Afternoon as did Doctr. Rumney also.

13. At home all day alone.

14. Went up to Alexandria to the Election where I was Chosen, together with Majr. Broadwater, Burgess. Staid all Night to a Ball.

Governor Dunmore, who had dissolved the assembly upon its protest of the Boston Port Bill in May 1774, had issued the writs for new elections on 16 June (*Va. Gaz.*, P&D, 16 June 1774, supp.).

Maj. Charles Broadwater (d. 1806) lived at Springfield, in northern Fairfax County. After serving for a number of years as a vestryman in Truro Parish, Broadwater was elected to the vestry of newly created Fairfax Parish in 1765. He served in the last session of the Virginia House of Burgesses and in the first four Virginia conventions of 1774–75 (SLAUGHTER [1], 45, 120; STETSON [2], 236–38; STANARD, 199, 201, 204).

An English visitor in Alexandria, who was present for the election, recorded in his diary: "*Thursday, July 14th, 1774.* An Election for Burgesses in town. . . . There were three Candidates, the Poll was over in about two hours and conducted with great order and regularity. The Members Col. George Washington and Major Bedwater. The Candidates gave the populace a Hogshead of Toddy (what we call Punch in England). In the evening the returned Member [GW] gave a Ball to the Freeholders and Gentlemen of the town. This was conducted with great harmony. Coffee and Chocolate, but no Tea. This Herb is in disgrace amongst them at present" (CRESSWELL, 27–28).

In his accounts GW entered £8 5s. 6d. for "my p[ar]t of the Electn. Ball" (LEDGER B, 126).

15.   Return'd home to a late Dinner.

16.   At home all day alone.

17.   Went to Pohick Church & returnd to Dinner. Colo. Mason came in the Afternoon & stayed all Night.

George Mason of Gunston Hall was a member of the Fairfax resolutions committee that GW chaired. He and GW probably spent this Sunday afternoon and evening perfecting a draft, probably Mason's, of resolutions to be presented the following day. The final draft submitted to the committee contained 24 separate resolutions regarding English liberty, American rights, taxation and representation, the boycotting of most British imports (including slaves), and "a Congress [that] shou'd be appointed, to consist of Deputies from all the Colonies, to concert a general and uniform Plan for the Defence and Preservation of our common Rights" (MASON [2], 1:205).

18.   Went up to Alexandria to a Meeting of the County. Returnd in the Evening—Mr. Magowan with me.

When GW arrived in Alexandria he first attended a meeting wherein "the Resolutions [were] revised, alterd, & corrected in the Committee" (GW to Bryan Fairfax, 20 July 1774, ViHi). Then the whole committee went "into a general Meeting in the Court House," where GW found an almost "perfect satisfaction, & acquiescence to the measures propos'd," though his friend Bryan Fairfax thought otherwise (see Fairfax to GW, 5 Aug. 1774, DLC:GW). These resolutions, approved on this day by the "General Meeting of the Freeholders and other Inhabitants of the County of Fairfax, at

Washington strongly backed the Fairfax Resolves, which he carried to a special meeting in Williamsburg. (Virginia State Library)

the Court House," thereafter were commonly known as the Fairfax Resolves (VAN SCHREEVEN, 1:127–33).

The meeting also chose a 25-man committee, headed by GW, which would "have power to call a General Meeting, and to Concert and Adopt such Measures as may be thought most expedient and Necessary" (VAN SCHREEVEN, 1:133; and see MASON [2], 1:201–10). This committee subsequently absorbed the role of the Alexandria committee of correspondence that had been formed the preceding May (PURVIANCE, 126–28).

There were meetings similar to this Fairfax County meeting in almost every county in Virginia during this summer, all of which passed resolutions and chose delegates (usually their burgesses) for the upcoming August convention (VAN SCHREEVEN, 1:105–168). Only a few of the preconvention meetings, however (including those of Fairfax, Dunmore, Frederick, and Stafford counties), formed county committees before the convention even met. While Dunmore and Frederick counties each chose committes of 6, Stafford County chose a 69-man committee, 5 of whom were cousins of GW (VAN SCHREEVEN, 1:161).

19.   At home all day.

20. Rid into the Neck. Mr. Piper, Mr. Ross & Mr. Gibson Dind & Lodgd here.

Mr. Gibson may be James Gibson, merchant of Suffolk, Nansemond County, with whom GW had some dealings (LEDGER A, 281, 283), or John Gibson, who in 1780 was a Colchester merchant (George Mason to James Mercer, 5 Feb. 1780, MASON [2], 2:617).

21. The Gentlemen who came Yesterday went after Breakfast. I contd. at home all day.

22. Mr. Magowan went away. I continued at home all day.

23. At home all day. Mr. Thoms. Johnson & Mr. Paca of Ann[ap]o[li]s & Mr. Digges & his Son George Dined here & went away afterwards.

Thomas Johnson, Jr. (1732–1819), the fifth child of Thomas Johnson, Sr. (d. 1777), and Dorcas Sedgwick Johnson (d. 1770), was born in Calvert County, Md. As a young man, Johnson read law in Annapolis with Stephen Bordley (1710–1764) and practiced law both in Annapolis and in frontier Frederick County, Md., where the Johnson family had interests in land and ironworks and where, by 1768, Johnson himself owned an interest in over

Thomas Johnson, of Maryland, was to nominate Washington to lead the army of the United Colonies. Portrait by John Hesselius. (Maryland Historical Society)

William Paca, who dined with Washington, was a fellow delegate to the Continental Congress. A Charles Willson Peale portrait. (Collection of the State of Maryland, Annapolis)

22,000 acres (DELAPLAINE, 67). In 1762 Johnson, an early and active promoter of commercial navigation on the upper Potomac, became a manager of the navigation company and began correspondence with GW on the feasibility of opening a canal above the great falls of the Potomac River (DELAPLAINE, 59–84; GW to Johnson [1762], DLC:GW). From 1762 until the Revolution, Johnson represented Anne Arundel County in the Maryland House of Delegates, becoming a moderate but firm leader in the popular resistance to British incursions upon American interests and rights.

William Paca (1740–1799), second son of John and Elizabeth Smith Paca, was born in Harford County, Md. From 1768 to the Revolution, Paca represented Talbot County in the Maryland House of Delegates, where he, like Johnson, actively fought the Proprietary party. Paca joined Johnson as a member of the Maryland committee of correspondence and became a Maryland delegate to the First Continental Congress.

24. Went up to Church at Alexandria. Returnd to Dinner.

25. At home all day alone.

26. Mr. Peake dind here. I continued at home.

27. At home all day. Doctr. Rumney Dined and lodged here.

28. Set of with Mr. Custis for Williamsburg. Dined at Tylers on Aquia and lodged at Colo. Lewis's.

29. Set out from Fredericksburg late. Dined at Roys and lodged at Hubbards.

30. Breakfasted at King Wm. Court Ho. Dined at Ruffins & reachd Colo. Bassetts.

31. At Colo. Bassetts all day.

Acct. of the Weather in July

July 1st. Very warm with but little Wind & that Southerly.

2. Warm. Wind Southerly but not much of it. About 6 Oclock a pretty smart Shower for a few Minutes.

3. Another Shower in the Night with appearance's of Rain throughout the day.

4.   Very warm with the Wind Southerly. Cloudy in the Afternoon & a good deal of Rain in the Night.

5.   Exceeding Warm, with little or no Wind.

6.   Again very hot with Clouds in the Afternoon & a fine Rain
in the Night.

7.   Very Warm with a Shower of Rain & pretty high Wind from
the No. West.

8.   A little Cool in the forenoon. Wind at No. West. Warm in
the middle of the day there being no Wind & cool again in the
Afternoon the Wind blowing pretty fresh from the Eastward.

9th.   Pretty warm in the forenoon with but little Wind. Cool
afterwards Wind being Eastwardly.

10.   Rather Cool all day altho there was but little Wind. That
however was Northerly.

11.   Clear and pleasand being rather cool. Without much wind.

12.   Wind Northerly in the forenoon and rather Cool but
warmer afterwards & clear all day.

13.   Clear with but little wind & rather Warm.

14.   Clear, and exceeding warm, especially in the Afternoon,
there being no Wind at the time.

15.   Warm Morning with fine Showers in the Afternoon.

16.   Very warm, with but little Wind, & that Southerly. Appearances of Rain with some thundr. & lightning but none fell
here or very little.

17.   Very warm with but little Wind & that Southerly. Night
very hot.

18.   Morning exceeding Warm. Evening Cooler.

19.   Cool all day, Wind Northerly & clear.

20. Pleasant, but not so Cool as yesterday. Cloudy.

21. Warm again. Wind Southerly but not much of it.

22. Very warm, & clear. Wind Southerly.

23. Wind fresh from the Southward, but very warm. Abt. 2 Oclock a fine Shower, & another in the Evening.

24. Cool Wind at No. West & Clear.

25. Again Cool Wind in the same place.

26. Wind Southerly & turnd a good deal Warmer.

27. Warmer than yesterday, Wind what little there was of it Southerly.

28. Exceeding warm with but little & clear Wind.

29. Clear forenoon with but little Wind & exceeding Warm. In the Afternoon Rain where I was.

30. Clear, and again very Warm, there being but little Wind.

31. Exceeding Warm with little or no Wind.

[August]

Where, how, or with whom my time is Spent

Augt. 1st. Went from Colo. Bassetts to Williamsburg to the Meeting of the Convention. Dined at Mrs. Campbells. Spent the Evening in my Lodgings.

After he arrived at the convention, GW wrote to Thomas Johnson: "We never before had so full a Meeting . . . as on the present Occasion" (5 Aug. 1774, MdHi). At least 108 delegates, most of whom were also burgesses, were present at some time during the convention, which met in the Capitol (see VAN SCHREEVEN, 1:109, 219–22).

2. At the Convention. Dined at the Treasurer's. At my Lodgings in the Evening.

The Capitol in Williamsburg as it appeared during the turbulent meetings in 1774. (Valentine Museum, Richmond)

WILLIAMSBURG, *August* 5.

ON Monday laft, the 1ft Inftant, there was a very general and full Meeting of the late Reprefentatives of this Colony, who ftill continue fitting upon the weighty Matters intrufted to their Deliberation by their feveral Conftituents. We cannot, with Certainty, at this Time, publifh any of their Councils and Determinations; but next Week we expect to be able to communicate the Whole to the Publick, which (at leaft as far as we are able to judge) will be fuch as will do Honour to the Colony, revive the Spirits of our fuffering Fellow Subjects to the Northward, and, in all Probability, fecure the Rights and Liberties of America, from every Invafion thereof.

The Refolves of the Conties of Fairfax, Mecklenburg, Prince Edward, Brunfwick, Lancafter, Suffex, Accomack, and Charles City, are come to Hand; which we fhould with much Pleafure have inferted in our Gazette, had it been poffible. We had neither Time, nor near Room enough, for them; and therefore can only obferve, that they contain the like patriotick Sentiments with the Refolutions of feveral Counties already publifhed, and profefs all due Obedience to the Sovereign of the Britifh Empire.

A brief report on the meeting of the Virginia Convention was carried in the *Virginia Gazette.* (Colonial Williamsburg Photograph)

3.   Dined at the Speaker's & Spent the Evening at my own Lodgings.

4.   Dined at the Attorneys & Spent the Evening at my own Lodgings.

5.   Dined at Mrs. Dawson's & Spent the Evening at my own Lodgings.

The *Virginia Gazette* reported: "FRIDAY, *August* 5. This Day the Commissioners on Behalf of this Colony, to attend the General Congress at Philadelphia the 5th of next Month, were appointed by Ballot, and are as follows, viz. The Honourable PEYTON RANDOLPH, Esq; Moderator of the present Meeting, RICHARD HENRY LEE, GEORGE WASHINGTON, PATRICK HENRY, RICHARD BLAND, BENJAMIN HARRISON, AND EDMUND PENDLETON, Esquires; and a Sum of Money, amounting nearly to [£]1000 (*Va. Gaz.*, P&D, 4 Aug. 1774). The convention voted to ask for a contribution of £15 from each of the 61 counties (MAYS, 1:277). GW's "proportion of the Sum voted" was £90 13s. 9d., which he received on the day he entered Philadelphia (LEDGER B, 30).

6.   Dined at Mrs. Campbells & Spent the Evening at my own Lodgings.

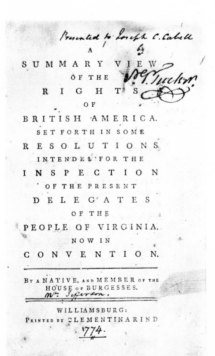

The Albemarle resolution before the Virginia Convention grew into Jefferson's famous *Summary View*. (Rare Book Division, Library of Congress)

On this day the convention adjourned, after a nonimportation, nonexportation association had been *"unanimously resolved upon and agreed to"* (VAN SCHREEVEN, 1:231–35). Unless Britain repealed its new laws applying to Boston and Massachusetts, Virginia would stop all British imports, including slaves (but excluding medicines), beginning 1 Nov. 1774, and would end all export of tobacco to Britain beginning 1 Aug. 1775. The associators also agreed to foster county enforcement committees, encourage all merchants to sign the association and boycott those who would not, prevent inflated prices, support Boston with contributions, refrain from drinking tea, and empower the moderator to reconvene the convention when he thought necessary. These articles of association became the basis for those adopted for all of the colonies by the First Continental Congress in Oct. 1774.

7. Left Williamsburg abt. 9 Oclock & got up to Colo. Bassets to Dinner where I stayd the remaining part of the Day & Night.

8th. Left Colo. Bassetts. Visited my own Plantn. in King Wm. & Mr. Custis's in King & Queen. Dind at King Wm. Ct. House & lodged at Tods Bridge.

9. Breakfasted at Roys Ord[inar]y. Dined and lodged at Colo. Lewis's in Fredericksburg.

10. Breakfasted at Tylers on Acquiae & Dined at home.

11. At home all day. Miss Calvert here.

12. At home all day. Miss Carlyle & her Sister Nancy came here. Mr. Willis also dind here, & went away afterwds.

13. I rid to the Neck Plantation & came home by Muddy hole.

14. Went to Pohick Church with Mr. Custis. Found Messrs. Carlyle, Dalton, Ramsay, Adam, & Doctr. Rumney here upon my return. Doctr. Craik also came in the Afternoon.

15. Went in Compa. with the aforementd. Gentlemen to Colo. Fairfax's Sale. Mr. Ramsay, Mr. Dalton, & Doctr. Craik came home with me—the Rest did not. Miss Carlyle & her Sister went aw[a]y.

Francis Willis, Jr. (1745–1828), had advertised a sale, to take place on this date, of the household and kitchen furniture from Belvoir. He also placed an advertisement for rental of the mansion house itself with its 2,000 acres and several fisheries (*Va. Gaz.*, P&D, 2 June 1774). GW wrote George William Fairfax that he feared the latter would be disappointed in Willis's estimate of the rental value of Belvoir and he was not optimistic about the prospects of leasing the house and land, for "there are very few People who are of ability to pay a Rent equivalent to the Interest of the Money which such buildings may have cost, who are not either already provided with a Seat, or would choose to buy one, in order to Improve it . . . & as to your Fishery at the Racoon Branch, I think you will be disappointed there likewise as there is no Landing on this side the River that Rents for more than one half of what you expect for that. . . . I have already advertiz'd the Publick of this matter, also of the Sale of your Furniture, as you may see by the Inclosed Gazette. . . . The advertisements are in Mr. Rinds Gazette also & the one relative to Renting shall be put into the Papers of Maryland & Pensylvania whilst the other is already printed in hand Bills, & shall be distributed in the several Counties & Parts round about us" (10–15 June 1774, PPRF).

16. Ramsay Dalton & the Doctr. went away after Breakfast.

On this day GW paid £4 to Col. Thomas Ludwell "for a Card Table wch. he bot. at Colo. Fairfaxs. Sale & let me have." He also received from Dr. Craik £8 "for a Wilton Carpet bot. at Colo. Fairfax's Sale" (LEDGER B, 121).

17. I rid to Doeg Run, Muddy hole, Mill, & Poseys Plantns.

18. Rid to the Plantation's in the Neck. Found Mr. Fitzhugh here upon my Return.

19. Mr. Fitzhugh went away after Breakfast.

20. Rid with Mrs. Washn. to Alexa. & returnd to Dinner.

21. At home all day. Mr. Moylan, Doctr. Craik, & Mr. Fitzgerald Dind here. The latter went away.

Mr. Moylan may be Stephen Moylan (1737–1811) or his brother James, merchants of Philadelphia (GRIFFIN, 2).

22. Doctr. Craik went away after Breakfast, & Mr. Moyland after Dinner havg. Rid with [him] to Shew Belvoir.

23. At home all day alone.

24. At home all day alone.

25. Ditto. Mrs. Slaughter dind here.

26. Ditto. All day alone.

27. Went to the Barbacue at Accatinck.

28. Went to Pohick Church. Messrs. Stuart, Herbert, Mease, Doctr. Jenifer Mr. Stone & Mr. Digges dind here. The first three stayed all Night.

Dr. Walter Hanson Jenifer (1751–1785) was a son of Daniel Jenifer (1727–1795) and grandson of Dr. Daniel Jenifer, of Charles County, Md. Jenifer's aunt, Elizabeth Jenifer, married David Stone (1709–1773) of Poynton Manor, Charles County, Md., by whom she had six sons, one of whom is probably the Mr. Stone who appears here.

29. The above Gentn. went away after Breakfast.

30. Colo. Pendleton, Mr. Henry, Colo. Mason & Mr. Thos. Triplet came in the Eveng. & stayd all Night.

Edmund Pendleton (1721–1803), a member of the House of Burgesses since 1752, was one of the most influential men in Virginia. Although a leader of the conservatives, he staunchly supported the rights of the colonists and was elected one of Virginia's delegates to the First Continental Congress. He and Patrick Henry, often political opponents, met by prearrangement at Pen-

Edmund Pendleton, in a miniature by William Mercer. (Virginia Historical Society)

Patrick Henry, in a portrait by Thomas Sully. (Virginia Historical Society)

dleton's plantation in Caroline County 29 Aug. to travel together to Philadelphia, stopping at Mount Vernon on the way (WILLISON, 232).

31.   All the above Gentlemen dind here, after which with Colo.
Pendleton, & Mr. Henry I set out on my journey for Phila. &
reachd uppr. Marlbro.

According to Pendleton, Mrs. Washington sent the delegates off with an
admonition to stand firm in their demands against the British ministry
(HENRY, 1:213).

Acct. of the Weather in August

1.   Exceeding Warm. About 4 Oclock a fine Shower of Rain
with thunder wch. Cool'd the Air a little.

2.   Tolerably pleasant in the forenoon—but Warm Afterwards
with but little Wind.

3.   Very warm and clear with but little Wind.

4.   Again warm with appearances of Rain but none fell.

5.   Warm with moderate Showers in the Afternoon & Night.

6.   Close & warm all day with frequent Shower's.

7.   Very hot with a heavy Rain abt. One Oclock. Still warm
afterwards.

8.   Close & warm with appearances of Rain but none fell.

9.   Raining more or less all the Morning. After noon warm.

10.   Foggy Morning but no Rain. Warm.

11th.   Clear and Warm, with but little Wind & that Southerly.

12.   Much such a day as yesterday.

13.   Cool in the Morning, and Evening with the Wind No.
Easterly with some Rain at Night. Midday warm.

14.   Lowering Morning but clear & very warm afterwards with very little Wind.

15.   No Wind, but clear & exceeding hot.

16.   Again warm with but little wind. In the Afternn. a Shower or two of Rain.

17.   Very warm with Rain at Night.

18.   Again warm with but little Wind & that Southerly.

19.   Warm again and clear, after the Morning which was lowering with some appearances of Rain.

20.   Very warm with little or No Wind.

21.   Much such a day as the former.

22.   Wind very fresh from the So. West—otherwise exceeding warm.

23.   Lowering in the Morning with fine Showers afterwards. Wind Northerly & a little Cool.

24.   Misting all day & sometimes Rain. In the Evening a settled Rain. Wind at No. East but not much of it.

25.   Cloudy in the Morning, but clear afterwards. Wind at No. West.

26.   Clear and very pleasant. Wind at No. West.

27.   Pleasant, & clear with but little Wind.

28.   Clear but turning Warm. Wind Southerly.

29.   Warm & clear. Wind Southerly.

30.   Very warm. Wind in the same place tho' not much of it.

31.   Exceeding hot with very little Wind & that Southerly.

[September]

Where, how, or with whom, my time is Spent.

Septr. 1. Breakfasted at Queen Anne. Dined in Annapolis, & lodged at Rock Hall.

Queen Anne was a small village on the Patuxent River in Prince George's County, Md., nine miles northeast of Upper Marlboro. It consisted of only a few houses and a tobacco warehouse in 1783 (SCHOEPF, 1:364; *Md. Gaz.*, 5 Aug. 1746). ROCK HALL: GW lists expenses "at Hodges" as 16s. 9d. (GW's Cash Memoranda, 24 Mar.–25 Oct. 1774, CSmH). A 30 Nov. 1775 advertisement in the *Maryland Gazette* for the rental of the "White Rock-Hall ferry" describes James Hodges as currently living on the ferry plantation. He probably ran the ferry-house where GW stayed.

2. Din'd at Rock Hall (waiting for my Horses) & lodg'd at New Town on Chester.

3. Breakfasted at Down's. Dind at the Buck Tavern (Carsons) & lodg'd at Newcastle.

DOWN'S: a tavern operated by William Down at Down's Cross Roads, now Galena, Md., 1½ miles south of Georgetown (W.P.A. [2], 365). The Buck Tavern was in New Castle County, Del., 11 miles south of the present city of Newark, Del. William Carson, a tavern keeper in New Castle County in 1778, was probably the proprietor at this time (W.P.A. [3], 461; CALENDAR [2], 316).

4. Breakfasted at Christeen Ferry. Dined at Chester & lodged at Doctr. Shippens's in Phila. after Supping at the New Tavern.

Arriving in Philadelphia for the 1774 Continental Congress, Washington took his first meal at the City Tavern. (Independence National Historical Park Collection)

Christina (Christiana) ferry crossed Christina (Christiana) River at Wilmington on the main road from New Castle to Philadelphia (LINCOLN, 83–84).

William Shippen, Jr. (1736–1808), son of Dr. William Shippen (1712–1801) and Susannah Harrison Shippen, was a Philadelphia physician and surgeon, educated at Edinburgh. In 1765 he was appointed professor of surgery and anatomy at the new medical school connected with the College of Philadelphia, and during the Revolution he was chief physician and director general of the military hospital of the Continental Army. Shippen was married to Alice Lee Shippen, sister of GWs fellow delegate, Richard Henry Lee. Lee had undoubtedly invited GW to stay at his brother-in-law's house until suitable lodgings were obtained.

The New Tavern, or City Tavern, was on the west side of Second Street, above Walnut. Designed in the style of the best London taverns, it contained several large club rooms. Daniel Smith was the proprietor at this time (SCHARF [1], 1:291).

5.   Breakfasted and Dined at Doctr. Shippen's. Spent the Eveng. at Tavern.

On this day the delegates to Congress met at City Tavern. The credentials of the various members were read, and Peyton Randolph of Virginia was elected chairman, or president, and Charles Thomson of Pennsylvania secretary. Carpenters' Hall, which has been offered by the Carpenters' Guild of Philadelphia, was chosen as the meeting place for Congress (JCC, 1:13–14). GW rarely mentions in his diaries anything concerning his presence in Congress, but he seems to have attended the sessions regularly. For information on the day-to-day transactions of the Congress, see JCC and LMCC.

Carpenters' Hall, where delegates to the First Continental Congress assembled. (Historical Society of Pennsylvania)

6.   Dined at the New Tavern—after being in Congress all day.

On this day GW spent 15s. for shoes, etc., for William Lee, his body servant, who accompanied him to Philadelphia (Cash Memoranda, 24 Mar.–25 Oct. 1774, CSmH). In Congress today the decision was made to keep secret the proceedings of the Congress (JCC, 1:25–26).

7.   Dined at Mr. Pleasants and spent the Evening in a Club at the New Tavern.

Mr. Pleasants is probably Samuel Pleasants, a Philadelphia Quaker, who was married to Mary (Polly) Pemberton, a member of another prominent Quaker family.

Most of the work of Congress during the next two weeks was done in two committees appointed this day, to neither of which GW was appointed (JCC, 1:26–27). Much of his time was spent becoming acquainted with delegates from the various colonies and exchanging views on important questions of the day.

8.   Dined at Mr. Andw. Allan's & spent the Evening in my own Lodgings.

Andrew Allen (1740–1825), a son of William Allen, chief justice of Pennsylvania until 1774, and Margaret Hamilton Allen, graduated from the College of Philadelphia and studied law in England as well as Philadelphia. He was at this time an influential Patriot active in opposing British policies. Allen was attorney general of Pennsylvania, a member of the provincial council, and in November of this year became one of the founders of the First Troop of Philadelphia City Cavalry. In 1775 he was elected to the Continental Congress. However, after the move toward independence seemed inevitable he resigned from Congress and fled behind British lines. Much of his property was confiscated and sold, and he spent most of his remaining years in England (KEITH [2], 361–65).

MY OWN LODGINGS: The location of GW's lodgings during his attendance at the First Continental Congress is uncertain. A mutilated entry in his cash memoranda book for 24 Oct., two days before he left Philadelphia, shows a payment of £34 2s. 6d. "at Carsons" (CSmH). The size of this expenditure would be commensurate with the cost of lodgings for himself and his servant, William, during his stay in the city. William Carson (b. 1728), an Irish immigrant, at this time ran a tavern called the Harp and Crown, on North Third Street just below Arch Street (DORLAND, 363).

9.   Dined at Mr. Tilghman's & spent the Evening at home (at my Lodgg.).

James Tilghman, Sr. (1716–1793), originally of Maryland, had moved to Philadelphia in 1765 and married Anna Francis, daughter of Tench Francis. He was a member of the provincial council and secretary of the proprietary land office. In May 1774 he had been sent to Williamsburg with James Allen to consult with Governor Dunmore about the Pennsylvania-Virginia boundary dispute, and GW probably had seen the two men there during the meeting of the House of Burgesses. Tilghman was a moderate and tried to preserve his neutrality during the Revolution. His son Tench was one of GW's most trusted friends and aides and another son, James Tilghman, Jr., of Alexandria, appears frequently at Mount Vernon (HANSON, 255; SCHARF [1], 2:1508).

10. Dined at Mr. Richd. Penn's.

Richard Penn was the former governor who had been superseded by his brother John (see main entry for 16 May 1773).

11. Dined at Mr. Griffen's.

GW visited a man named Samuel Griffin in Philadelphia several times in 1775. This may be Samuel Griffin of Williamsburg (1746–1810), a lawyer who was appointed aide-de-camp to Gen. Charles Lee in 1775. He later became deputy adjutant general of the Flying Camp and a member of the Virginia Board of War. After the Revolution, Griffin served in the Virginia House of Delegates 1787–88 and the United States House of Representatives 1789–95.

12. Dined at Mr. James Allan's.

James Allen (c.1742–1778), son of William and Margaret Hamilton Allen, was a lawyer and a member of the common council of Philadelphia. In May 1776 he was elected to the Pennsylvania assembly from Northampton, where his country seat, Trout Hall (near Allentown, Pa.), was located. Although a Patriot at this time, he, like his father and brothers, could not accept the Declaration of Independence and in the late summer of 1776 left the assembly to retire to Trout Hall (ALLEN, 176–77, 188–91).

13. Dined at Mr. Thos. Mifflins.

Thomas Mifflin (1744–1800), a Philadelphia merchant, was at this time a member of the provincial assembly and of the First Continental Congress. In June 1775 he was chosen GW's first aide-de-camp and later served as a general, quartermaster general, member of the Board of War, and president of the Continental Congress. After the Revolution, Mifflin was president of Pennsylvania and later governor.

14. Rid over the Provence Island, & dind at Mr. Wm. Hamiltons.

Province Island was a low island of 342 acres near the mouth of the Schuylkill River. On it the province of Pennsylvania had erected a "pest house" for the quarantine of sick immigrants and rented a portion of it for truck farms.

William Hamilton (1745–1813), son of Andrew Hamilton the younger, owned Woodlands, an estate on the Schuylkill River three miles from Philadelphia. Although he supported the colonists in their dispute with Britain, he disapproved of the Declaration of Independence. Hamilton was greatly

Thomas Mifflin, as portrayed by Charles Willson Peale. (Independence National Historical Park Collection)

interested in horticulture and after the Revolution introduced from England many specimens of plants and flowers (WARD [1], 160–62; BLACK [1], 1:242).

15. Dined at my Lodgings.

16. Dined at the State House at an Entertainment given by the City to the Members of the Congress.

The State House, later called Independence Hall, was to become the meeting place for the Second Continental Congress in 1775. "On Friday last the Honourable Delegates, now met in General Congress, were elegantly entertained by the gentlemen of this city. Having met at the City Tavern about 3 o'clock, they were conducted from thence to the State House by the Managers of the entertainment, where they were received by a very large company composed of the Clergy, such genteel strangers as happened to be in town, and a number of respectable citizens, making in the whole near 500. After dinner . . . toasts were drunk, accompanied by musick and a discharge of cannon" (*Pa. Packet,* 19 Sept. 1774).

17. Dined at Mr. Dickensons about 2 Miles from Town.

John Dickinson (1732–1808) was a representative to the Continental Congress from Pennsylvania. He had gained fame by his "Letters from a Farmer in Pennsylvania" and had drafted the petition to the king from the Pennsylvania legislature in 1771. During the First Continental Congress, Dickinson drew up Congress's petition to the king and was on the committee that prepared an address to the people of Canada. Dickinson lived at Fair Hill, north of Philadelphia on the Germantown Road.

18. Dined at Mr. Hills about 6 Miles from Town.

Henry Hill (1732–1798), son of Richard Hill of Maryland, was a Philadelphia merchant engaged largely in the Madeira wine trade. He became a member of the Pennsylvania Constitutional Convention of July 1776 and in 1780 subscribed £5,000 for relief of the Continental Army. Hill's home was on the Germantown Road near the Schuylkill Falls. GW had met Hill in 1773 when he atended the meeting of the Jockey Club in Philadelphia with Jacky Custis (JACKSON, facing p. 118).

19.   Rid out in the Morning. Dined at Mr. Ross's.

Mr. Ross is either George Ross (1730–1779), a Pennsylvania delegate to the Continental Congress 1774–77 and member of the colonial legislature, or John Ross (c.1725–1800), a Scottish-born Philadelphia merchant who was active in the cause of the colonies before and during the Revolution.

20.   Dined with Mr. Fisher the Mayor.

William Fisher, a Quaker merchant, was mayor of Philadelphia 1773–74. He had been a member of the common council of Philadelphia 1767–70 and of the board of aldermen 1770–76 (LOYALIST, 105, n.1).

21.   Dined with Mr. James Mease.

22.   Dined with Mr. Chew the Chief Justice.

Benjamin Chew (1722–1810), son of Dr. Samuel Chew (1693–1743) and Mary Galloway Chew of Maryland, moved from Delaware to Philadelphia c. 1754. He held a number of posts in the provincial government, including attorney general from 1755–69, member of the council from 1755 to the Revolution, and Speaker of the assembly of the Lower Counties in 1756. In 1774 he replaced William Allen as chief justice of Pennsylvania. He remained a moderate Loyalist during the Revolution but retained GW's friendship. In 1791 he became president of the High Court of Errors and Appeals in Pennsylvania. Chew lived on South Third Street between Walnut and Spruce.

23.   Dined with Mr. Joseph Pemberton.

Joseph Pemberton, son of Israel Pemberton, Jr., was a member of a prominent Philadelphia Quaker family. He was married in 1767 to Ann Galloway of Maryland.

24.   Dined with Mr. Thos. Willing and Spent the Eveng. at the City Tavern.

Thomas Willing (1731–1821), merchant, was a partner of Robert Morris in the Philadelphia firm of Willing, Morris & Co. He held a number of posts including that of commissioner for trade with the western Indians 1758; mayor of Philadelphia 1764; member of the provincial assembly 1767; justice of the Supreme Court of Pennsylvania 1767–77; and a member of the Continental Congress 1775–76. He refused to support the move for independence and remained neutral during the Revolution.

25.   Went to the Quaker meeting in the Forenoon & St. Peters in the Afternoon. Dind at my lodgings.

QUAKER MEETING: It cannot be determined which Quaker meetinghouse GW attended. According to Toner, it was probably the meetinghouse at Second and High streets (Toner Transcripts, DLC).

St. Peter's, an Anglican church located at Third and Pine streets, was completed in 1761. From 1762 to 1775 both St. Peter's and Christ churches, called the United Churches, were under the rectorship of Rev. Richard Peters.

26.   Dined at the old Doctr. Shippens & went to the Hospital.

William Shippen (1712–1801) was a Philadelphia physician and father of Dr. William Shippen, Jr. (1736–1808). He was one of the founders of the College of Philadelphia, a member of the American Philosophical Society, and a member of the Continental Congress 1778–80. Among the guests at Dr. Shippen's on this evening, in addition to GW and some of the other Virginia delegates, were Dr. William Shippen, Jr., Rev. and Mrs. Samuel Blair, John Adams, and the New Jersey delegates (ADAMS [1], 2:137).

The Pennsylvania Hospital, the first of any importance in the colonies, was bounded by Eighth and Ninth and Spruce and Pine streets. It had been completed in 1756, partly by money voted by the assembly of Pennsylvania and partly by subscription. According to John Adams, on this visit to the hospital young Dr. Shippen gave him, GW, and the other guests a lecture on anatomy. John Adams had also visited the hospital earlier with young Dr. Shippen: "We saw in the lower Rooms under Ground, the Cells of the Lunaticks, a Number of them, some furious, some merry, some Melancholly. . . . We then went into the Sick Rooms which are very long, large Walks with rows of Beds on each side, and the lame and sick upon them—a dreadfull Scene of human Wretchedness" (ADAMS [1], 2:116).

27.   Dined at the Tavern with the Virga. Gentn. &ca.

VIRGA. GENTN: the Virginia delegates.

28.   Dined at Mr. Edward Shippens. Spent the afternn. with the Boston Gentn.

Edward Shippen, Jr. (1729–1806), the son of Edward Shippen of Lancaster, Pa., was a lawyer in Philadelphia and at this time was prothonotary of the Pennsylvania Supreme Court, a member of the provincial council, and judge of the court of vice admiralty. Although a moderate Loyalist in the Revolution, he became chief justice of Pennsylvania in 1791. He was married to Margaret Francis, daughter of Tench Francis of Philadelphia.

The Boston gentlemen were the Massachusetts delegates to the Congress: Thomas Cushing, Samuel Adams, John Adams, and Robert Treat Paine, all from Boston. Richard Henry Lee and young Dr. Shippen were also present. John Adams made this entry in his diary: "Spent the Evening at Home, with Coll. Lee, Coll. Washington and Dr. Shippen who came in to consult with us" (ADAMS [1], 2:140).

29. Dined at Mr. Allan's and went to the Ball in the aftern.

30. Dined at Doctr. Cadwalladers.

Dr. Thomas Cadwalader (c.1708–1799) was one of the founders of the Pennsylvania Hospital, a vice-president of the American Philosophical Society, and a member of the provincial council from 1755 until the Revolution.

An Acct. of the Weather in Septr.

Sepr. 1. Exceeding Hot, with but little wind from the Southward. In the Night Rain (where I was).

2. Again very warm with but little wind & that Southerly. In the Night Rain.

3. Cloudy & Cool, Wind fresh from the Northward.

4. Again Cloudy & Cool. Wind about No. East & fresh.

5. Cloudy all day & now and then Misting. Wind at No. Et.

6. Clear & pleasant with but little Wind.

7. Clear and Warm with but little Wind & that Southerly.

8. Again Warm & clear, wind in the same place.

9. Warm & close, Weather lowering, & in the Afternoon Rain, tho little of it.

10. Clear & cool, Wind Westwardly & tolerably fresh.

11. Pleasant, but growing warmer, there being but little Wind.

12. Warmer than yesterday and clear.

13th. Lowering most part of the day—with a little Rain in the Evening.

14. Wind a little fresh from the Northward & day clear & somewhat Cooler.

15. A little lowering & dull in the forenoon—but cool.

16. Rather warm being clear with little Wind.

17. Warm & clear with but little Wind & that Southerly.

18. Warm in the forenoon with a brisk Southwest Wind. In the Afternoon Rain.

19. Pleasant, and clear with but little Wind.

20. Very pleasant and clear as also a little Cool.

21. Much such a day as yesterday.

22. Ditto. Ditto.

23. Clear but Pleast. and Cool. Wind Northerly.

24. Clear and pleasant but somewhat cool. Wind in the same Quarter.

25. Very pleasant and somewhat [warmer], there being no Wind.

26. Clear and pleasant but rather warm there being no wind.

27. Again clear and warm with but little or no wind.

28. Very warm. Foggy in the Morning but clear afterd.

29. Very warm again, being clear with no Wind.

30. Still warm with some appearances of Rain.

[October]

Where, how, or with whom my time is Spent

Octr. 1st.   At the Congress till 3 Ocl. Din'd with Mr. Hamilton at Bush Hill.

Christ Church in Philadelphia, where Washington attended a service. *Columbian Magazine*, Nov. 1787. (New-York Historical Society)

James Hamilton (c.1710–1783) of Bush Hill, north of Philadelphia, was the son of Andrew Hamilton (d. 1741) and Anne Brown Preeson Hamilton. He had held various public positions including those of mayor of Philadelphia, member of the provincial council, lieutenant governor of Pennsylvania, and acting governor of the colony in 1771 and 1773. Hamilton was arrested as a Tory during the Revolution.

2. Went to Christ Church & dined at the New Tavern.

Christ Church, the oldest Anglican church in Philadelphia, was located on the corner of Second and Market streets. On this day, one of the assistant rectors, Rev. Thomas Coombe, preached upon "Judge not according to the Appearance, but judge righteous Judgment" (ADAMS [1], 2:146).

3. At Congress till 3 Oclock. Dined at Mr. Reed's.

Joseph Reed (1741–1785), a lawyer in Philadelphia, had been educated at the Middle Temple. In 1773–75 he carried on an extensive correspondence with the British secretary of state for colonial affairs, Lord Dartmouth, attempting to acquaint him with conditions and attitudes in the colonies and to warn him against instituting oppressive measures in dealing with America. In Nov. 1774 Reed was appointed to the committee of correspondence in Philadelphia, and in 1775 he became president of the provincial congress and a lieutenant colonel in the Pennsylvania militia. In June of that year GW appointed him his first military secretary. Reed became adjutant general of the Continental Army in 1776, a delegate to the Continental Congress 1777–78, and president of Pennsylvania 1778–81.

4. At Congress till 3 Oclock. Dined at young Doctr. Shippens.

5. At Congress as above, Dined at Doctr. Bonds.

Dr. Thomas Bond (1712–1784), physician and surgeon, was a native of Maryland who began practicing medicine in Philadelphia around 1734. He was influential in the establishment of the Pennsylvania Hospital and was a member of the staff until his death.

6. At Congress. Din'd at Mr. Saml. Meridith's.

7. At Congress. Dined at Mr. Thos. Smiths.

Thomas Smith (1745–1809) was deputy surveyor of the frontier area around Bedford, Pa., in 1769. After the formation of Bedford County in 1771, he held the offices of prothonotary, recorder of deeds, and clerk of the sessions and orphans courts. Smith later became colonel of the 2d Battalion of Bedford County Associators and a member of the Pennsylvania legislature 1776–80. He served in the Continental Congress 1780–82 and in 1794 was appointed to the Pennsylvania Supreme Court.

8. At Congress. Dined with Mr. John Cadwallader.

9.   Went to the Presbeterian Meeting in the forenoon and Romish Church in the Afternoon. Dind at Bevans's.

PRESBETERIAN MEETING: Which Presbyterian church GW attended is un-known, although prevailing opinion favors the Presbyterian meetinghouse at Third and Arch streets. However, GW may have been with John Adams, who on this day attended the Presbyterian meetinghouse on Market Street between Second and Third streets and heard Dr. Francis Alison or Allison (1705–1779) deliver a sermon on the Lord's Supper (ADAMS [1], 2:149).

The Catholic church which GW attended was St. Mary's, built in 1763 and located at Fourth and Spruce streets.

10.   At Congress. Din'd at Doctr. Morgan's.

John Morgan (1735–1789), a graduate of Edinburgh, had also studied medi-cine and anatomy in England, France, and Italy. In 1765, shortly after his return to Philadelphia, Morgan was responsible for founding at the College of Philadelphia the first medical school in the American colonies. At the outbreak of the Revolution he aligned himself with the Patriots, and in Oct. 1775 he was appointed director general of hospitals and physician-in-chief of the Continental Army. Feuds and jealousies caused Morgan's removal from office in 1777.

11.   Din'd at my Lodgings & Spent the Evening at Bevan's.

12.   At Congress all the forenoon. Dined at Mr. Josh. Whartons & went to the Govrs. Club.

JOSH. WHARTONS: This man is more likely to be Joseph Wharton, Jr. (1734–1816), a merchant of Philadelphia, than his father, Joseph Wharton (1707–1776), who was living in retirement outside Philadelphia at his country place, Walnut Grove.

GOVRS. CLUB: An earlier visitor to Philadelphia described the Governor's Club as "a Select Number of Gentlemen that meet every Night at a certain Tavern, where they pass away a few Hours in the Pleasures of Conversation and a Cheerful Glass" (SCHARF [1], 1:235). The club at this time probably met at Peggy Mullen's Beefsteak House on Water Street at the corner of Tun Alley (JACKSON, 122).

13.   Dined at my lodgings–after being at Congress till 4 Oclk.

This long day in Congress was caused by an extended debate "about the Parliamentary Power of regulating Trade. 5 Colonies were for allowing it, 5. against it, and two divided among themselves, i.e., Mass. and Rhode Is-land" (ADAMS [1], 2:151).

14.   Dined at Mr. Thos. Barclay's and Spent the Evening at Smiths.

Thomas Barclay (1728–1793) was a partner in the Philadelphia mercantile house of Carson, Barclay & Mitchell and was a member of the Philadelphia committee of correspondence. He was appointed to the state navy board in 1777 and in 1780 subscribed £5,000 for supplies for the Continental Army. Barclay was appointed consul in France in 1781. SMITHS: the City Tavern, run by Daniel Smith. GW's cash memoranda book for this date lists "club at Smiths—.6.3" (CSmH). GW clubbed frequently at Smith's as well as at other taverns during his stay in Philadelphia.

15. Dined at Bevans's. Spent the Evening at home.

On this day GW gave £1 14s. to his old Indian acquaintance Guyasuta, who was on a mission from the tribes in the Illinois and Ohio country to Guy Johnson, superintendent of Indian affairs for the Northern Department (GW's Cash Memoranda, 25 Mar.–25 Oct. 1774, CSmH; WHARTON LETTER BOOKS, 450).

16. Went to Christ Church in the forenoon. After which rid to, & dind in the Provence Island. Suppd at Byrns's.

17. After Congress dind on board Captn. Hamilton. Spent the Evening at Mr. Miflins.

Although Hamilton has been identified elsewhere as Capt. W. Hamilton of the ship *Union* (DIARIES, 2:168n), that vessel had cleared the port of Philadelphia before 3 Oct. (*Pa. Packet,* 3 Oct. 1774).

18. Dined at Doctr. Rush's and Spent the Evening at the New Tavern.

Benjamin Rush (1745–1813), the best-known American physician and medical writer of his day, was a professor of chemistry at the College of Phila-

Benjamin Rush, by Charles Willson Peale after a painting by Thomas Sully. (Independence National Historical Park Collection)

delphia and a member of the American Philosophical Society. Rush was elected to the Continental Congress in 1776. In April 1777 he became surgeon general of the hospital for the Middle Department and, in July, physician general for the same department.

19.   Dined at Mr. Willings & Spent the Evening at my own lodgings.

20.   Dind at the New Tavern with the Pensa. Assembly. Went to the Ball afterwards.

DIND AT THE NEW TAVERN: "On Thursday last an elegant entertainment was given at the City Tavern, by the Assembly of this province, to the Gentlemen of the Congress" (*Pa. Packet,* 24 Oct. 1774). GW's cash memoranda book shows a payment of 7s. for the ball ticket and a 1s. offering to Christ Church (CSmH).

21.   Dined at my lodging & Spent the Evening there also.

22.   Dined at Mr. Griffins & drank Tea with Mrs. Roberdeau.

Mary Bostwick Roberdeau (d. 1777), daughter of Rev. David Bostwick of New York, was the wife of Daniel Roberdeau, a Philadelphia merchant and Patriot.

23.   Dined at my lodgings and spent the Evening there.

24.   Dined with Mr. Mease & Spent the Evening at the New Tavern.

25.   Dined at my lodgings.

26.   Dined at Bevans's, and Spent the Evening at the New Tavern.

After approving an address to be printed for distribution among the inhabitants of Quebec, the First Continental Congress adjourned (JCC, 1:113–14). GW and Richard Henry Lee were the only members of the Virginia delegation still remaining in Philadelphia at the time of the adjournment. The other Virginia delegates had left on 23 Oct. for Virginia, where the House of Burgesses was due to meet on the first Thursday in November.

27.   Set out on my return home. Dined at Chester and lodged at Newcastle.

28.   Breakfasted at the Buck Tavern. Dined at Downs's & lodged at New town upon Chester.

29.   Breakfasted at Rockhall & reachd Annapolis in the Afternoon.

30.   Breakfasted at Mr. Calverts & reachd home abt. 3 Oclock.

31.   At home all day.

Acct. of the Weather in October

Octr. 1st.   Very warm & lowering all day. In the Evening much Rain fell.

2.   Lowering but much Cooler. Wind at West.

3.   Cool. Wind fresh from the No. West.

4.   Cool, but not quite so much so as yesterday.

5.   Warm without wind & being clear at the same time.

6.   Little or no Wind. Clear & Warm.

7.   Again warm—wind notwithstanding Easterly.

8.   Warm, but somewhat lowering.

9.   Rather warm in the forenoon with appearances of Rain abt. 2 Oclock but none fell. However it turnd Cool.

10.   Much Cooler than Yesterday. Wind Northerly.

11.   Still cool, but pleasant notwithstanding.

12.   Rather warm being clear with but little Wind.

13.   Much such a day as yesterday.

14.   Thick & close Morning with Appearances of Rain. Very warm afternoon.

15.   Clear with very little wind & warm.

16. Lowering forenoon but no Rain. Wind fresh from the Southwest.

17. Somewhat Cool especially towards the Evening Wind being westerly.

18. Pretty cool—a large white Frost.

19. Again cool & somewhat lowering.

20. Warm, & lowering, but no rain fell.

21. Warm and still lowering but no Rain.

22. Very foggy & lowering Morning but clear and warm afterwards. In the Evening Rain.

23d. Foggy Morning but clear and warm afterwds.

24. Foggy again in the forenoon, but clear afterwds. & Warm.

25. Again foggy in the forenoon but clear and warm afterwards.

26. Foggy & misting all the forenoon. In the Evening Rain.

27. Much such a day as yesterday.

28. Showery through the day. Wind Easterly.

29. Clear and cool. Wind Westerly & fresh in the forenoon but less of it afterwds.

30. Clear and pleasant. Wind westerly.

31. Much such a day as the preeceding one.

[November]

Where, how, or with whom my time is, Spent

Novr. 1. At home all day. Mr. Ramsay, Mr. Muir, Mr. Rob. Harrison & Doctr. Rumney came here to Dinner & stayed all Night.

2. The Gentlemen went away after Breakfast. I rid to the Mill. Mr. Ben. Dulany & Wife came here to Dinner & stayd all Night as did Mr. R. Thompson.

Richard Thompson was living on the Maryland side of the Great Falls of the Potomac, where he was trying to establish a business in the manufacturing and sale of smoking tobacco, chewing tobacco, and snuff. In 1774 he was appointed to be the clerk for the trustees for Potomac navigation (*Va. Gaz.*, R, 8 Oct. 1772; *Va. Gaz.*, D, 7 Jan. 1775).

3. I went up to Alexandria after the Company abovementioned Went away. Returnd in the Aftern.

4. At home all day alone.

5. Ditto. Mr. Piercy a Presbeterian Minister dined here.

Mr. Piercy was probably William Piercy (Percy), a Calvinistic Methodist and disciple of George Whitefield. Piercy was chaplain to Selina Hastings, countess of Huntingdon, a devoted follower of the new Methodist movement. In order to give protection to Methodist preachers, she appointed large members of them to the nominal position of chaplain in her household. She had sent Piercy from London to Georgia in 1772 to act as president of Whitefield's Orphan House, or college, at Bethesda, near Savannah, and to preach wherever he could collect an audience in the colonies. Piercy had preached at various locations in Philadelphia during the year. He had given a farewell sermon in late October at the Arch Street Presbyterian meeting-house, and was probably at this time on his return to his headquarters in Georgia (KNIGHT, 213; HILTZHEIMER, 30–32; SPRAGUE, 5:293–96).

6. Went to Pohick Church. Mr. Triplet & Mr. Peake & Daughter dined here.

Probably Humphrey Peake's younger daughter, Elizabeth, still a minor in 1774. GW commonly referred to a child of a friend as a "son" or "daughter" while still a minor and as a "Mr." or "Miss" after the age of about 16. Thus Humphrey Peake's elder daughter, Ann (Nancy), would be a "Miss" by this time.

7. Mr. Martin Cockburn & Mr. Geo. Mason Junr. dined here.

George Mason, Jr. (1753–1796), was the eldest son of George and Ann Eilbeck Mason of Gunston Hall. He married Elizabeth Mary Ann Barnes Hooe and settled at Lexington in Mason's Neck.

8. At home all day alone.

9. At home all day.

10.	At home all day. Doctr. Craik came here in the Evening and stayed all Night.

11.	At home all day. Mr. Bryan Fairfax came here & stayed all Night.

12.	I went up to George Town To an intended meeting of Trustees for openg. Potomack River. None Met. Returnd home at Night.

After inspecting canal works in England, John Ballendine had returned to the Potomac valley in the late summer of 1774 with a plan for opening navigation of the Potomac River "at and above the Lower Falls" to boats that could carry wheat and iron downriver to the ports of Georgetown and Alexandria (*Md. Gaz.*, 8 Sept. 1774). At a meeting held in the early fall, probably at Georgetown, 37 trustees were chosen from the subscribers to Ballendine's project, among whom was GW. Today's meeting was scheduled to choose an executive committee of 10 trustees, but because the notice for the meeting did not appear in the *Maryland Gazette* until 10 Nov. 1774, there probably was not a quorum present.

13.	Went up to Alexandria Church. In the Evening Colo. Blackburn Mr. Lee, & Mr. Richd. Graham came here as a Committee from the Prince Wm. Independ. Compy.

Mr. Lee was Philip Richard Francis Lee (died c.1834), son of Squire Richard Lee of Blenheim, Charles County, Md. Philip Richard, a merchant in Dumfries, was a captain in the Prince William Independent Company, which was absorbed into the 3d Virginia Regiment early in 1776 (vsp, 8:216; LEE [1], 347).
	PRINCE WM. INDEPEND. COMPY.: On 21 Sept. 1774 a meeting of local men in Alexandria formed an agreement to organize the Fairfax Independent Company of Volunteers, which was probably the first "Independent Company" so organized in a Virginia county (MASON [2], 1:210–11). On 11 Nov. 1774 the Independent Company of Cadets of Prince William County appointed the three men who appeared here today as a delegation to "wait upon Collonel George Washington, and request of him to take the command of this Company as their Field Officer, and that he will be pleas'd to direct the fashion of their uniform," which request GW accepted (HAMILTON [1], 5:68–69). By the late spring of 1775 GW had also accepted the commands of the independent companies of Fairfax, Fauquier, Richmond, and Spotsylvania counties (photostat, Vi). In contemporary military terminology an independent company was a company unattached to any regiment. These independent companies were also independent of the militia system, and were usually founded independently of the county committees of inspection, although some men were members of both organizations.

14.	At home all day. Those Gentn. Went away after Dinnr.

15.	At home all day alone.

16. Ditto. Ditto.

17. At home. Mr. Francis Willis Junr. dined here, & went to B[elvoir].

18. Captn. Dalton dined here and went away afterwards.

19. At home all day.

20. Set out for Wests Ordinary in order to attend Colo. Mercers Sale of the Bull run Land. Dined at New Gate & lodged at Colo. Fras. Peytons.

GW did more than "attend" the sale; he was in charge of the auctions to settle the estate of James Mercer's late father, John. Francis Peyton, son of Valentine Peyton, was a justice and burgess for Loudoun County. Peyton accompanied GW to the sale the next day (GW to John Tayloe, 11 Dec. 1775, WRITINGS, 37:515).

21st. Attended at Wests Ordy. with Mr. James Mercer & sold all the Bull run Lands. Returnd to Colo. Peytons.

GW found his role in the auctioning of the Mercer land, which had "a good deal of exceeding poor and broken ground in it," to be a frustrating experience. As the auction proceeded, he saw he was not getting prices anywhere near the original estate inventory valuation made in 1767. "But," he reported to his fellow executor, John Tayloe, "there was no help for it; everything that could be done, was done, to dispose of it to the best advantage; in attempting which, I had three Lots of the Land (by endeavouring to raise [the price of] them) left upon my hands" (30 Nov. 1774, WRITINGS, 37:508).

22. At Colo. Peytons all day taking Bonds & making Conveyances.

23. Set out for Frederick, in order to sell Colo. Mercers Estate in that County. Dind at Morgan Alexanders Ordy. & lodged at Colo. Warner Washington's.

Morgan Alexander (1746–1783), originally of Gloucester County, moved to the Shenandoah Valley in the late 1760s and married Sarah Snickers (b. 1756). As she was a daughter of Edward Snickers, whose home and ordinary, in Frederick (now in Clarke) County, were on the Shenandoah River near the gap in the Blue Ridge that bore his name, Alexander may have been running the ordinary for Snickers at this time.

Warner Washington's home was Fairfield in Frederick County, a few miles north of the present town of Berryville (WAYLAND [1], 171–73).

24. Went to the Sale, which began at the Middle Plantation, at Willm. Dawson's, the Head Overseers. Lodged there.

Having held the land sale at a spot convenient to buyers from both sides of the Blue Ridge Mountains, GW was now auctioning off the slaves, stock, and tools which were gathered together at the main Mercer plantation for examination by the bidders. GW was disturbed at finding "only 90 instead of 110 Negroes, and a proportionate difficency of Horses and stock; and few or no Plantation utensils" (GW to John Tayloe, 30 Nov. 1774, WRITINGS, 37:508).

25. Sale continued at the same place where I again lodged.

In the margin of his Virginia almanac for this month, GW, apparently as a reminder, noted for 21 Nov. "Mercer's sale at Wests" and for 24 Nov. "do. at Snicker's," but the latter sale seems to have been held at Dawson's. Edward Snickers had a home where the road from Snickers's ferry to Winchester crossed Buck Marsh Run, about three miles due south of Warner Washington's home, Fairfield (CHAPPELEAR [1], 37).

26. Sale again—remained there.

27. Still continued to sell at the same place where I again lodged.

28th. Dined at Mr. Booths and returned to my Lodgings at Dawson's.

As no sales were held on Sunday, GW went to visit an old friend from the Nomini region of Westmoreland County, William Booth, who had recently settled on upper Buck Marsh Run, about two miles southwest of Fairfield.

29th. Continued the Sale at Dawson's & finishd at that Plantation.

GW was becoming increasingly suspicious about his host's honesty regarding the estate. His suspicions were confirmed when he was later told by Edward Snickers that Dawson had been selling off timber and stock at reduced prices; this, GW thought, would "account for the deficiency we found in the Articles of Horses & Stock" (GW to James Mercer, 12 Dec. 1774, DLC:GW).

30. Concluded the whole Sales at all the Plantations & went to, and dined at Alexanders where I also lodged.

Acct. of the Weather in Novr.

Novr. 1st. Clear & pleasant, but somewhat Cool till Eveng. then Rain.

2. Again cool & somewhat lowering.

3. Clear & pleasant but little Wind.

4. Cool but clear with but little Wind.

5. Very pleasant with but little [wind].

6. Clear & pleasant in the forenoon but lowering & cold in the Afternoon. Wind Easterly.

7. Lowering and cold.

8. Tolerably pleasant not being so cool.

9. Cold Wind hard at West or No. West all day.

10. Clear, & not quite so cold notwithstanding the Wind kept in the same place but not quite so hard.

11. Clear, warm and pleasant with but little Wind and that Southerly.

12. Exceeding pleasant, being clear and without wind.

13. Clear and pleasant being quite warm.

14. Warm and pleasant with but little Wind. Lowering in the Evening.

15. A little Rain in the Night & lowering in the forenoon. Clear afterwards.

16. Rain in the Night & this Morning. Clear afterwards & windy from the No. West. Cold.

17. Clear with not much Wind & that Southerly.

18. Hard Wind all day from the No. West and very cold. Weather clear.

19. Clear and Cold. Wind hard at No. West all day.

20.   Not so cold as the two preceeding days wind not being so fresh—but in the same place.

21.   Snowing and raining all day and the greatest part of the Night. Wind at No. Et. & fresh.

22.   Flying Clouds, & Wind fresh from the Northwest but not very cold.

23.   Wind in the same Quarter but more moderate & not cold.

24.   Southerly Wind, after a very white frost & Cloudy.

25.   Raining more or less till abt. one Oclock—then clear.

26.   Clear and pleasant, with but very little Wind.

27.   Pleasant day, being clear with little or no Wind.

28.   Very pleasant after a very white frost. Southerly wind & Warm.

29.   Another very white frost. Wind fresh from the Southward. Rain at & all Night.

30.   It Continued Raining on & off till Noon then a close & Wet Snow till Night.

[December]

Where, how, or with whom my time is spent

Decr. 1st.   At Alexanders till 12 oclock taking Bonds &ca. then set of for, & lodged at Leesburg.

2.   Breakfasted at Moss's and dined at home.

3.   At home all day alone.

4.   At home all day. Mr. Willis and a Mr. Harrison dind here & Parson Morton lodged here.

Andrew Morton, or Moreton (died c.1776), was minister of Drysdale Parish in King and Queen County and Caroline County in 1774 (*WMQ,* 5 [1896–97], 202). He was at Mount Vernon to try to lease Belvoir from GW, who was acting as George William Fairfax's agent. GW refused a seven-year lease on the house without a bond for payment of the rent; but Morton arrived at Belvoir before Feb. 1775, with the bond unexecuted, and seems to have persuaded GW to let him live there for a year without a lease (GW to Morton, 21 Dec. 1774, CtY; Morton to GW, 1 Feb. 1775, ViMtV). He died some time before Sept. 1775, while still living at Belvoir (Fairfax County Will Book, D-1, 94–95).

5.   Went to Colo. Fairfax's Sale at Belvoir. Returnd in the Evening alone.

A second sale at Belvoir was advertised for this day. It consisted of two rooms of household furniture, kitchen furniture, cattle, plantation utensils, etc. The mansion house and land were also again advertised for lease on this date, as was a small plantation and two fisheries (*Va. Gaz.,* P&D, 20 Oct. 1774).

6.   At home all day alone.

7.   Rid to the Mill, Morris's & Muddy hole. In the Afternoon Mr. & Mrs. Calvert came.

8.   At home all day with the above Company. Mr. Willis lodged here.

9.   At home all day. The foregoing Company continuing.

10.   Mr. & Mrs. Calvert—together with Mr. & Mrs. Custis went to Maryland. Mr. Willis continued.

11th.   At home all day. Mr. Willis went to Alexandria after breakfast.

12.   At home all day alone.

13.   At home. Doctr. Craik and Miss Nancy McCarty came here in the Evening.

14.   I went up to Alexandria, to an intended meeting of the Committee but was disappointed. Found Doctr. Craik & Mr. Willis here upon my return.

15.   At home all day.

16.   Ditto—Do. Mr. Willis went away.

In GW's ledger under date of 17 Dec. is a payment to Mr. Willis of £47
10s. for 200 barrels of wheat. He received from Willis at the same time £9
4s. 9d. "for Sundrys sold at Belvoir for Cash" (LEDGER B, 128).

17.   Early this Morning my Brother and Mr. Phil Smith came
here—as did Mr. Booth.

MY BROTHER: John Augustine Washington, whose wife's sister, Elizabeth
Bushrod, married Philip Smith (d. 1782), of Washington Parish, Westmoreland County.

18.   At home all day.

19.   Went with Mrs. Washington my Brother & Mr. Smith to
Alexandria and stayed all Night. Mr. Booth went to Mary[lan]d.

GW went to town on committee business: "at a meeting of the committee
for Fairfax County, in the town of Alexandria, on Monday the 19th day of
December, 1774, Messieurs [John] Fitzgerald and [Valentine] Peers, informed
the committee that the ship Hope . . . had arrived in this colony . . . from
Belfast, with sundry packages of Irish linen, amounting . . . to £1101 4s. 8d.
sterling, their property, and requesting that the same should be sold, agreeable to the 10th article in the continental association . . . ordered, that the
said goods be sold by the package, to the highest bidder . . . and if any
profit shall arise from such sale, that [it be used] for relieving and employing
such of the poor inhabitants of the town of Boston as are sufferers by the
Boston port bill, subject to the direction of the committee for the said county
of Fairfax" (*Va. Gaz.*, Pi, 29 Dec. 1774).
   While in Alexandria, GW also met with several other trustees of John
Ballendine's Potomac navigation project and authorized Ballendine to hire
50 slaves as laborers (*Va. Gaz.*, D, 7 Jan. 1775).

20.   Returnd in the Afternoon. Found Mr. Booth & Captn. Chs.
Smith here.

21st.   At home all day with my Brothr. Jno. & Mr. Smith.

22.   In the Afternoon my Brother & Mr. Smith went away.

23.   Doctr. Rumney & Mr. Thos. Triplet dined here.

24.   At home all day. Mr. Richd. Washington came here to Dinner, as did Mrs. Newman.

Richard Washington, a London merchant to whom GW apparently believed
he was distantly related, had been a correspondent and tobacco dealer for
GW from 1755 to 1763. GW warmly assured him that "in the Event of your

ever visiting America . . . Mrs. Washington and I both woud think ourselves very happy in the oppertunity of shewing you the Virginia Hospitality
. . . and I must . . . add, that I shall think myself very happy in seeing
you at Mt. Vernon where you might depend upon finding the most cordial
entertainment" (27 Sept. 1763, 10 Aug. 1760, DLC:GW). The other guest was
possibly the Mrs. Newman who was employed by George Mason of Gunston
Hall as a schoolmistress for his daughters at this time (ROWLAND [2], 1:97).

25. At home all day with the above.

26. At home all day.

27. Ditto. Ditto. Colo. Carlyle & his Son George came here and
stayed all Night.

28. They went away again after Dinner and Mr. Robt. Graham
came and stayed all Night.

This was probably Robert Graham (1751–1821), son of John Graham of
Graham Park near Dumfries, Prince William County. Robert succeeded his
father as Prince William County clerk in 1777 (HAYDEN, 162–63).

29. Mr. Graham went away after breakfast. I contind. at home
all day.

30. At home all day. In the Afternoon Genl. Lee, & Mr. Jno.
Ballendine came here.

Charles Lee (1731–1782) was a veteran English soldier, who, having recently
embraced the American cause, was publicly defending the rights of the
colonists and encouraging them to believe that they could successfully fight
British or other professional troops if war came. A member of the English
gentry by birth, he had served with distinction during the Seven Years' War
in America and Portugal, but at the end of the war he had been retired on
half pay with the rank of major. His title of general derived from later
service under the king of Poland, who had commissioned him a major
general in his army in 1769. After returning to America in the fall of 1773,
Lee had traveled extensively, talking to many colonial leaders. At this time
he was on the way to Williamsburg, having come from Annapolis where,
according to his former army friend Josiah Martin, now royal governor of
North Carolina, he had been "employed in diciplining or rather drilling a
set of people to arms . . . and by the most extravagant discourse exciting
contempt of the Troops and power of Great Britain and of every character
and act related to Government sparing not the most sacred" (Martin to the
earl of Dartmouth, 10 Mar. 1775, N.C. COL. REC., 9:1155–59). GW had seen
Lee in Philadelphia while attending the First Continental Congress but may
have met him first during the Braddock expedition of 1755 in which both
men participated. Their conversation during Lee's stay at Mount Vernon
probably included a discussion of a plan that Lee had devised for organizing

A caricature of Major General Charles Lee. (Prints Division, New York Public Library)

American troops into battalions and may have touched on the subject of western lands, in which Lee was also much interested (ALDEN, chaps. 1–5).

31.   At home all day. In the Afternoon Doctr. Craik came.

Acct. of the Weather in Decr.

Decr. 1st.   Clear and pleasant, with but little Wind and that Southerly.

2.   Cool & frosty in the Morning but very pleasant afterwards with but little Wind & that South.

3.   Clear & calm in the forenoon but lowering afterwards. Wind blowing fresh from So. Wt.

4.   Lowering Morning but Warm. Clear afterwards. Wind still Southerly.

5.   Wind in the same place & Warm. Abt. Noon Cloudy with a few drops of Rain.

6.   Clear and very pleasant with little or no Wind & warm.

7.   Lowering all day with but little Wind. Warm.

8.   Much such a day as the preceeding one. In the Evening Rain which contd. all Night.

9.   Fine Rain all day, with but little Wind. Rather Raw & cool but not Cold.

10.   Clear after the Morning with the Wind fresh & cold from No. Wt.

11th.   Clear and very cold. Wind very fresh from the North West.

12.   Clear and Cold, wind continuing in the same place.

13.   More moderate, but Snowing fast all the forenoon.

14.   Clear and not unpleast. with but little Wind.

15.   Much such a day as yesterday.

16.   Very pleasant.

17.   Ditto.

18.   Warm and pleasant. Wind Southerly very little.

19.   Still Warm with Showers of Rain, & Wind fresh from the So. West. In the Afternn. it chang'd to No. Wt. & blew hard.

20.   Wind still at No. West but not very hard or Cold, clear.

21.   Calm all the forenoon and very warm and pleasant in the Afternoon. Wind at No. Et.

22.   Again calm & pleasant. Afternoon hazy & Wind Easterly.

23.   A little Snow in the forenoon. Wind continuing in the same place.

24.   Clear and pleasant. Wind Northerly.

25.   Remarkably pleasant Morning with little or no Wind. Afternoon hazy with a little Rain.

26.   Clear, and neither very cold, or unpleasant, although the Wind blew fresh from the No. West.

27.   Clear and pleasant forenoon. Cloudy afterwards with Snow in the Afternoon. Wind at No. East.

28.   Lowering, and Snowing now and then throughout the day. Wind abt. No. West but not very Cold.

29th.   Clear and tolerably moderate and pleasant notwithstanding the Wind was pretty fresh at So. Wt.

30.   Calm and exceeding pleasant—being clear in the forenoon. Somewhat lowering afterwards.

31.   Clear but pretty cool. Wind fresh from No. West.

A Call to Service

1775

[January]

Where, how, or with whom, my time is Spent.

Jan. 1st. At home all day. Doctr. Craik went away after Breakfast.

2. Genl. Lee and myself rid up to Alexandria & returnd in the Afternoon. Mr. Richd. Washington went away after Dinner.

3. At home all day.

4. Genl. Lee went away after Breakfast. A Mr. Tarrant Breakfasted & Dined here. And Mr. & Mrs. Custis, & Miss Calvert came here in the Afternoon.

Leonard Tarrant was visiting GW as a representative of the firm of Balfour & Barraud, of Hampton, seeking to obtain from GW "about a Thousand Barr[el]s flour & a few hundred Bar[rel]s of bread" (Balfour & Barraud to [GW], 25 Dec. 1774, DLC:GW). Tarrant got his contract.

GW today lent Charles Lee £15 cash, probably for traveling expenses to Williamsburg. According to a memorandum that GW wrote for Fielding Lewis on 30 April 1775, the debt was to be discharged by Col. William Byrd, with whom Lee supposedly left money for that purpose (PHi: Gratz Collection). Nevertheless, the £15, plus £9 12s. which GW lent Lee in June of this year, remained unpaid until four years after Lee's death, when the account was settled without interest by the executor of his estate (LEDGER B, 137).

5. At home all day.

6. Mr. George Digges & three of his Sisters—to wit Tracy; Nancy & Jenny, and Mr. Danl. Carroll & Nancy Peake came here & stayed all Night.

7. Mr. Digges & his Sisters and Mr. Carroll went away after Breakfast.

8. Miss Nancy Peake went away after Breakfast. Doctr. Rumney Dined and lodged here.

9th.   At home all day. Doctr. Rumney & Mrs. Newman went away after Breakfast.

10.   At home all day, Mr. Stone dined here.

11.   Again at home and alone.

12.   Went a Fox hunting—found but did not kill.

13.   At home all day alone.

14.   Ditto—Ditto.

15.   Went to Pohick Church & returnd to Dinner. Colo. Mason & Son, Mr. Dulany & Mr. Cockburn came home with me & stayed all Night.

16.   Went up to Alexandria to a review of the Independant Company & to choose a Com[mitt]ee for the County of Fairfax.

When first organized in Sept. 1774, the company agreed to limit its number to 100 men, to elect its own officers, to drill from time to time, and to supply its own ammunition. Each volunteer was to carry "a good Fire-lock and Bayonet, Sling Cartouch-Box, and Tomahawk" and to dress in "a regular Uniform of Blue, turn'd up with Buff" (MASON [2], 1:211).

Although most of the Virginia county committees that had been formed before the Continental Association transferred their authority to meet and act from the Virginia Association to the Continental Association in the fall of 1774, there was strong sentiment to hold new elections for county committees as called for by the 11th article of the Continental Association. Many counties simply reelected the old committees or changed them slightly; some other counties took advantage of these new elections to expand the membership of their committees.

17.   Under Arms this day also and in Committee in the Eveng.

Today the committee, chaired by GW, passed resolutions to assess 3s. for every tithable in the county to pay for powder, to keep a list "of such persons as shall refuse to pay the same," and to organize a countywide militia system of 68-man companies (MASON [2], 1:212–13).

18.   In Committee all day.

No contemporary reference has been found during the period covered by GW's diaries to any county committee in Virginia being called a committee of safety, each committee usually referring to itself merely as "the committee" for the county.

19.   Returnd home to Dinner alone.

20.   At home all day. Miss Calvert returnd home.

21.   Went a hunting with Mr. Custis. Killd a Dog Fox & returnd to Dinner.

22.   At home all day. Danl. Jenifer Adams came here abt. 11 Oclock, & went away. Price Posey came—Dined and stayd all Night.

Adams was still trying to settle his debts to GW growing out of his role in the 1772 voyage of the brig *Fairfax* to the West Indies (see main entry for 22 July 1772). GW was pressing "that worthless young Fellow" Adams for possession of about 550 acres of Adams family lands in Charles County, Md., which GW accepted later in the year as "all I am likely to get for my debt" (GW to Robert McMickan, 10 May 1774, DLC:GW; LEDGER B, 99; Daniel Jenifer Adams to GW, 4 Feb. 1775, DLC:GW; GW to Thomas Pollock, 29 Nov. 1773, DLC:GW).

23.   At home all day. Doctr. Rumney came here in the Afternoon.

24.   Doctr. Rumney visited the Sick—returnd to Dinner & stayed all Night. Mr. Alexr. Ross dind & went away after it.

25.   Doctr. Rumney visited the Sick & returnd to Dinner. I went a hunting. Found a fox but did not kill it.

26.   Went up to Alexandria to an intended meeting of the Trustees for opening the Rivr. Potomack. None met. Stayd in Alexandria all night & bo[ugh]t a parcel of Servants.

This meeting had been called to "form and digest proper Plans to be laid before the Assemblies of *Virginia* and *Maryland*" in the hope of raising capital for John Ballendine's Potomac navigation project (*Va. Gaz.*, D, 7 Jan. 1775).

27.   Went up to four Mile run to view the Land bought of Mr. Mercer. Lookd at part of it, & returnd home at Night.

Four Mile Run is a small stream, about eight or nine miles long, which flows into the Potomac approximately four miles north of Hunting Creek. The land GW bought from James and George Mercer consisted of two patents, one for 378 acres and the other for 790 acres. These lands were deeded to GW 12 Dec. 1774 and proved 15 Oct. 1775. GW paid £892 for the two tracts (STETSON [1], 39–60).

28.   At home all day alone.

29.   At home all day. Ditto. Mr. & Mrs. Custis went to Pohick
Church & from thence to Colo. Masons.

30.   Rid into the Neck to see the Sick People—came home by
Muddy hole. A Mr. Bruce dined here.

Normand Bruce (d. 1811), of Frederick County, Md., brought a letter of introduction from Thomas Johnson, who wrote: "his Drift is to persuade people in general to manufacture *coarse* Linnens in earnest, to shew that Hemp
is the proper material for us to rely on much in preference of Flax. . . . he
wishes for your Encouragement of a Work so well intended" (17 Jan. 1775,
DLC:GW).

31.   At home all day. Miss Dent & a daughter of Captn. Marshalls dind here.

The daughter of Capt. Thomas Hanson Marshall of Marshall Hall was Mary
Marshall (1767–1789). Miss Dent is probably Mary's aunt, Sarah Dent, a
sister of Mary's mother, Rebecca Dent Marshall, who died in 1770 (NEWMAN,
35).

Acct. of the Weather in January

Jan. 1.   Calm, clear, warm, & exceeding pleasant.

2.   Very pleasant again, with but little Wind, and that Southerly.

3.   Exceeding pleasant, being clear, warm, & Calm.

4.   Just such a day as yesterday.

5.   Very pleasant in the Morning, and calm. Towards Noon the
wind sprung up Northerly, but neither cold or hard.

6.   Calm & pleasant in the Morning, but Wind at No. Et. afterwards.

7.   Calm & clear Morning, but Wind from the No. West afterwards but neither hard or Cold.

8.   Clear & pleasant in the Morning but the Wind coming out
fresh from the No. Wt. it turnd Cool.

9th.   Clear & pleasant though a hard frost in the Morning being calm. Wind Southerly afterwards & a little lowering.

10.   Calm & clear in the forepart of the day—hard frost. Wind Southerly in the Afternoon & somewhat lowering again.

11.   Clear all the forepart of the day & calm—lowering afterwards & Wind fresh from the Southward.

12.   Rain fell last Night. Morning still & calm, Afternoon very windy from the No. West. Day cloudy.

13.   Very cold in the forepart of the Day. Wind fresh from the No. West—Southerly towards Night.

14.   A little smoky & hazy. Wind fresh from the So. Wt. all day. Warm.

15.   Exceeding pleasant but rather too warm—there being but little wind & that Southerly.

16.   Warm, but lowering wind fresh from the Southwd.

17.   Lowering all day & Wind Southerly. At Night a good deal of Rain.

18.   Cloudy but little or no Rain till Night. Wind Easterly.

19.   Raining, or Snowing, more or less all day—with the Wind at East.

20.   Foggy in the Morning, but clear, warm, & pleasant afterwards.

21.   Calm, warm, and exceeding pleasant in the forenoon with a White frost. In the Afternoon the wind got to No. West but neither blew hard or cold.

22.   Very white frost but clear, Calm, & remarkably pleast. all day.

23.   Calm, but lowering all day and warm.

24.   Warm and pleasant, but rather lowering.

25. Very warm and pleasant. Evening lowering, & Night Raining.

26. Clear, & very pleasant after the Morning—wind Southerly.

27. Calm, clear, warm, and exceeding pleasant till the Afternoon then lowering.

28. In the Night Rain. Misting all day with the Wind at No. East.

29. Cloudy all day, and somewhat raw & cold. Wind at No. West but not hard.

30. A very white frost—clear & very pleasant with but little Wind & that Southerly.

31. Clear, warm, & pleasant. Wind pretty fresh from So. Wt.

[February]

Where, how, or with whom, my time is Spent.

Feby. 1st. Went into the Neck to see the Sick. Also went a fox huntg. Found nothing.

2. At home all day. In the Afternn. Mr. Calvert, Mr. Bordley, & Mr. Jacques from Maryland and Mr. Wagener, Mr. Mills, Doctr. Rumney, & Mr. Rutherford came here.

John Beale Bordley (1727–1804), of Baltimore and Wye Island, Md., pursued an avid interest in all areas of agriculture, including crop rotation, farm industry, and proper diet. Like GW, he turned from tobacco to wheat as a cash crop and practiced extensive experimental farming at his farms on Wye Island, on Maryland's Eastern Shore.

Launcelot Jacques (d. 1791) was apparently a descendant of French Huguenots who had settled in England. Jacques immigrated to Maryland and in the 1760s settled on the Potomac River at Green Spring, in Frederick (now Washington) County, Md. There he developed several ironworks in partnership with Thomas Johnson, both of whom had been working for years to open up the navigation of the upper Potomac (SCHARF [3], 2:1293–97). MR. MILLS: possibly John Mills (died c.1784), a merchant of Alexandria (*Va. Gaz.*, D&N, 10 July 1779).

3. Mr. Wagener, & Mr. Mills went away after Breakfast.

4.   Mr. Calvert & the Gentlemen from Maryland went away after Breakfast. Colo. Nathl. Harrison & a Mr. Murdock came to Dinner.

Mr. Murdock is possibly John Murdock (1733–1791), who inherited land in Frederick County, Md., and in the fall of 1774 was chosen a trustee of John Ballendine's Potomac Navigation Company (*Va. Gaz.*, 10 Nov. 1774).

5.
6. } They contd. here.

7.   Colo. Harrison, Mr. Murdock & Mr. Rutherford went away after Breakfast.

8.   Mr. Willm. Milner came to Dinner & went over to Mr. Digges's in the Aftern.

William Milnor continued to do business with GW, although there is no record of his buying fish after May 1774. Milnor was a Quaker, but he was an ardent supporter of the colonists against the British ministry and, on GW's orders, furnished drums, fifes, and colors for the Fairfax and Prince William Independent companies, as well as a number of muskets. He also furnished GW with an officer's sash, gorget, epaulettes, and sword knots, a treatise on military discipline, and several political pamphlets (LEDGER B, 123; Milnor to GW, 29 Nov. 1774, DLC:GW).

9.   At home all day alone.

10.   Doctr. Jenifer & his Brother dind here, & Mr. Milner Lodged here.

11.   Mr. Milner went away. Mr. Custis & myself went a hunting but killd nothing although we found a Fox. Robt. Ashby & bro. lodgd here.

12.   Ashby & his brother went away. I contd. at home all day.

13th.   At home all day. Mr. Geo. Digges came in the Afternoon.

14.   Went a Fox hunting—found & killd a Fox. Robt. Phil, & George Alexander came home with us. Mr. Muir Doctr. Rumney & Cap. Harper lodgd here.

15.   Went a Huntg. again—found Nothing. None but Mr. Digges came home with me. Doctr. Rumney contd. here all day.

16.   At home all day. The Doctr. went away after Breakfast, & Mr. Digges after Dinner.

17.   At home all day alone.

18.   Went up to Alexandria to meet & exercise the Independant Company.

19.   At home all day alone.

20.   Went up to Alexandria to the Choosing of Delegates to go to Richmond. Doctr. Rumney.

Pursuant to a resolution by the First Virginia Convention (1–6 Aug. 1774) authorizing the moderator, Peyton Randolph, to call another convention when he thought necessary, Randolph issued a call on 19 Jan. 1776 for each county to choose two delegates to a convention to be convened in Richmond on 20 Mar. (VAN SCHREEVEN, 2:245–54).

21.   At home all day. Doctr. Rumney & Captn. Marshall Dined here. Mr. Grayson & Mr. Henderson came in the Afternoon & lodgd.

On 16 Feb., James Scott, Jr. (1742–1779), of Fauquier County, wrote to GW that he and Capt. Thomas Marshall were "the persons chosen by our [Fauquier County] Independent company, to wait on you for the purpose of offering you the command," but Scott was not able to join Marshall in this visit (DLC:GW).
   William Grayson was at this time head of the Prince William County Independent Company. He served as aide-de-camp to GW from Aug. 1776 to Jan. 1777, when, promoted to colonel, he raised Grayson's Additional Regiment, which he commanded until he retired from the service in 1779 (BERG, 48; W.P.A. [1], 91–92).

22.   The whole went away after Breakfast. Went with Mrs. Washington to Mr. Digges & Dind. Mr. Custis and wife went to Maryland. Doctr. Craik came in the Aftern.

23.   Doctr. Craik staid all day. Mr. Rutherford came to Dinner & also stayd all Night. A Mr. Corse dind & went away afterwds.

Mr. Corse may have been John Corse, a captain in the Delaware Regiment during the Revolution (see DIARIES, 2:186n).

24.   Doctr. Craik went away early in the Morning & Mr. Rutherfd. after Dinner.

25.   Mr. Danl. Jenifer came to Dinnr. & went away afterwards.

26.   Mrs. Washington & self went to Pohick Church. Dind at Captn. McCartys. Mrs. Craik came home with us.

27.   Mrs. Craik went away after Breakfast—the Doctr. coming for her.

28.   Went up with Mrs. Washington to Alexandria—returnd to Dinner.

Acct. of the Weather in Feby.

Feby. 1.   Pleasant with but little Wind, & that Near No. West.

2.   A White frost but clear & very pleast. with but little wind & that Southerly.

3.   Calm, warm, & pleasant all day—being also clear.

4.   Pleasant & clear in the Morning, but lowering afterwards with some rain in the Evening & Night.

5.   Quite calm and Pleasant being warm.

6.   Very little wind, but lowg. & like for falling weather.

7.   Cloudy & calm, & something like Snow in the forenoon. Afternoon clear & exceeding pleasant. Wind Southerly.

8.   Wind blowing very fresh from the So. West all day & for the most part clear.

9.   Cloudy all day, with the wind fresh from the No[rth]ward. In the Afternoon Snowing & wind at No. Et.

10.   Snowing & Raining till 12 or one Oclock then clear—wind getting to No. West at Night.

11.   Cloudy for the most part and Raw. Wind at No. Et. with Snow.

12.   Snowing all the forenoon but not fast. Afternoon clear and Cold. Wind at No. Wt.

13.   But little Wind, and that Southerly. For the most part clear.

14.   Cool & raw all day—the fore part at least. Wind Northerly.

15.   Clear but cool. Wind fresh from the So. West.

16.   Calm, at least very little Wind & that Southerly. Clear & exceeding pleasant.

17.   Rather lowering with but little Wind & that at East.

18.   Cloudy a little in the forenn. but clear afterwards & warm with very little wind.

19.   Cloudy all day, but not Cold with but little wind, and that variable. At Night Rain.

20.   Clear & very warm with but little wind & that Southerly.

21.   Again very warm and pleast. with but little wind.

22.   Quite warm with little or no Wind and Clear.

23.   Clear and warm with the wind pretty fresh from the Southward. At Night Rain.

24.   Raining more or less till the Afternoon, then clear, wind fresh all day from the Southward.

25.   Clear and a little Cool—Wind fresh all day from the West & So. Wt.

26.   Wind pretty fresh from the Northwest and a little cold towards Noon.

27.   Wind fresh from the Southward. Raw & cool and lowering towards Eveng.

28.   Lowering Morning but clear, warm, & exceeding pleasant afterwards—till the Evening when it Clouded & look like Rain. Wind blowing fresh from the Southwd.

[March]

Where, how, or with whom, my time is Spent.

Mar. 1st.   Cloudy all the forenoon with a little Rain. Clear afterwards. Wind very fresh all day from the No. West. Mrs. Barnes, & Miss Betcy Ramsay came in the Eveng. as did Mr. Morda. Red.

Betcy Ramsay was Mrs. Sarah Barnes's granddaughter.

2.   Morda. Red went away after Breakfast. Doctr. Jenifer & wife & Mrs. McCarty came to Dinner & stayd all Night.

Dr. Walter Hanson Jenifer's wife Ann was commonly called Nancy.

3.   They went away after Breakfast. I contd. at home all day.

4.   Went a Hunting but found nothing. Colo. Harrison and Captn. Wood came here to Dinner.

5.   At home all day. Colo. Richd. Lee came to Dinner and Doctr. Craik in the Evening.

6.   Colo. Harrison & Colo. Lee went away, as did Mrs. Barnes & Miss Ramsay after Breakfast.

7.   I set my People off for the Ohio under the care of Willm. Stevens. Captn. Wood went away and Doctr. Craik went up with Lund Washington to see Jas. Cleveland. Colo. Harrison returnd. Mr. Whiting, & Mr. Catesby Woodford came to Dinner also & Stayed all Night.

GW was making his second attempt in two years to seat his frontier lands on the Ohio and Kanawha rivers, for which he had gathered, through purchase and hire, a collection of black and white artisans and laborers. He was now sending them west under the temporary direction of William Stevens, who had replaced the ailing James Cleveland. In his instructions to Stevens dated 6 Mar. 1775, GW wrote: "I cannot pretend to say with certainty, when I shall be with you; but hope it may happen in May—if not in May, it shall be so soon after as I can make it convenient" (DLC:GW).

Mr. Whiting is probably Francis Whiting, who died in this year.

Catesby Woodford (1738–1791), a younger brother of Brig. Gen. William Woodford of the Revolution, was born in Caroline County. Catesby married Mary Buckner in 1771 and settled in Fauquier County (STEWART, 1:70, 238, 276, 313; CROZIER [3], 171).

John Hoskins Stone, copied from an unknown artist by Charles Willson Peale. (Collection of the State of Maryland, Annapolis)

8th. The above Gentlemen went away after Breakfast. Docter Craik came to Dinner & wt. away afterwards.

9. At home all day. Lewis Lemart & George Chin came & stayd all Night.

10. At home all day. Mr. Custis who came over on Sunday returnd again to Maryland.

11. At home all day. Mrs. Slaug[h]ter dind here.

12. Went to Pohick Church & returnd to Dinner. Found Mr. Jno. Stone here who went away afterwards. Jas. Cleveland came in the Afternoon.

John Hoskins Stone (1745–1804), of Charles County, Md., had come to Mount Vernon to pay £300 for 3,000 bushels of GW's corn (LEDGER B, 190).

13. At home all day. Capt. Mc[Car]ty dind here.

14. At home all day. Doctr. Craik came in the Afternn. Cleveland still here.

15. Set of for Richmond. Dind in Colchester with Mr. Wagener & lodgd at Colo. Blackburns.

16. Went to Dumfries to review the Independant Company there. Dind & lodged with Mr. Leitch. Spent the Evg. at an Entertt. at Grahams.

GW reviewed the Independent Company of Cadets of Prince William County. Andrew Leitch, a merchant of Dumfries, was a member of the Prince William County Committee (VAN SCHREEVEN, 2:204).

The entertainment at "Grahams" may have been in the 60-by-28-foot "Assembly room" which was constructed about 1769 under the management of Richard Graham and financed by subscription in Dumfries for assembly balls, celebrations, and entertainments on public occasions (*Va. Gaz.*, R, 23 Mar. 1769).

17.   Reachd Fredericksburg first dining at Mr. James Hunters—detaind by Wind.

GW's host was probably James Hunter, Sr. (d. 1785), then of King George County.

18.   Clear and pleasant—in Fredericksburg all day.

19.   Dined at Roys at the Bolling green and lodged at Hanovr. Court House.

Hanover Court House, now Hanover, is 15 miles north of Richmond. In 1781 there was a "very fine and large inn here" (RICE, 2:101).

20.   Reach'd Richmond abt. 11 Oclock. Dind at Mr. Richd. Adam's. Went to Col. Archy Carys abt. 7 Miles in the Aftern.

The Second Virginia Convention was called to order at the Henrico Parish Church in Richmond, built in the 1740s on Indian Town Hill and set in a yard which in time became bounded by Broad, Grace, Twenty-fourth and Twenty-fifth streets. In 1772 a north wing was added, and it was in this building that the Second Virginia Convention met. Indian Town Hill, which was also called Richmond Hill, came in time to be called Church Hill, after the church building, which itself was variously called Indian Town Church, New Church, Old Church, Henrico Parish Church, and the Town Church. The present name, St. John's Church, first appeared in the early nineteenth century (RAWLINGS, 165–68).

The house of Richard Adams (c.1726–1800) was about a block from the church (SCOTT, 12). Adams, who bought up so many lots in the area that Church Hill was sometimes called Adams Hill, became a successful merchant and entrepreneur (SCOTT, 12–13; HEADS OF FAMILIES, VA., 112, 115; MORDECAI, 45, 137). He represented Henrico County in the House of Burgesses 1769–75 and in all five Virginia conventions.

Col. Archibald Cary (1720–1787) lived at Ampthill, on the south side of the James River in Chesterfield County, the county he represented in the House of Burgesses 1756–75 and in the Virginia conventions. The Ampthill house and major dependencies have since been moved to a site in Richmond (WATERMAN, 212–16; ROTHERY, 254–56).

21.   Dind at Cooleys Tavern in Richmd. & returnd to Colo. Carys.

Col. Archibald Cary of Ampthill.
(Virginia State Library)

The convention spent this day's session hearing reports from their seven delegates to the First Continental Congress and discussing the proceedings of that congress (VAN SCHREEVEN, 2:353). Cowley's (Cooley's, Coley's) tavern, inherited in 1769 by Abraham Cowley, was located near the intersection of what later became Main and Twenty-second streets.

22.　Dined at Galts Tavern & lodgd at a House of his providing.

The convention concluded the day's deliberations by voting unanimous approval to "the proceedings and Resolutions of the American Continental Congress" and unanimous thanks to their seven delegates (VAN SCHREEVEN, 2:361). Gabriel Galt (1748–1788) ran the City Tavern, on the northwest corner of Nineteenth and Main streets below Church Hill (HEADS OF FAMILIES, VA., 116; REPS, 277).

23.　Dined at Mr. Patrick Cootes & lodgd where I had done the Night before.

At this day's session Patrick Henry proposed resolutions "that this Colony be immediately put into a posture of Defence." After much debate, in the course of which Henry gave his "liberty or death" speech, the resolutions passed by a close vote. GW was appointed to a committee to "prepare a Plan for embodying, arming and disciplining" such an armed force, after which the convention adjourned for the day (VAN SCHREEVEN, 2:366–69; also see FREEMAN, 3:403–5; MAYS, 2:4–11; MEADE [1], 2:25–40).

At this time Patrick Coutts (d. 1776), a Richmond merchant, was living on Shockoe Hill, later the site of the state Capitol (*Va. Gaz.*, D&H, 4 Nov. 1775; REPS, 274, 277).

24. Dined at Galts & spent the Evening & lodgd at Mr. Saml. Duvals.

The convention decided on this day to send seven delegates to the Second Continental Congress (VAN SCHREEVEN, 2:371).

Samuel Du Val (1714–1784) lived near Shockoe Creek at Mount Comfort, then situated northwest of Richmond but since incorporated into the city limits. From 1772 he had represented Henrico County in the House of Burgesses and the first two Virginia conventions (GRABOWSKII, 171–81; VAN SCHREEVEN, 2:171–72).

25. Returnd to the Convention in Richmond. Dined at Galts & went to Mrs. Randolphs of Wilton.

Today the convention accepted an amended report of the defense committee, which recommended that each county "form one or more voluntier Companies of Infantry and Troops of Horse," that every infantryman have a rifle or firelock and a tomahawk and "be cloathed in a hunting Shirt by Way of Uniform," while the county committees were to be in charge of raising the money for munitions from among the local citizenry (VAN SCHREEVEN, 2:374–75). The convention also appointed a committee to report on manufactures, to which GW was appointed, and then chose the same seven delegates who had attended the First Continental Congress to attend the second Congress set for May. In the polling GW stood second to Peyton Randolph (VAN SCHREEVEN, 2:376).

Anne Harrison Randolph, a daughter of Benjamin and Anne Carter Harrison of Berkeley, was the widow of William Randolph (1710–1761). Since her husband's death she had presided over Wilton, which was built in the early 1750s about six miles south of Richmond on the north side of the James River. The house was later moved to the west end of Richmond (DU BELLET, 4:133).

26. Stay'd at Wilton all day.

27. Returnd to Richmond. Dined at Mr. Richd. Adam's.

Today, in its final session the Second Virginia Convention made Thomas Jefferson, delegate from Albemarle County, Peyton Randolph's alternate delegate to the Second Continental Congress (VAN SCHREEVEN, 2:385–86).

28. Left Richmond. Dined at Hanover C[our]t Ho[use] & Lodged at Roys at the Bolling Green.

29. Got to Fredericksburg abt. 11 Oclock. Dined at Colo. Lewis's & spent the Evening at Weedons.

George Weedon was described by an English traveler who stopped at his tavern about this time as "very active and zealous in blowing the flames of sedition" (SMYTH, 2:151). Weedon was indeed a vigorous advocate of the American position; by April 1776 he had rented his tavern to another innkeeper and had accepted a commission as a lieutenant colonel in the Continental Army (*Va. Gaz.*, P, 6 Oct. 1775 and 5 April 1776). He became a brigadier general in Feb. 1777 and served until 1783, seeing action at Brandywine, Germantown, and Yorktown. After the Revolution he returned to Fredericksburg, where he died in 1793.

30.   At Fredericksburg all day. Dined at Colo. Lewis's.

31.   Set of from thence. Dined at Dumfries & reachd home about Sun Set.

Acct. of the Weather in March

March 1st.   Cloudy all the forenoon with a little Rain—clear afterwards. Wind very fresh all day from the No. West & towards Night cold.

2.   Clear, with little or no Wind in the forenoon but Southerly afterwards.

3.   Clear & very pleasant all day. In the forenoon the Wind was a little fresh from the Southward but quite calm afterwards.

4.   Warm, Calm, and pleasant. In the Afternoon a little Wind from the Southward.

5.   A very foggy Morning but Calm, warm, & pleasant afterwards.

6.   Clear, Warm, & Calm in the forenoon, but the Wind a little fresh from the Southward afterwards.

7.   Calm and Lowering in the forenoon with but little wind. At Night Rain.

8.   Clear and pleasant with but little Wind. Warm also.

9th.   Wind very fresh all day from the No. West but not Cold —though clear.

10.   Clear and very pleasant with little or no Wind all day. In the Eveng. it was fresh from the Southward.

11.   Foggy in the Morning & very Smoaky all day with but little Wind & that Southerly.

12.   Clear warm and very pleasant with but little wind & that Southerly.

13.   Again warm & pleasant but lowering.

14.   Misting with Rain now and then through the day. Wind at So. West.

15.   Clear but somewhat Cool. Wind very fresh from the Westward, and No. West.

16.   Cloudy with Rain now & then through the day. Wind very fresh first from the No. East—then No. West.

17.   A frost & cold—Wind very hard all day from the No. Wt.

18.   A White as well as a black frost.

19.   Clear and very pleasant with but little Wind and Southe[rly].

20.   Lowering and very warm with the Wind fresh from the So. West.

21.   Very Windy all day from the West, & turnd much Cooler.

22.   Cold all day with the Wind fresh from the No. Wt.

23.   Cloudy & Chilly—with appearances of Snow—wind being Easterly but none fell. Afternn. clear.

24.   Clear & warm in the forenoon—Wind very fresh from the So. West. In the afternoon Wind shifting to the No. West & Cooler.

25.   Wind Northerly & somewhat Cool but not unpleasant.

26.   Wind Easterly with Misting Rain all day.

27.   Raining in the Afternoon with the wind fresh at No. Et. In the Evening it got to No. Wt.

28. Very Cold with a Frost—Wind fresh from the No. West.

29. Severe Frost. White & Black. Fruit distroyd.

30. A tolerable pleasant day with but little Wind.

31. Cool with the Wind at No. West but not very hard.

Memm.

[March 10 1775].   On the 10th. of March when the Cherry buds were a good deal Swell'd, & the White part of them beginning to appear, I grafted the following Cherries viz.

In the Row next the Quarter & beginning at the end next the grass walk, 13 May Duke & next to those 12 Black May Cherry both from Colo. Masons and cut from the Trees yesterday.

In the Row next to these 6 Cornation, and 6 May Cherry from Colo. Richd. Lees but I do not know which is first as they were not distinguishd.

March 11th.   At the head of the Octagon—left hand side—in the first Row, next the gravel walk 5 Peach Kernals fine sort from Philadelphia. In the next 4 Rows to these 130 Peaches also of a fine kind from Phila.—same as Colo. Fairfax white Peach. Row next these 25 Missisippi Nuts—something like the Pignut— but longer, thiner shelld & fuller of Meat.

OCTAGON: GW had four small octagonal buildings incorporated into the newly finished brick walls of his upper (north) and lower (south) gardens. Two of these were located on either side of the west lawn near the mansion house. The other two were at the far end of the two garden walls facing the lawn. GW referred to these houses variously as garden houses, seed houses, and necessaries.

MISSISSIPPI NUTS: *Carya illinoensis,* pecan. GW also called this species the Illinois nut and "pekan."

[April]

Where, how, or with whom, my time is Spent.

Aprl. 1.   At home all day, Mr. Magowan came here.

2.   At home all day. Mr. Magowan went to church & returnd to Dinner. Mr. Wilper came in the Afternoon—as did Captn. Curtis also.

Philip Curtis was the captain of GW's brig *Farmer,* just arrived at Mount Vernon from a voyage that had carried 4,000 bushels of "Indian Corn" to Lisbon and returned with 3,000 bushels of salt from the Turks Islands in the Caribbean (P.R.O., T.1/512, ff. 196, 197).

3. Mr. Wilper went away. Mr. Magowan & self walkd into the Neck.

4. Mr. Tilghman Mr. Buchanan, Mr. Herbert, Mr. Danl. Carroll & Mr. Fitzgerald came down to Dinner & the two last returnd in the Aftern.

5. At home all day with the above Gentleman.

6. All the above Gentlemen except Mr. Magowan went away after Breakfast. Mr. R. Adam came in the Evening & stayd all Night.

7. Mr. Adam went away after Breakfast. I continued at home all day.

8. Mr. Magowan went away after Breakfast. Mrs. Washington & self rid to the Mill.

9. Went to Pohick Church & returnd to Dinner. Doctr. Craik and Mr. Danl. Jenifer came in the Afternoon and stayed all Night.

10. At home all day alone.

11. At home. Captn. Saunders came and lodged here.

CAPTN. SAUNDERS: probably either Joseph Saunders (died c.1792), a merchant of Philadelphia, or his son John Saunders, who was settling in Alexandria in this year (Fairfax County Wills, Book F-1, 251–55, Vi Microfilm; Fairfax County Deeds, Book M, 41–46, Vi Microfilm).

12. Captn. Saunders went away after Dinner. A Lloyd from Pen[n]s[ylvani]a Came to Dinner & stayd all Night. Mr. Andw. Stewart also came to Dinr. & returnd.

This Lloyd may be John Lloyd (1751–1811), who was traveling through Pennsylvania, Maryland, and Virginia at this time as a partner of his brother-in-law, Osgood Hanbury (1731–1804), of London (SAYERS, 5–12, 348; *Pa. Mag.,* 35:502–5, 249; GW to Osgood Hanbury & Co., 4 Aug. 1774, DLC:GW).

13. Mr. & Mrs. Custis, & Mrs. Newman came to Dinner. Mrs. Slaughter also.

14. Doctr. Rumney Mr. Adam & Captn. Broadstreet came to Dinner. The two first stayd all Night—the other went away.

CAPTAIN BROADSTREET: was probably Capt. Lyonel Bradstreet, who apparently brought GW the acceptance by Thomas Contee of GW's offer to sell his brig *Farmer*. Contee assured GW that "Capt. Bradstreet will take her in Charge when or as Soon as you please" (Contee to GW, 11 April 1775, DLC:GW; see also Lyonel Bradstreet to GW, 26 April 1785, DLC:GW).

15. Went up to Alexandria to the Muster of the Independt. Company. Returnd late at Night.

16. At home all day. Genl. Lee Mr. Harry Lee Junr. Mr. Geo. Mason, Mr. Thompson, & Mr. McDonald came to Dinner. The three last went away afterwards. Colo. Mason came in the Afternn.

Charles Lee was returning north from Williamsburg to be present in Philadelphia when the Second Continental Congress convened there in May. Henry Lee (1756–1818), later known as Light Horse Harry Lee for his exploits as a cavalry officer in the Revolution, was the eldest son of Col. Henry Lee of Leesylvania and no relation to Charles Lee. He had graduated in the fall of 1773 from the college at Princeton, N.J., where he had acquired a lifelong passion for Latin classics, and now he was developing a second great passion: soldiering. Much impressed by Charles Lee, he was soon to write him, requesting the privilege of serving under him and learning the art of war (ALDEN, 72).

Henry Lee, soon to command mounted troops and earn the nickname of Light Horse Harry. (The Society of the Lees of Virginia)

Mr. Thompson is probably William Thompson, a merchant, originally from King George County but established in Colchester by 1773.

Mr. McDonald is probably Angus McDonald (c.1726–1778) who immigrated to America from Scotland after the Battle of Culloden in 1746. In the 1760s he built his home, Glengary, near Winchester in Frederick County, where he was a rent collector for Lord Fairfax and in 1774 performed a similar service for GW (MCDONALD, 357–76).

17.   Colo. Mason & myself went up to Alexa. to a Committee & to a New choice of Delegates. I returnd at Night.

This meeting was called in Alexandria for election of delegates to the Virginia Convention from Fairfax County. GW and Charles Broadwater were again elected. By early May GW and the other Virginia delegates to the Second Continental Congress, all of whom were also Virginia Convention delegates, had advised their Virginia constituents to replace them in the convention "during their necessary Absence" at the Congress in Philadelphia (*Va. Gaz.*, D&H, 13 May 1775). On 12 July a "meeting of the freeholders" of Fairfax County chose George Mason to replace GW in the Third Virginia Convention which convened in Richmond five days later (George Mason to William Ramsay, 11 July 1775; MASON [2], 1:239). GW was the only one of the Virginia delegates to the Continental Congress who had not resumed his seat in the Third Virginia Convention by mid-August (STANARD [1], 203–5).

18.   Walkd with Genl. Lee to Mr. Adams's Fishing Landg. Mrs. Blackburn & Mrs. Brown Dined & stayd all Night here.

Mrs. Thomas Blackburn, of Rippon Lodge, and Mrs. William Brown, of Alexandria, were sisters.

19.   Mrs. Blackburn & Mrs. Brown went away after Dinner. Mr. Rutherford who came yesterday to Dinnr. went away after Breakfast today. Dr. Rumney came in the Afternn.

20.   Genl. Lee, & Doctr. Rumney both went away after Breakft.

21.   Captn. Curtis dind here. In the Afternoon my Brother Jno. Billy Washington, & George & Charles Lewis came.

Capt. Philip Curtis and GW were settling the accounts of the brig *Farmer*, which GW sold ten days later to Thomas Contee, of Maryland (LEDGER B, 192). Billy was William Augustine Washington (1767–1785), son of GW's brother John Augustine Washington. George and Charles Lewis were sons of GW's sister Betty and her husband Fielding Lewis.

22.   I rid with my Brother to Alexa. & returnd to Dinner.

23.   At home all day. In the afternoon Mr. Leitch & his Wife & Mr. Robt. Adam came.

24.   My Brother John, Mr. Adam & Mr. Leitch & his Wife went away. I continued at home.

25.   At home all day. A Mr. Johnson—a Muster Master dind here & went away afterwds. Thos. Davis came Express & returnd.

William Johnson was sent by the Fairfax County Independent Company to consult GW on its new uniform. The members wrote GW to ask if they could "take the fashion of the Hunting shirt Cap and Gaiters from you," and inquired "whether you Intend to send yours up that we may get the fashion" (Fairfax County Independent Company to GW, 25 April 1775, DLC:GW). Thomas Davis (Davies) was sent from Fredericksburg to GW with £4 16s. to buy gunpowder for the Spotsylvania Independent Company (LEDGER B, 192).

26.   Went up to Alexa. to meet the Indt. Company. Mr. Hepburn came home with me & Mr. Loyd I found there.

William Hepburn, of Alexandria, owned a ropewalk from which GW had bought rope for refitting his brig *Farmer* (HEADS OF FAMILIES, VA., 16; LEDGER B, 117).

27.   At home all day—those Gentlemen continuing.

28.   Mr. Hepburn & Mr. Loyd both went away.

29.   At home all day.

30.   Went up to Alexandria & returnd in the Afternoon.

Acct. of the Weather in April

Apl. 1.   Cool, with the Wind at No. Wt.

2.   Wind in the same place, and weather Cool.

3.   Wind at No. Wt.—fresh & Cool all the forepart of the day—latter part moderate—Wind Southerly.

4.   Misting, & Raining more or less all day with but little Wind and that Southerly.

5.   Wind very fresh and Cold from the No. West all day.

6.   A hard frost—day colder & wind harder from the same Quarter than yesterday.

7.   Pleasant forenoon, but rather cool & Raw afterwards notwithstandg. the Wind was Southerly.

8.   Rather Cool, Wind, what there was of it at No. East.

9.   Again Cool, & Wind still at No. East.

10.   Lowering all day with the wind at No. Et.

11.   Misting all day and a good deal of Rain in the Night—with the Wind at No. Et.

12.   Raining in the forenoon but clear afterwards.

13.   Clear but Windy from the No. West & Cool.

14.   Very Cool & Wind very hard at No. West.

15.   Very pleasant. Wind what little there was Southerly.

16.   Warm & towards the Evening lowering. Wind very fresh from the So. West.

17.   Wind very fresh from the Southwest with Rain in the Night.

18.   A little Rain in the Morning but clear, & the wind hard, & cold from the Westward afterwards.

19.   Wind hard from the same Quarter till Night & clear.

20.   Wind very hard from the Southwest. Clear.

21.   Wind more moderate from the Eastward.

22.   Not much Wind in the forenoon but pretty fresh afterwards from the Southward and very warm.

23.   Wind Southerly and very warm all day.

24.   Wind, what little there was of it, Easterly but warm notwithstanding.

25.   Wind fresh from the Westward all day & rather hard from thence in the Morng.

26.   Clear & pleasant but rather warm.

27.   Lowering & Misting with rain at Night.

28.   Clear and a little warm. Wind Southerly.

29.   Wind Southerly & warm.

30.   Lowering—Wind Easterly with Showers of Rain.

[May]

Where, how, or with whom, my time is Spent.

May 1.   Went up to Alexa. to meet the Independt. Company. Mr. Herbert came at Night.

2.   Messrs. Hendks. Dalton & others Breakfasted here & Majr. Gates & Mr. B. Fairfax dind & lodgd here.

James Hendricks, an Alexandria merchant, was one of ten Alexandrians who formed a town committee of correspondence in May 1774; he later served in the Revolution as a major and colonel with the Virginia troops (VAN SCHREEVEN, 2:88; HEITMAN [2], 217).

Horatio Gates (1727–1806) had been a captain in the British army in 1755 when he was wounded in Braddock's Defeat. After serving in the French and Indian War he returned to Great Britain, where he subsequently retired on half pay with the rank of major. In 1772 he and his family moved to America and settled on a farm near Opequon Creek, about six miles northwest of Charles Town in the Shenandoah Valley. This home, which he named Traveller's Rest, was situated in newly formed Berkeley County (now in Jefferson County, W.Va.), where he served with GW's brother Samuel Washington as a county justice of the peace (NORRIS [1], 292).

Gates probably used this visit at Mount Vernon to discuss with GW the recent battles of Lexington and Concord, the current seige of Boston by New England troops, and the prospects for the two serving in an American army against Lt. Gen. Thomas Gage, with whom they had both served in Braddock's campaign, and who was now commander of the British troops in Boston.

3.   Mr. Fairfax went away. Majr. Gates stayd all day. In the Afternoon Colo. Richd. H. Lee & Brothr. Thoms. as also Colo. Chas. Carter came here.

Richard Henry Lee as painted by Charles Willson Peale in 1795. (National Portrait Gallery, Smithsonian Institution, Washington, D.C.)

Horatio Gates, an old comrade in arms, became Washington's adjutant general. (Print Division, Library of Congress)

Richard Henry Lee (1732–1794) married Anne Aylett (1738–1768), whose half sister, also named Anne Aylett, had married GW's half brother Augustine Washington, of Pope's Creek, Westmoreland County. Lee built his home, Chantilly, just a few miles down the Potomac River from Pope's Creek and Stratford Hall and across Nomini Bay from Bushfield, home of GW's brother John Augustine Washington.

Lee and GW entered the House of Burgesses the same year (1758), and Lee represented Westmoreland County as a burgess until the Revolution, distinguishing himself for an accomplished command of the English language. He had been one of the leading Virginia delegates to the First Continental Congress in 1774 and was now on his way to the second Congress, where in June 1776 he moved a resolution that resulted in the Declaration of Independence.

Colonel Carter is probably Charles Carter, Jr. (1733–1796), eldest son of Charles Carter of Cleve (1707–1764). He was variously referred to as Colonel Carter, Charles Carter, Jr., and Carter of Ludlow and Nanzatico. Carter served as burgess from King George County 1756–71. During part of his service two other Charles Carters also served in the House of Burgesses—his father, Charles Carter of Cleve, also representing King George County, and a cousin, Charles Carter of Corotoman and Shirley, representing Lancaster County. Charles Carter, Jr., was at this time living on his Stafford County property, Ludlow, and representing that county in the House of Burgesses. Carter had been in serious financial difficulties even before his father's death and acted for a time as manager of one of his uncle Landon Carter's farms

(CARTER [3], 2:817, 856). In later years Carter borrowed money from GW for the education and establishment of his sons (GW to Carter, 10 June 1797, Carter to GW, 3 Mar. 1795, GW to Carter, 10 Mar. 1795, DLC:GW).

4.   Set out for the Congress at Phila. Dind in Alexa. & lodgd at Marlborough.

GW left Mount Vernon in his chariot, probably accompanied by Richard Henry Lee. He may have met several of the other delegates on the road between Mount Vernon and Baltimore, because GW, Lee, Peyton Randolph, Edmund Pendleton, and Benjamin Harrison of Virginia and Joseph Hewes and Richard Caswell of North Carolina all arrived in Baltimore on the same day (SCHARF [2], 132; FREEMAN, 3:418).

GW evidently dined with friends in Alexandria, for there are no expenses posted in his ledger for this date except 7s. 6d. for the ferry at Alexandria (LEDGER B, 195). On this trip to Philadelphia, GW tried a different route. He had on earlier trips north used either Posey's ferry or Johnston's ferry on Clifton's Neck. The ferry crossing at Alexandria was probably located on West's Point (Point West), at the foot of Oronoco Street, and terminated on Thomas Addison's land just south of Oxon Creek in Prince George's County, Md. Addison had run the ferry, but he had died the previous September and the ferry building and the land adjoining it were for rent (*Md. Gaz.*, 1 June 1775). From the ferry, GW journeyed to Marlboro and from there across the Patapsco ferry to Baltimore. From Baltimore he followed the road across the Gunpowder River to Susquehanna Lower Ferry (now Havre de Grace), on the west bank of the Susquehanna River. He then crossed the Susquehanna to Perryville in Cecil County and continued on to Charlestown, and from there to Head of Elk and Wilmington, Del.

5.   Breakfasted at Mrs. Ramsays & Lodged at Baltimore.

Although GW had traveled the Baltimore-Marlboro road on his return south in 1773, he still was unfamiliar with the route and paid 7s. 6d. for a guide to Baltimore (LEDGER B, 193). The roads in this part of Maryland ran through farms, and much time was lost in stopping to open and close gates each time the road passed from one field to another. Ebenezer Hazard complained in 1777 that he passed through 32 gates in one day on his way from Baltimore to Marlboro (HAZARD, 48–50).

Upon their arrival at Baltimore, GW and the other Virginia and North Carolina delegates who arrived on this day were met by three companies of militia and escorted to the Fountain Inn (SCHARF [2], 132). This inn and tavern, run by a former Philadelphian, Daniel Grant, was a "large and commodious house, lately built by Mr. GOUGH, in Market-street, BALTIMORE" (*Md. Journal*, 20 Aug. 1773). The Fountain Inn was moved in 1782 a short distance to a new edifice built by Grant on Light Lane between Market Street and Ellicott's Wharf (*Md. Journal*, 3 Dec. 1782). GW stayed at the inn several times on later trips to Baltimore.

6.   At Baltimore all day. Reviewd the Companies there & dind at an Entertainmt. given by the Townsmen.

"Four companies of the town militia were drawn upon the Common, where they were reviewed by Col. Washington . . . accompanied by the other delegates. . . . In the afternoon the delegates, accompanied by the Rev. Clergy and principal gentlemen of the town, preceded by Capt. [Mordecai] Gist's independent company, and the officers of the other companies, walked from the Fountain Inn to the new Court-house, where an entertainment was provided" (SCHARF [2], 132). Pursuant to a resolution by the Second Maryland Convention (8–12 Dec. 1774), Baltimore County organized 68-man militia companies in each district or "Hundred" of the county (*Md. Journal*, 2 Jan. 1775; *Md. Gaz.*, 19 Dec. 1774, 26 Jan. 1775). GW may also have reviewed a company of Baltimore Independent Cadets, which had been formed in December (*Md. Hist. Mag.*, 4:372).

7.   Breakfasted at Cheyns's. Dind at Rogers's & lodged at Stevensons this side Susqueha[nna].

CHEYNS'S: probably the tavern located about 13 miles east of Baltimore at the head of Bird River, a tributary of the Gunpowder River. It was operated for a number of years by a series of different keepers, and at one time was called the Red Lion Tavern.

John Rodgers (c.1726–1791), a Scot who came to America about 1760, opened a tavern at Susquehanna Lower Ferry, Harford County, Md., in 1774. About 1778 he moved across the river to Perryville, in Cecil County, where he ran a tavern and the ferry for several years. Rodgers was captain of a troop of Maryland militia during the Revolution and a member of the Harford County committee of correspondence. Since he was always referred to in later years as Colonel Rodgers, he probably was promoted to the higher rank sometime during the Revolution (PAULLIN, 16–19).

William Stephenson, a Scottish emigrant, and his wife, Rachel Barnes Stephenson, kept a hotel or tavern during the Revolution at Perryville, in Cecil County, Md., directly across the Susquehanna River from Rodgers's establishment at Susquehanna Lower Ferry (HARFORD, 374). A traveler in 1777 called Stephenson's and Rodgers's the two best public houses between Philadelphia and Edenton, N.C. (HAZARD, 53).

8.   Breakfasted at Charles Town & Dined & lodged at Wilmington.

Charlestown, a flourishing port on the Northeast River, was the county seat of Cecil County, Md., until 1786, when the courthouse was moved to Elkton (Head of Elk).

The road followed by GW from Charlestown to Wilmington led him through Christiana Bridge, or Christiana (LEDGER B, 193). Another traveler who passed this way in the same year described the village as lying "in a Bottom at the head of Christeen creek over which there is a Bridge here & to which the Tide flows, bringing up sloops & such like vessels" (HONYMAN, 11). On later trips, GW alternated between this route and the road closer to the coast which led through New Castle and the Christina (Christiana) ferry.

9th.   Breakfasted at Chester, & dined at the City Tavern Phila. Supped at Mr. Jos. Reads.

The arrival in Philadelphia of the delegates from Virginia and other southern colonies was celebrated, according to Christopher Marshall, by a large reception and parade at the outskirts of the city (MARSHALL [1], 25). However, since Marshall himself was not present at the scene, and no other contemporary accounts have been found that mention any such reception, it seems probable that he confused this with the enthusiastic reception and parade accorded the New England delegates on the following day. The reception of the New England delegates was described by numerous participants and eyewitnesses, but is not mentioned by Marshall.

Samuel Curwen, a Loyalist, also spent this evening at Joseph Reed's house "in company with Colonel Washington a fine figure, and of a most easy and agreeable address," Richard Henry Lee, Benjamin Harrison, and others. "I staid till 12 o'clock, the conversation being chiefly on the most feasible and prudent method of stopping up the Channel of Delaware to prevent the coming up of any large King's ships to the City. I could not perceive the least disposition to accomodate matters or even risk" (CURWEN, 1:7–8).

10.   Dined at Mr. Thos. Mifflins & spent the Eveng. at my lodgings.

MY LODGINGS: GW's cash memorandum lists a payment of £17 13s. 3d. in Pennsylvania currency "By Mr. Randolph Bd. &ca." on 22 June, the day before he left Philadelphia (Cash Memoranda, DLC:GW). Benjamin Randolph was a cabinetmaker who lived on Chestnut Street between Third and Fourth streets. Thomas Jefferson also lodged with Randolph when he went to Philadelphia later in the year (JEFFERSON [1], 1:293n).

GW today attended the first meeting of the Second Continental Congress, held in the State House. Peyton Randolph and Charles Thomson were again unanimously chosen president and secretary (JCC, 2:11–12).

11.   Dined at Young Doctr. Shippens—spent the Eveng. at my Lodgings.

In Congress the credentials of the delegates were read and the decision was again made to keep the proceedings secret. A letter was read from colonial agents in London reporting the rejection of the colonists' petition to the king, the failure of the earl of Chatham's plan for reconciliation, and the embarkation of more British troops for America. Massachusetts delegates laid before Congress numerous documents concerning the recent troubles at Lexington and Concord (JCC, 2:13–44).

12.   Dined and Supped at the City Tavern.

GW's expenses on this day include 6s. 7d. in Pennsylvania currency for "Club at Smith's" (Cash Memoranda, DLC:GW). George Read, Delaware delegate, wrote his wife a description of these dinners at Daniel Smith's City Tavern: "I then dine at the City Tavern, where a few of us have established a table for each day in the week, save Saturday, when there is a general dinner. Our daily table is formed by the following persons, at present, to wit: Messrs. Randolph, Lee, Washington, and Harrison, of

Virginia, Alsop of New York, Chase of Maryland, and Rodney and Read. A dinner is ordered for the number, eight, and whatever is deficient of that number is to be paid for at two shillings and sixpence a head, and each that attends pays only the expense of the day" (LMCC, 1:92).

13. Dined at the City Tavern with the Congress. Spent the Eveng. at my Lodgings.

This was Saturday, the day all members of Congress met together for dinner at the City Tavern.

14. Dined at Mr. Willings, & Spent the Evening at my Lodgings.

15. Dined at Burns's & Spent the Evening at my Lodgings.

In Congress a question was raised by the New York delegates on how the colony was to conduct itself in regard to the British troops expected there. Recommendations were made in Congress and a resolution passed for appointing a committee to consider what posts in that colony should be occupied and how many troops should be necessary to guard them. It was further "resolved, That Mr. Washington, Mr. Lynch, Mr. S. Adams, and the delegates from New York, be the committee for the above service, and that they be desired to report as speedily as possible" (JCC, 2:49–53).

16. Dined at the City Tavern & Spent the Evening at Doctr. Shippens.

17. Went to the Commencemt. at the College and dined at Mr. Saml. Griffins—after wch. attended a Comm[itt]ee at the Conistoga Waggon.

GW attended the ceremony at the College of Philadelphia in his role as a member of the Continental Congress, which attended as a group. For a description of the commencement, see *Pa. Packet*, 15, 22, 29 May 1775.

The Conestoga Wagon was a small inn on Market, or High, Street, between Fourth and Fifth. After the Revolution it was run by Maj. Samuel Nichols, or Nicholas, but at this time the proprietor may have been Charles Jenkins (SMITH [2], 39–56; SCHARF [1], 2:995–96).

The committee was to consider posts to be occupied in New York and the number of troops to be used there.

18. Dined at the City Tavern, and attended a Comee. afterwards at the State House.

The president of Congress on this day gave Congress news of the capture of Ticonderoga, which he had received by messenger the evening before. Congress resolved to recommend to New York that the cannon and stores be removed from Ticonderoga to the south end of Lake George, where a strong post should be established (JCC, 2:55–56).

19.   Dined at Mr. Allans. Spent the Evening in my own lodgings.

The committee of Congress to consider the defense of New York, which had occupied much of GW's time for two days past, brought in its report. The report was read and referred to the committee of the whole, which made its resolutions regarding New York's defense on 25 May (see JCC, 2:57).

20.   Dined at the City Tavern & Spent the Evening at my Lodg.

21.   Dined at Mr. Richd. Willings and Spent the Evening at my Lodgings.

Richard Willing (1745–1798) was a captain in the Philadelphia Associators during the Revolution (WALKER [3], 24:422).

22.   Dined at Mr. Griffins & spent the Evening at my Lodgings.

23.   Dined at Mr. Jno. Cadwalladers & spent the Evening in my own Room.

24.   Dined at Mr. Andw. Allan's & Spent the Evening at the Gov[e]r[nor']s Club.

25.   Dined at Mr. Tilghman's, & Spent the Evening at the City Tavern.

26.   Dined at Mr. Meridiths and Spent the Evening at the City Tavern.

27.   Dined at the City Tavern & spent the Evening at my own Lodgings.

GW, Philip Schuyler, Thomas Mifflin, Silas Deane, Lewis Morris, and Samuel Adams were named a committee to "to consider of ways and means to supply these colonies with Ammunition and military stores and to report immediately" (JCC, 2:67).

28.   Rid out to the Provence Island & dind there in Compy. with sevl. other Gentlemen.

29.   Dined at the City Tavern. Spent the Evening in my own Room.

30.   Dined at Mr. Mease's, & after setting a while with the Boston Gentlemen retird to my own Room.

BOSTON GENTLEMEN: GW is referring to the Massachusetts delegates to Congress.

31.   Dined with Mr. Jno. Rutlidge. Spent the Evening in my Chambers.

John Rutledge (1739–1800) was the elder of two Rutledge brothers representing South Carolina in the Continental Congress at this time. He had served in the South Carolina House of Commons for a number of years and in the Stamp Act Congress in 1765. During the Revolution Rutledge was president of South Carolina 1776–78, governor of the state 1779–82, and again a member of Congress 1782–83.

Acct. of the Weather in May

May 1st.   Exceeding hot. Wind southerly.

2.   Also warm, but not so hot as yesterday.

3.   Again warm & clear. Wind Southerly.

4.   Very warm indeed with but little wind & clear.

5.   Again very Warm with a violent Gust abt. 5 Oclock in the Evening.

6.   Somewhat Cool. Wind Easterly.

7.   Cool & pleasant. Wind Northerly.

8.   Still Cool & lowering with Rain now and then.

9.   Clear & pleasant. Wind Westerly.

10.   Clear and pleasant not being very warm.

11.   Clear but rather Cool wind being Westerly.

12.   Clear & pleasant, but rather Cool.

13.   Lowering with a little Rain in the forenoon. Clear afterwards.

14.   Clear & pleasant – rather warm.

15.   Clear in the afternoon. A little lowering in the forenoon.

16.   Clear & pleasant. Evening a little Cool.

17.   Clear and pleasant in the forenoon but Cloudy & dropping of Rain afterwds.

18.   Clear and Warm all day.

19.   Clear & warm in the forenoon, but lowering & Cool afterwards.

20.   Clear and pleasant. Rathr. cool.

21.   Clear in the forenoon with a good deal of Rain afterwards.

22.   Lowering in the forenoon with Rain in the Afternoon.

23.   Lowering most part of the day.

24th.   Clear and pleasant with but little Wind.

25.   Clear & pleasant but growing warmer.

26.   Clear and Warm. Wind Southerly but not fresh.

27.   Clear and very Sultry. Wind still Southerly.

28.   Clear and warm. Wind pretty fresh from the South.

29.   Warm with some appearances of Rain but none fell.

30.   Lowering all day & warm. Wind fresh from the So[uth]-ward.

31.   Warm, & somewhat lowering. Wind pretty fresh from the Southward.

[June]

Where, how, or with whom my time is Spent.

June 1.   Dined at Burns's and Spent the Evening in my own Room.

GW's committee on ways and means of supplying ammunition and military stores to the colonies read its report, which was referred to the committee of the whole (JCC, 2:74).

2. Dined at Mr. Josh. Shippens & spent the Evening at Mr. Tilghman's.

Shippen was probably Joseph Shippen, Jr. (1732–1810), son of Edward and Sarah Plumley Shippen of Lancaster, Pa. He had graduated from Princeton in 1753 and served as an officer in the Pennsylvania Regiment during the French and Indian War. He was with Gen. John Forbes on the Fort Duquesne expedition and probably knew GW at that time. From 1762 until its dissolution in 1775, Shippen served as secretary of the Pennsylvania council and in 1786 was appointed a judge of the Lancaster County Court of Common Pleas (SHIPPEN, 36:367; BALCH [2], 28:399).

3. Dined at the City Tavern & spent the Evening at my lodgings.

Congress appointed a number of committees, including one composed of GW, Philip Schuyler, Silas Deane, Thomas Cushing, and Joseph Hewes, "to bring in an estimate of the money necessary to be raised" (JCC, 2:79–80).

4. Dined at Mr. Robt. Morris's on the Banks of Schoolkill & Spent the Eveng. at the City Tavn.

Robert Morris (1734–1806), born in England, came in his youth to Maryland where his father was engaged in the tobacco export business. The younger Morris settled in Philadelphia and in 1754, as a partner in the firm of Willing, Morris & Co., eventually became one of America's wealthiest

Robert Morris, a Charles Willson Peale portrait. (Independence National Historical Park Collection)

merchants. Morris signed the nonimportation agreement in 1765 and in 1775 was a member of the council of safety. He was a member of the Continental Congress Nov. 1775–78, and he served as superintendent of finance 1781–84. After the Revolution, Morris and his wife, Mary White Morris of Maryland, became close friends of the Washingtons. At the convening of the Constitutional Convention in 1787, GW gratefully accepted the hospitality of the Morrises, and later they gave up their handsome town house for the use of GW and his family during the presidential years. Morris's country home, called The Hills, where GW dined on this day, is located on the east side of the Schuylkill River, in what is now Fairmount Park.

5.   Dined at Mr. Richard Penns. On a Committee all the Afternn.

This was the committee appointed on 3 June to estimate the amount of money needed to be raised.

6.   At Mr. Willm. Hamiltons & Spent the Evening at my Lodgings.

7.   Dined at the City Tavern and spent the Evening at home.

GW's committee to estimate the amount of money to be raised today gave its report, which was referred to the committee of the whole (JCC, 2:81). GW made a number of purchases on this day, including "5 Books—Military" (Cash Memoranda, DLC:GW).

8.   Dined at Mr. Dickensons and spent the Evening at home.

9.   Dined at Mr. Saml. Pleasants and went to hear Mr. Piercy preach.

10.   Dined at Mr. Saml. Griffens. Spent the Evening in my own Room.

11th.   Went to Church in the forenoon & then went out & Dined at Mr. H. Hills. Returnd in the Afternoon.

12.   Dined at the City Tavern & Spent the Evening at my lodgings.

13.   Dined at Burn's in the Fields. Spent the Evening at my Lodging's.

14.   Dined at Mr. Saml. Merediths. Spent the Evening at home.

After Congress resolved that "six companies of expert rifflemen, be immediately raised in Pensylvania, two in Maryland, and two in Virginia . . . That each company, as soon as compleated, shall march and join the army near Boston, to be there employed as light infantry, under the command of the chief Officer in that army," it named GW, Schuyler, Deane, Cushing, and Hewes to a committee to draw up rules for the regulation of the army (JCC, 2:89–90).

15.   Dined at Burns's in the Field. Spent the Eveng. on a Committee.

Congress resolved today "that a General be appointed to command all the continental forces, raised, or to be raised, for the defence of American liberty" (JCC, 2:91). GW, nominated by Thomas Johnson of Maryland, was unanimously elected. For a discussion of GW's election and the reasons behind it, see FREEMAN, 3:432–40; ADAMS [1], 3:321–23.

   The committee which occupied GW all the evening was the one on drafting army regulations.

16.   Dined at Doctr. Cadwaladers. Spent the Evening at my lodgings.

GW was informed officially in Congress of his appointment as general and commander in chief, and he read his acceptance speech "standing in his place." He refused the salary which Congress had voted, asking only that his expenses be paid. Other resolutions on this day set up an establishment of major generals, brigadiers, aides, secretaries, etc. (JCC, 2:92–94).

17.   Dined at Burns's in the Fields. Spent the Evening at my Lodgings.

18.   Dined at Mullens upon Schoolkill. Spent the Evening at my lodgings.

Thomas Mullen opened a tavern called Vauxhall, at Passyunk on the Schuylkill River, in 1775. His wife, Peggy Mullen (d. 1774), had run the famous Beefsteak House on Water Street which GW probably had visited the previous year (see entry for 12 Oct. 1774; JACKSON, 122; SCHARF [1], 2:996).

19.   Dined at Colo. Rieds. Spent the Evening at Mr. Lynch's.

Thomas Lynch, Sr. (1727–1776), a South Carolina planter, was a member of the Continental Congress 1774–76. He had served for many years in the South Carolina legislature and was a member of the Stamp Act Congress in 1765. Silas Deane, a Massachusetts delegate for Congress, wrote that Lynch was "plain, sensible, above ceremony, and carries with him more force in his very appearance than most powdered folks in their conversation" (LMCC, 1:18).

   On 18 June, perhaps while he was alone in his room during the evening,

Phila. June 23d 1775.

My dearest,

As I am within a few Minutes of leaving this City, I could not think of departing from it without dropping you a line; especially as I do not know whether it may be in my power to write again till I get to the Camp at Boston — I go fully trusting in that Providence, which has been more bountiful to me than I deserve, & in full confidence of a happy meeting with you sometime in the Fall — I have not time to add more, as I am surrounded with Company to take leave of me — I retain an unalterable affection for you, which neither time or distance can change my best love to Jack & Nelly, & regard for the rest of the Family; concludes me with the utmost truth & sincerity

Yr entire Go Washington

On 23 June 1775, as he was leaving Philadelphia for Boston, Washington penned a farewell to Martha. (Mount Vernon Ladies' Association of the Union)

GW wrote to Mrs. Washington: "My Dearest: I am now set down to write to you on a subject, which fills me with inexpressible concern. . . . Believe me my dear Patsy . . . that I should enjoy more real happiness and felicity in one month with you, at home, that I have the most distant prospect of reaping abroad, if my stay was to be seven times seven years. . . . I shall rely therefore, confidently, on That Providence which has heretofore preserved, and been bountiful to me, not doubting but that I shall return safe to you in the fall" (owned by Armistead Peter 3rd, Washington, D.C.). In the letter GW enclosed his will.

On 19 June, John Hancock, president of the Continental Congress, signed GW's commission as "General and Commander in Chief of the army of the United Colonies" (DLC:GW). Meanwhile, GW was writing more letters home to Virginia, including one to his closest brother, John Augustine, wherein he "bid adieu to you, & to every kind of domestick ease, for a while. I am Imbarked on a wide Ocean, boundless in its prospect & from whence, perhaps, no safe harbour is to be found. I have been called upon by the unanimous Voice of the Colonies to take the Command of the Continental Army. An honour I neither sought after, nor desired, as I am thoroughly convinced, that it requires greater Abilities, and much more experience, than I am Master of" (20 June 1775 DLC:GW).

During this week, while Congress was choosing 13 new generals, drafting GW's initial instructions, and deciding how to finance the campaign, GW was preparing for his trip to Massachusetts to form the thousands of citizen-soldiers surrounding Boston into an army of the united colonies. He chose Joseph Reed as his secretary and Thomas Mifflin as his first aide-de-camp. He queried the Massachusetts delegates about what arrangements their government had made for supporting the army and whom he would be dealing with (Massachusetts Delegates to GW, 22 June 1775, DLC:GW). And he sent his chariot home.

On 23 June the new commander in chief left Philadelphia, accompanied by Generals Charles Lee and Philip Schuyler and their aides. While he was but "a few Minutes of leaving this City" and "surrounded with Company to take leave of me," GW wrote again to Mrs. Washington: "My Dearest. . . . I could not think of departing . . . without dropping you a line. . . . I retain an unalterable affection for you, which neither time or distance can change. . . . I go fully trusting in that providence, which has been more bountiful to me than I deserve, & in full confidence of a happy meeting with you some time in the fall" (ViMtV). He then rode off to a campaign that would last for more than seven years, during which he saw Mount Vernon only in his 1781 visits during the Yorktown campaign.

For the period between 19 June 1775 and January 1780, no diaries of GW have been found; his opening remarks in his 1781 Yorktown diary indicate that no other war journals were kept.

Acct. of the Weather in June

June 1st.   Warm and clear in the forenoon—Cool afterwards.

2.   Clear & rather Cool.

3. Clear and tolerably pleasant.

4. Lowering in the Forenoon, & Raining in the Afternoon. Cool all day.

5. Raining more or less all day. Wind abt. No. Et.

6. A little lowering and in the Mid day warm.

7. Lowering all day—especially in the Evening. Cool.

8. Lowering in the forenoon but clear afterwards and warm.

9. Clear after the Morning and very warm.

10. Lowering Morning but clear afterwards. A [   ]

11. Very warm with little or no wind in the forenoon—a thunder gust in the Afternoon & cooler.

12. Warm with Showers about Noon—Cooler afterwards.

13th. Clear but somewhat Cool.

14. Very warm—being clear & the wind Southerly.

15. Clear, and Cooler than Yesterday.

16. Cooler, wind Easterly, & somewhat lowering.

17. Clear and warm with but little Wind & that So.

18. Very warm, and but little wind—clear.

19. Very warm in the forenoon but cooler much afterwds. Wind shifting Northerly.

The Weather at Headquarters

1780

EDITORIAL NOTE: The following weather diary for the first five months of 1780 was kept at Morristown, N.J., during GW's second winter encampment there during the Revolution. It is one of the two surviving diaries for the war period. It represents one of the earliest instances of GW's interest in keeping a weather record while away from Mount Vernon. The manuscript is neat, uniform, showing some attempt at decorative lettering, and appears to be copied from an earlier original. Because it shares some calligraphic characteristics with the 1781 diary, we assume that both were rendered into fair copies by GW after 1781 — probably after the war.

In terms of hardship and the bitterly cold weather, the winter at Morristown (1779–80) was the story of the earlier Valley Forge experience all over again. Many persons who lived through both encampments declared that it was far worse. The blizzard of 2–4 Jan. was one of the most severe on record, with high winds and heavy drifts. Although GW shows little inclination to dwell upon the rigors of the storm in his notations for early January, his correspondence adds a few details. He wrote to Congress 5 Jan. that the late violent storm "has so blocked up the Roads that it will be some days before the scanty supplies in this quarter can be brought to Camp" (DNA: PCC, Item 152). And to the Magistrates of New Jersey, 8 Jan.: "The distress we feel is chiefly owing to the early commencement and uncommon rigor of the Winter, which have greatly obstructed the transportation of our supplies" (DLC:GW).

As spring approached, GW looked back on a period of remarkable travail and wrote to Lafayette, 18 Mar.: "The oldest people now living in this Country do not remember so hard a Winter as the one we are now emerging from. In a word, the severity of the frost exceeded anything of the kind that had ever been experienced in this climate before" (DLC:GW).

He was describing the only winter in recorded American history during which the waters around New York City froze completely and closed down navigation for several weeks. Jefferson reported that Chesapeake Bay froze solid from its head to the mouth of the Potomac (LUDLUM, 111–18).

January

1st.   Clear—cold & freezing with little wind.

2d.   Very cold—about noon it began to Snow, & continued without intermission through the day, & night. The wind high & variable, but chiefly from the west & No. West.

3d.   The same weather as yesterday—to wit cold & stormy—wind from the same point.

4th.   Very cold with high winds from the west & No. West and intermitting Snow.

5th.   Cloudy till the afternoon—when the Sun appeared.

6th.   Snowing & Sunshine alternately—cold with the Wind and west & No. West & encreasing—Night very stormy. The Snow which in general is Eighteen Inches deep, is much drifted—roads almost impassable.

7th.   Very boisterous, from the West & No. West & sometimes Snowing, which being very dry drifted exceedingly. Night intensely cold and freezing—Wind continuing fresh.

8th.   Morning cold & Windy from the No. West. Mid-day and afternoon more moderate and less Windy—Weather clear. After Sunset it again turned very cold the Wind freshning from the No. West.

9th.   Morning clear and cold the Wind (though not high) from the No. West—Mid-day moderate with but little Wind—the evening cold though the wind had shifted to the Southward.

10th.   Morning clear and Mild—Wind at So. East. Before noon it clouded & about two began to Snow & continued to do so all the afternoon & evening.

11th.   Clear and moderate with little or no Wind in the foren[oo]n but rather cloudy—variable Wind in the afternoon.

12th.   Variable weather with a little Snow in the day & more in the Night. In the whole a fall of about three Inches. In the afternoon it turned very cold.

13th.   Wind fresh at No. West and exceeding cold. Weather clear and frost very severe.

14th.   Clear & cold—Wind steadily from the West—but not hard.

15th.   Wind at No. West—Weather clear but not cold. Of a sameness through the day.

16th.   Fine morning, and pleast. day though cool—but little Wind & that Southerly.

17th.   Morning cloudy and great appearances of Snow. Mid day clear with a disposition to thaw, but the wind shifting to No. West it turned exceeding cold & froze hard.

18th.   Clear & cold—Wind at No. Wt. but not very fresh.

19th.   Clear—Morning tolerably pleasant—Evening cold—Wind at No. West but not very fresh.

20th.   Intensely cold & freezing—Wind very fresh from the No. West the whole day.

21st.   In the Night the Wind shifted to the Southward & the severity of the cold abated. The day pleasant with but little Wind & that abt. So. Wt. till the evening when it got more to the Westward blew fresh, & grew colder.

22d.   Tolerably pleasant with but little wind from the westward. At Night it grew cold & froze severely.

23d.   Wind westerly & little of it. Air fresh & no thawing even in the Sun South of the House.

24th.   Clear in the forenoon and cloudy afternoon—Cold but little or no Wind—but that Westerly—No thaw.

25th.   Clear and pleasant, yet cold—wind contg. to the Westwd.

26th.   Wind for the most part of the day Southerly—but cold & sharp air notwithstanding—Weather clear.

27th.   Cold in the Morning with a little Snow—clear Midday & afternoon with the Wind at West.

28th.   Very cold—the Wind being fresh from the No. West—Frost severe.

29th.   Clear and cold without much wind—which in the forenoon was Westerly & in the afternoon to Southwd.

30th.   Warm and clear in the forenoon with the Wind at South & thawing fast—afternoon cold & freezing. Wind getting to the No. West and blowing fresh particularly in the Night.

31st.   Very cold & freezing—Wind being fresh from the No. West the whole day.

February

1st.   More mild—especially in the forenoon. Wind variable but mostly Southerly. Afternoon chilly with appearances of Snow.

2d.   Clear & tolerably pleasant in the Morning. In the afternoon a keen air from the Westward.

3d.   Moderate—rather warm & thawing—Wind for the most part of the day Southerly. Eveng. cold.

4th.   Clear and cold—Wind Westerly—little or no thawing.

5th.   Wind at No. West & cold—frost very severe. In the evening the Wind shifted to the Southward & moderated.

6th.   Clear and tolerably pleasant—wind rather South of West—Snow melting.

7th.   Clear, mild and moderate in the forenoon but little Wind—afternoon rather lowering and cooler.

8th.   A fall of nine or 10 Inches Snow in the Night from the No. Et. Wind continuing in the same quarter all the forenoon with a little Snow and some rain. In the afternoon the wind got westerly & in the evening cleared.

9th.   Wind fresh in the Night from the Westward—day clear & not very cold. The wind continued Westerly all day.

10th.   Wind Southerly—Weather moderate but somewhat lowering.

11th.   Wind at So. West and pretty fresh—forepart of the day very lowering & dropping rain—Snow much softened & beginning to dissolve. Afternoon clear & pleasant.

12th.   Clear & pleasant with but little wind—rather cooler than yesterday—Snow dissolving a little—Frost at Night.

13th.   Clear and pleasant with but little wind & that at No. East thawing a little in the middle of the day.

14th.   Air keen, though but little Wind—forenoon clear, afternoon a little lowering.

15th.   A kind of Sleet in the Morning, & moderate rain all the remaining part of the day with but little wind—Snow much dissipated.

16th.   Clear & quite warm in the forenoon. Snow yielding fast to the Sun. Much Water in the roads & brooks and the thick beds of Snow over which good sleighing had been were now too soft to bear and too difficult & dangerous to Horses to pass. Afternoon lowering.

17th.   Clear and pleasant with but little wind—thawing all day pretty considerably.

18th.   Wind fresh from the No. West but moderate with respect to cold, notwithstanding it continued to blow from that quarter all day.

19th.   In the Morning it was a little Cool. In the afternoon somewht. raw, but upon the whole pleasant. Wind at West & No. Wt. but not fresh.

20th. Clear & pleasant Morning. Wind about So. West in the forepart of the day, but shifted to the west & No. West afterwards & tho' pleasant got a little cooler.

21st. Ground where bare, and top of the Snow pretty hard frozen. But little wind in the morning or any part of the day— the first part of which was clear. The latter part lowering.

22d. Wind at No. Et. and raining moderately all day—beginning about 7 Oclock with fine hail. In the Night the Wind freshned from the same quarter.

23d. Lowering Morning with a little snow in the forenoon— Wind at So. West. But shifting to the No. West abt. 3 Oclock & blowing hard it cleared and grew cold and began to freeze very hard.

24th. Hard frost—flying clouds in the forenoon but clear afterwards. Wind fresh from the No. West & very cold. No thawing even in the Sun at Mid day though the roads & fields in many places were uncoverd.

25th. Perfectly clear—Wind westerly, fresh, & cool but thawing nevertheless.

26th. Hazy & lowering in the Morning—clear about Noon—but moderately raining by intervals afterwards till eight Oclock at Night when it cleared & the wind blew pretty fresh from the westward. There was but little wind in the day and that Southerly.

27th. Clear and pleasant morning with the wind at west—the day much of a sameness throughout. Thawing pretty considerably.

28th. A great Hoar frost—quite clear. Wind still westerly and pleasant—thawing—the Snow having dissipated very considerably in the course of the last two or three days.

29th. Clear, warm and exceeding pleasant with but little Wind & that Southerly. Snow almost wholly gone off the fields & Roads —the latter of which is beginning to get deep.

March

1st.   Raining in the morning and drizling all day with very little Wind but a thick fog. Roads very deep.

2d.   Wind coming out very fresh at West. In the Night it cleared, & froze a little. Continued boisterous thro' the day & towards evening grew cold.

3d.   Ground hard frozen. Morning clear & pleasant with but little wind and that from the South. Mid-day cloudy & lowering— variable afterwards—sometimes snowing, at other times Sunshine —Wind getting westerly. The Northern lights or aurora Borealis was seen last evening but not in a very conspicuous degree.

4th.   Cloudy in the Morning with flying clouds all day. Wind Westerly and pretty fresh in the forenoon. Less so afterwds. and milder.

5th.   Clear—warm and pleasant with but little wind—that however was Westerly.

6th.   A little rain fell in the Night. Morning lowering but clear & warm afterwards without wind except a little breeze from the Southwestward. Roads deep.

7th.   Morning soft and lowering without Wind. About 11 O'clock it began to rain with the wind from the No. East & con- tinued to do so & at times hard through the day. In the evening it cleared the wind shifting to the westward without blowing hard.

8th.   Flying clouds—wind pretty fresh from the westward but not cold.

9th.   Lowering Morning—Wind at No. East all day, but not fresh. A little rain in the forenoon, afterwards Sunshine then cloudy with a good deal of rain in the Night.

10th.   Wind and Weather variable but upon the whole warm.

11th.   A hoar frost. Morning clear & pleasant with the Wind Westerly. Mid-day cloudy with the Wind at East. Afternoon very lowering & cold. Roads very deep.

12th.　Snowing & hailing in the Night, with the Wind fresh from the No. East. In the Morning the ground was covered about two Inches deep. The wind continuing in the same place was accompanied by a rain and mist the whole day. In the evening it cleared the wind having shifted to the Westwd.

13th.　Clear and pleasant morning with but little wind & that at west. Variable afterwards with squals of rain & wind from the same quarter. In the Night it became very high and turned colder.

14th.　Ground pretty hard froze. Morning clear and cool. Wind fresh from the Westward & continued so through the day, with flying clouds.

15th.　Ground frozen again. Morning cold & a little cloudy with the wind fresh from the No. Wt. where, & westerly, it continued briskly & cool all day. About Noon it grew very cloudy with appearances of Snow, & towards dusk turned warmer.

16th.　Ground was frozen again. About Sunrise it began to Snow from the North or North a little westerly and continued without intermission the whole day—at the same time cold. Snow abt. 9 Inchs. deep.

17th.　Lowering in the morning but clear afterwards. Wind Westerly & rather cool.

18th.　Ground hard froze. Morning clear & rather cool. Warmer afterwards, wind getting to the Southward. Afternoon lowering with much appearance of Rain—spitting Snow.

19th.　Morning clear, but raw & lowering afterwards—Wind southerly. The grd. was pretty hard froze in the morning. In the evening the wind shifted to the Westward & blew hard all Night.

20th.　Rather cool in the Morning but the Wind getting to the Southward it grew warmer. The ground was hard froze in the morning.

21st.　Wind Southerly but not high—clear & pleasant in the forenoon—lowering afterwards or rather hazy. In the Night it shifted to the West or No. West & blew fresh. Ground froze.

22d.   Clear but rather cool the wind being pretty fresh from the No. West all day. Ground froze again.

23d.   Pleasant Morning but rather cool. Wind in the forenoon westerly afterwd. Easterly & raw with much appearance of Rain.

24th.   Lowering Morning and Wind at East. About Noon it began to rain and continued drizzling all the latter part of the day and till some time in the night the wind continuing to blow pretty fresh.

25th.   Morning fine, being clear, warm, pleasant—the Trees and Earth being glazed looked beautiful. About the hour of nine the wind came fresh from the West & shifting to the No. West blew very hard & became very cold towards Evening.

26th.   Ground very hard frozen & day cool. The Wind continuing rather fresh from the No. West—Weather clear. Towards evening the wind seemed to be shifting round to the Southward.

27th.   Morning lowering & raw the wind being pretty fresh from South. About Noon it blew exceeding hard from the same point with much appearances of Rain. After Sun down the wind shifted round to the West or No. West blew fresh—cleared & became cold.

28th.   Clear & cool—Wind fresh from the No. West, all day.

29th.   Ground hard frozen—Morning clear & cold, wind fresh from the Westward—the Northern light conspicuous.

30th.   Clear & cool—Wind continuing to blow from the same pt. —Ground froze again.

31st.   Snowing more or less all day & generally pretty fast. Wind tho not much of it abt. No. East.

April

1st.   The Snow which fell yesterday & last night was about 9 or 10 Inches deep upon a level. The Morning and remainder of the day clear & pleasant overhead. Wind Westerly but thawing never-theless. Pretty good Sleighing in the forenoon.

2d.   Hard frost—clear & very cold—wind fresh from the No. West & continued so all day. Towards evening it began to freeze hard. The Snow but little dissipated.

3d.   Clear and more moderate than yesterday—though the ground was very hard froze in the morning. Wind still fresh from the West & No. West.

4th.   Lowering in the Morning with little or no Wind. Clearer afterwards with the wind pretty fresh from the No. East.

5th.   Morning clear & rather cold wind being pretty fresh from the No. East. In the evening it turned warmer.

6th.   Grey morning and warm—clear afterwards and rather hot, there being but little wind & that Southerly.

7th.   Warm & pleasant morning. About Noon the Wind began to blow pretty fresh from the southward.

8th.   Clear & pleasant in the morning with little or no Wind. Afterwards the Wind freshned from the Eastward. Grew rather cool and in the evening began a misty kind of Rain.

9th.   In the night there fell a good deal of Rain accompanied with lightning & thunder. The day vareable—sometimes sunshine & clear—at other times cloudy & rain. Wind though not much of it, was for the most part westerly.

10th.   Wind fresh from the West or No. West & cold—the ground being pretty hard froze.

11th.   Cold—raw & cloudy in the forenoon with the Wind fresh from the westward. Afternoon it began to rain, & continued to do so moderately till 9 or 10 O'clock at Night when it cleared.

12th.   Clear & pleasant, but cool Wind still fresh from the West-ward.

13th.   Ground frozen—weather clear & cool but pleasant. Wind at No. West.

14th.   Ground frozen again. Morning cool but pleasant, the Wind in the forepart of the day being Westerly the latter part Southerly.

15th.   Cold & raw—Wind very fresh from the Eastward. Weather lowering with appearances of Snow or Rain.

16th.   Lowering all the forenoon with rain afternoon. Cold and raw again. Wind northerly.

17th.   Wind at No. West & cold—day clear. Frost in the Morning.

18th.   Morning clear and tolerably pleasant. Mid-day warm and afternoon very lowering & very likely to rain. Wind also at No. East.

19th.   A little rain fell last night. This day lowering & dripping quite throughout, with the Wind, for the most part disagreeably fresh from No. West.

20th.   Wind still at No. West & fresh; the Morning lowering and dripping, but clearer afterwards and cold.

21st.   Clear & cool—Wind fresh from the No. West all day.

22d.   Morning a little lowering but clear afterwards. Wind about West.

23d.   Wind Westerly and very fresh—at the same time clear & cold for the Season.

24th.   Wind in the same place but not fresh; day clear & pleasant but rather cool.

25th.   Morning very pleasant but cold raw and cloudy afterwards with appearances of rain. Wind fresh from the Southward or So. Et. afternoon.

26th.   Lowering & cloudy all day the forepart of it without much wind but fresh afterwards, with a little rain from the Northward and, for the season, very cold and disagreeable.

27th.   Cold in the Morning and Evening but warm about Mid-day. In the Morning the Wind was fresh from the Westward. In the Evening it had got Easterly.

28th.   Cold & disagreeable in the forenoon. With clouds & a little rain in the afternoon. Wind getting Southwardly.

29th.   Clear & very pleasant Morning with little or no Wind & warm. In the afternoon it grew a little lowering & showery.

30th.   Morning pleasant and clear, with the Wind Southerly— afternoon Showery and foggy.

May

1st.   Raining moderately all the forenoon with a little thunder —thick and misty afterwards—wind Northerly.

2d.   Foggy & misting all day at the same time cold & raw. Wind still in the same quarter as yesterday.

3d.   Close and misting—the Wind being at West in the Morning & continuing so all day. Abt. 9 it cleared.

4th.   Very pleasant and clear. Wind being Southwardly & Warm.

5.   Clear & pleasant—Wind being rather variable, it was cooler than could be wished. In the Morning the Wind was Northerly & southerly in the afternoon.

6th.   The forenoon was clear & Warm with little or no Wind. In the afternoon the Wind was fresh from the Eastward & became raw & cold.

7th.   Clear morning, & not unpleasant but rather cool. Mid-day lowering & raw. Wind at East.

8th.   Lowering all day with the Wind at East, or So. East & a small sprinkle of Rain.

9th.   Clear, warm, and pleast. with the Wind at South, and in the evening pretty fresh.

10th.   Morning very pleasant & warm. Wind fresh from the Southward afterwards.

11th.   Clear but too cool for the Season the Wind being fresh from the No. West.

12th.   As yesterday in Wind and Weather.

13th.   Clear & more pleasant, being warmer till the afternn. when it again turned cool. Wind in the forenoon tho there was not much of it was Southerly. In the afternoon it got more to the Eastward.

14th.   Pleasant & clear, being neither cool nor warm—Wind southerly.

15th.   Clear and pleasant Wind, though not much of it hanging to the Southward & growg. warm.

16th.   A very great dew & fog. With little wind in the forenoon & very warm. In the afternoon it was pretty fresh from the Southward and about dusk came out from the Northward.

17th.   Clear (except being smoky) & morning rather cool—wind being Northerly—but shifting afterwards to East it grew raw & disagreeably cool.

18th.   Heavy & uncommon kind of Clouds—dark & at the same time a bright and reddish kind of light intermixed with them—brightning & darkning alternately. This continued till afternoon when the sun began to appear. The Wind in the Morning was Easterly. After that it got to the Westward.

19th.   Lowering with but little Wind and that Southerly—weather grown warmer.

20th.   Wind Southwardly with some appearances of Rain but none fell—day warm & very dusty.

21st.   Appearances of Rain but none fell—warm and dry.

22d.   Very little wind and rather Warm in the forenoon but cooler afterwards the Wind coming out pretty fresh from the Northward.

23d.   Lowering with some drops of Rain, but not enough to lay the dust. The Wind what there was of it was Northerly.

24.   Clear Morning with but little wind, but pretty fresh afterwards and from the Eastward.

25th.   Warm—The Wind blowing fresh from the West, or So. West—Exceeding dry and dusty with appearances of rain in the afternoon—but none fell.

26th.   Wind fresh from the Westwd. Very warm—dusty & dry— Also hazy with appearances of Rain but none fell.

27th.   Very warm and extreme⟨ly⟩ dusty. The Wind in the forepart of the day blew fresh from the South West. Afterwards it got more to the West or No. West. Clouds & appearances of Rain but none fell here.

28th.   Clear morning and rather Cooler than yesterday—the wind being pretty fresh from the No. West—but warm afterwards with but little of it.

29th.   Clear with but little wind in the forenoon, but more refreshing afterwards, tho' from the Southward—exceeding dry & dusty—grass beginning to decline.

30th.   Warm with appearances of Rain but none fell here but little wind & that at So. or So. West.

31st.   Raining more or less all day. The showers were moderate & exceedingly refreshing as the Earth imbibed the moisture as it fell & the Earth became well penetrated. Very little wind accompanied the Rain.

June

1st.   Clear and very pleasant being also warm. But little Wind & that Southerly.

2d.   Clear & cooler than yesterday—the wind in the forenoon being abt. No. West & continued in the same way all day.

3d.   Rather cool—Wind fresh from the Westward with a little Rain about 3 Oclock.

4th.   Clear and rather Cool—Wind being fresh from the Westward.

Yorktown: A Victor's View

1781

May 1781

I begin, at this Epoch, a concise Journal of Military transactions &ca. I lament not having attempted it from the commencement of the War, in aid of my memory and wish the multiplicity of matter which continually surround me and the embarrassed State of our affairs which is momently calling the attention to perplexities of one kind or another, may not defeat altogether or so interrupt my present intention, & plan, as to render it of little avail.

To have the clearer understanding of the entries which may follow, it would be proper to recite, in detail, our wants and our prospects but this alone would be a Work of much time, and great magnitude. It may suffice to give the sum of them—wch., I shall do in a few words—viz.—

Instead of having Magazines filled with provisions, we have a scanty pittance scattered here & there in the different States. Instead of having our Arsenals well supplied with Military Stores, they are poorly provided, & the Workmen all leaving them. Instead of having the various articles of Field equipage in readiness to deliver, the Quarter Master General (as the denier resort, according to his acct.) is but now applying to the several States to provide these things for their Troops respectively. Instead of having a regular System of transportation established upon credit or funds in the Qr. Masters hands to defray the contingent Expences of it, we have neither the one nor the other and all that business, or a great part of it, being done by Military Impress, we are daily & hourly oppressing the people—souring their tempers and alienating their affection. Instead of having the Regiments compleated to the New establishment (and which ought to have been So by the [   ] of [   ] agreeably to the requisitions of Congress, scarce any State in the Union has, at this hour, an eighth part of its quota in the field and little prospect, that I can see, of ever getting more than half. In a word—instead of having everything in readiness to take the Field, we have nothing—and instead of having the prospect of a glorious offensive campaign before us, we have a bewildered, and gloomy defensive one—unless we should receive a powerful aid of Ships—Land Troops and

Money from our generous allies & these, at present, are too contingent to build upon.

May 1st.   Induced by pressing necessity—the inefficacy, & bad tendency of pushing Military Impresses too far and the impracticability of keeping the Army supplied without *it,* or *money,* to pay the transportation I drew for 9000 dollars of the Sum sent on by the State of Massachusetts for payment of their Troops; and placed it in the hands of the QM General [1] with the most positive orders to apply it solely to this purpose.

Fixed with Ezekiel Cornell Esqr. a member of the Board of War (then on a tour to the Eastward to inspect some of the Armoury's &ca.) on certain articles of Cloathing—arms and Military Stores which might be sent from hence to supply the wants of the Southern Army.[2]

Major Talmadge was requested to press the C——s Senr. & Junr. to continue their correspondence and was authorized to assure the elder C—— that he should be repaid the Sum of 100 Guineas, or more, with interest; provided he advanced the same for the purpose of defraying the expence of the correspondence, as he had offered to do.[3]

Colo. Dayton was also written to, and pressed to establish a correspondence with New York, by way of Elizabeth Town for the purpose of obtaining intelligence of the Enemys movemts. and designs; that by a comparison of Accts. proper & just conclusions may be drawn.[4]

1. Timothy Pickering (1745–1829) had been appointed quartermaster general in Aug. 1780.

2. Ezekiel Cornell (1733–1800), was a delegate to the Continental Congress from Rhode Island 1780–83 and member of the Board of War. In the spring of 1781 he had received leave from Congress "for visiting the military Magazines, Laboratories, etc., and causing some necessary reforms" (LMCC, 6:65). See also GW to Board of War, 8 May 1781 (DLC:GW). Cornell reported back to GW on 24 May 1781 (DLC:GW).

3. Maj. Benjamin Tallmadge (1754–1835), a native of Brookhaven, N.Y., conducted secret service operations for GW in the New York area, operating under the name of John Bolton, from 1778 to the end of the war.

Samuel Culper was the name used by two New York intelligence agents who furnished information on British troops and naval movements in the area of New York and Long Island. Samuel Culper, Sr., was Abraham Woodhull (c.1750–1826) of Setauket, Long Island. Samuel Culper, Jr., was Robert Townsend (1753–1838) of Oyster Bay, Long Island. From 1778 to the end of the war, both, usually reporting to GW through Benjamin Tallmadge, gave invaluable information on British activities. For the operation of this intelligence ring, see PENNYPACKER, BARBER, and FORD [4].

Tallmadge had written to GW, 25 April, stating that the Culpers had decided Townsend should take up residence in New York City if his frequent trips back and forth from Long Island to the city were not to lead to enemy suspicion. A sum of money was therefore necessary to defray his expenses and Woodhull had volunteered to advance 100 guineas (DLC: GW). GW's letter to Tallmadge concerning the Culpers is dated 30 April 1781 (DLC:GW).

4. On 1 May, GW wrote to Elias Dayton (1737–1807), a colonel in the New Jersey Line, stressing the importance of intelligence from New York (Kunglia Biblioteket, Stockholm).

Elizabethtown is now Elizabeth, N.J.

May 2d. No occurrence of note. A very fresh and steady gale of Wind all day from the So. East. Upon its shifting (about dusk) it blew violently, & continued boisterous through the Night or greatest part of it.

4th. A Letter of the Baron de Steuben's from Chesterfield Court House Virga. dated the 21st. Ulto. informs that 12 of the Enemys Vessels but with what Troops he knew not, had advanced up James River as high as Jamestown—that few Militia were in arms and few arms to put into their hands—that he had moved the public Stores from Richmond &ca. into the interior Country.[1]

A Letter from the Marqs. de la Fayette, dated at Alexandria on the 23d., mentioned his having commenced his march that day for Fredericksburg—that desertion had ceased, & that his detachment were in good Spirits.[2]

1. Friedrich Wilhelm Augustus von Steuben (1730–1794), after an extensive military career in Europe, came to the United States bearing somewhat inflated European references in Dec. 1777. Joining GW at Valley Forge in Feb. 1778, he quickly proved his value to the Continental forces as an instructor in discipline and tactics, his "blue book"—*Orders and Discipline of the Troops of the United States*—becoming the manual of instruction in the U.S. Army for many years. On 5 May 1778 he was appointed inspector general of the army with the rank of major general (JCC, 11:465). In Oct. 1780, when Maj. Gen. Nathanael Greene replaced Horatio Gates as commander of the Southern Department, Steuben accompanied Greene in order to aid in the restoration of the army in the South. Setting up headquarters at Chesterfield Court House, Va., about 12 miles south of Richmond, he attempted to organize Virginia's defenses and arrange for men and supplies for Greene in the Carolinas. In Dec. 1780 Sir Henry Clinton dispatched to Virginia from New York a fleet and over 1,500 British soldiers under the command of Benedict Arnold, now a brigadier general in the British army. The force landed at Hampton Roads 30 Dec. 1780 and, moving up the James River, took Richmond 5–7 Jan. 1781, then withdrawing to Westover. Steuben participated in the attempt to halt the British in Virginia in the spring of 1781 (see PALMER, 237–72). In mid-April, Arnold and Maj. Gen. William Phillips, now in command of British

forces in Virginia, moved against the Continental troops in Richmond and Chesterfield Court House. Lafayette arrived at Richmond 29 April with reinforcements in time to force Phillips's withdrawal to the area of Jamestown Island. Steuben's letter to GW of 21 April is in DLC:GW.

2. The marquis de Lafayette (1757–1834) had been selected by GW in Feb. 1781 to lead a force of 1,200 light infantry to Virginia to halt Arnold's advance. Lafayette was to cooperate with a French fleet under Admiral Destouches. The plan to capture Arnold's forces failed, partly because the damage inflicted on Destouches's fleet by a British naval force under Admiral Marriot Arbuthnot in an engagement on 16 Mar. had sent the French back to Newport, R.I. Arnold himself had been substantially reinforced by the arrival of British transports. Lafayette and his troops remained in Virginia, and on 6 April 1781 GW ordered him to march south to reinforce Greene (DLC:GW). On 21 April he reached Alexandria.

5th.   Accounts from Brigadr. Genl. Clinton at Albany, dated the 30th. ulto. & 1st. Inst., filled me with anxious fears that the Garrison of fort Schuyler would be obliged to evacuate the Post for want of Provisions and that a Mutiny in the other Troops was to be apprehended.[1] In consequence of this alarming information, I directed the Q. M. Gl. to send 50 Barls. of flour & the like qty. of Salted Meat immy. up for the Garrison of Fort Schuyler—but of the latter there being only 24 in Store, no more could be sent.[2]

1. Brig. Gen. James Clinton (1733–1812), brother of Gov. George Clinton of New York, had become commander of the Northern Department in 1780. Clinton's letter, from his headquarters at Albany, dated 30 April with a postscript of 1 May, informed GW of reports from Maj. Gen. Philip Schuyler that Saratoga, Fort Schuyler, and indeed almost every post in the area had had almost no beef for nearly a month. "The spirit of desertion has sometime past prevailed" (DLC:GW). Fort Schuyler, in the area of present-day Rome, N.Y., was the former Fort Stanwix, rebuilt and renamed in 1776.

2. GW to Timothy Pickering, 4 May 1781 (DLC:GW). On 5 May, GW wrote to Clinton informing him that the supplies for Fort Schuyler were on the way but that the other posts would have to be relieved "from the Counties of Massachusetts, which are nearest to you" (CSmH).

6th.   Colo. Menonville,[1] one of the Adjutt. Generals in the French Army came to Head Quarters by order of Count de Rochambeau to make arrangements for supplying the Troops of His Most Christian Majesty with certain provisions contracted for by Doctr. Franklin. This demand, tho' the immediate compliance with it, was not insisted upon, comports illy with our circumstances; & is exceedingly embarrassing.[2]

The D[eputy] Q[uarter] M[aster] at Sussex C[our]t House,[3]

conceiving that the Provision Magazine, & other stores at that place were exposed to a surprize, and in danger of being destroyed by the Indians & Tories who were infesting the Settlement at Minisink,[4] I directed Colo. Dayton to send a guard there from the Jersey Brigade near Morristown.

Mr. John Flood (at present a liver at lower Salem) whom I had sent for to obtain from him an acct. of the Harbours in the Sound from Frogs point Eastward, arrived; and gave the information wch. is filed in my Office.[5]

Other letters arriving this Evening late (more expressive of the wants of the York Troops at Albany, & the Posts above) I ordered 100, out of 131 Barrls. of Flour which were in Store, to be immediately sent up; & again called upon the Q. M. Genl. in the most pointed terms to send active men to forward on, by every means they could devise, the Salted provs. in Connecticut; & flour from Sussex Ct. Ho. &ca.[6]

That the States might not only know our Wants, which my repeated & pressing letters had recently, & often communicated, but, if possible, be impressed with them and adopt some mode of Transporting it to the Army, I resolved to send Genl. Heath (2d. Offr. in Commd.) to make to the respective legislatures East of York State, pointed representations; & to declare explicitly that unless measures are adopted to supply transportation, it will be impossible to subsist & keep the Troops together.[7]

1. François Louis Arthur Thibaut, comte de Ménonville (1740–1816), was appointed lieutenant colonel in the French army in 1772 and came to America as aide to the French general staff.

2. The French army at Newport was encountering the same problems in obtaining supplies as the American army. Although the French army had usually paid for its supplies—some estimates of expenditures run as high as $6 million—locating adequate provisions remained a problem. From France, Benjamin Franklin reported to Congress in Dec. 1780 that he had made an arrangement with the French ministry to have delivered for the use of the French troops in America "such Provisions as may be wanted from time to time, to the Amount of 400 thousand Dollars . . . the said Provisions to be furnished at the current Prices for which they might be bought with Silver Specie" (Franklin to Samuel Huntington, 2 Dec. 1780, DNA: PCC, Item 82). On the assumption that Franklin had signed the contract as a form of payment to the French government for funds furnished him by France to discharge bills of exchange drawn on him by Congress, that body confirmed the contract and agreed to provide the supplies (JCC, 19:372–73; 20:528).

GW's interview with Ménonville lasted several days, after which GW referred him to Congress for a decision. For the negotiations with Ménonville, see WRITINGS, 22:43–45, 56–58; Ménonville to GW, 8 May 1781 (Aff. Etr., Corr. Pol., Etats-Unis, supp. vol. 15); GW to the President of Congress, 8

May 1781 (DNA: PCC, Item 152). Ménonville then conferred with Robert Morris, superintendent of finance, who informed him that the prospects for supplying the French army were not promising. By late July, however, Morris wrote Franklin that he would endeavor to carry out the commitment to France (Morris to Franklin, 21 July 1781, DLC: Robert Morris Papers).

3. Newton, N.J.

4. GW may be referring to the site of a ford across the Delaware River in Sullivan County, N.Y., which had been the scene of a battle between the Mohawks and Tories and the Patriots in July 1779, or to the village of Minisink some 25 miles east of the ford (BOATNER [2], 265).

5. Flood, a sea captain, who had "formerly lived at Maroneck," apparently carried out minor intelligence errands for GW in the Long Island area. A copy of his report, in GW's handwriting, is in DLC:GW.

Lower Salem was in Westchester County, N.Y. In 1840 the name was changed to Lewisboro.

6. See William Heath to GW, 6 May 1781, James Clinton to GW, 4 May 1781, and George Clinton to GW, 6 May 1781 (DLC:GW). GW wrote to Timothy Pickering concerning the desperate need of provisions at the New York posts, 6, 7 May 1781 (DNA: RG 93, MS File Nos. 26368, 26372).

7. At this time Maj. Gen. William Heath (1737–1814) was in command of the area of the lower Hudson. GW's instructions, 9 May 1781, are in DLC:GW.

7th.   The Wind which blew with great force from the So. East the last two days was accompanied this day by incessant Rain and was a most violent Storm & is supposed to have done damage to Ships on the Coast.

9th.   Went to the Posts at West point, and found by enquiry of General Heath, that all the Meat deposited in the advanced redoubts for contingent purposes would not, if served out, serve the Army two days—that the Troops had drawn none that day & that none remained in the common Magazine.

10th.   The Q. M. Genl. representing, that it was not in his power to get the Salt Meat of Connecticut transported—even for the Money that was put into his hands for this purpose—the people now alledging that they had no forage—when the badness of the roads was an excuse when they were called upon by the Executive of their State in the Month of March and that nothing but Military force could affect the transport for our present wants. Parties were ordered out accordingly and the Officers commanding them directed to receive their Instructions from him.[1]

1. Timothy Pickering to GW, 9 May 1781 (DLC:GW). GW's instructions to Pickering, 10 May 1781, are in MHi: Pickering Papers.

11th.   Major Genl. Heath set out this day for the Eastn. States, provided with Instructions, and letters couched in strong terms— representing the distresses of the Army for want of provisions and the indispensable necessity of keeping up regular supplies by the adoption of a plan, which will have system & permanency in't.[1]

This day also I received advice from Colo. Dayton that 10 Ships of the line, and 3 or 4000 Troops had sailed from New York. The intelligence was immediately communicated to Congress, and to the French Genl. & Admiral at R. Isld.[2]

1. See entry for 6 May 1781. Heath carried with him a circular letter of 10 May to the New England states from GW stressing the army's need for supplies: "From the Post of Saratoga, to that of Dobbs Ferry inclusive, I believe there is not (by the Returns & Reports I have received) at this moment, one day's supply of Meat for the Army on hand. Our whole dependence for this Article is on the Eastern States: their resources of it, I am persuaded are ample. . . . I have struggled to the utmost of my ability, to keep the Army together; but all will be in vain, without the effectual assistance of the States" (DLC:GW).

2. Elias Dayton to GW, 9 May 1781 (DLC:GW). GW received Dayton's letter on 10 May. On 11 May he ordered Dayton "either to confirm or contradict, as speedily as possible and with as much precision as you can, as to the number of Ships of War, Troops and destination" (DLC:GW). Dayton's letter was forwarded to the president of Congress on 11 May with GW's comment that "it does not carry the strongest marks of credibility" (DNA: PCC, Item 152). The information was sent to the comte de Rochambeau, in command of the French forces at Newport, 11 May 1781, with a request that it be transmitted to Charles René Dominique Gochet, chevalier Destouches (1727–1794), temporarily commanding the French fleet at Newport (DLC:GW).

12th.   Colo. Dayton's intelligence, so far as respected the Sailing of Troops, was confirmed by two sensible deserters from Kings- bridge; which place they left yesterday Morning at two Oclock. They add the detachment consisted of the Grenadrs. (Bh.) —the Corps. of Anspach (two Battalions) & the 37th. & 43d. British regiments, amounting, as is supposed, to about 2000 Men under the Command of Majr. Genl. Redeisel.[1]

1. In spite of opposition from Arnold and Cornwallis, Clinton planned to move operations to the Delaware Neck (see CLINTON, 274–75; MACKESY, 408–9). The "Corps of Anspach" consisted of mercenary troops hired by the British from the German principality of Ansbach-Bayreuth. When in Jan. 1776 the duke of Brunswick agreed to provide some 4,000 mercenaries to the British for the American campaign, he placed Friedrich Adolf von Riedesel, Baron von Eisenbach (1738–1800), in command of the first of his troops to sail for America. In Oct. 1777 Riedesel was among those who sur-

rendered at Saratoga. According to the terms of the Convention of Saratoga, the British and Hessian forces were to be allowed to sail to England with the stipulation they would not again serve in America. Fearing that their return to Britain would free other troops for service in America, the Continental Congress refused to honor the agreement, and Riedesel and the other British and Hessians from Saratoga became the so-called Convention Army. Quartered first in Boston, the Convention troops were later shifted to Charlottesville, Va. Riedesel and his family remained in Charlottesville until Oct. 1780, when he was exchanged. After his exchange Riedesel was then given a command on Long Island by the British (see RIEDESEL, xxi–xli).

13th.   Received Letters from Count de Rochambeau advising me of the arrival of his Son [1] & from Count de Barras [2] informing me of his appointment to the Command of the French Squadron at Rhode Island—both solliciting an Interview with me as soon as possible. Appointed, in answer, Monday the 21st. Inst. & Wethersfield, as the time & place of Meeting.

1. Rochambeau to GW, 11 May 1781 (DLC:GW). Rochambeau's son, Donatien Marie Joseph de Vimeur, vicomte de Rochambeau (1755–1813), served with his father in America as *mestre de camp en second* of the Régiment de Bourbonnais, commanding a battalion of grenadiers at the Battle of Yorktown. In May 1781 the younger Rochambeau had just returned from France, where he had gone in Oct. 1780 in the hope of obtaining additional supplies for the American campaign. The French frigate *Concorde* had brought the comte de Rochambeau dispatches from the minister of war and the minister of marine informing him that the antici-

Sir Henry Clinton, Washington's military opponent, in a miniature by Thomas Day. (R. W. Norton Art Gallery, Shreveport, La.)

pated reinforcement of troops would not be available for the campaign and that the present army under Rochambeau would serve under GW's orders. A sum of six million livres tournois had been granted for the supply of the American army (DONIOL, 5:466–70). In addition, he learned that Admiral de Grasse's fleet had been ordered to the West Indies and would be available to support the upcoming summer campaign. In light of this new information Rochambeau urgently requested a conference with GW (see also CLOSEN, 78). GW agreed to meet with Rochambeau and Admiral Barras at Wethersfield, Conn., on 21 May (GW to Ralph Pomeroy, 14 May 1781, DLC:GW).

2. Jacques Melchior Saint-Laurent, comte de Barras, had replaced Admiral de Ternay as commander of the French naval squadron at Newport. Admiral Destouches had been in temporary command. Barras's letter to GW, 11 May 1781, is in DLC:GW.

14th.   About Noon, intelligence was recd. from Genl. Patterson at West point, that the Enemy were on the No. side of Croton in force – that Colo. Green, Majr. Flag, & some other officers with 40 or 50 Men were surprized & cut off at the Bri⟨dg⟩e & that Colo. Scammell with the New Hampshire Troops had Marched to their assistance. I ordered the Connecticut Troops to move in & support those of New Hampshire.[1]

In the evening, information was brot. that the enemy (consisting of about 60 horse, & 140 Infantry) had retreated precipitately & that several of our Soldiers had been inhumanly murdered.

1. John Paterson (1744–1808) had served first as a colonel in the Massachusetts militia and after Jan. 1776 in the Continental Army, attaining the rank of brigadier general Feb. 1777. In 1781 he was in command of the 2d Massachusetts brigade, operating around West Point (EGLESTON, 124). Paterson's two letters of 14 May to GW containing this information are in DLC:GW. Col. Christopher Greene, commanding the 1st Rhode Island Regiment, and Maj. Ebenezer Flagg, of the same regiment, were part of a small force guarding a ford on the Croton River in Westchester County, N.Y. Both men were killed in a surprise attack just after sunrise on 13 May by a troop of James De Lancey's Tories. The Americans were particularly incensed by rumors that Greene, wounded in the first attack, was "carried into the woods and barbarously murdered" by the Tories (THACHER, 262). See also MOORE [2], 2:427–28; GW to Samuel Huntington, 17 May 1781, DNA: PCC, Item 152. A copy of GW's letter to Paterson, 14 May, ordering him to dispatch troops of the Connecticut Line to reinforce Col. Alexander Scammell's New Hampshire forces is in DLC:GW. On the same day Paterson informed GW that De Lancey's force had withdrawn (DLC:GW).

Alexander Scammell (1747–1781) was adjutant general on GW's staff Jan. 1778–Jan. 1781. He was mortally wounded during the siege of Yorktown under conditions of considerable controversy, the Americans charging that he had been shot after surrendering to a party of British soldiers (see THACHER, 280; TUCKER, 381). At this time he was in command of the 1st New Hampshire Regiment.

15th.   Information, dated 12 oclock yesterday reports 15 Sail of Vessels & a number of Flatboats to be off Fort Lee.[1] Ordered a detachment of 200 Men to March immediately to support the Post at Dobbs's. ferry—countenance the Militia, & cover the Country in that Neighbourhood.[2]

Intelligence from C—— Senr., dated 729[3]—a detachment is expected to Sail tomorrow from New York, & said to consist of the Anspach Troops's 43d. B. Regiment, remainder of the 76th., 80th., 17th. Dragoons, & Infantry of the same—to be conveyed by 7 Ships of the line, 2 fifties, & 3 forty fours which are to cruize of the Capes of Virginia. He gives it as the opinion of C—— Junr. that the above detachmt. does not exceed 2000 Men—that not more than 4000 remain—wch. is only (he adds) to be accounted for on the supposition of their expecting a reinforcement immediately from Europe.[4]

1. Fort Lee was on the New Jersey side of the Hudson River, opposite Fort Washington.
2. GW to John Paterson, 15 May 1781 (DLC:GW).
3. "729" was the cipher for Setauket, Long Island, where Samuel Culper, Sr., was operating (see entry for 1 May 1781).
4. See entry for 12 May 1781.

16th.   Went to the Posts at West point. Received a particular acct. of the surprize of Colo. Green & the loss we sustained which consisted of himself & Major (Flag) killed—three officers & a Surgeon taken prisoners (the latter & two of the former wounded) —a Sergeant & 5 R[ank] & F[ile] killed—5 left wounded & 33 made Prisoners & missing—in all 44 besides Officers.[1]

The report of the number of Shipping &ca. at Fort Lee was this day contradicted in part—the number of Vessels being reduced, & said to be no higher than Bulls ferry.[2] In consequence of this intelligence Lt. Colo. Badlam[3] who marched with the detachment of 200 Men pursuant to the order of Yesterday & had reached Stony point halted—but was directed not to return till the designs of the enemy were better understood.

1. For the attack on Greene's force, see entry for 14 May 1781.
2. Bull's Ferry was approximately two miles below Fort Lee.
3. Ezra Badlam (d. 1788) was lieutenant colonel of the 8th Massachusetts Regiment. See entry for 15 May 1781.

17th.   Received a letter from Captn. Lawrence, near Dobbss ferry, informing me that abt. 200 Refugees were building a block house & raising other works at Fort Lee.[1] Order'd the detachment

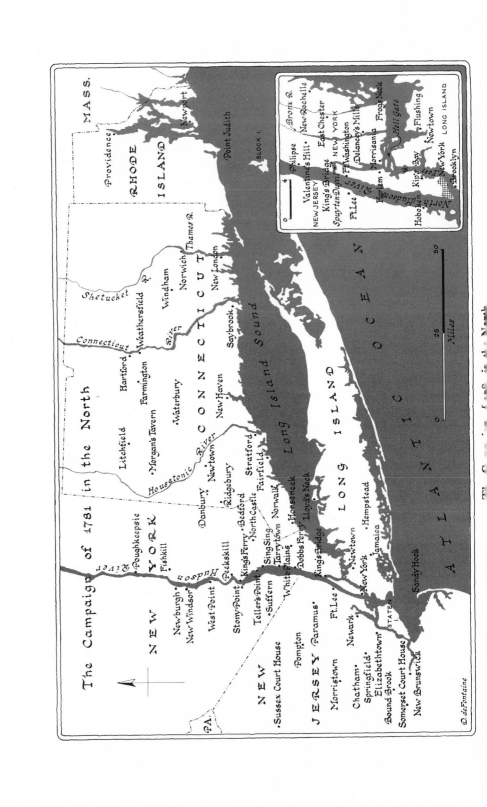

The Campaign of 1781 in the North

which had halted at Kings Ferry² & another forming under Colo. Scammel to advance down & endeavour to annoy, if they could not prevent them.

A Letter from Genl. Foreman of Monmouth (dated the 14th. Instt.) informs me that the British fleet from New York consisting of Seven Ships of 60 Guns & upwards – 12 large Transport Vessels, & 10 topsail Schooners & Sloops made Sail from Sandy hook the 12th., with the wind at So. East. but veering round to the Southward, & Westward, it returned within the hook & lay there till 10 o'clock next day when it again Sailed. By two oclock it was clear of the hook and steering Southward.³

1. Jonathan Lawrence, Jr. (d. 1802), was a captain in the Corps of Sappers and Miners. His letter to GW, 16 May 1781, is in DLC:GW. On receipt of this letter, GW ordered Alexander Scammell to incorporate Lawrence's New York Levies and any available New Jersey militia in his command and, if possible, attack the British party of refugees at Fort Lee (GW to Scammell, 17 May 1781, DLC:GW). The British received intelligence reports of GW's plans and Sir Henry Clinton ordered the refugees to withdraw from the post (MACKENZIE [2], 2:526–27).

2. King's Ferry was the Hudson River crossing between Verplanck's Point and Stony Point.

3. David Forman (1745–1797) was a brigadier general in the New Jersey militia. Forman's letter to GW is in DLC:GW.

18th.   Received Letters from Generals Schuyler and Clinton giving an acct. of the threatened Invasion of the Northern Frontier of this State from Canada, and of the unfavourable prospects from Vermont and of the destruction of the Post of Fort Schuyler – the indefensible State of the Works occasioned thereby & submitting for considn. the propriety of removing the Garrison to the German Flatts which he (that is Clinton) was requested to do if it appear'd to be the sense of the Governor & other principal Gentn. of the State that it would be eligible.¹

Set out this day for the Interview at Weathersfield with the Count de Rochambeau & Admiral Barras. Reached Morgans Tavern 43 Miles from Fishkill Landing after dining at Colo. Vandebergs.²

1. After his resignation from the Continental Army in 1779, Philip Schuyler (1733–1804) was a delegate to the Continental Congress from New York 1779–80 and served in the New York Senate 1780–84. Although at this time Schuyler was involved principally in the management of his New York estates and his business affairs, his advice was frequently sought about military matters in northern New York. In Mar. 1781 he was appointed state surveyor general and in an unofficial capacity was active in procuring supplies for the army in New York State (GERLACH, 156–59). Schuyler's letter,

15 May 1781, is addressed to Brig. Gen. James Clinton and was enclosed, with other correspondence, in Clinton's letter to GW, 16 May 1781 (DLC: GW). At the beginning of May 1781 the barracks at Fort Schuyler had been partially destroyed by fire and further devastated by a heavy rainstorm which followed. On 27 May, GW informed Congress that the post had been abandoned and the garrison and stores removed to German Flats (in the area of present-day Herkimer, N.Y.), since a post at that location "would be more easily supported, and equally advantageous to the security of the Frontier" (GW to Samuel Huntington, 27 May 1781, NjP: deCoppet Collection).

2. The Connecticut assembly was meeting at Hartford, so the conference with the French was held at nearby Wethersfield. Morgan's tavern was probably the establishment kept by Gideon Morgan, who was licensed in 1781 as a tavern keeper in Washington, Litchfield County, Conn. (CROFUT, 1:442). Also in GW's party were Brig. Gen. Henry Knox (1750–1806), chief of artillery for the Continental Army, and the French engineer Brig. Gen. Louis Le Bègue Duportail, who had been serving with the American forces since 1777.

19th. Breakfasted at Litchfield – dined at Farmington & lodged at Weathersfield at the House of Joseph Webb Esqr. (the Quarters wch. were taken for me & my Suit).[1]

1. GW may have breakfasted at Samuel Sheldon's tavern in Litchfield. In Wethersfield, GW and his suite lodged at Webb House, owned at this time by Col. Joseph Webb (1749–1815) and his wife, Abigail Chester Webb. Webb's brother, Samuel Blachley Webb (1753–1807), had served as GW's aide-de-camp from June 1776 to Jan. 1777. The officers in the French party lodged at Stillman's tavern. See also *Conn. Courant*, 29 May 1781.

20th. Had a good deal of private conversation with Govr. Trumbull who gave it to me as his opinion that if any important offensive operation should be undertaken he had little doubt of our obtaining Men & Provision adequate to our wants.[1] In this opinion Colo. Wadsworth & others concurr'd.[2]

1. Jonathan Trumbull, Sr. (1710–1785), served as governor of Connecticut from 1769 to 1784. He was closely involved with the state's heavy responsibilities in supplying the Continental Army. Although GW and Trumbull generally worked well together, the commander in chief was occasionally impatient with the governor's difficulties in raising provisions.

2. Jeremiah Wadsworth (1743–1804), a native of Hartford, Conn., had already become established as a merchant when he was appointed in 1775 commissary of the Connecticut militia. In 1777 the Continental Congress named him deputy commissary general of purchases, and from April 1778 to Dec. 1779 he served as commissary general of the army. In 1780 he agreed to act unofficially as advance purchasing agent for the supply of Rochambeau's army and later, in partnership with John Barker Church (operating under the alias of John Carter), contracted to become provisioning agent for much of the French army in America (see DESTLER, 50–54; CHASTELLUX, 1:258).

21st.   The Count de Rochambeau with the Chevr. de Chastellux arrived about Noon.[1] The appearance of the British Fleet (under Adml. Arbuthnot) off Block Island prevented the attendance of the Count de Barras.[2]

1. François Jean le Beauvoir, chevalier de Chastellux (1734–1788), entered the French army at the age of 13, reaching the rank of colonel by 1759, and serving with some distinction in the Seven Years' War. After 1763, while he retained his position in the army, his literary activities earned him a place among the Encyclopedists and philosophes (see Howard Rice's introduction to CHASTELLUX, 1:1–25). In 1780 Chastellux was promoted to *maréchal de camp* and named a major general in Rochambeau's army. He arrived in America in July 1780 with Admiral de Ternay's fleet, served in the Yorktown campaign, and remained in America until Jan. 1783. His relations with GW were excellent, and they remained in correspondence after the war.

2. Marriot Arbuthnot (c.1711–1794) was an admiral in the British navy and commander of the American station. Baron von Closen, writing at Newport, noted in his journal on 18 May that at "11 o'clock, 10 sails were discovered, which were signalled a little later to be warships. They anchored off Judith Point and Block Island [Rhode Island]" (CLOSEN, 79). These were probably ships of the fleet which had sailed from New York on 9 May (see entry for 12 May 1781) to escort British and Hessian troops to the Chesapeake. Frederick Mackenzie noted on 25 May that "There has been no account from the fleet since it sailed from hence. 'Tis supposed that after seeing the transports with the troops for the Chesapeak, safe past the Delaware, the Admiral returned to cruize off Rhode-Island" (MACKENZIE [2], 2:530). Barras was reluctant to leave Newport for Wethersfield after the arrival of the British fleet, partly because the French were in daily expectation of the arrival of a convoy from France and he had hoped to sail to meet the French ships (RICE, 1:27; CLOSEN, 79).

22nd.   Fixed with Count de Rochambeau upon a plan of Campaign—in Substance as follows. That the French Land force (except 200 Men) should March so soon as the Squadron could Sail for Boston—to the North River & there, in conjunction with the American, to commence an operation against New York (which in the present reduced State of the Garrison it was thought would fall, unless relieved; the doing which wd. enfeeble their Southern operations, and in either case be productive of capital advantages) or to extend our views to the Southward as circumstances and a Naval superiority might render more necessary & eligable. The aid which would be given to such an operation in this quarter—the tardiness with which the Regiments would be filled for any other—the insurmountable difficulty & expence of Land transportation—the waste of Men in long marches (especially where there is a disinclination to the Service—objections to the climate &ca.) with other reasons too numerous to detail, induced to this opinion. The heavy Stores & Baggage of the French Army were to be deposited at Providence under Guard of 200 Men (before mentioned) & Newport Harbour & Works were to be secured by 500 Militia.[1]

1. The Wethersfield Conference was held in the Webb House. Rochambeau informed GW of the probability that the combined French and American forces would be able to count on the arrival of de Grasse's fleet in American waters later in the summer. The main question to be considered at Wethersfield was where the summer campaign should take place. Rochambeau contended that Virginia offered the best hope for a successful campaign, while GW stressed the advantages of an attack on the British in New York. "The Enemy by several detachments from New York having reduced their force at that Post to less than one half of the number which they had at the time of the former conference at Hartford in September last; it is thought advisable to form a junction of the French & American Armies upon the North [Hudson] River as soon as possible, and move down to the vicinity of New York to be ready to take advantage of any oppertunity which the weakness of the enemy may afford" ("Conference with Comte de Rochambeau," 23 May 1781, DLC:GW). See also the more complete report of the interview in the Rochambeau Papers, Paul Mellon Collection, Upperville, Va.; KEIM, 381–83; and an account in Arch. des Aff. Etr., Corr. Pol., Etats-Unis, supp. vol. 15. In Mar. 1781 GW and Rochambeau had determined at a conference at Hartford that the French fleet would remain at Newport, a decision that conflicted with Admiral Barras's orders which had stipulated that after Rochambeau marched to join GW the fleet would sail for Boston. In light of the possible transfer of the fleet it was decided at the meeting that the entensive stores and munitions which had been collected at Providence for the use of the fleet at Newport "may safely remain there under the Guard of 200 French Troops" (DLC:GW). Later, however, a council of war of French officers at Newport decided that Barras's fleet would remain at Newport rather than move operations to Boston. See also Rochambeau to GW, 31 May 1781, DLC:GW; DONIOL, 5:477–86.

Governor Trumbull dined with GW on 22 May (WEBB [2], 2:340–41).

23d.   Count de Rochambeau set out on his Return to Newport,[1] while I prepared and forwarded dispatches to the Governors of the four New England States calling upon them in earnest & pointed terms, to compleat their Continental Battalions for the Campaign, at least, if it could not be done for the War or 3 Years—to hold a body of Militia (according to the Proportion given them) ready to march in one Week after being called for and to adopt some effectual mode to supply the Troops when assembled with Provisns. & Transportation.[2]

I also sollicited the Governors of the States of Massachusetts & Connecticut earnestly for a Loan of Powder & the means of Transporting it to the Army.[3]

A Letter from Genl. St. Clair came to hand with accts. of an apparent intention of the enemy to evacuate New York.[4]

1. Rochambeau reached Newport on 27 May (CLOSEN, 80).

2. A copy of GW's circular letter to the governors of the New England states, dated 24 May 1781, is in DLC:GW.

3. On 25 May 1781 GW wrote to Massachusetts governor John Hancock requesting that "as great a loan of powder from the State of Massachusetts as can possibly be spared" be sent to Fishkill, N.Y. A similar letter was sent to Connecticut governor Jonathan Trumbull, Sr., on the same day (Ct).

4. In May 1781 Maj. Gen. Arthur St. Clair (1736–1818) was at Headquarters at New Windsor. His letter to GW, 21 May 1781, also transmitted a report that Sir Henry Clinton had been making inquiries "whether there was any probability that Congress would listen to Terms of Accommodation separately from France" (anonymous donor).

24th.   Set out on my return to New Windsor—dined at Farmington and lodged at Litchfield.[1]

1. GW's lodgings in Litchfield were probably at Samuel Sheldon's tavern or at Capt. William Stanton's tavern in Kilbourn House, both on North Street (CROFUT, 1:62).

25th.   Breakfasted at Squire Cogswells[1]—dined at Colo. Vandeburgs & reached head Quarters about Sunset where I found letters from Generls. Schuyler & Clinton, full of uncertain information respecting the enemys landing at Crown point & intention to penetrate on the Hudson & Mohawk Rivers.[2] This uncertainty respects the number, not the fact—the latter seeming to be beyond a doubt. In consequence of this information I ordered the Companies of Vanscaicks Regiment[3] at West point to hold themselves in readiness to Move at an hours warning.

1. The tavern kept by William and Anna Whittlesey Cogswell was "near the village of New Preston, in the town of Washington" (CROFUT, 1:63).

2. The letters from James Clinton and Philip Schuyler to GW, both dated 22 May 1781, are in DLC:GW. Schuyler's letter relayed a report that "four thousand of the Enemy are actually come to crown point and Tyconderoga."

3. Goose Van Schaick (1736–1789) became colonel of the 2d New York Regiment in June 1775. Van Schaick's regiment at this time was the 1st New York Regiment, of which he served as colonel from Nov. 1776 to Nov. 1783 (BERG, 84).

26th.   Received a Letter from the Honble. Jno. Laurens Minister from the United States of America at the Court of Versailles —informing me that the Sum of 6,000,000 of Livres was granted as a donation to this Country—to be applied in part to the purchase of Arms—Cloaths &ca. for the American Troops and the ballance to my orders, & draughts at long sight and that a Fleet of 20 Sail of the Line was on its departure for the West Indies 12 of which were to proceed to this Coast where it was probable they might arrive in the Month of July.[1] He also added that the Courts of Petersbg. & Vienna had offered their Mediation in settling the present troubles wch. the King of France, tho' personally pleas'd with, could not accept without consulting his Allies.[2] A Letter from Doctr. Lee – inclosing extracts of one from his Brother Wm. Lee Esqr. dated the 20th. of Feby. holds out strong assurances of Peace being restored in the course of this Yr.[3]

1. John Laurens (1754–1782), of South Carolina, son of Henry Laurens, former president of the Continental Congress, had been appointed aide-de-camp to GW in 1777. In Dec. 1780 John Laurens was made a special envoy to France to obtain additional aid for the United States. When he returned from his mission to France he rejoined the army, participated in the York-town campaign, and was killed in a minor skirmish with the British at Combahee Ferry, S.C., in Aug. 1782. For the objectives of Laurens's mission to France, see his memorial to the comte de Vergennes (WHARTON, 4:318–21). His letter to GW, written from Paris, 24 Mar. 1781, is in DLC:GW.

2. Vergennes had told Laurens that "The Courts of Petersburg & Vienna have offered their mediation. The King has answered that it would be personally agreeable to him, but that he could not as yet accept it, because he has Allies whose concurrence is necessary. Mr. Franklin is requested to communicate the Overture and Answer to Congress, and to engage them to send their instructions to their plenipotentiaries. It is supposed the Congress

Lt. Col. John Laurens, Washington's valuable aide and envoy. (Independence National Historical Park Collection)

will accept the mediation with eagerness" (Laurens to GW, 24 Mar. 1781, DLC:GW). For the mediation attempts of Russia and Austria and Vergennes's maneuvers, see BEMIS, 172–88; MORRIS, 173–90. The Austro-Russian mediation offer was transmitted to Congress by the French minister on 26 May 1781 (JCC, 20:560–63).

3. Arthur Lee (1740–1792), a member of the powerful Lee family of Virginia, was educated at Eton and studied medicine at the University of Edinburgh, receiving the M.D. degree in 1764. After practicing medicine for a short time in Williamsburg, he returned to England in 1768 and studied law at Lincoln's Inn and the Middle Temple. His brother, William Lee (1739–1795), accompanied him to England and entered on a successful mercantile career in London. In 1773 William was made a sheriff of London and in 1775 an alderman. Both Lees became prominent in London literary and political circles. After 1777 William Lee embarked on a series of unsuccessful diplomatic missions on behalf of the United States to various European courts. Arthur Lee was appointed in 1776, with Benjamin Franklin and Silas Deane, one of the three commissioners to France and, after stormy controversies with his fellow commissioners, was recalled by Congress to America in 1779. After his return he served in the Virginia House of Delegates and in 1781 was elected to the Continental Congress. William had been recalled from his diplomatic missions in 1779 but remained in Europe until 1783. GW had been connected with both Lees in the Mississippi Company before their departure for England. Arthur Lee's letter has not been found, but on 7 June, GW acknowledged Lee's letter of 19 May thanking him "for the extract taken from the letter of Mr. Lee of Feby. 20th. The information contained in it is important, and went to some matters which were new to me. I suspt. with you, that Mr. Lee is rather too sanguine in his expectation of a genl. Peace within the year" (DLC:GW). The extracts were probably taken from William Lee to Richard Henry Lee, 20 Feb. 1781, written from Brussels and containing William's anticipation of impending peace "unless some unexpected and unforeseen occurrences in America should happen, that may induce the King of Great Britain to risque every thing elsewhere, in hopes of obtaining his favorite object, the Subjugation of America. You have the game therefore in your hands" (LEE [2], 3:843–48).

28th.   The Commanding Officer of Artillery & the chief Engineer were called upon to give in estimates of their wants for the intended operation against New York.[1] The intention of doing this was also disclosed to the Q. M. General who was desired to give every attention toward the Boats, that a number of them might be prepared; & provide other matters necessary to such an undertaking—especially those things which might be called for by the Artillery, & the Engineering departments.[2]

1. GW to Henry Knox, 28 May 1781 (MHi: Knox Papers) and to Louis Le Bègue de Presle Duportail, 28 May 1781 (DLC:GW). Duportail (1743–1802) became an officer of engineers in the French army in 1762 and by 1773 had risen to rank of captain. Sent to America by Franklin in 1777, he was made "Colonel in Chief of Engineers" of the Continental Army and

promoted to brigadier general in Nov. 1777 (JCC, 8:539, 571, 9:932). In April 1780 he was attached with the rank of lieutenant colonel to the newly arrived French army.

2. GW's instructions to Timothy Pickering may have been verbal. No letter has been found.

31st.   A Letter from Count de Rochambeau informed me that the British fleet had left Block Island—that Adml. de Barras would Sail with the first fair Wind for Boston (having 900 of his Soldiers on Board to Man his fleet) and that he should commence his March as soon as possible, but would be under the necessity of Halting a few days at Providence.[1]

A Letter from Major Talmage, inclosing one from C—— Senr. & another from S. G. dated the 27th. were totally silent on the subject of an evacuation of New York;[2] but speak of an order for Marching the Troops from Long Island and the Countermand of it after they had commenced their March; the cause for either they could not assign. Neither C. Senr. nor S. G. estimate the Enemys regular force at New York or its dependencies at more than 4500 men including the New Levies; but C—— says it is reported that they can command five & some add 6,000 Militia & refugees. S. G. disposes of the Enemys force as follow.

At Fort Washington[3] & towards New York —2 Hessn. Regts.	2
Laurel Hill[4]—Fort George. 57th B.	1
Haerlam—at a place called Laurel Hill—38 Do.	1
At Hornes hook,[5] & towds. the City—22d. & 42d. B. Regts.	2
In the City Hessian Regimts.	2
On Staten Island	2
Total on this Isld. 1200	
On Long Island	
1st. B. Grenadrs. ... New Town	1
2d. .... Ditto ... Jamaica	1
Worms Hessian Yagers[6] (called by him 6 or 700) No. side of the Plains	1
Light Dragns. ... 17th. Regt. at Hempstead Plains	1
Loyds Neck—detachmets. from New Corps Abt. 6, or 700	14

The detachment which left Sandy hook the 13th Instt. according to the S. G.'s acct.—consisted of the Troops on the other side

—though it is thought he must be mistaken in naming the 46th. & 86th. Regimts.—the first of them being a convention Regimt.[7] and the other not in America. By Accts. from Deserters the 37th. Regt. went with the detachment and must be in place of the 46th. as the 80th. must be that of the 86th.

	suppos'd
43 British Regiments	300
Anspach—2 Battalions	700
part of the 86th.	150
part of the 46th.	150
Hessian Yagers—abt.	150
	1450[8]

1. Rochambeau's letter to GW, 29 May 1781, partly in cipher, is in DLC:GW.

2. Benjamin Tallmadge to GW, 29 May 1781 (DLC:GW). "C——— Sen." (Samuel Culper, Sr.) was an alias for Abraham Woodhull (see entry for 1 May 1781). "S. G." was the code name for another American spy, George Smith of Nissequogue, Long Island, who before he joined the Culper spy ring had served in a Suffolk County militia regiment as a lieutenant (see FORD [4], 277, 322). Both enclosures are in DLC:GW.

3. Fort Washington was located in the vicinity of present W. 183d Street in Manhattan. It had been captured by the British in Nov. 1776.

4. Laurel Hill was at present 192d Street and Audubon Avenue on the west bank of the Harlem River. After the American withdrawal from Manhattan, the British had constructed Fort George on the site of the earlier American works. The fort was about half a mile east of Fort Washington.

5. Horn's Hook, a strip of land extending into the East River near E. 88th Street in Manhattan.

6. Lt. Col. Ludwig Johann Adolph von Wurmb's Jaeger Corps.

7. That is, part of the so-called Convention Army, consisting of British and Hessian troops surrendered Oct. 1777 after the battles of Saratoga.

8. On 31 May 1781 GW wrote to the marquis de Lafayette in Virginia that "Upon a full consideration of our affairs in every point of view, an attempt upon New York with its present Garrison . . . was deemed preferable to a Southern operation as we had not the Command of the Water." The letter contained considerable detail on the proposed campaign, including the vital information that "above all, it was thought that we had a tolerable prospect of expelling the enemy or obliging them to withdraw part of their force from the Southward, which last would give the most effectual relief to those States" (MiU-C: Clinton Papers). This letter was among a number of others, including some of GW's dispatches to Congress and correspondence of the French command, which were captured by the British on 3 June. British Ens. John Moody arrived at Clinton's headquarters in New York City with the captured mail and was rewarded by the elated Clinton with 200 guineas. "The Capture of this Mail is extremely consequential, and gives the Commander in Chief the most perfect knowledge of the designs of the Enemy" (MACKENZIE [2], 2:536; CLINTON, 305–6).

June 1781

1st.   Received Letters from Generals Schuyler & Clinton,[1] containing further but still indistinct accts, of the enemys force at Crown point. Letters from Doctr. Smith of Albany,[2] & —— Shepherd[3] principal armourer at that place, were intercepted, going to the enemy with acct. of our distresses—the strength & dispositon of our Troops—The disaffection of particular Settlements—the provision these Settlemts. had made to subsist them—their readiness to join them—the genl. temper of the people and their earnest wishes for their advance in force—assuring them of the happy consequences which would derive to the Kings arms if they would move rapidly to Albany. In consequence of this information I directed the Q. M. General to provide Craft for, & the 6 Companies of Vanscaicks Regiment & Hazens to proceed immediately to Albany & put themselves under General Clintons orders.[4]

1. James Clinton to GW, 30 May 1781, enclosing Philip Schuyler to Clinton, 24 May 1781 (DLC:GW).

2. Dr. George Smith of Albany had been arrested in Aug. 1780, charged with aiding a British spy through American lines. Smith was released shortly after his arrest, but he remained under suspicion and his movements were sharply curtailed. In May 1781 the board of commissioners for detecting and defeating conspiracies decided that "Doctor George Smith and his son Terence Smith are Persons whose going at large at this Time may prove detrimental to the Safety of the State." Dr. Smith attempted to flee to Canada but was apprehended at Bennington, Vt., 30 May 1781. In Aug. 1781 he was implicated in a plot to take Philip Schuyler prisoner (PALTSITS, 2:477, 479, 545, 561, 720–21, 726, 728, 765).

3. William Shepherd. His name appears several times as bailsman for individuals in Albany suspected of Tory activities (PALTSITS, 1:216; 2:572, 597).

4. Tench Tilghman, one of GW's aides-de-camp, sent these orders to Timothy Pickering, 1 June 1781 (DLC:GW).

4th.   Letters from the Marqs. de la Fayette of the 25th Ulto. informs that Lord Cornwallis had formed a junction with Arnold at Petersbourg[1]—that with their United force he had Marched to City point[2] on James River and that the detachment which sailed from New York the 13th of May had arrived in James River and were debarking at Westover and that he himself had removed from Wilton[3] to Richmond.

The Duke de Lauzen arrived this afternoon with Letters from Count de Rochambeau & Admiral Count de Barras, with the proceedings of a Council of War held on Board the Duke de Burgoyne proposing to continue the Fleet at Rhode Island under the protection of 400 French Troops & 1000 Militia in preference to the plan adopted at Weathersfield; requiring my opinion thereon which was given to the effect—that I conceived the first plan gave a more perfect security to the Kings fleet than the latter, & consequently left the Land force more at liberty to act, for which reason I could not change my former opinion but shou'd readily acquiesce to theirs if upon a re-consideration of the matter they adhered to it. Accordingly, that delay might be avoided, I inclosed letters (under flying Seals) to the Governors of Rd. Island & Massachusetts, to be made use of or not, requesting the Militia; & pressed the March of the Land Troops as soon as circumstances would admit of it.[4]

1. This information was contained in a letter from Lafayette to GW, dated 24 rather than 25 May 1781 (DLC:GW).

2. City Point, Va., now part of Hopewell, is near the confluence of the James and Appomattox rivers.

3. Wilton was an estate on the north side of the James River, six miles south of Richmond in Henrico County. Lafayette had established his headquarters there in May 1781. Westover was the estate of Col. William Byrd III.

4. Armand Louis de Gontaut Biron, duc de Lauzun (1747–1793), served in the French guards and in 1767 in the French campaign in Corsica. In 1780 he was appointed brigadier general in command of the legion of horse which bore his name and in July 1780 arrived with his troops at Newport, R.I. He was in the Yorktown campaign in 1781 and carried the news of the capitulation at Yorktown to Paris.

See also entry for 22 May 1781. For the minutes of the council of war held on board Barras's flagship, the *Duc-de Bourgogne*, 31 May 1781, see DONIOL, 5:477–79. Rochambeau sent a copy of the minutes to GW, 31 May 1781 (DLC:GW). Apparently Lauzun, who had been in favor of transferring the French fleet to Boston, left GW under the impression that the council of war's decision to keep the fleet at Newport was subject to the commander in chief's approval (see CARSON [1], 91). GW also wrote letters on 4 June to William Greene, governor of Rhode Island (DLC:GW), and to John Hancock, governor of Massachusetts (M-Ar), requesting 500 militia from each to support the French establishment at Newport. Both letters were sent to Rochambeau and closed with a "flying seal," that is, a seal attached but not closed, so that Rochambeau might examine the contents and forward the letters if necessary. A second council of war, held on board the *Neptune* 8 June 1781, confirmed the decision to hold the fleet at Newport (DONIOL, 5:484–86; Rochambeau to GW, 9 June 1781, DLC:GW). See also GW to the chevalier de Chastellux, 13 June 1781 (DLC:GW).

5th.   Governor Rutlidge of South Carolina came to Head Qrs. with representations of the situation of Southern affairs, & to sollicit aids. I communicated the plan of Campaign to him & candidly exposed the true State of our Circumstances which convinced him—or seemed to do so—that no relief cd. be given from this army till we had acquired a Naval Superiority and cd. transport Troops by Water.[1]

1. John Rutledge was at this time governor of South Carolina. Rutledge had left Philadelphia 23 May to visit Headquarters at New Windsor, N.Y., before returning to South Carolina (LMCC, 6:96). Presumably his mission was to relay to GW the hopes of the southern delegates in the Continental Congress for a summer campaign in the South rather than an attack on New York.

7th. A Letter from the Govr. of Virginia dated at Charlottesville the 28th. Ulto. representing the distressed State of Virginia & pressing my repairng thither, was received[1]—other letters (but not official) speak of Lord Cornwallis's advance to Hanover Court House—that the Marquis was retreating before him towards Fredericksburg and that General Leslie[2] was embarked in James River with about 1200 Men destined, as was supposed, to Alexandria whither it was conjectured by the letter writers Lord Cornwallis was pointing his March.

Accts. from Pittsburg were expressive of much apprehension for that quarter as a force from Canada was expected thither by way of the Lakes and the Alligany River.

A Letter from the Executive of Pennsylvania afforded little hope of assistance in the article of Provision or other things from that State and was more productive of what they had done, than what they meant to do.[3]

1. Thomas Jefferson's letter to GW, 28 May 1781, is in DLC:GW. Jefferson joined other southerners in pressing for a summer campaign in the South. In May 1781 Cornwallis had moved north from the Carolinas to reinforce Gen. William Phillips and Benedict Arnold in Virginia. Jefferson now informed GW that Cornwallis's army had joined forces with troops under Arnold at Petersburg, Va. The combined force had evacuated Petersburg and, with reinforcements sent by Sir Henry Clinton from New York, marched on Richmond, then held by Lafayette with 3,000 regulars and militia. Jefferson's intelligence reports estimated that some 7,000 British troops were operating in Virginia. On 8 June, GW wrote to Jefferson, giving his reasons for remaining in the North to direct an attack on New York City, in expectation that such an attack would compel the British to recall at least part of their forces in the South (PHi: Gratz Collection).

2. Maj. Gen. Alexander Leslie (1740–1794) was active in British campaigns in the South in 1780 and 1781 and was in command at Charleston at the end of the war.

3. Joseph Reed, president of Pennsylvania, to GW, 17 May 1781 (MH: Sparks Transcripts).

9th.   A Captn. Randolph—sent by General Clarke from Pittsburg, arrived here with letters & representations of his disappointments of Men, and the prospect of failure in his intended Expedition against Detroit unless he could be aided by the 9th. Virginia Regiment & Heths Company at Pittsburg—but the weakness of the Garrison & other considerations would not admit this—nor did it appear to me that this reinforcement would enable him to undertake & prosecute the Plan.[1]

1. At this time George Rogers Clark (1752–1818) was at Pittsburgh. Clark had mounted successful campaigns against Vincennes in 1778 and 1779 and was largely responsible for forestalling British plans to recapture the Illinois country and the Ohio Valley in 1779–80. In Dec. 1780 he began to plan for a new campaign against British-held Detroit and Lake Erie and in Jan. 1781 was made brigadier general of the Virginia forces in the West. Preparations for the expedition, however, were constantly thwarted by shortages of men and supplies (see CLARK [1], 8:cxlii–cxlvii). The two letters from Clark to GW are dated 20 and 21 May 1781 (DLC:GW). GW replied to Clark on 8 June 1781 (DLC:GW).

Capt. Henry Heth's company was one of two independent companies raised after Feb. 1777 to garrison Fort Pitt and Fort Randolph. Each consisted of a captain, two lieutenants, one ensign, and 100 enlisted men (see BERG, 100–101; JCC, 7:21).

11th.   Received Letters from the Marqs. de la Fayette, containing information of Lord Cornwallis's movements from Westover, and that, at the date of his letter—the 3d. Instt.—he had advanced to the North Anna—but his design was not sufficiently understood

A mezzotint of the marquis de Lafayette, after Charles Willson Peale. (Mount Vernon Ladies' Association of the Union)

—supposed Fredericksburg. The Marqs. was retreating before him with abt. 3000 Men Militia included—the Enemys force exclusive of Leslies detachment being estimated at five or 6000 Men, 600 of wch. were Horse.

13th.   To facilitate the building, and repairing of Boats, a number of Carpenters was ordered from the line of the army to the Q. M. G. to aid the artificers of his department in this important business and Major Darby with a Captain 5 Subs & 6 Sergts. and 100 Rank & file were drawn from the army in order to collect and take care of the public Boats.[1]

   1. Samuel Darby (d. 1807) had served as a captain in various Massachusetts regiments and was promoted to major in the 7th Massachusetts in 1778. Darby's instructions were contained in General Orders, 19 June 1781 (DLC:GW).

14th.   Received agreeable acts. from General Greene, of his Successes in South Carolina [1]—viz.—that Lord Rawden [2] had abandoned Cambden with precipitation, leaving all our wounded taken in the action of the 25th. of April last, together with 58 of his own too bad to remove—that he had destroy'd his own Stores —burnt many buildings and in short left the Town little better than a heap of Rubbish—That Orangeburg, Forts Mott. & Granby, had surrendered; [3] their Garrisons including officers consisting of near 700 Men—That Ninety Six & Fort Augusta were invested [4]—that he was preparing to March to the Former and that, Lord Rawden was at Nelsons ferry [5] removing the Stores from that place which indicated an Evacuation thereof.

   1. GW had just received Maj. Gen. Nathanael Greene's letter of 16 May 1781, enclosing a copy of Greene's letter of 14 May to Congress announcing his successes in the South (DLC:GW). News of Greene's victories was relayed to the army in General Orders, 15 June 1781 (DLC:GW).
   2. Francis, Lord Rawdon (1754–1826), had commanded a company at Bunker Hill and served on the staffs of Burgoyne and Cornwallis. In 1778 he was promoted to lieutenant colonel and in 1780 was ordered south for the campaign against Charleston, S.C. By Jan. 1781 Rawdon was left in virtual command of some 8,000 troops to face Greene's army in South Carolina and Georgia while Cornwallis moved into North Carolina. It was on 25 April 1781 Rawdon defeated Greene at the Battle of Hobkirk's Hill, S.C., suffering heavy casualties. He then moved on to capture Camden, S.C., but finding it impossible to hold, he withdrew to Monck's Corner.
   3. These forts were in South Carolina: Orangeburg in Orange County, taken by Brig. Gen. Thomas Sumter 11 May; Fort Motte on the Congaree River in Orange County, captured 12 May by Lt. Col. Henry Lee and Brig. Gen. Francis Marion; Fort Granby, on the Congaree River, taken by Lee on 15 May.

June 1781

4. Ninety Six, Greenwood County, S.C., was under siege from 22 May to 19 June 1781. Rawdon had ordered the fort abandoned but his instructions miscarried. Ninety Six was on the verge of surrender to the Americans when Rawdon mustered 2,000 men and marched to its relief. On 20 June, Greene pulled back from the fort and was briefly pursued by the British. Rawdon then ordered Ninety Six abandoned and the evacuation was completed by 3 July.

Fort Augusta on the Savannah River, Richmond County, Ga., was under siege by Henry Lee and Andrew Pickens 22 May–5 June 1781. The fort surrendered on 5 June.

5. Nelson's Ferry was on the Santee River about five miles from Eutaw Springs, S.C.

16th.   Directed that no more Invalids be transferred till further Orders[1]—that a detachment be formed of the weakliest Men for garrisoning of West point & that a Camp be marked out by the Chief Engineer & Q. M. Genl. near Peekskill to assemble the Troops on.

1. GW's command that no men were "to be transferred to the Corps of Invalids untill further orders" is in General Orders, 15 June 1781 (DLC: GW). The Corps of Invalids had been established 16 July 1777 for the utilization of veterans who were not fit for active service but were still able to perform such assignments as garrison duty (JCC, 8:554–56).

18th.   Brigaded the Troops, and made an arrangement of the Army, which is to March for the New Camp in three divisions— the 1st. on Thursday the 21st.—the 2d. on the 23d. and the 3d. on the 24th. Instt.[1] To strengthen the detachment intended for the Garrison of West point, I had previously called upon the State of Connecticut for 800 Militia.

1. Headquarters was being moved from New Windsor, N.Y., to Peekskill, N.Y. (see General Orders, 19 June 1781, DLC:GW).

20th.   Recd. Letters from Genl. Clinton at Albany inclosing the examination of two Prisoners taken at Crown point by wch. and other intelligence it appears that no Troops had landed at that place and that the enemys Shipping *only,* had ever been there.[1] In consequence, the Continental Troops to the No[rth]ward were ordered to be in readiness to join the army on the shortest notice & Governor Clinton informed thereof that the New levies of the State, & nine months, men might be hastened to relieve them.[2]

1. James Clinton to GW, 15 June 1781 (DLC:GW), enclosing examinations of William Empie and Randal Hewit, taken prisoner by one of Clinton's scouts.
2. GW to George Clinton, 21 June 1781 (CSmH). Because of rumors

of a British attack on the New York frontier, GW had sent reinforcements to the area. See entries for 18, 25 May, 1 June 1781. GW informed Governor Clinton that from "the examination of two Prisoners who were lately taken . . . it appears the Enemy in Canada, have not made any Movements in force, or preparations for an incursion; and indeed this intelligence corresponds so exactly with that, which has been received through other channels, that I cannot but regret having sent the Reinforcement to the Northward, at a time when the aid of every Man was so essential to the success of the operations in contemplation."

24th.　A Letter from the Count de Rochambeau dated at Windham the 20th. advises me of his having reached that Town, that day, with the first division of his army—that the other 3 divisions were following in regular succession—that he expected to Halt the Troops two days at Hartford, but would come on to my Camp from that place after the arrival of the division with which he was.[1]

By a Letter from Govr. Trumbull it appear'd that the assembly of Connecticut had passed some salutary Laws for filling their Battalions, & complying with my requisition—but it is to be feared that their list of deficiencies, which the respective Towns are called upon to make good by drafts to compleat the Battalions is short of the number wanting for this purpose.[2]

1. Rochambeau's letter is in DLC:GW. The main body of the French army had left Newport between 10 and 12 June 1781 and arrived in the vicinity of White Plains 6 July (RICE, 1:27, 32, 246). For the march, see RICE, 1:26–32, 246–49, 2:9–36; CLOSEN, 82–91.

2. Jonathan Trumbull, Sr., to GW, 20 June 1781, enclosing a resolution of the Connecticut council of safety, 19 June 1781, and two acts of the Connecticut legislature (DLC:GW).

25th.　A Letter from Genl. Heath of the 18th. holds up favourable Ideas of the disposition prevaling in the State of Massachusetts Bay to comply with every thing required of them.[1]

Joined the Army at its Encampment at Peekskill. Mrs. Washington set out at the same time towards Virginia but with an intention to Halt at Philadelphia if from information & circumstances it was not likely she should remain quietly at Mt. Vernon.[2]

A Letter from Count de Rochambeau informs me that he shall be with his first division at Newtown on the 28th. where he purposed to assemble his force & March in Brigades while the Duke de Lauzens Legion continues to move on his Left flank.[3]

Had an interview with Govr. Clinton, Lieut. Govr. Courtlandt,[4] & Generals Schuyler & Tenbrook;[5] in which I pressed the necessity of my recalling the Continental Regiments from Albany,

This handsome miniature of Martha Washington was made by Charles Willson Peale in 1776. (Mount Vernon Ladies' Association of the Union)

& the Posts above, & of the States hastening up their Levies for 3 Years & Nine months and agreed to order 600 Militia (part of the quota required of Massachusetts bay) from the Counties of Berkshire and Hampshire to March immediately to Albany which was accordingly done & Govr. Hancock advised of it.[6]

Genl. Stark was directed to repair to Saratoga & take command of the Troops on the Northern & western frontier and Genl. Clinton called upon in pointed terms to have the Continental Troops under his command in the most perfect readiness to join the Army.[7]

Recd. a Letter from the Minister of France advising me of the arrival of between 3 & 4000 Troops abt. the 4th. Inst. at Charles Town[8]—that 2000 of them had debarked & that the rest were said to be destined for St. Augustine & New York—that George Town was evacuated & the Enemy in Charles town weak (not exceeding 450 Men before the reinforcement arrived—which latter must be a mistake, as the Ministers informant added, that Lord Rawden had got there after a precipitate retreat from a Post above and that the American parties were within 5 Miles of the Town. Lord Rawdens Troops alone amounted to more than the Number here mentioned).

Having suggested to the Count de Rochambeau the advantages which might be derived to the common cause in general and the Southern States in particular, if by arming the Fantasque & bringing the 50 gun ship to Rhode Isld. (which then lay at Boston) the fleet of his most Christian Majesty at Newport could appear in Chesapeak bay.[9] I received an answer from the French Admiral through the General that he was disposed to the measure provided he could obtain a loan of the French Guard (of 400 Men which were left at Newport & which were granted) and 4 pieces of heavy artillery at Brentons point[10] which the Count could not spare but that the fleet could not be ready to Sail under 20 days from the date of his letter (the 21st.) —thus, uncertain, the matter stands.

1. William Heath to GW, 18 June 1781 (DLC:GW).

2. On 17 June 1781 GW wrote Joseph Webb that "Upon my return from Weathersfield I found Mrs. Washington extremely unwell, she still continues low & weak, but will set out for the Southward as soon as she can bear the fatigue of the journey" (DLC:GW). By 21 June she had "so perfectly recovered, as to be able to set out for Virginia in a day or two" (GW to Martha Mortier, 21 June 1781, MiU-C: Clinton Papers). Although she was well enough to start south on 25 June, GW wrote Fielding Lewis on 28 June that she "left me on Monday last in a very low and weak state

having been sick for more than a Month with a kind of Jaundice" (PU: Armstrong Photostats).

3. Rochambeau to GW, 23 June 1781 (DLC:GW).

4. Pierre Van Cortlandt (1721–1814) was lieutenant governor of New York from 1777 to 1795.

5. Abraham Ten Broeck (d. 1810) was mayor of Albany.

6. GW wrote John Hancock 25 June 1781 (M-Ar). See entries for 18, 25 May, 1, 20 June 1781.

7. When rumors of a threatened British invasion of the New York frontier had proved unfounded, GW had recalled the reinforcements which had been sent to the area (see entry for 20 June 1781). In informing Gov. George Clinton of the withdrawal, GW noted that the recall of the Continental troops might be ameliorated by sending a Continental officer to superintend military activities in the area and suggested Brig. Gen. John Stark (1728–1822) of New Hampshire as "a proper person [to] employ on this service" (GW to Clinton, 21 June 1781, CSmH).

8. Anne César, chevalier de La Luzerne (1741–1791), served as French minister plenipotentiary to the United States 1779–84. His undated letter to GW enclosing an intelligence report with this information is in DLC:GW.

9. GW to Rochambeau, 17 June 1781 (DLC:GW). Rochambeau had already informed GW that the French admiral de Grasse had confirmed his intention of bringing his fleet north from the West Indies during the summer to aid the French and American armies in an attack against the British and had estimated the fleet would arrive in American waters around 15 July at the earliest (Rochambeau to GW, 10 June 1781, DONIOL, 5:487–88). On 13 June, in addition to urging Rochambeau to march as rapidly as possible to join the American army at White Plains, GW requested that Rochambeau persuade de Grasse not only to use his fleet to support the attack on New York but to bring a substantial body of troops with him (DLC:GW). A similar request was made to La Luzerne, the French minister in the United States (GW to La Luzerne, 13 June 1781, Aff. Etr., Mémoires et Documents, Etats-Unis, vol. 6). Rochambeau replied, 20 June, that de Grasse had been informed "that Your Excellency preferred that he should make his first appearance at New York . . . that I submitted, as I ought, my opinion to yours" (DLC:GW). In expressing his own views to de Grasse, however, Rochambeau was not as submissive as his letter to GW would indicate. He had not given up his preference for a Virginia campaign and clearly hoped that his apprehensions for the success of operations against the British in New York City would influence de Grasse to make the Chesapeake his destination (DONIOL, 5:395).

For information on French maneuvers at this time, see also DONIOL, 5:489–90, 495; WEELEN, 104–5, 217–19; WHITRIDGE, 131–40; FREEMAN, 5:296. Barras's reply to GW's request to arm the *Fantasque* is in Barras to Rochambeau, 23 June 1781, enclosed in Rochambeau to GW, 23 June 1781 (DLC:GW).

10. Brenton's Point is at the entrance of Newport harbor.

28th. Having determined to attempt to surprize the Enemys Posts at the No. end of Yk. Island, if the prospt. of success continued favourable, & having fixed upon the Night of the 2d. of July for this purpose [1] and having moreover combined with it an attempt to cut off Delancy's [2] And other light Corps without Kingsbridge and fixed upon Genl. Lincoln to Commd. the first detachment & the Duke de Lauzen the 2d. every thing was put in train for it and the Count de Rochambeau requested to file of from Ridgebury to Bedford & hasten his March—while the Duke de Lauzen was to do the same & to assemble his command (which was to consist of abt. 3 or 400 Connecticut State Troops under the Command of Genl. Waterbury [3]—abt. 100 York Troops under Captn. Sacket [4]—Sheldons Legion [5] of 200, & his own proper Corps.). Genl. Lincolns command was to consist of Scammells light Troops and other detachments to the amt. of 800 Rank & file properly officerd—150 watermen and 60 artillerists.

1. As the British had detached troops into Monmouth County, N.J., to forage for horses and cattle, GW thought it a propitious moment to launch an attack on the relatively unprotected posts at the northern end of Manhattan Island. Maj. Gen. Benjamin Lincoln was to bring his two regiments and a detachment of artillery from Peekskill to attack Fort Tryon, Fort Knyphausen, and Fort George (GW to Lincoln, 1 July 1781, MH). If this plan proved unsuccessful, he was to move across the river and support the duc de Lauzun's cavalry in an attack on James De Lancey's Loyalists at Morrisania. Rochambeau was to "put your first Brigade under march to-morrow Morning, the remaining Troops to follow as quick as possible, and endeavour to reach Bedford by the evening of the 2d. of July, and from thence to proceed immediately towards Kingbridge should circumstances render it necessary" (GW to Rochambeau, 30 June 1781, DLC:GW). Although GW's report to Congress on the affair puts it in the most favorable

Washington's irreplaceable drillmaster, Baron Frederick Wilhelm von Steuben. A painting by Ralph Earl. (Yale University Art Gallery)

light, it is evident that the attack was anything but successful in spite of the cooperation of the French. The forts along the Hudson were unexpectedly reinforced by the return of British foraging parties from New Jersey, one of which encountered Lincoln's men, costing the Americans the element of surprise. Lauzun's forces arrived too late and most of the outlying British posts were withdrawn across the Harlem River to safety. The only material result of the raid was the opportunity of "reconnoitring the works upon the north end of the Island and making observations which may be of very great advantage in future" (GW to Samuel Huntington, 6 July 1781, DNA: PCC, Item 152). For a description of the raid from the British side, see MACKENZIE [2], 2:556–59; Rivington's *Royal Gazette,* 14 July 1781. See also RICE, 1:32, 248–49; STEVENS [3], 6–10; CLOSEN, 88–91. Preliminaries to the attack are discussed in the exchange of letters, 30 June (DLC:GW) between GW and his aide David Cobb, who was with the French forces at this time.

2. Lt. Col. James De Lancey (1746–1804) commanded a Loyalist partisan corps operating in the vicinity of New York from 1776 to the end of the war. The corps was generally known as De Lancey's Refugees or Westchester Refugees.

3. David Waterbury (d. 1801) was brigadier general of Connecticut state troops. GW's instructions to him, 30 June, are in DLC:GW.

4. William Sackett, a captain of New York state levies, was in command of three companies of New York state troops at Bedford. GW's instructions to him, 30 June, are in DLC:GW.

5. Elisha Sheldon was colonel of the 2d Continental Light Dragoons.

29th.   Recd. a letter from the Marqs. de la Fayette informing me that Lord Cornwallis after having attempted to surprise the Virginia Assembly at Charlottesville and destroy some Stores at the Forks of James River in which he succeeded partially had returned to Richmond without having effected any valuable purpose by his manoeuvers in Virginia.[1] In a private letter he complains heavily of the conduct of the Baron de Steuben whom he observes has rendered himself extremely obnoxious in Virga.[2]

1. Lafayette was referring to the raid by British cavalry leader Banastre Tarleton on Charlottesville, Va., 4 June 1781, and the attack by Lt. Col. John Graves Simcoe on Point of Fork, at the confluence of the James and Rivanna rivers in Virginia, 5 June 1781. At this time the Virginia legislature was meeting in Charlottesville and Thomas Jefferson and the members of the legislature whom he was entertaining at Monticello barely escaped capture. Aside from a few prisoners taken, including seven members of the legislature, the principal result of the raids was the capture by the British of a considerable store of arms and ammunition at Point of Fork and the destruction of a similar store at Charlottesville (TARLETON, 296–99; SIMCOE, 212–23; MALONE [2], 1:355–58).

2. Lafayette contended that Steuben's military tactics during the British raids on Point of Fork and Charlottesville had come under so much criticism that "Every man woman and Child in Virginia is Roused against him. They dispute even on his Courage" (Lafayette to GW, 18 June 1781, DLC:GW).

Steuben believed that his first priority was preparations for the support of Nathanael Greene in the Carolinas and his policy, unchanged by renewed British military threats in Virginia in May 1781, was to leave the defense of the state to Lafayette. When the two detachments under Simcoe and Tarleton moved up the James in the direction of Point of Fork and Charlottesville, Steuben was still more concerned with protecting the recruits destined for Greene than with guarding the state stores at Point of Fork. On the morning of 4 June, Steuben moved most of his men to positions of safety, leaving only a token force to defend the Fork. For Steuben's movements at this time, see CHASE, 228–46; PALMER, 272–82. On 13 July, GW wrote Lafayette that "What you say in confidence of the conduct of a certain Officer shall be kept a profound secret, and I will contrive means of removing him from the quarter where he is so unpopular" (DLC:GW).

[July 1781]

July 2d. Genl. Lincoln's detachment embarked last Night after dark, at or near Tellers point;[1] and as his operations were to be the movement of two Nights he was desired to repair to Fort Lee this day & reconnoitre the enemy's Works—Position and strength as well as he possibly could & take his ultimate determination from appearances—that is to attempt the surprize if the prospect was favourable or to relinquish it if it was not, and in the latter case to land above the Mouth of Spikendevil[2] & cover the Duke in his operation on Delancys Corps.[3]

At three o'clock this Morning I commenced my March with the Continental Army in order to cover the detached Troops and improve any advantages which might be gained by them. Made a small halt at the New bridge over Croton abt. 9 Miles from Peekskill—another at the Church by Tarry Town till Dusk (9 Miles more) and compleated the remaining part of the March in the Night—arriving at Valentines Hill[4] (at Mile square) about Sun rise.

Our Baggage & Tents were left standing at the Camp at Peekskill.

1. Teller's Point (Croton Point) is on the Hudson River below Verplanck's Point.
2. Spuyten Duyvil, a creek connecting the Hudson River with the Harlem River.
3. See entry for 28 June 1781.
4. Valentine's Hill, north of Spuyten Duyvil in present Yonkers.

3d. The length of Duke Lauzens March & the fatiegue of his Corps, prevented his coming to the point of Action at the hour appointed. In the meantime Genl. Lincolns Party who were ordered to prevent the retreat of Delancy's Corps by the way of Kg. Bridge & prevent succour by that Rout were attacked by the Yagers and others but on the March of the Army from Valentines Hill retired to the Island. Being disappointed in both objects from the Causes mentioned I did not care to fatiegue the Troops any more but suffered them to remain on their Arms while I spent good part of the day in reconnoitering the Enemys works.

In the afternoon we retired to Valentines Hill & lay upon our Arms. Duke Lauzen & Waterbury lay on the East side of the Brunxs [Bronx] river on the East Chester road. Our loss in this days skirmishing was as follows—viz.—[   ]

4th.   Marched & took a position a little to the left of Dobbes ferry & marked a Camp for the French Army upon our left. Duke Lauzen Marched to the Whitepl[ai]n & Waterbury to Horseneck.[1]

1. The area called Horseneck is now the borough of Greenwich, Fairfield County, Conn.

5th.   Visited the French Army which had arrived at North-castle.[1]

1. On 4 July, GW had suggested that Rochambeau rest his troops for a day at North Castle (now Mount Kisco, N.Y.) before marching to join the Americans at White Plains, requesting him to "give me notice of your approach that I may have the happiness of meeting and conducting you to your Camp which will be about 4 Miles on this side the Village of White Plains" (DLC:GW). The French army had arrived at North Castle on 3

Anne César, chevalier de La Luzerne, another portrait by Charles Willson Peale. (Independence National Historical Park Collection)

July, finding few amenities (see RICE, 1:248). On his arrival at North Castle, GW inspected the French troops and spent some five hours in conference with Rochambeau. He dined with the French officers, who then escorted him for several miles on his return to the American camp at Philipsburg (CROMOT DU BOURG, 296).

6th. The French Army formed the junction with the American on the Grounds marked out.[1] The Legion of Lauzen took a position advanced of the plains on Chittendens hill[2] west of the River Brunx [Bronx]. This day also the Minister of France arrived in Camp from Philadelphia.

1. The French reached Philipsburg about six o'clock on the evening of 6 July and camped about a quarter of a mile from the American camp (CLOSEN, 91–92). The allied camp is described in detail in Louis Alexandre Berthier's journal (RICE, 1:249). GW's Headquarters was at the house of Joseph Appleby, "on the cross-road from Dobbs' Ferry to White Plains, and about three and a half miles from the ferry" (BAKER [1], 226). Rochambeau's headquarters was at the Odell house, about 1½ miles east of the Appleby house (see CAMPBELL [2], 46–47).
2. Chatterton's Hill was at White Plains, Westchester County, N.Y.

8th. Began a Work at Dobbs's ferry with a view to establish a communication there for the transportation of provision and Stores from Pensylvania.[1]

1. At this time fortifications were being erected on both sides of the Hudson to command passage of the river. The fortifications on the left bank had recently been constructed under the direction of Louis Le Bègue Duportail (CLOSEN, 94). Work on the fortifications on the right bank was to be supervised by Jean Baptiste Gouvion, a French engineer who held the rank of lieutenant colonel in the Continental Army (General Orders, 8 July 1781, DLC:GW).
On 8 July, GW reviewed the French and American armies. This was the first glimpse for many of the French officers of the American forces. One of them, Jean François Louis, comte de Clermont-Crèvecoeur, noted in his journal: "In beholding this army I was struck, not by its smart appearance, but by its destitution: the men were without uniforms and covered with rags; most of them were barefoot. They were of all sizes, down to children who could not have been over fourteen. There were many negroes, mulattoes, etc. Only their artillerymen were wearing uniforms. These are the élite of the country and are actually very good troops, well schooled in their profession" (RICE, 1:33). See also CROMOT DU BOURG, 299; CLOSEN, 91–92.

9th. Received a Letter from the Marqs. de la Fayette informing me of Cornwallis's retreat to Williamsburg—that he had pushed his rear and had obtained advantages—having killed 60 & wounded an hundred with small loss.[1]

Southern accts. though not official speak of the reduction of Augusta and Ninety Six by the arms of Major Genel. Greene.[2]

1. Lafayette to GW, 28 June 1781 (DLC:GW). In mid-June, after some weeks of skirmishing with Lafayette and Wayne, Cornwallis moved toward Williamsburg in what was less a retreat than a planned withdrawal, although Lafayette harassed the British forces all the way. Reaching the town on 25 June, he waited orders from Sir Henry Clinton in New York and by 26 June received directions from him to establish a base in Virginia for operations against the Americans. In the midst of a confusion of orders and counterorders from Clinton in New York and Lord George Germain in England, Cornwallis in August selected Yorktown as his headquarters. Entrenchments were also established at Gloucester, across the York River from Yorktown. For the British maneuvers at this time, see WICKWIRE, 325–53; CLINTON, 299–331; CORNWALLIS, 1:95–112.

2. See entry for 14 June 1781.

10th.   A Letter from Governor Trumbull, inclosing the proceedings of a convention of Eastern Deligates gives better hope of a regular supply of provision than we have been accustomed to for more than two years as the business seem to be taken up Systematically and regular modes adopted to furnish supplies at stated periods.[1]

General Heath also writes very favourably of the disposition of the Eastn. States but still we are without the reinforcements of Men required of them.[2]

The Boats undertaken by General Schuyler, are, by his letters, in a promising way [3]—as those at Wappings Creek also are by the Q. Mr. Genls. report.[4]

John Trumbull's portrait of his father, Gov. Jonathan Trumbull, Sr. (Yale University Art Gallery, gift of the artist, 1821)

Hazen's, and the 1st. York Regimt. who had been ordered to West point arrived there, but not till the latter had mutinied on acct. of their pay & several had deserted. The other York Regiment were detained at Albany to bring down the Boats & boards.[5]

1. Jonathan Trumbull, Sr., to GW, 9 July 1781 (DLC:GW). The enclosure was the minutes of "a Meeting of Commissioners from the New England States convened at Providence the 26th Day of June 1781 to agree on some regular method of sending on supplies of Beef &c to the army during the present year" (DLC:GW).

2. William Heath to GW, 4 July 1781 (DLC:GW). See entry under 6 May 1781. For his reports on his mission, see HEATH PAPERS, 3:196–225.

3. Philip Schuyler to GW, 1 and 6 July 1781 (DLC:GW). In June 1781 Schuyler had agreed to superintend the construction of 100 bateaux at Albany for the projected campaign against New York, at an estimated price of $35 to $40 per vessel (GW to Schuyler, 19 June 1781, Schuyler to GW, 20 June 1781, Jonathan Trumbull, Jr., to Timothy Pickering, 28 June 1781, DLC:GW). On 28 June 1781 GW wrote the president of Congress, urging that funds be forwarded promptly for the construction of the boats (DNA: PCC, Item 152). Schuyler encountered serious problems in obtaining supplies and qualified workmen; money was not forwarded promptly by Congress and Schuyler had to meet most of the expense from his own resources. He was not reimbursed by Congress until October (see GERLACH, 160).

4. Two new whaleboats were under construction at Wappings Creek, south of Peekskill, N.Y. (GW to Alexander McDougall, 6 July 1781, CSmH).

5. Hazen's Regiment (2d Canadian) and the 1st New York arrived in Albany 5 July and were to embark almost immediately for West Point (Philip Schuyler to GW, 6 July 1781, DLC:GW). For the disaffection of the troops, see James Clinton to GW, 10 July 1781, DLC:GW.

13th.   The Jersey Troops arrived at Dobbs's Ferry agreeable to orders. Some French Frigates made an attempt on the Enemy's Post at Loyds Neck but without success not being able to Land in the Night.[1]

1. The raid on the British fort at Lloyd's Neck (also called Fort Franklin), on the Cold Spring Harbor side of Huntington Bay, had been discussed as early as April 1781. GW had pointed out to the French commanders that possession of the post would cut off communication between the British army on Long Island and Loyalists on the mainland (GW to Rochambeau and Destouches, 8 April 1781; NcD: Francis Warrington Dawson Papers). The plan was revived in early July and on the evening of 10 July the French vessel *Romulus* and three frigates left Newport for the Lloyd's Neck post. The French were unable to land their troops at night as had originally been planned, and when the attack was launched against the fort at daybreak it was easily repulsed by the British, who had already been warned of the French enterprise (CLOSEN, 93–94). For an eyewitness account of the raid, see the Verger journal in RICE, 1:130–43.

14th.   Near 5000 Men being ordered to March for Kings bridge, to cover and secure a reconnoitre of the Enemys Works on the No. end of York Island, Harlaem river, & the Sound were prevented doing so by incessant rain.[1]

1. These troops were being held in readiness for a reconnaissance by French and American forces of the New York defenses. See "Instructions for Reconnoitering the Enemy's Post at the North End of York Island," 13 July 1781 (owned by Mr. Richard Maass, White Plains, N.Y.).

15th.   The Savage Sloop of War of 16 Guns—the Ship Genl. Washington, lately taken by the Enemy—a row Galley and two other small armed Vessels passed our post at Dobbs Ferry (which was not in a condition to oppose them).[1] At the same time three or four river Vessels with 4 Eighteen pounders—stores &ca. had just arrivd at Tarry town and with infinite difficulty, & by great exertion of Colo. Sheldon, Captn. Hurlbut, (who got wounded)[2] —Captn. Lieutt. Miles[3] of the artillery & Lt. Shayler[4] were prevented falling into the hands of the Enemy as they got a ground 100 yards from the Dock and were set fire to by the Enemy but extinguished by the extraordinary activity & spirit of the above Gentn. Two of the Carriages however were a good deal damaged by the fire. The Enemy however by sending their armed Boats up the River took the Vessel of a Captn. Dobbs laden with Bread for the French Army—Cloathing for Sheldons Regiment & some passengers. This was done in the Night—it being after Sunset before the Vessels passed the Post at Dobs ferry.

1. These British vessels were dispatched to attack American supply depots at West Point and Tarrytown and American supply boats plying the Hudson River. During the night the British ships "captured a small vessel, laden with flour and clothing for Sheldon's Dragoons, and they had put nearly all their crews into their boats to attempt a descent and carry off the rest of the supplies which were at Tarrytown; but a sergeant of the Regiment of Soissonnois who was there with twelve men kept up so brisk a fire that he prevented the landing; a half hour later the Americans arrived, who lost a sergeant and had one of their officers severely wounded. On our arrival the Americans placed two eighteen pounders on the right of Tarrytown, and we placed ours on the left" (CROMOT DU BOURG, 300–301). The British captured 1,000 rations of bread on board a small vessel commanded by William Dobbs of Fishkill and a negligible amount of military supplies (CLOSEN, 96). See also RICE, 1:34–35; MOORE [2], 2:459–60.
2. George Hurlbut (d. 1783) of Connecticut was a captain in the 2d Continental Dragoons.
3. John Miles of New York was a captain lieutenant in the 2d Continental Artillery.
4. Joseph Shaylor (d. 1816) of Connecticut was a lieutenant in the 4th

Continental Regiment. These officers were thanked for their actions by GW in General Orders, 17 July 1781 (DLC:GW).

16th.   The Cannon & Stores were got out of the Vessels & every thing being removed from Tarry town, two french twelve pounders, & one of our 18 prs. wer[e] brought to bear upon the Ships which lay of Tarry town, distant about a Mile, and obliged them to remove lower down & move over to the West shore.

17th.   The Vessels being again fired at in the position they took yesterday run up the River to Tellers point & there came to burning the House of the Widow Noy⟨e⟩ll.

18th.   I passed the North River with Count de Rochambeau Genl. de Beville [1] his Qr. Mr. Genl. & Genl. Duportail in order to reconnoitre the Enemy Posts and Encampments at the North end of York Island. Took an Escort of 150 Men from the Jersey Troops on the other side.

From different views the following discoveries were made—viz.—

That two Ships of 20 Guns & upwards lay opposite to the Mouth of spikendevil—one pretty near the East Shore the other abt. the same distance from the West; the first is intended to guard the Mouth of Spikendevil equally with the No. River. Below these, & directly opposite to Fort Washington (or Knyphausen) lay two transports with about 6 Guns & few Men in each. The Eastermost Ship seems designed to Guard the landing at the little bay above Jefferys Rock.[2] About the center of the Ground leading to Jeffreys Rock or point a Guard Mounts. It appears to be no more than a Sergeants guard with one centry in front where there is a small Work—the Guard House standing within.

These are all the Guards and all the security I could discover upon the No. River—on the right flank of the Enemy. The Shore from Jeffreys rock downwards, was quite open, and free—without Hutts of any kind—Houses or Troops—none being encamped below the heights. There did not even appear springs, or washing places any where on the face of the Hill which were resorted to.

The Island is totally stripped of Trees, & wood of every kind; but low bushes (apparently as high as a Mans waste) appear in places which were covered with Wood in the year 1776.

The Side of the Hill from the Barrier below Fort Tryon,[3] to the Bay opposite to fort Knyphausen,[4] is difficult of access; but there seems to be a place abt. 200 yds. above the bay, which has the best appearance of a landing, and is most private—but a hut or two on the heights abt. 200 yds. above Fort Knyphausen, & a little above the old long Battery, which was thrown up in 1776 must be avoided by leaving it on the left in getting to the Fort last mentioned.

In the hollow below Morris's heights[5] (between that & Haerlam) is a good place to land but near the York Road opposite there appeared to be a few Tents and many Dragoon Horses seemed to be at Pasture in the low land between the heights. A landing perfectly concealed, but not so good, might be made a little higher up the river, and nearer to those heights which ought to be immediately occupied— (between the old American lines and the aforesaid hollow).

From the point within the Mouth of Spiken devil, the way to the Fort on Cox's Hill[6] seems difficult, and the first part of it covered with bushes. There is a better way up from the outer point, but too much exposed to a discovery from the Ship which lays opposite to it, and on acct. of its being less covered with wood.

The ground round the Fort on Cox's hill is clear of Bushes. There is an abatis round the Work, but no friezing; nor could I discover whether there is a ditch. At the No. Et. corner there appeared to be no Parapet & the whole seemed to be in a decaying State. The gate is next the No. River.

Forts Tryon, Knyphausen & Ft. George on Laurell, with the Batteries in the line of Pallisading across from River to river appeared to be well friezed, ditched & abattied—In a word to be strong and in good repair.

Fort No. 8[7] is also abatied & friezed at the Top. The gate is next Haerlam River. There are no Houses or Huts on the side of the Hill from this work till you come near old Fort Independence.

On McGowans heights[8] there appears (by the extent of the Tents) to be two Battns. Encamped—supposed to be the British Grenadiers. A little in the rear of this, and on the (enemys) left, are a number of Huts but whether they are Inhabited or not could not be ascertained there being different opinions on this point, from the nearest view we could get of it. On the height opposite to Morris's white House there appeared to be another Regt. (supposed to be the 38th. British). Between this and Fort Knyphausen (abt. half way) are two small Encampments contiguous to each other—both together containing two or 3 and 40 Tents—Hessians. On Laurel Hill near Fort George is another Encampment in view abt. 40 Tents & huts which appear to be Inhabited also—by (it is said) —the 57th. Regiment. The other, and only remaining Encampment in View, & discoverable from the West side of the river, is betwn. the Barrier and Kings bridge —in the Hollow between Cox's hill and the heights below. One hundred Tents could be counted in view at the same time, and others might be hid by the Hills. At this place it is said the Jagers—Hessian & Anspach lay.

1. Pierre François, chevalier de Béville, was quartermaster general to the French army during its American tour. Jean Nicolas, vicomte Désandroüins (1729–1792), commander of Rochambeau's corps of engineers, also accompanied the party, which left camp at daybreak. "After pushing as far as Fort Lee, and after distinguishing very clearly six small camps on that side of the island, they returned in the evening" (CLOSEN, 96–97).

2. The British had constructed Fort Knyphausen on the site of the American works at Fort Washington.

3. Jeffrey's Rock or Jeffers' Hook, just below Fort Washington in the area of the George Washington Bridge.

4. Fort Tryon was a British fort on upper Manhattan. The site was west of 190th Street.

5. Morris's Heights was the area around Roger Morris's house (later the Morris-Jumel Mansion) at Edgecombe Avenue and 160th Street in Manhattan.

6. Cox's Hill was at the extreme northern tip of Manhattan near Spuyten Duyvil Creek.

7. Fort No. 8, was a British fort in the Bronx on the Harlem River, now within the campus of New York University.

8. McGowan's Heights were above McGowan's Pass at the northeast end of present Central Park.

19th.   The Enemys Shipping run down the river, and left the Navigation of it above once more free for us.[1] In passing our Battery at Dobbs's where were 2 Eighteen & 2 twelve pounders and two Howitzers, they recd. considerable damage; especially the Savage Sloop of War which was frequently hulled, and once set on fire; occasioning several of her people, and one of our own (taken in Dobbes Sloop, and) who gives the Acct. to jump over board. Several people he says were killed & the ship pierced through both her sides in many places and in such a manner as to render all their pumps necessary to free the Water.

1. The British ships involved included the *General Monk*, the *Savage*, and several other vessels. A British account states that the Americans fired red-hot shot from the New Jersey shore, hitting the masts and rigging of both

vessels and blowing up an arms chest on board the *Savage,* killing several men. See MACKENZIE [2], 2:569; CLOSEN, 97; and the entry for 15 July 1781.

20th.   Count de Rochambeau having called upon me, in the name of Count de Barras, for a definitive plan of Campaign, that he might communicate it to the Count de Grasse[1]—I could not but acknowledge, that the uncertainties under which we labour —the few Men who have joined (either as recruits for the Continental Battns. or Militia) & the ignorance in which I am kept by some of the States on whom I mostly depended—especially Massachusetts from whose Govr. I have not received a line since I addressed him from Weathersfd. the 23d. of May last—rendered it impracticable for me to do more than to prepare, first, for the enterprize against New York as agreed to at Weathersfield[2] and secondly for the relief of the Southern States if after all my efforts, & earnest application to these States it should be found at the arrivl. of Count de Grasse that I had neither men, nor means adequate to the first object. To give this opinion I was further induced from the uncertainty with respect to the time of the arrival of the French Fleet & whether Land Troops would come in it or not as had been earnestly requested by me & inforced by the Minister of France.

The uncertainty of sufficient aids, of Men & Means from the States to whom application had been made, and the discouraging prospects before me of having my requisitions complied with— added to an unwillingness to incur any expence that could be avoided induced me to desire Genl. Knox to suspend the Transport of the heavy Cannon & Stores from Philadelphia lest we should have them to carry back again or be encumbd. with them in the field.

1. See entry for 25 June 1781. Rochambeau had written to GW 19 July, relaying Barras's request and inviting GW to confer with him (DLC:GW). On the same day the commanders met at Dobbs Ferry and Rochambeau posed a series of questions concerning plans for the coming campaign. GW replied that in case the comte de Grasse should delay in joining the American and French forces in the North or should bring few land troops with him, the allies should leave a garrison at West Point and a small force in the New York area and march the remainder of their troops to Virginia for a late summer or early fall campaign. "But should the Fleet arrive in Season, not be limited to a short Stay; should be able to force the Harbour of N York, and in addition to all these, should find the British Force in a divided State, I am of Opinion that the Enterprize against N York & its Dependencies shou'd be our primary Object" (DLC:GW). See also DONIOL, 5:514–16.

2. See entry for 22 May 1781.

21st.   Wrote to the Count de Grasse in a Cypher of the Count de Rochambeau's, giving information of the junction of the allied armys—the Position they had taken—our strength and that of the enemy's—our hopes & fears & what we expected to do under different circumstances.[1] This letter was put under cover to Genl. Forman, who was requested to have look outs on the heights of Monmouth, and deliver it himself upon the arrival of the Fleet and who was also requested, to establish a chain of Expresses for quick communication between Monmouth and Dobbs's ferry—the Expence of which I would see paid.[2]

Again ordered abt. 5000 Men to be ready to March at 8 oclock, for the purpose of reconnoitering the enemys Posts at Kings bridge and to cut off, if possible, such of Delancys Corps as should be found without their lines.[3]

At the hour appointed the March commenced in 4 Columns, on different roads. Majr. Genl. Parsons[4] with the Connecticut Troops & 25 of Sheldon's horse formed the right column (with two field pieces) on the No. River road. The other Two divisions of the Army, under the Majr. Generals Lincoln & Howe,[5] together with the Corps of Sappers and Miners, and 4 field pieces, formed the next column on the Sawmill river road.[6] The right column of the French (on our left) consisted of the Brigade of Bourbonnis, with the Battn. of Grenadiers and Choissairs, 2 field pieces & 2 twelve pounders. Their left column was composed of the Legion of Lauzen—one Battn. of Grenadiers, & Choissairs of Soussonnis,[7] 2 field pieces & 2 Howitzers. General Waterbury with the Militia and State Troops of Connecticut, were to March on the East chester Road and to be joined at that place by the Cavalry of Sheldon, for the purpose of Scouring Frogs Neck.[8] Sheldons Infantry was to join the Legion of Lauzen for the purpose of Scouring Morrissania,[9] and to be covered by Scammells light Infantry who were to advance thro' the fields & way lay the Roads —stop all communication & prevent Intelligence getting to the Enemy.

At Mile Square (Valentine's hill) The left column of the American Troops, and right of the french formed their junction, as did the left of the French also, by *mistake* as it was intended it should cross the Brunx by Garrineaus,[10] & recross it at Williams's bridge.[11]

The whole Army (Parson's division first) arrived at Kingsbridge about day light & formed on the heights back of Fort Independance[12]—extending towards delancy's Mills[13]—While the Legion of Lauzen & Waterbury proceeded to scour the Necks of

Morrissania & throgs to little effect, as most of the Refugees were fled, & hid in such obscure places as not to be discovered; & by stealth got over to the Islands adjacent, & to the enemys shipping which lay in the East River. A few however were caught and some cattle & Horses brought off.

1. GW to the comte de Grasse, 21 July 1781 (DLC:GW).

2. GW to David Forman, 21 July 1781 (NHi).

3. Although a definite decision had not yet been reached to implement the earlier plans for the attack on New York, both GW and Rochambeau carried on extensive reconnaissance of British defenses in the area. A reconnaissance in force by the French and American armies of the British posts had been scheduled for the evening of 13 July, but was delayed by bad weather. For the order of march, see "Instructions for Reconnoitering the Enemy's Posts at the North End of York Island," 13 July 1781 (owned by Mr. Richard Maass, White Plains, N.Y.). For contemporary maps of the reconnoitered area, see RICE, 2:nos. 43 and 44. For contemporary descriptions of the reconnaissance, see CLOSEN, 97–102; CROMOT DU BOURG, 301–3.

4. Samuel Holden Parsons (1737–1789) was in command of the Connecticut divisions.

5. Maj. Gen. Robert Howe (1732–1786) of North Carolina.

6. The Sawmill River Road paralleled the Sawmill or Nepperhan River on the east, turning east north of Philipse's toward Valentine's Hill.

7. The French regiments referred to by GW in this entry were the Bourbonnais and the Soissonnais, both of which were sent to America in 1780. Chasseurs were light cavalry trained for rapid maneuvering. Lauzun's Legion was composed of infantry and cavalry units under the command of the duc de Lauzun. The legion had arrived at Newport, R.I., in July 1780.

8. Frog's (Throg's or Throck's) Neck is a peninsula extending into the East River from the Westchester shore.

9. Morrisania, the estate of the Morris family, in southern Westchester County.

10. Garineau's was about 16 miles north of the mouth of the Bronx River (DLC: Toner Collection).

11. Williams's Bridge crossed the Bronx River in southern Westchester.

12. Fort Independence, later called Fort No. 4 by the British, "was located between the old Boston and the Albany Post Roads . . . just within the old line of Yonkers" (HUFELAND, 104).

13. De Lancey's Mills was on the Bronx River near West Farms in Westchester County.

22d. The enemy did not appear to have had the least intelligence of our movement or to know we were upon the height opposite to them till the whole Army were ready to display.[1]

After having fixed upon the ground, & formed our line, I began, with General Rochambeau and the Engineers, to reconnoitre the enemy's position and Works first from Tippets hill[2] opposite to their left and from hence it was evident that the small redoubt (Fort Charles)[3] near Kings bridge would be absolutely at the command of a battery which might be erected thereon. It also appeared equally evident that the Fort on Cox's hill was in bad repair, & little dependence placed in it. There is neither ditch nor friezing to it, and the No. East Corner appears quite easy of access (occasioned as it would seem by a Rock). The approach from the inner Point (mentioned in the Reconnoitre from the Jersey shore) is secured by a ledge of Rocks which would conceal a party from the observation & view of the ship till it got within abt. 100 Yds. of the Fort round which for that, or a greater distance the ground has little covering upon it of bushes. There is a house on this side under Tippets hill but out of view, I conceive of the crossing place most favourable to a partizan stroke. From this view, and every other I could get of Forts Tryon, Knyphausen & Laurel hill the Works are formidable.

There is no Barracks or huts on the East side of the Hill on which Fort Tryon and Knyphausen stands—nor are there any on the hill opposite except those by Fort George. Near the Blew bell [4] there is a number of Houses but they have more the appearance of Stables than Barracks. In the hollow, near the Barrier gate, are about 14 or 15 Tents; which is the only Encampment I could see without the line of Pallisading as the large one discovered on the 18th. through the brake of the Hill betwn. Fort Tryon & Coxss hill was not to be seen from any view I had.

A continued Hill from the Creek, East of Haerlam River, & a little below Morris's White House,[5] has from every part of it, the command of the opposite shore, & all the plain adjoining, within range of shot from batteries which may be erected thereon. The general width of the river along this range of Hills, appears to be from one to two hundred yards. The opposite shore (tho' more or less marshy) does not seem miry, & the banks are very easy of access. How far the Battery, under cover of the block Ho[use] on the hill No. West of Harlaem town is capable of scouring the plain, is difficult to determine from this side, but it would seem as if the distance was too great to be within the range of its shot on that part of the plain nearest the Creek before mentioned & which is also nearest the height back of our old lines thrown up in the year 1776. It unfortunately happens that in the rear of the (continued) hill before mentioned, there is a deep swamp, and the grounds East of that swamp, are not so high as the heights near Harlaem river. In the rear of this again is the Brunx which is not be crossed without Boats below De Lancys Mills.

1. The appearance of the Americans at Morrisania was so unexpected that the Loyalist troops there were forced to pull back hurriedly to the British

lines "but had not time to bring off their stock, which the Rebels seized upon and drove off" (MACKENZIE [2], 2:570). See also RICE, 1:36; CLINTON, 321.

2. Tippett's Hill, on the bank of Tippett's Brook, a tributary of Spuyten Duyvil Creek.

3. Fort Charles, or Fort Prince Charles, was located on the top of Marble Hill, overlooking King's Bridge.

4. The Blue Bell Tavern was located on the west side of the road from New York City to King's Bridge. The land had been owned since 1769 by Blasius Moore, a New York City tobacconist, but the tavern was apparently operated during the Revolution by Jacob Moore (*Magazine of American History*, 7 [1881], 375–76).

5. Presumably the Morris-Jumel Mansion at 160th Street and Edgecombe Avenue in Manhattan.

23d.   Went upon Frogs Neck, to see what communication could be had with Long Isld. The Engineers attending with Instrumts. to measure the distance across found it to be [   ] Yards.[1]

Having finished the reconnoitre without damage—a few harmless shot only being fired at us—we Marched back about Six o'clock by the same routs we went down & a reversed order of March and arrived in Camp about Midnight.

This day letters from Genls. Greene and the Marqs. de la Fayette came to hand, the first informing of his having taken all the Enemy's posts in Georgia except Savanna and all those in So. Carolina except Charles Town & Ninety Six—the last of wch. he was obliged to abandon the siege of, on acct. of the relief which was marching to it, consequent of the late reinforcemt. received at Charles Town. The second, that Waynes affair with Lord Cornwallis on the 6th. Instt. was partial on our side, as a part of our force was opposed to the enemys whole Army—that on our Side the loss in killed, wounded & missing, amounted to 5 Capt. 1 Captn. Lieutt. 4 Lieutts. 11 Sergts. & 118 R. & file—that the enemys loss was computed at 300 at least—that our loss of two field pieces proceeded, from the horses belonging to them being killed and that Lord Cornwallis had retreated to the South side of James River from the Peninsula at James Town.

1. Rochambeau described this incident in his memoirs: "While our engineers carried out this geometrical operation, we slept, worn out by fatigue, at the foot of a hedge, under fire from the cannon of the enemy's ships, who wished to hinder the work. Waking first, I called General Washington, and remarked to him that we had forgotten the hour of the tide. We hurried to the causeway of the mill on which we had crossed this small arm of the sea which separated us from the mainland; we found it covered with water. We were brought two little boats, in which we embarked, with the saddles and trappings of the horses; they then sent back two American dra-

goons, who drew by the bridle two horses, good swimmers. These were followed by all the others, urged on by the lashes of some dragoons remaining on the other shore, and for whom we sent back the boats. This maneuver was made in less than an hour, but happily our embarrassment was unnoticed by the enemy" (ROCHAMBEAU, 1:283–84).

29th. A Letter from the Marqs. de la Fayette (commanding in Virginia) [1] informed me that after Lord Cornwallis had crossed James River he detached Tarlton with a body of horse into Amelia County with a view, as was supposed, to destroy some Stores which had been deposited there but which had been previously removed—that after this the enemys whole force removed to Portsmouth with a design it was said to embark part of them and that he had detached Generl. Wayne to the South side of James River to cover the Country, while the enemy lay in it, & to March Southerly if they did not—he himself with the Main body of his Army having taken a position at a place called Malvin hill not far from Shirley.[2]

Part of the Second York Regiment came down from Albany with such of the Boats as had been undertaken by Gen. Schuyler, & were finished. The light Infantry Company of the Regiment were ordered down with the next Boats & the remainder of the Regiment to bring down the rest when done.[3]

About this time, the discontents in the Connecticut State line, occasioned by some disappointment of a Committee sent from it to the Assembly, in settling an Acct. of Subsistence &ca. began to increase, & put on a more serious face; which induced me to write a second letter to the Govr. of that State. The distress of the Line for want of a small portion of the pay due it contributed not a little to irritate them.[4]

1. Lafayette to GW, 20 July 1781 (DLC:GW). This is one of two letters written by Lafayette on this date.
2. Banastre Tarleton (1754–1833) was lieutenant colonel of the British Legion, composed primarily of Loyalists. In 1779 the legion served in the North but was transferred to the southern theater in 1780, and it was here that Tarleton's ability as a cavalry leader and raider rendered him indispensable to Cornwallis. Lafayette was referring to the raids carried out by Tarleton between 9 and 24 July to destroy public and private stores in the area between Prince Edward Court House and New London, Va. (see BASS, 180–81; TARLETON, 358–59).
By 16 July, Lafayette had received intelligence reports that Tarleton and some 900 men were moving toward South Carolina, presumably to attack Greene. Lafayette then ordered Maj. Gen. Anthony Wayne and the Pennsylvania and Virginia troops under his command to march south (Wayne to Joseph Reed, 16 July 1781, MH: Sparks Transcripts).

Malvern Hill was a plantation on the James River in Henrico County, Va. Shirley plantation, also near the James, was in Charles City County.

3. See entry for 10 July 1781. Schuyler wrote GW from Albany, 21 July, that 84 bateaux were virtually completed and at least half were ready to be sent forward to the army (DLC:GW).

4. This is probably the letter to Trumbull which GW dated 3 Aug. 1781, suggesting that the "Money for the Pay of The Troops of your Line will be exceedingly welcome—the sooner it arrives the more salutary will be its Consequences" (Ct: Trumbull Papers). Governor Trumbull's son, Jonathan Trumbull, Jr., who was GW's aide, had urged his father as early as 13 July to send "a sum of money for our poor suffering Connecticut lads, who are in want beyond your or any other man's conception who have not seen them" (TRUMBULL PAPERS, 3:247–48).

30th.   Ordered the Jersey Militia, who were directed to Assemble in the first instance at Morristown to Dobbs ferry and there join the remains of the Jersey Brigade and receiving Letters from Govr. Clinton & Genl. Clinton complaining that none of the Massachusetts Militia had repaired to Albany agreeable to my requisition I again addressed Govr. Hancock in pointed terms to send them on & complained of not having recd. answers from him to any of my letters since the Conference with Count de Rochambeau and a communication of the plan of operation which was agreed on at Weathersfield the 22d. of May last.[1]

Received a Letter from the Count de Barras,[2] refering me to one written by him to Genl. Rochambeau in Cypher; pointing, in stronger terms than heretofore, his disinclination to leave Newport till the arrival of Adml. de Grass. This induced me to desist from further representing the advantages which would result from preventing a junction of the enemy's force at New York; & blocking up those which are now in Virginia, lest in the Attempt any disaster should happen, & the loss of, or damage to his fleet, should be ascribed to my obstinacy in urging a measure to which his own judgment was oppos'd, & the execution of which might impede his junction with the West India fleet, & thwart the views of the Count de Grasse upon this Coast—especially as he gave it as a clear opinion, that the West India fleet might be expected by the 10th. of Next Month.

1. On 25 June 1781 GW had written to Gov. John Hancock of Massachusetts informing him that he had ordered the Massachusetts militia quotas from the counties of Berkshire and Hampshire, numbering some 600 men, to Albany to be placed under the command of Brig. Gen. John Stark (M-Ar). See also entry for 25 June 1781, n.7. After receiving letters from George Clinton, 28 July, and James Clinton, 20 July (DLC:GW), complaining that the troops had not yet arrived, GW wrote Hancock again on 30 July, reminding him that he had received no reply to his letter of 25 June and

informing him that reports had come in from the Massachusetts frontier that "the Orders for raising your Militia but recently received in that Part of the State; and that no Orders had been received for any Part to march to Albany" (DLC:GW). On 15 Aug., Hancock replied that the orders had miscarried but he had now given the necessary orders to the Berkshire and Hampshire militia to march immediately to Albany (DLC:GW).

For the Wethersfield Conference, see entry for 22 May 1781.

2. Barras to GW, 25 July 1781, enclosing a copy of a letter from Barras to Rochambeau of the same date (DLC:GW).

31st. Governor Trumbull informed me, that in order to facilitate the Collection of a Specie Tax for the purpose of sending Money to the Troops of the Connecticut line Gentlemen were sent to the different Towns of the State to try by personal influence & exertion to hasten it to the Army and that he & some of his Council had removed to Hartford to forward on the Recrts. for the Continental Regiments and the Militia and in a word to promote the operations of the Campaign as much as in them lay.[1]

1. Gov. Jonathan Trumbull, Sr., to GW, 31 July 1781 (DLC:GW). On 8 Aug., Trumbull wrote GW that £3,500 had been collected to pay the Connecticut Line. The money was to be ready at Danbury by 15 Aug. (DLC:GW). See also entry for 29 July 1781.

[August 1781]

1st. By this date all my Boats were ready—viz.—One hundred New ones at Albany (constructed under the direction of Genel. Schuyler) and the like number at Wappings Creek by the Qr. Mr. Genl.; besides old ones which have been repaired. My heavy ordnance & Stores from the Eastward had also come on to the North Rivr. and every thing would have been in perfect readiness to commense the operation against New York, if the States had furnished their quotas of men agreeably to my requisitions but so far have they been from complying with these that of the first, not more than half the number asked of them have joined the Army; and of 6200 of the latter pointedly & timously called for to be with the Army by the 15th. of last Month, only 176 had arrived from Connecticut, independant of abt. 300 State Troops under the Command of Genl. Waterbury, which had been on the lines before we took the field, & two Companies of York levies (abt. 80 Men) under similar circumstances.

Thus circumstanced, and having little more than general assurances of getting the succours called for and energetic Laws & resolves or Laws & resolves energetically executed, to depend upon – with little appearance of their fulfillment, I could scarce see a ground upon wch. to continue my preparations against New York – especially as there was much reason to believe that part (at least) of the Troops in Virginia were recalled to reinforce New York and therefore I turned my views more seriously (than I had before done) to an operation to the Southward and, in consequence, sent to make enquiry, indirectly, of the principal Merchants to the Eastward what number, & in what time, Transports could be provided to convey a force to the Southward if it should be found necessary to change our plan & similar application was made in a direct way to Mr. Morris (Financier) to discover what number cd. be had by the 20th. of this Month at Philadelphia or in Chesapeak bay.[1] At the sametime General Knox was requested to turn his thoughts to this business and make every necessary arrangement for it in his own Mind – estimating the ordnance & Stores which would be wanting & how many of them could be obtained without a transport of them from the North River. Measures were also taken to deposit the Salt provisions in such places as to be Water born. More than these, while there remained a hope of Count de Grasses bringing a land force with him, & that the States might yet put us in circumstances to prosecute the original plan could not be done without unfolding matters too plainly to the enemy & enabling them thereby to Counteract our Schemes.

1. GW to Robert Morris, 2 Aug. 1781 (DLC:GW).

4th. Fresh representations of the defenceless State of the Northern frontier, for want of the Militia so long called for and expected from Massachusetts bay; accompanied by a strong expression of the fears of the People that they should be under the necessity of abandoning that part of the Country & an application that the Second York Regiment (Courtlandts) [1] at *least* should be left for their protection induced me to send Major Genl. Lincoln (whose influence in his own State was great) into the Counties of Berkshire & Hampshire to enquire into the causes of these delays & to hasten on the Militia. I wrote at the same time to the Governor of this State consenting to suffer the 4 Companies of Courtlandts Regiment (now at Albany) to remain in that Quarter till the Militia did come in, but observed that if the States instead of filling their Battalions & sending forth their

Militia were to be calling upon, & expecting me to dissipate the sml. operating force under my command for local defences that all offensive operations must be relinquished and we must content ourselves (in case of compliance) to spend an inactive and injurious Campaign which might—at this critical moment—be ruinous to the common cause of America.[2]

1. Col. Philip Van Cortlandt (1749–1831) commanded the 2d New York Regiment from Nov. 1776 to the end of the war.

2. Brig. Gen. James Clinton wrote to GW on 30 July and Gov. George Clinton on 1 Aug. 1781; both men enclosed letters from other officers complaining of the precarious state of the northern frontier (DLC:GW). GW's letter to George Clinton, 5 Aug. 1781, is in N: Clinton Papers. For GW's problems with the militia from these counties, see the entries for 25 June, 30 July 1781.

6th.   Reconnoitred the Roads and Country between the North River and the Brunxs from the Camp to Philip's[1] and Valentines Hill and found the ground every where strong—the Hills 4 in Number running parallel to each other with deep ravines between them—occasioned by the Saw Mill river—the Sprain branch and another more Easterly. These hills have very few interstices or Breaks in them, but are more prominent in some places than others. The Saw mill River, & the Strain branch occasion an entire seperation of the hills above Philips's from those below commonly called Valentines hills. A strong position might be taken with the Saw Mill (by the Widow Babcocks)[2] in Front, & on the left flank and the No. River on the right Flank and this position may be extended from the Saw Mill river over the sprain Branch.

A Letter from the Marqs. de la Fayette of the 26th. Ulto. gives the following acct.—That the two Battalions of light Infantry— Queens Rangers—the Guards & one or two other Regiments had Embarked at Portsmouth & fallen down to Hampton Rd. in 49 Transports—that he supposed this body of Troops could not consist of less than 2000 Men—That Chesapeak bay & Potomack River were spoken of as the destination of this detachment—but he was of opinion that it was intended as a reinforcement to New York. Horses were laid for the speedy communication of Intelligence and an officer was to be sent with the acct. of the Fleets Sailing.[3]

1. The Philipse manor house was at Yonkers, Westchester County. At this time it was owned by the third lord of the manor, Frederick Philipse (1720– 1786).

2. Widow of Rev. Luke Babcock, a Loyalist minister, Mrs. Babcock lived in Babcock's House, the parsonage of St. John's Episcopal Church in West-

chester (see SHONNARD, 443–44). Her residence was some five miles below Dobbs Ferry at the eastern foot of Wild Boar Hill.

3. A copy of Lafayette's letter to GW, 26 July 1781, is in DNA: PCC, Item 156.

7th.   Urged Governor Greene of Rhode Island to keep up the number of Militia required of that State at Newport & to have such arrangements made of the rest as to give instant & effectual support to the Post, & the Shipping in the harbour, in case any thing should be enterprized against the latter upon the arrival of Rodney; who, with the British fleet, is said to be expected at New York, & in conjuction with the Troops which are Embarked in Virginia & their own Marines are sufficient to create alarms.[1]

1. GW to William Greene, 7 Aug. 1781 (DLC:GW). GW wrote Greene that "It is reported in New York, perhaps not without foundation, that Rodney's Fleet may be expected upon this Coast. In such case we may suppose that the Count de Grasse would follow him: But can we say which would arrive first." At this time Admiral Sir George Rodney (1719–1792) was in command of the British fleet in the West Indies. Although British intelligence reports indicated that the French fleet was about to sail for the Chesapeake, Rodney gambled on the assumption that de Grasse would divide his fleet, taking part to the Chesapeake and leaving the remaining ships to guard the French West Indies. When de Grasse left the West Indies (6 Aug.), taking with him his entire fleet, Rodney had already (1 Aug.) sailed for England, leaving command of the fleet in southern waters to Rear Admiral Sir Samuel Hood. For the circumstances surrounding the British failure to pursue de Grasse's fleet in force to American waters, see WILLCOX [2], 21–23.

8th.   The light Company of the 2d. York Regiment (the first having been down some days) having joined the Army, were formed with two Companies of Yk. levies into a Battn. under the Command of Lieutt. Colo. Hamilton [1] & Major Fish [2] & placed under the orders of Colo. Scammell as part of the light Troops of the Army.

1. Lt. Col. Alexander Hamilton (1755–1804) had resigned as GW's aide-de-camp in Feb. 1781 after a dispute with the commander in chief (see HAMILTON [2], 2:563–68), and in July 1781 he was successful in securing command of a battalion composed of New York levies (General Orders, 31 July 1781, DLC:GW).

2. Nicholas Fish (1758–1833), of New York City, was at this time a major in the 2d New York Regiment and during the Yorktown campaign served as Alexander Hamilton's second-in-command.

9th.   A Letter from the Marqs. de la fayette of the 30th. Ulto., reports, that the Embarkation in Hampton Road still remained there – that there were 30 Ships full of Troops chiefly red Coats in the fleet—that Eight or ten other Vessels (Brigs) had Cavalry on Board—that the Winds had been extremely favourable—notwithstanding which they still lay at anchor & that the Charon & several other frigates (some said Seven) were with them as an escort. The Troops which he now speaks of as composing the detachment are the light Infantry—Queens Rangers and he thinks two British & two German Regiments—no mention of the Guards as in his former Acct.[1]

  1. Lafayette to GW, 30 July 1781 (DLC:GW).

10th.   Ordered the first York, and Hazens Regiments immediately to this place from West point—The Invalids [1] having got in both from Philadelphia & Boston and more Militia got in from Connecticut, as also some from Massachusetts bay giving with 4 Companies of Courtlandts Regiment in addition to the detachment left there upon the March of the Army perfect security to the Posts.

  1. That is, troops from the Corps of Invalids (see entry for 16 June 1781).

11th.   Robt. Morris Esqr. Superintendant of Finance & Richd. Peters Esqr. a Member of the Board of War, arrived at Camp to fix with me the number of Men necessary for the next Campaign and to make the consequent arrangements for their establishment and Support.[1]

A Fleet consisting of about 20 Sail, including 2 frigates & one or two prizes, arrived within the harbour of New York with German recruits—to the amount—by Rivington—of 2880 but by other, & better information to abt. 1500 sickly Men.[2]

  1. The Continental Congress had appointed, 26 July 1781, a committee consisting of Daniel Carroll, Theodorick Bland, and James Mitchell Varnum to confer with GW, Superintendent of Finance Robert Morris, and Secretary of the Board of War Richard Peters on the arrangements for the army for 1782 (JCC, 21:791). On 13 Aug., Morris and Peters sent GW a number of queries in preparation for drawing up the 1782 arrangement, touching on such matters as the contribution of the states to the military establishment, the possibility of reducing the numbers of officers and men required, and the settlement of periods of enlistment (DLC:GW). GW replied to the committee of conference on 21 Aug., advising against a reduction of the Continental Army in the new arrangement, considering "how much more expensive & less servicable Militia are than Continental Troops" (DLC:GW).
  2. GW was clearly not aware of all of the facts noted in this entry as early as 11 Aug. In the evening of that day Brig. Gen. David Forman wrote GW from Freehold, N.J., that his observers had sighted a British fleet of 20 sail off Sandy Hook but weather conditions prevented identification of the

vessels. At first it was conjectured that the fleet was carrying part of Cornwallis's troops from Virginia to reinforce Clinton in New York (Forman to GW, 11 Aug. 1781, GW to Forman, 13 Aug. 1781, DLC:GW). The fleet observed by Forman, however, consisted of 2 British armed ships and 23 transports carrying German recruits. According to a "Return of the troops arrived from Germany. 11th Augt 1781," 2,750 Hessian troops arrived (MACKENZIE [2], 2:585). The soldiers were under the command of Col. Friedrich von Benning, and "a little more than one hundred and thirty sick, most of them suffering from scurvy, of which they will soon be cured, were disembarked earlier and taken to hospitals." Twenty-two men had died during the 13-week voyage (BAURMEISTER, 457).

The arrival of the transports was reported in the 15 Aug. issue of the *Royal Gazette* by editor James Rivington (1724–1802). Rivington, a native of London who emigrated to America in 1760, had established *Rivington's New York Gazetteer* in 1773, after a varied career as printer and bookseller. Openly supporting the crown when the Revolution broke out, he was appointed the king's printer in New York in 1776, and his newspaper, now operating under various titles, became a leading Tory organ until he suspended publication in 1783. After the war he remained in New York City, but his business ventures failed to prosper and he died in comparative poverty. For his secret career during the Revolution as an agent for GW's intelligence system in New York, see CRARY, 61–72; FORD [4], 323–24.

12.   By accounts this day received from the Marqs. de la Fayette it appeared that the Transports in Hampton road had stood up the Bay & came too at the distance of 15 Miles and, in conseqe. he had commenced his March toward Fredericksburg that he might more readily oppose his operations on Potomack or up Chesapeak bay.[1]

1. Lafayette to GW, 1 Aug. 1781 (DLC:GW).

14th.   Received dispatches from the Count de Barras announcing the intended departure of the Count de Grasse from Cape Francois with between 25 & 29 Sail of the line & 3200 land Troops on the 3d. Instant for Chesapeake bay and the anxiety of the latter to have every thing in the most perfect readiness to commence our operations in the moment of his arrival as he should be under a necessity from particular engagements with the Spaniards to be in the West Indies by the Middle of October— At the same time intimating his (Barras's) Intentions of enterprizing something against Newfoundland, & against which both Genl. Rochambeau and myself remonstrated as impolitic & dangerous under the probability of Rodneys coming upon this Coast.[1]

Matters having now come to a crisis and a decisive plan to be determined on—I was obliged, from the Shortness of Count de

Grasses premised stay on this Coast—the apparent disinclination in their Naval Officers to force the harbour of New York and the feeble compliance of the States to my requisitions for Men, hitherto, & little prospect of greater exertion in future, to give up all idea of attacking New York; & instead thereof to remove the French Troops & a detachment from the American Army to the Head of Elk[2] to be transported to Virginia for the purpose of cooperating with the force from the West Indies against the Troops in that State.[3]

    1. De Grasse's letter to Rochambeau, 28 July 1781, announcing his plans to sail to the Chesapeake is in DONIOL, 5:520–22. The original letter is in the collection of Mr. Paul Mellon, Upperville, Va. The letter arrived at Newport on board the frigate *Concorde* on 11 Aug. and was immediately dispatched by Barras to Rochambeau at Philipsburg where it arrived on 14 Aug. (see RICE, 1:40).

    Barras's letter to GW, 8 Aug. 1781, is in DLC:GW. Upon receipt of the news of de Grasse's projected departure from Cap Français in Saint Domingue, Barras concocted a scheme whereby, instead of joining de Grasse in the Chesapeake, he would launch a naval attack on Newfoundland (Barras to Rochambeau, 11, 12 Aug. 1781, DONIOL, 5:522–23). On 15 Aug., Rochambeau wrote to Barras, remonstrating against this plan and pointing out that if Rodney should bring his fleet north and join Admiral Graves, de Grasse's vessels would be outnumbered (DONIOL, 5:523–24). GW added a postscript to this letter, urging compliance with Rochambeau's request "that you would form the junction, and as soon as possible, with the Count de Grasse in Chesapeak bay" (DLC:GW). In face of this opposition, Barras agreed to abandon the attempt on Newfoundland and join de Grasse (Barras to Rochambeau, 17 Aug. 1781, DONIOL, 5:524–26). Barras's squadron left Newport for the Chesapeake on 23 Aug. with the French siege artillery and most of the troops which had been left at Newport under the command of the marquis de Choisy.

    2. Now Elkton, Md.

    3. "In consequence of the dispatches received from your Excellency by the Frigate La Concorde," GW wrote de Grasse, 17 Aug., "it has been judged expedient to give up for the present the enterprise against New York and to turn our attention towards the South, with a view, if we should not be able [to] attempt Charles town itself, to recover and secure the States of Virginia, North Carolina and the Country of South Carolina and Georgia. We may add a further inducement for giving up the first mentioned enterprise, which is the arrival of a reinforcemt. of near 3000 Hessian Recruits. For this purpose we have determined to remove the whole of the French Army and as large a detachment of the American as can be spared to Chesapeake, to meet Your Excellency" (DLC:GW).

15.   Dispatched a Courier to the Marquis de la Fayette with information of this matter—requesting him to be in perfect readiness to second my views & to prevent if possible the retreat of Cornwallis toward Carolina. He was also directed to Halt the

Troops under the Command of General Wayne if they had not made any great progress in their March to join the Southern Army.[1]

1. GW to Lafayette, 15 Aug. 1781 (DLC:GW). Presumably the courier was Louis Le Bègue Duportail (see GW to Lafayette, 17 Aug. 1781, DLC:GW).

16th.   Letters from the Marqs. de la Fayette & others, inform that Lord Cornwallis with the Troops from Hampton Road, had proceeded up York River & landed at York & Gloucester Towns where they were throwing up Works on the 6th. Inst.[1]

1. Lafayette to GW, 11 Aug. 1781 (DLC:GW).

19th.   The want of Horses, or bad condition of them in the French army delayed the March till this day. The same causes, it is to be feared, will occasion a slow and disagreeable March to Elk if fresh horses cannot be procured & better management of them adopted.

The detachment from the American [army] is composed of the light Infantry under Scammell—two light companies of York to be joined by the like Number from the Connecticut line—the remainder of the Jersey line—two Regiments of York—Hazens Regiment & the Regiment of Rhode Island—together with Lambs regiment of Artillery with Cannon and other Ordnance for the field & Siege.[1]

Hazens regiment being thrown over at Dobbs's ferry was ordered with the Jersey Troops to March & take Post on the heights between Spring field & Chatham & Cover a french Battery at the latter place to veil our real movement & create apprehensions for Staten Island.[2] The Quarter Master Genl. was dispatched to Kings ferry—the only secure passage—to prepare for the speedy transportation of the Troops across the River.

Passed Singsing[3] with the American column. The French column marched by the way of Northcastle, Crompond & Pinesbridge being near ten miles further.

1. GW's General Orders for 31 July 1781 had stated that the light infantry companies "of the first and second regiments of New York (upon their arrival in Camp) with the two companies of [New] York Levies under command of Captains [William] Sackett and [Daniel] Williams will form a Battalion under command of Lieutenant Colonel [Alexander] Hamilton and Major [Nicholas] Fish.

"After the formation of the Battalion Lieutenant Colonel Hamilton will join the Advanced Corps under the Orders of Colonel [Alexander] Scammell" (DLC:GW).

Charles Cornwallis, second Earl Cornwallis, the general defeated by the Americans and French at Yorktown, sat for this Thomas Gainesborough portrait in 1783. (National Portrait Gallery, London)

At this time Hazen's 2d Canadian Regiment was acting as the 4th Battalion of Lafayette's Light Division under the command of Lt. Col. Edward Antil.

Lamb's Regiment was the 2d Battalion of Continental Artillery, organized in 1777 and composed of companies from New York, Connecticut, New Hampshire, and Rhode Island. It was commanded by Col. John Lamb of New York.

For the army's movement to the rendezvous at Head of Elk, see TRUMBULL [1], 331–33.

2. Elaborate plans were made to deceive the British concerning the army's movements. Thirty boats were mounted on carriages and taken with the troops to give the appearance of preparations for an attack on Staten Island. Jonathan Trumbull, Jr., one of GW's aides-de-camp, noted: "French ovens are building at Chatham in Jersey. Others were ordered to be prepared at a place near the Hook. Contracts are made for forrage to be delivered immediately to the French Army on their arrival at the last mentioned place. Here it is supposed that Batteries are to be erected for the security and aid of the Fleet, which is hourly expected. By these maneuvres and the correspondent march of the Troops, our own army no less than the Enemy are completely deceived" (TRUMBULL [1], 332). Clinton was apparently not completely deceived about GW's intentions toward New York; but as long as de Grasse's destination was uncertain, he believed that the allies would probably not move their entire force south. It was not until 6 Sept., when Clinton received Cornwallis's letter of 4 Sept. announcing de Grasse's arrival off the Capes, that "Mr. Washington's design in marching to the Southward remained no longer an object of doubt" (CLINTON, 327–29). See also STEVENS [4], 2:151; MACKENZIE [2], 2:596, 605–6. For GW's later recollections of events at this time, see his letter to Noah Webster, 31 July 1788 (SPARKS, 9:402–4).

3. Ossining, N.Y.

20th. The head of the Americans arrived at Kings ferry about ten O'clock & immediately began to cross.

21st. In the course of this day the whole of the American Troop, all their baggage, artillery & Stores, crossed the river. Nothing remained of ours but some Waggons in the Commissary's & Qr. Mr. Generals departmt., which were delayed, that no interruption might be given to the passage of the French Army.

During the passing of the French Army I mounted 30 flat Boats (able to carry about 40 Men each) upon carriages—as well with a design to deceive the enemy as to our real movement, as to be useful to me in Virginia when I get there.

Some of the french Artillery wch. preceeded their Infantry got to the ferry & crossed it also.[1]

1. Both the French and American armies left camp at Philipsburg on 19 Aug. but took different routes to King's Ferry (Clermont-Crèvecoeur in

RICE, 1:40). For descriptions of the march, see CLOSEN, 106–8; TRUMBULL [1], 331–32; DEUX-PONTS, 121–24.

22d. 23d. 24th. & 25th.   Employed in transporting the French Army, its baggage & Stores over the river.[1]

1. On 23 Aug., GW and Rochambeau visited West Point (CROMOT DU BOURG, 307).

[25th.]   The 25th. the American Troops marched in two Columns—Genl. Lincoln with the light Infantry & first York Regiment pursuing the rout by Peramus to Springfield—while Colo. Lamb with his Regiment of Artillery—the Parke[1]—Stores and Baggage of the Army covered by the Rhode Island Regt. proceeded to Chatham by the way of Pompton & the two bridges.

The Legion of Lauzen & the Regiments of Bourbonne & Duponts[2] with the heavy Parke of the French Army also Marched for percipony[3] by Suffrans Pompton & [   ].

1. That is, gun or artillery park.
2. The Deux-Ponts Regiment was composed primarily of officers and men from the duchy of Deux-Ponts on the Franco-German border. Its colonel was Christian, comte de Deux-Ponts, with Guillaume, comte de Deux-Ponts, as lieutenant colonel. The regiment came to America with Admiral de Ternay's fleet in the spring of 1780.
3. Parsippany, Morris County, N.J., is six miles northeast of Morristown.

[26th.]   The 26th. the remainder of the French army, its baggage & Stores, moved from the ferry and arrived at Suffrans—the ground the others had left.

28th.   The American columns and 1st. division of the French Army arrived at the places assigned them.

29th.   The Second division of French joined the first. The whole halted—as well for the purpose of bringing up our rear—as because we had heard not of the arrival of Count de Grasse & was unwilling to discover our real object to the enemy.

30th.   As our intentions could be concealed one March more (under the idea of Marching to Sandy hook to facilitate the entrance of the French fleet within the Bay), the whole Army was put in motion in three columns—the left consisted of the light Infantry, first York Regiment, and the Regiment of Rhode Island—the Middle column consisted of the Parke Stores & Bag-

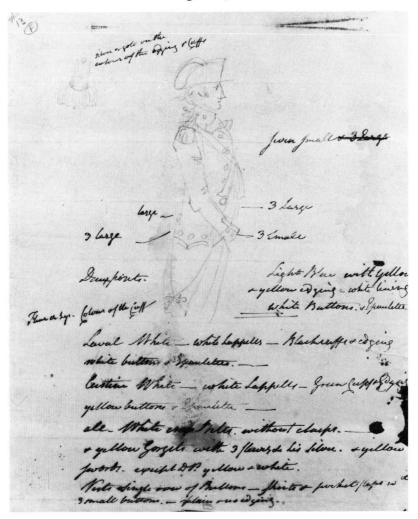

A French officer, Guillaume, comte de Deux-Ponts, with notes about his uniform, done by John Trumbull. (Yale University Art Gallery)

gage—Lambs Regt. of Artillery—Hazens & the Corps of Sappers & Miners—the right column consisted of the whole French army, Baggage Stores &ca. This last was to march by the rout of Morristown—Bullions Tavern[1]—Somerset C[our]t House[2] & Princeton. The middl. was to go by Bound brooke[3] to Somerset &ca. and the left to proceed by the way of Brunswick to Trenton, to which place the whole were to March Transports being ordered to meet them there.

I set out myself for Philadelphia to arrange matters there—provide Vessels & hasten the transportation of the Ordnance Stores, &ca.—directing before I set out, the secd. York Regiment (which had not all arrived from Albany before we left Kings ferry) to follow with the Boats—Intrenching Tools &ca. the French Rear to Trenton.

1. Bullion's Tavern was at Liberty Corner, N.J.

2. Somerset Court House is now Millstone, Somerset County, N.J., eight miles west of New Brunswick.

3. Bound Brook is on the Raritan River, Somerset County, N.J., six miles northwest of New Brunswick.

31st.   Arrived at Philadelphia to dinner and immediately hastened up all the Vessels that could be procured—but finding them inadequate to the purpose of transporting both Troops & Stores, Count de Rochambeau & myself concluded it would be best to let the Troops March by land to the head of Elk, & gave directions accordingly to all but the 2d. York Regiment which was ordered (with its baggage) to come down in the Batteaux they had in charge to Christiana bridge.[1]

1. The *Pa. Packet,* 2 Sept. 1781, TRUMBULL [1], 332, and CLOSEN, 116, all give 30 Aug. as the date of arrival in Philadelphia where GW, Rochambeau, and their entourage were "received by crowds of people with shouts and acclamations" (TRUMBULL [1], 332). On 28 Aug., Robert Morris had offered GW his house for the commander in chief's stay in Philadelphia since the city was "filled with Strangers" and private lodgings were almost impossible to acquire (DLC:GW). The French officers lodged at the residence of the chevalier de La Luzerne, "where M. de Rochambeau and his staff were housed like princes." In the evening they dined with Robert Morris (CLOSEN, 116). GW's main purpose in visiting Philadelphia was to arrange for supplies and transport for the march to Virginia (see GW to Robert Morris, 17, 24, 27 Aug. 1781, GW to de Grasse, 17 Aug. 1781, DLC:GW; for the conference between Morris and GW on supplying the campaign, see Morris's diary, 31 Aug. 1781, DLC: Robert Morris Papers).

For GW's orders of march, see his two letters to Benjamin Lincoln, 31 Aug. 1781 (MH). For the progress of the French army to Head of Elk, see RICE, 1:40–51, 253–55; CLOSEN, 107–15.

September 1781

5th.   The rear of the French army having reached Philadelphia and the Americans having passed it—the Stores having got up & every thing in a tolerable train here; I left this City for the head of Elk to hasten the Embarkation at that place and on my way—(at Chester) —received the agreeable news of the safe arrival of the Count de Grasse in the Bay of Chesapeake with 28 Sail of the line & four frigates—with 3000 land Troops which were to be immediately debarked at James town & form a junction with the American Army under the command of the Marqs. de la Fayette.[1]

Finding upon my arrival at the head of Elk a great deficiency of Transports, I wrote many letters to Gentn. of Influence on the Eastern shore,[2] beseeching them to exert themselves in drawing forth every kind of Vessel which would answer for this purpose and agreed with the Count de Rochambeau that about 1000 American Troops (including the Artillery Regiment) and the Grenadiers & Chasseurs of the Brigade of Bourbonne with the Infantry of Lauzen's legion should be the first to Embark and

Comte de Rochambeau, the French commander in chief, in a painting by Charles Willson Peale. (Independence National Historical Park Collection)

The chevalier de Chastellux, Washington's French friend and comrade in arms, by Charles Willson Peale. (Independence National Historical Park Collection)

that the rest of the Troops should continue their march to Baltimore proceeding thence by Land, or Water according to circumstances. The Cavalry of Lauzen, with the Saddle horses & such
teams of both armies as the Qr. Masters thereof might judge
necessary to go round by Land to the place of operation.

Judging it highly expedient to be with the army in Virginia as
soon as possible, to make the necessary arrangements for the
Siege, & to get the Materials prepared for it, I determined to set
out for the Camp of the Marqs. de la Fayette without loss of time
and accordingly in Company with the Count de Rochambeau
who requested to attend me, and the Chevr. de Chastellux set out
on the [3]

1. In Philadelphia, GW was engaged in last-minute preparations for the
march south (see GW to Lafayette, 2 Sept. 1781, DLC:GW). Between 31
Aug. and 5 Sept. there was also considerable uneasiness about the movements
of both the British and French fleets. On 31 Aug., Brig. Gen. David Forman
wrote GW from his observation post in Freehold, N.J., that two British
squadrons under Admirals Graves and Hood were in process of setting sail
from New York City (DLC:GW). Barras's fleet had sailed from Newport,
R.I., on 23 Aug. carrying siege guns and provisions for Yorktown and no
word had since been received from him. If he were intercepted by the British
fleet before he joined de Grasse in the Chesapeake, the results could be
disastrous to the allied campaign in the South.

On 5 Sept., GW informed the president of Congress that he had received
a letter from Brig. Gen. Mordecai Gist announcing the arrival of de Grasse's
fleet (DNA: PCC, Item 152). Gist's letter, dated Baltimore, 4 Sept. 1781, is
in DLC:GW. See also David Humphreys to Gist, 5 Sept. 1781 (NN: George
Washington Papers, facsimilies and transcripts). By 7 Sept., GW was able
to report that the French fleet from Rhode Island was "hourly expected" to
join de Grasse's fleet ("Circular to Gentlemen on the Eastern Shore of
Maryland," 7 Sept. 1781, DLC:GW). According to Jonathan Trumbull's
journal, GW had left Philadelphia with his suite and about three miles below Chester met the express from de Grasse. He then returned to Chester
to inform Rochambeau and Congress of the French fleet's arrival (TRUMBULL
[1], 332). Rochambeau had decided to come from Philadelphia to Chester
by water. As the ship approached Chester, "We discerned in the distance
General Washington, standing on the shore and waving his hat and a white
handkerchief joyfully. . . . MM. de Rochambeau and Washington embraced
warmly on the shore" (CLOSEN, 123).

2. GW is referring to his circular letter, dated 7 Sept. 1781, to "Gentlemen
on the Eastern Shore of Maryland." Copies were sent to Christopher
Birchead, Robert Goldsborough, James Lloyd Chamberlaine, Richard Barn-
aby, Nicholas Thomas, John Bracco, and James Hindman (DLC:GW).

3. GW made no entries for 6 and 7 Sept., but Jonathan Trumbull, Jr.,
his aide-de-camp, made notations on these days: "6. Breakfast at Christiana
Bridge, where our boats, stores, &c. are brought from Delaware Water
through Christiana Creek, debarked and carried a[c]ross by land about 12
miles to the head of Elk. Here they are again embarked up the Elk River

and transported down the Chesapeake. The General proceeds to the Head of Elk where the troops and a great part of the stores are arrived and beginning to embark.

"The want of water craft obliges part of the troops to march by land to Baltimore, and eventually as far as An[n]apolis. Many ox and horse teams are sent on by land, the General expecting to find little or no means of land transportation in Virginia. The many rivers and great abundance of water communication almost superceeding the necessity of that convenience.

"7. At Elk writing letters, forwarding troops, stores &c. The country through which we have passed greatly pleased with the prospect of our Expedition" (TRUMBULL [1], 332–33).

8th.   and reached Baltimore where I recd. and answered an address of the Citizens.[1]

1. While GW and his party were in Baltimore they stayed at Daniel Grant's Fountain Inn. For a description of GW's reception in Baltimore, see *Md. Journal*, 11 Sept. 1781. The address of welcome of the citizens of Baltimore to GW and his reply, both dated 8 Sept. 1781, are in DLC:GW. The address was presented to GW at a banquet held on the evening of 8 Sept. at Lindsey's Coffeehouse in honor of the arrival of the French fleet (SCHARF [2], 189–90).

9th.   I reached my own Seat at Mount Vernon (distant 120 Miles from the Hd. of Elk) where I staid till the 12th. and in three days afterwards that is on the 14th. reached Williamsburg. The necessity of seeing, & agreeing upon a proper plan of co-operation with the Count de Grasse induced me to make him a visit at Cape Henry where he lay with his fleet after a partial engagement with the British Squadron off the Capes under the Command of Admiral Graves whom he had driven back to Sandy hook.[1]

1. GW, who had not seen his home since his departure in May 1775, was accompanied to Mount Vernon by Lt. Col. David Humphreys, one of his staff, while the "rest of the family jogg on easily" (TRUMBULL [1], 333). GW's aides arrived at midday on 10 Sept. and Rochambeau and his staff in the evening. Chastellux and his aides came the next day (see GW to Chastellux, 10 Sept. 1781, NjP). Trumbull noted: "A numerous family now present. All accommodated. An elegant seat and situation, great appearance of oppulence and real exhibitions of hospitality & princely entertainment." On 13 Sept. the party left Mount Vernon for Williamsburg and "between Colchester and Dumphries meet letters giving an account of an action between the two Fleets, & that the French were gone out from the Bay in pursuit of the English. The event not known. Much agitated" (TRUMBULL [1], 333). In light of the news from the Capes, troops moving south were temporarily halted (see CLOSEN, 129).

After Rodney's departure from the West Indies for England (see entry for

7 Aug. 1781), Sir Samuel Hood had sailed for New York, joining Graves there on 28 Aug. The combined fleets of Graves and Hood, consisting of 19 ships of the line, did not sail from New York until 31 Aug. Both admirals underestimated de Grasse's strength. Still unaware of the arrival of de Grasse, the British fleet reached the Chesapeake on 5 Sept. and virtually stumbled into the French fleet anchored just inside the bay (see Verger journal, RICE, 1:137–38). The two fleets met on 5 Sept. off the Chesapeake in a 2½-hour action. The results were inconclusive, but the two fleets remained in contact, 6–7 Sept., drifting south to the vicinity of Cape Hatteras, which allowed Barras's fleet from Newport to sail into Chesapeake Bay unmolested. By 11 Sept. the French fleet was back in the Chesapeake, and on 14 Sept. the British fleet sailed for New York. For a description of the engagement off the Capes, see Graves to Philip Stevens, 14 Sept. 1781 (GRAVES PAPERS, 61–69; RICE, 1:137–38; GOUSSENCOURT, 69–75; JOURNAL OF AN OFFICER, 155–58; HOOD, 28–36).

On the way to Williamsburg, Trumbull noted that the party heard "rumours of the return of the French Fleet, with some advantage, which relieved our fears" (TRUMBULL [1], 333). Both GW and Trumbull mistakenly date the party's arrival in Williamsburg as 15 Sept. rather than 14 Sept. St. George Tucker states that GW reached the city about four o'clock in the afternoon. "He had passed our camp which is now in the rear of the whole army, before we had time to parade the militia. The French line had just time to form. The Continentals had more leisure. He approached without any pomp or parade attended only by a few horsemen and his own servants. The Count de Rochambeau and Gen. Hand with one or two more officers were with him. . . . The Marquis [de Lafayette] rode up with precipitation, clasped the General in his arms and embraced him with an ardor not easily described. The whole army and all the town were presently in motion. The General—at the request of the Marquis de St. Simon—rode through the French lines. The troops were paraded for the purpose and cut a most splendid figure. He then visited the Continental line" (St. George Tucker to Frances Tucker, 15 Sept. 1781, COLEMAN, 70–71). In Williamsburg, GW lodged at George Wythe's house. In the evening "an elegant supper was served up" and "an elegant band of music played an introductive part of a French Opera" (BUTLER, 106).

On 15 Sept., GW wrote to de Grasse, expressing his desire for a conference aboard the admiral's flagship, the *Ville de Paris*, and requesting de Grasse to send some form of conveyance for GW and his officers (DLC:GW). In the evening he dined with Lafayette and on 16 Sept. with Baron von Steuben (BUTLER, 106).

17th. In company with the Count de Rochambeau—the Chevr. Chastellux—Genls. Knox & Duportail, I set out for the Interview with the Admiral & arrived on board the Ville de Paris (off Cape Henry) the next day by Noon and having settled most points with him to my satisfaction except not obtaining an assurance of sending Ships above York and one that he could not continue his fleet on this Station longer than the first of November I embarked on board the Queen Charlotte (the Vessell I went down in) but by hard blowing; & contrary Winds, did not reach Williamsburg again till the 22d.[1]

1. On 17 Sept. de Grasse sent a small vessel, the *Queen Charlotte,* captured from the British, to convey GW and his party to the *Ville de Paris* for the conference. Also accompanying GW were aides David Cobb and Jonathan Trumbull, Jr. (TRUMBULL [1], 333). For an amusing but perhaps apocryphal account of GW's reception by de Grasse aboard the flagship, see CUSTIS, 235–36. See also TRUMBULL [1], 333–34. GW's revolutionary accounts record the expenses of the trip to and from the French flagship as £25 (DLC:GW).

De Grasse had already warned Rochambeau and GW that the stay on the Chesapeake of his fleet and Saint Simon's troops would be limited, probably not extending beyond mid-October (see DONIOL, 5:520–22). The question uppermost in GW's mind was whether de Grasse would be able to extend his stay until the British could be forced to surrender, particularly if the siege of Yorktown proved to be protracted. The series of questions dealing with the campaign posed by GW at the conference and de Grasse's replies are in DNA: PCC, Item 152.

22d.   Upon my arrival in Camp I found that the 3d. Maryland Regiment had got in (under the Command of Colo. Adam) [1] and that all except a few missing Vessels with the Troops from the head of Elk were arrived, & landing at the upper point of the College Creek [2] – where Genl. Choisy [3] with 600 Fr. Troops who had from R. Isld. had arrived in the Squadron of Count de Barras [4]

had done before them during my absence.

1. Lt. Col. Peter Adams was in command of the 3d Maryland Regiment.
2. College Creek is a branch of the James River.
3. Claude Gabriel, marquis de Choisy (b. 1723), a brigadier general in the French army, had commanded the French troops left behind in Newport to guard Barras's fleet and the French artillery (DONIOL, 5:493). In Aug. he sailed with Barras's fleet to the Chesapeake and was now ordered to "take command of the Troops ordered to besiege the village of Gloucester, a post opposite the town of York held by the English, in which they had 1,100 men in addition to their hospitals and stores. The troops under M. de Choisy included the Lauzun Legion, 800 men from the garrisons of our ships, and 1,500 militia" (Clermont-Crèvecoeur's journal in RICE, 1:56).
4. At this point the page of the diary ends. Since the words that follow do not appear to belong to the previous sentence, a page or pages containing entries for the 23 and 24 Sept. may be missing.

25th.   Admiral de Barras having Joined the Count de Grasse with the Squadron and Transports from Rhode Island, & the latter with some Frigates being sent to Baltimore for the remr. of the French army arrived this day at the usual port of debarkation above the College Creek and began to land the Troops from them.

28th.   Having debarked all the Troops and their Baggage—Marched and Encamped them in Front of the City and having with some difficulty obtained horses & Waggons sufficient to move our field Artillery—Intrenching Tools & such other articles as were indispensably necessary—we commenced our March for the Investiture of the Enemy at York.

The American Continental, and French Troops formed one column on the left—the first in advance—the Militia composed the right column & marched by the way of Harwoods Mill. Half a mile beyond the halfway Ho[use] [1] the French & Americans seperated. The former continued on the direct road to York, by the Brick House. [2] The latter filed of to the right for Murfords bridge, [3] where a junction with the Militia was to be made. About Noon the head of each column arrived at its ground, & some of the enemys Picquets were driven in on the left by a Corps of French Troops, advanced for the purpose, which afforded an oppertunity of reconnoitering them on their right. The enemy's Horse on the right were also obliged to retire from the ground they had Encamped on, & from whence they were employed in reconnoitering the right column.

The line being formed, all the Troops—Officers & Men—lay upon their arms during the Night.

1. Halfway House was operated as a tavern on the old Williamsburg Road and, as its name implies, was halfway between Williamsburg and Yorktown.
2. The Brick House appears on a number of contemporary maps on the road between Williamsburg and Yorktown approximately four miles west of Yorktown and six miles east of Williamsburg, in York County.
3. Murford's Bridge crossed Skiffes Creek, which flows into the James River.

29th.   Moved the American Troops more to the right, and Encamped on the East side of Bever dam Creek, [1] with a Morass in front, about Cannon shot from the enemys lines. Spent this day in reconnoitering the enemys position, & determining upon a plan of attack & approach which must be done without the assistance of Shipping above the Town as the Admiral (notwithstanding my earnest sollicitation) declined hazarding any Vessells on that Station.

1. Beaver Dam Creek, or Great Run, is about halfway between Yorktown and Wormley Creek. The creek and its branches formed a marsh about the

middle of the allied lines which stretched from the edge of the York River above Yorktown to Wormley Creek.

30th.   The Enemy abandoned all their exterior works, & the position they had taken without the Town; & retired within their Interior works of defence in the course of last Night—immediately upon which we possessed them, & made those on our left (with a little alteration) very serviceable to us.[1] We also began two inclosed Works on the right of Pidgeon Hill[2]—between that & the ravine above Mores Mill.[3]

From this time till the 6th. of October nothing occurred of Importance—much deligence was used in debarking, & transporting the Stores—Cannon &ca. from Trebells Landing (distant 6 Miles) on James Riv., to Camp; which for want of Teams went on heavily and in preparing Fascines, Gabions, &ca. for the Siege —as also in reconnoitering the Enemys defences, & their situation as perfectly as possible, to form our parallels & mode of attack.

The Teams which were sent round from the head of Elk, having arrived about this time, we were enabled to bring forward our heavy Artillery & Stores with more convenience and dispatch and every thing being prepared for opening Trenches 1500 Fatiegue men & 2800 to cover them, were ordered for this Service.[4]

1. On the night of 29 Sept. the British abandoned the outer defenses in the area between Yorktown Creek and Wormley's Pond and withdrew into positions within the town. The British decision to abandon the outlying works was prompted by a letter to Cornwallis from Clinton, 24 Sept. 1781, informing him that considerable reinforcements were to sail from New York by 5 Oct. (CORNWALLIS, 1:120). Cornwallis replied on the 29th that "I shall retire this night within the works, and have no doubt, if relief arrives in any reasonable time, York and Gloucester will be both in possession of his Majesty's troops" (CORNWALLIS, 1:120–21).

2. Among the other defenses, the British had abandoned the redoubts at Pigeon Quarter and Pigeon Hill approximately two miles southwest of the town. Clermont-Crèvecoeur's journal notes that GW "immediately sent the grenadiers and chasseurs to take possession of them. We converted a redan they had also abandoned into a redoubt and built a fourth to tie them all together" (RICE, 1:57).

3. Moore's Mill was on Wormley's Pond at the head of Wormley Creek.

4. On 27 Sept., GW had received welcome news from de Grasse, suggesting that he had abandoned the prospect of cruising to intercept British Admirals Digby and Hood and was willing to commit his fleet to the investiture of Yorktown (de Grasse to GW, 25 Sept. 1781, WASHINGTON AND DE GRASSE, 51–52). GW also requested and received 600 to 800 marines from the French ships. On the 27th de Grasse had reluctantly agreed to GW's request for the French troops, but added "I earnestly beseech Your Excellency to

dispense in future with the necessity of demanding men from my vessels. I am mortified that I can not do all that I would wish, but there is no doing impossibilities" (WASHINGTON AND DE GRASSE, 56–57).

During this period GW also ordered construction and fortification of a trench commanding the main British defenses. He personally inspected the ground selected for this first parallel on 1 Oct., narrowly escaping fire from the British defenses 300 yards away. The parallel was not occupied until the siege guns could be transported from Trebell's Landing on the James River six or seven miles from Yorktown. A minor contretemps was presented to GW by Lafayette when he requested command of the right wing of the siege army in place of Benjamin Lincoln, who held the position by right of seniority. GW refused as tactfully as possible (Lafayette to GW, 30 Sept. 1781, DLC:GW). On 3 Oct. the marquis de Choisy moved his troops in tighter formation about Gloucester Point. In the process the duc de Lauzun, one of his officers, encountered Banastre Tarleton's Dragoons, resulting in an action also involving the Virginia militia which GW described somewhat excessively in General Orders as a "brilliant success." On 5 Oct. the army rejoiced at the news of Nathanael Greene's success at Eutaw Springs, S.C. Jonathan Trumbull, Jr., notes that during these days there was almost no fire from the British on the Americans busily digging in on the Yorktown perimeter. "A matter of Speculation. The General determined to return no fire upon the enemy till our batteries are all ready to play to some purpose" (TRUMBULL [1], 335).

October 1781

6th.   Before Morning the Trenches were in such forwardness as to cover the Men from the enemys fire.[1] The work was executed with so much secresy & dispatch that the enemy were, I believe, totally ignorant of our labor till the light of the Morning discovered it to them. Our loss on this occasion was extremely inconsiderable, not more than one Officer (french) & about 20 Men killed & Wounded—the Officer & 15 of which were on our left from the Corps of the Marqs. de St. Simond, who was betrayed by a deserter from the Huzzars that went in & gave notice of his approaching his parrallel.[2]

1. The trenches were opened between 500 and 600 yards from the British works, and the first parallel, supported by four redoubts (two on American ground, two on French), ran from the center of the enemy's works to the York River (TILGHMAN [3], 104). On the night of 6 Oct. the British concentrated their fire on a trench opened on the French left and on the redoubts on Pigeon Hill and the Hampton road and apparently were unaware of the work continuing on the first parallel during the night (CROMOT DU BOURG, 283).

2. Claude Anne Rouvroy, marquis de Saint Simon Montbleru (1743–1819), was in command of the 3,000 troops which de Grasse had transported from

the West Indies. On the night of 6 Oct. he launched a diversionary attack against the British defenses on lower Yorktown Creek.

7th. & 8th.   Was employed in compleating our Parallel—finishing the redoubts in them and establishing Batteries.

9th.   About 3 o'clock P.M. the French opened a battery on our extreme left, of 4 Sixteen pounders, and Six Morters & Hawitzers and at 5 oclock an American battery of Six 18s & 24s; four Morters & 2 Hawitzers, began to play from the extremity of our right —both with good effect as they compelled the Enemy to withdraw from their ambrazures the Pieces which had previously kept up a constant firing.[1]

1. According to Dr. James Thacher, "his Excellency General Washington put the match to the first gun, and a furious discharge of cannon and mortars immediately followed, and Earl Cornwallis has received his first salutation" (THACHER, 283).

10th.   The French opened two batteries on the left of our front parallel—one of 6 twenty four pounders, & 2 Sixteens with 6 Morters & Hawitzers—the other of 4 Sixteen pounders and the Americans two Batteries between those last mentioned & the one on our extreme right the left of which containing 4 Eighteen pounders— the other two Mortars.
    The whole of the batteries kept an incessant fire—the Cannon at the Ambrazures of the enemy, with a view to destroy them— the Shells into the Enemy's Works, where by the information of deserters they did much execution.
    The French battery on the left, by red hot shot, set fire to (in the course of the Night) the Charon frigate & 3 large Transports which were entirely consumed.

11th.   The French opened two other batteries on the left of the parallel, each consisting of 3 Twenty four pounders. These were also employed in demolishing the Ambrazures of the enemys Works & advancd Redoubts.
    Two Gentlemen—a Major Granchien & Captn. D'Avilion being sent by Admiral de Grasse to reconnoiter the Enemys Water defences, & state of the River at and near York, seemed favourably disposed to adopt the measure which had been strongly urged of bringing Ships above the Town & made representations accordingly to the Count de Grasse.[1]

1. Guillaume Jacques Constant de Liberge de Granchain (1744–1805) had served as *major général de l'escadre* in the fleet, under the command

of Admiral de Ternay, which brought Rochambeau to America. While at Newport he had been influential in planning French strategy. The other officer, a M. de la Villeon (see GW to de Grasse, 11 Oct. 1781, DLC:GW), is listed as a *lieutenant de vaisseau* on board de Grasse's flagship, the *Ville de Paris* (COMBATTANTS FRANÇAIS, 109).

12th. Began our second parallel within abt. 300 yards (& in some places less) of the enemys lines and got it so well advanced in the course of the Night as to cover the Men before morning. This business was conducted with the same secresy as the former & undertaken so much sooner than the enemy expected (we should commence a second parallel) that they did not by their conduct, & mode of firing, appear to have had any suspicion of our Working parties till day light discovered them to their Picquets; nor did they much annoy the Trenches in the course of this day (the Parallel being opened last Night from the ravene in front, and on the right flank of the Enemy till it came near to the intersection of the line of fire from the American 4 Gun Battery to the enemy's advanced redoubts on their left. The french Batteries fired over the second parallel.[1]

1. The second parallel was opened "1152 feet from the main fortifications" (CLOSEN, 147). It was soon apparent that the guns in two advanced British redoubts on the left would have to be silenced before work on the parallel could proceed effectively. The distance from the first parallel to the redoubts (some 650 yards) was too great to allow a frontal assault, and the suggestion of the engineers to reduce the distance by terminating "the right by a shoulder (épaulement) projection one hundred and twenty yards distant from one of their redoubts" was followed (CROMOT DU BOURG, 451–52).

13th. The fire of the enemy this Night became brisk—both from their Cannon and royals[1] and more injurious to us than it had been; several Men being killed, and many wounded in the Trenches, but the works were not in the smallest degree retarded by it. Our Batteries were begun in the course of the Night and a good deal advanced.

1. A royal was a small mortar carrying a shell with a diameter of 5.5 inches.

14th. The day was spent in compleating our parallel, and maturing the Batteries of the second parallel. The old batteries were principally directed against the abattis & salient angles of the enemys advanced redoubts on their extreme right & left to prepare them for the intended assault for which the necessary dispositions were made for attacking the two on the left and,
At half after Six in the Evening both were carried—that on

their left (on the Bank of the river) by the Americans and the other by the French Troops. The Baron Viominel commanded the left attack & the Marqs. de la fayette the right on which the light Infantry were employed.[1]

In the left redoubt (assaulted by the Americans) there were abt. 45 men under the command of a Major Campbell;[2] of which the Major a Captn. & Ensign, with 17 Men were made Prisoners— But few were killed on the part of the Enemy & the remainder of the Garrison escaped. The right Redoubt attacked by the French, consisted of abt. 120 Men, commanded by a Lieutenant Colo.—of these 18 were killed, & 42 taken Prisoners—among the Prisoners were a Captain and two Lieutenants. The bravery exhibited by the attacking Troops was emulous and praiseworthy—few cases have exhibited stronger proofs of Intripidity coolness and firmness than were shown upon this occasion. The following is our loss in these attacks and since the Investiture of York.

American

Periods	Killed								Wounded								Total
	Colo.	Lt. Colo.	Maj.	Captn.	C. Lieu.	Lieut.	Sergt.	R & F	Colo.	Lt. Colo.	Majr.	Captn.	C. Lt.	Lieut.	Sergt.	R & F	
From the Investe. to openg. 1st. parall.	1						1	4							8		14
To the opening of the 2d. parl.								2							6		8
To the Storm on the 14th.				1				6	1						14		22
At the Storm								8	2	1	2	1	1	1	28		44
Total	1			1		1		20	2	1	3	1	1	1	56		88

The loss of the French from the Investiture to the Assault of the Redoubts Inclusive, is as follows—viz.—

Officers—killed 2
Wounded . . . . . . 7 . .
9
Soldiers . . Killed 50
Wounded 127
177
Total 186

1. Antoine Charles du Houx, baron de Vioménil (1728–1792), was at this time Rochambeau's second-in-command in America. Ever since the épaulement had been started on 12 Oct., American and French guns had been pounding at the advanced British redoubts. By the evening of the 14th the engineers reported that the two British works had been sufficiently damaged by the shelling to make an assault practicable. It was decided that the redoubt on the extreme left would be attacked by American light infantry under the command of the marquis de Lafayette and the other by French grenadiers and chasseurs under Vioménil. In the midst of preparations for the attack, GW was forced to settle a squabble between Lafayette's two ranking subordinates, Alexander Hamilton and the chevalier de Gimat, as to which was to command the attack on the extreme left redoubt. GW decided in Hamilton's favor on grounds of seniority. Hamilton's subordinates in the attack were Maj. Nicholas Fish and Lt. Col. John Laurens; Guillaume, comte de Deux-Ponts, and baron d'Estrade were over the French assault force. Diversionary fire was ordered from Gloucester and from Saint Simon's troops on the left flank. For descriptions of the attack, see FREEMAN, 5:368–72; CARRINGTON, 638–39; Hamilton to Lafayette, 15 Oct. 1781, DLC:GW; DEUX-PONTS, 142–48.

2. Maj. James Campbell was an officer in the 71st Regiment.

Lt. Col. Alexander Hamilton in a detail from John Trumbull's "Surrender of Lord Cornwallis." (Copyright, Yale University Art Gallery)

15th.   Busily employed in getting the Batteries of the Second parallel compleated, and fixing on New ones contiguous to the Redoubts which were taken last Night. Placed two Hawitzers in each of the Captured Redoubts wch. were opened upon the enemy about 5 oclock in the Afternoon.

16th.   About four O'clock this Morning the enemy made a Sortee upon our Second parallel and spiked four French pieces of Artillery & two of ours—but the guards of the Trenches advancing quickly upon them they retreated precipitately. The Sally being made upon that part of the parallel which was guarded by the French Troops they lost an officer & 12 Men killed and 1 Officer taken prisoner. The American loss was one Sergeant of Artillery (in the American battery) Wounded. The Enemy, it is said, left 10 dead and lost 3 Prisoners.[1]

About 4 Oclock this afternoon the French opened two Batteries of 2. 24s. & four 16s. each. 3 pieces from the American grand battery were also opened—the others not being ready.

1. The British sortie, about 4:00 A.M., against the second parallel was led by Lt. Col. Robert Abercrombie with 350 men of the light infantry and Guards (see TUCKER, 390; WICKWIRE, 382–83). Although the British attackers succeeded in spiking the guns in two allied batteries, the spikes were quickly removed by the defenders (Cornwallis to Clinton, 20 Oct. 1781, CLINTON, 583–87). On the 16th, after the failure of Abercrombie's sortie had become apparent, Cornwallis made a last desperate attempt to escape the siege. He planned an attack on Choisy on Gloucester, hoping to break through his lines and march his troops north. Tarleton, already entrenched on Gloucester, sent 16 large boats across the river to ferry the British forces to Gloucester, since Cornwallis "hoped to pass the infantry during the night, abandoning our baggage and leaving a detachment to capitulate for the townspeople and for the sick and wounded, on which subject a letter was ready to be delivered to General Washington." At this point a violent storm broke, driving the boats down the river. When the American batteries opened fire at daybreak, a substantial portion of Cornwallis's troops were marooned at Gloucester; he was not able to get them back across the river until just before noon (Cornwallis to Clinton, 20 Oct. 1781, CLINTON, 583–87).

17th.   The French opened another Battery of four 24s. & two 16s. and a Morter Battery of 10 Morters and two Hawitzers. The American grand Battery consisting of 12 twenty fours and Eighteen prs.—4 Morters and two Hawitzers.

About ten Oclock the Enemy beat a parley and Lord Cornwallis proposed a cessation of Hostilities for 24 hours, that Commissioners might meet at the house of a Mr. Moore (in the rear of our first parallel) to settle terms for the surrender of the Posts of York and Gloucester.[1] To this he was answered, that a desire to spare the further effusion of Blood would readily incline me to treat of the surrender of the above Posts but previous to the meeting of Commissioners I wished to have his proposals in writing and for this purpose would grant a cessation of hostilities two hours—Within which time he sent out A letter with such proposals (tho' some of them were inadmissable) as led me to believe that there would be no great difficulty in fixing the terms.[2] Accordingly hostilities were suspended for the Night & I proposed my own terms to which if he agreed Commissioners were to meet to digest them into form.

1. Cornwallis's letter, 17 Oct. 1781, is in DLC:GW.

GW is referring to the Moore House, 1½ miles below Yorktown on Temple Farm. At this time the house was owned by Augustine Moore (d. 1788), a leading York County landowner. See also LOSSING, 2:530.

2. Cornwallis's letter, 17 Oct. 1781, is in DLC:GW. In his reply, GW agreed that the garrisons of Yorktown and Gloucester should be considered prisoners of war but Cornwallis's suggestion that the British and German troops should be returned to Europe was clearly inadmissible; instead the troops would be marched to whatever section of the country was best prepared to receive them. British shipping in the area was to be delivered to an officer of the navy and all British armament except officers' small arms was to be surrendered (GW to Cornwallis, 18 Oct. 1781, P.R.O. 30/11/74, ff. 124–25). Cornwallis's reply to GW, 18 Oct. 1781, agreeing to most of the proposed terms is in DNA: PCC, Item 152.

18th.   The Commissioners met accordingly; but the business was so procrastinated by those on their side (a Colo. Dundas & a Majr. Ross) that Colo. Laurens & the Viscount De Noailles who were appointed on our part could do no more than make the rough draft of the Articles which were to be submitted for Lord Cornwallis's consideration.[1]

1. The British commissioners were Lt. Col. Thomas Dundas of the 80th Regiment of Foot (Royal Edinburgh Volunteers) and Maj. Alexander Ross, Cornwallis's aide-de-camp. The American commissioners were Lt. Col. John Laurens and the vicomte de Noailles, *mestre de camp en second* of the Soissonnais Regiment and brother-in-law of Lafayette. The discussions dragged on through the day, and in late evening the commissioners reported that negotiations had been so protracted that an extension of the truce until 9:00 the next morning had been necessary.

19th.   In the Morning early I had them copied and sent word to Lord Cornwallis that I expected to have them signed at 11 Oclock and that the Garrison would March out at two O'clock— both of which were accordingly done.[1] Two redoubts on the Ene-

The surrender at Yorktown as seen by a German artist. (Metropolitan Museum of Art)

mys left being possessed (the one by a detachment of French Grenadiers, & the other by American Infantry) with orders to prevent all intercourse between the army & Country and the Town—while Officers in the several departments were employed in taking acct. of the public Stores &ca.

1. The final articles of capitulation, signed 19 Oct. by GW, Rochambeau, and Barras (signing for himself and de Grasse) for the allies and Cornwallis and Thomas Symonds for the British, contained customary conditions of honorable surrender. In addition, British officers were permitted to return to Europe or to any British-held American port on parole. Land troops were to be considered prisoners of the United States; naval prisoners would be in the custody of the French. British soldiers were "to be kept in Virginia, Maryland or Pennsylvania, and as much by Regiments as possible, and supplied with the same Rations of provisions as are allowed to Soldiers in the service of America." The sloop of war *Bonetta* was to be left at the disposal of Cornwallis to carry dispatches to Clinton "and such Soldiers as he may think proper to send to New York to be permitted to sail without examination" (P.R.O. 30/11/74, ff. 128–33). As GW probably surmised, the soldiers sent to New York aboard the *Bonetta* were principally deserters from the American army who had joined the British (see MACKENZIE, 2:685). The text of the capitulation is conveniently printed in WASHINGTON AND DE GRASSE, 104–11.

On this day GW wrote to Congress announcing the British surrender and enclosing his correspondence with Cornwallis and commissioned his aide Lt. Col. Tench Tilghman to carry the victory dispatch to Congress (DNA: PCC, Item 152).

At 2:00 P.M. French and American troops began to move into British positions at the east end of the town. With American troops lined up on the right and French on the left, the British began their march through the lines, "their Drums in Front beating a slow March. Their Colours furl'd and Cased . . . General Lincoln with his Aids conducted them—Having passed thro' our whole Army they grounded their Arms & march'd back again thro' the Army a second Time into the Town—The sight was too pleasing to an American to admit of Description" (TUCKER, 392–93). French army officer baron von Closen noted that in passing through the lines the British showed "the greatest scorn for the Americans, who, to tell the truth, were eclipsed by our army in splendor of appearance and dress, for most of these unfortunate persons were clad in small jackets of white cloth, dirty and ragged, and a number of them were almost barefoot" (CLOSEN, 153). Cornwallis, claiming illness, did not accompany his troops, and the surrender was carried out by Brig. Gen. Charles O'Hara, who had accompanied Cornwallis through the Carolina campaign. The British officer's sword was accepted by Maj. Gen. Benjamin Lincoln.

Descriptions of the Yorktown surrender ceremonies are legion. For details, see Clermont-Crèvecoeur in RICE, 1:61; DUMAS, 1:52–53; BUTLER, 111; THACHER, 288–90; LEE [4], 512–13. See also FREEMAN, 5:378–93; JOHNSTON [3], 151–61. For O'Hara's attempt, probably unintentional, to present his sword to Rochambeau instead of GW, see DUMAS, 52–53; ROCHAMBEAU, 1:295. The tradition that the British band played "The World Turned Upside Down" is discussed in FREEMAN, 5:388 n.47.

On the evening of the 19th Cornwallis was invited to dine at Headquarters "but excuses himself on account of health. Keeps his Quarters." O'Hara came in his place "very social and easy" (TRUMBULL [1], 337).

20th.   Winchester & Fort Frederick in Maryland, being the places destined for the reception of the Prisoners they were to have commenced their March accordingly this day, but were prevented by the Commissary of Prisoners not having compleated his Accounts of them & taken the Paroles of the Officers.[1]

1. On 20 Oct., GW was informed by the marquis de Choisy that the surrender of Gloucester by Tarleton was progressing smoothly (DLC:GW).

Estimates of prisoners taken at Yorktown vary slightly. A "General Return of Officers and Privates taken Prisoner, 19 Oct. 1781" (DNA: RG 93, Manuscript File no. 31604), made by Thomas Durie, deputy commissary of prisoners, lists the number as 7,171, not counting naval prisoners. Another return by Durie is in DNA: PCC, Item 152, enclosed in GW to Congress, 27 Oct. 1781. An unsigned "List of Prisoners taken at York & Gloucester" in DLC: Breckinridge Family Papers gives the number of prisoners as 6,935, with 2,000 seamen turned over to de Grasse, and 80 "followers of the army." A "Return of Prisoners Taken at the Surrender of the British Garrison of York and Gloucester in Virginia Octob. 19th 1781 exclusive of Marine Prisoners and of Officers and Soldiers Taken during the Siege" (DNA: RG 93, Manuscript File no. 31603) gives a total of 7,050. See also BOATNER [1], 1248–49; FREEMAN, 5:513–16.

21st.   The prisoners began their March & set out for the Fleet to pay my respects, & offer my thanks to the Admiral for his important Services and to see if he could not be induced to further co-operations before his final departure from this Coast. Despairing from the purport of my former conferences with him, & the tenor of all his letters, of obtaining more than a Convoy, I contented myself with representing the import, consequences and certain prospect of an attempt upon Charles town and requesting if his orders or other Engagements would not allow him to attend to that great object, that he would nevertheless transport a detachment of Troops to, & cover their debarkation at Wilmington that by reducing the enemy's post there we might give peace to another State with the Troops that would afterwards join the Southern army under the Command of Majr. Genl. Greene.[1]

Having promised the Command of the detachment destined for the Enterprize against Wilmington to the Marqs. de la Fayette in case he could engage the Admiral to convey it & secure the debarkation I left him on Board the Ville de Paris to try the force of his influence to obtain these.

In this French print, Washington holds the Declaration of Independence and the treaty of alliance with France. (Anne S. K. Brown Military Collection, Brown University Library)

1. GW's plan was presented in a letter to de Grasse, 20 Oct. 1781 (DLC: GW). De Grasse's reply, 23 Oct., agreeing in principle to the attack on Wilmington, is in DLC:GW. On further reflection, de Grasse decided that it would be impossible for him to transport American troops, supplies, and ammunition for the Wilmington expedition and still be certain of keeping his other engagements, although he was still willing to provide a convoy (de Grasse to Lafayette, 26 Oct. 1781, DNA: PCC, Item 152). For the circumstances of de Grasse's refusal, see also WASHINGTON AND DE GRASSE, 128–40.

23d.   The Marqs. returned with assurances from the Admiral, that he would countenance, & protect with his fleet, the Expedition against Wilmington. Preparations were immediately [begun] for Embarking Wayne's & Gists [1] Brigades with a sufficiency of Artillery, Stores, & provisions for this purpose.

1. Mordecai Gist (1743–1792) served as brigadier general in the Maryland Line, 9 Jan. 1779 to 3 Nov. 1783.

24th.   Received advice, by Express from General Forman, of the British Fleet in the Harbour of New York consisting of 26 Sail of the line, some 50s. & 44s.—Many frigates—fire Ships & Transports mounting in the whole to 99 Sail had passed the Narrows for the hook, & were as he supposd, upon the point of Sailing for Chesapeak.[1] Notice was immediately communicated to the Count de grasse.

From this time to the 28th. was employed in collecting and taking an acct. of the different species of Stores which were much dispersed and in great disorder.

All the Vessels in public employ in the James River were ordered round for the purpose of receiving and transporting Stores &ca. to the Head of Elk.

1. David Forman to GW, 17 Oct. 1781 (DLC:GW). In New York, Clinton and Graves, increasingly alarmed by Cornwallis's reports from Yorktown, had since mid-October been in the midst of preparations to send a fleet to his relief. For the difficulties and delays surrounding these preparations, see WILLCOX [3], 436–39; CLINTON, 338–46. Vessels of the British navy and transports carrying British troops began straggling out of New York on 17 Oct., but it was the 19th before the fleet was completely under way. By the 24th, when Graves had arrived at the Chesapeake, "he found Comte de Grasse's superior fleet of thirty-three ships of the line and two fifty-gun ships at anchor in a position of defense. Since they were so stationed that he could not attack them without first running past a formidable land battery, he thought it foolhardy to stake everything" (BAURMEISTER, 475–76). The fleet was back in New York by 3 Nov. (MACKENZIE [2], 686).

28th.   Began to Embark the Ordnance and Stores for the above purpose.

Received a Letter from the Count de Grasse, declining the Convoy he had engaged to give the detachment for Wilmington & assigning his reasons for it. This after a suspence & consequent delay of 6 or 7 days obliged me to prepare to March the Troops by Land under the command of M. Genl. St. Clair.[1]

In the Evening of this day Intilligence was received from the Count de Grasse that the British fleet was off the Capes, & consisted of 36 Ships 25 of which were of the line & that he had hove out the Signal for all his People to come on board & prepare to Sail—but many of his Boats & hands being on Shore it could not be effected.

1. See entry for 21 Oct. 1781. GW's instructions to Maj. Gen. Arthur St. Clair (1736–1818), dated 29 Oct. 1781, are in the Ohio State Library.

29th.   The British Fleet still appeared in the offing without the Capes, but the Wind being unfavourable, and other causes preventing, the French Fleet kept to their Moorings within. In the Evening of this day the former fleet disappeared, & Count de Grasse engaged to remain a few days in the Bay to cover the Water transport of our Stores & Troops up the Bay to the River Elk.

From this time to the 5th. of Novr. was employed in embarking the ordnance & Stores, & the Troops which were returning to the Northward—preparing the detachment for the Southward—providing Cloathing & Stores for the Army commanded by Majr. Genl. Greene—depositing a Magazine at Westham for the use of the Southern States and making other necessary arrangements previous to the division of the army and my return to the North river—also in marching off 467 Convalescents from the British Hospital under escort of Courtlandts York Regiment for Fredericksburg on their way to join their respective Regiments at Winchester & Fort Frederick in Maryland.

November 1781

5th.   The detachment for the Southward, consisting as has been before observed, of Waynes & Gists Brigades (excepting such Men of the Maryland & Virginia lines whose terms of Service would expire before the first of Jany.). Began their March and were to be joined by all the Cavalry that could be equiped of the first—third & fourth Regiments at [   ].[1]

1. At this point GW's 1781 diary abruptly ends. By 3 Nov. most of the American troops and supplies which GW was moving north were on their way to Head of Elk. The main body of Rochambeau's army was to go into winter quarters in Virginia. Cornwallis and those British officers who were going to New York and directly to Europe left Yorktown on 4 Nov. "The Prisoners who are to remain in the Country are all marched to Winchester & Fort Frederick, except such Sick as remain too bad to remove—of these there are still a considerable Number" (GW to Nathanael Greene, 16 Nov. 1781, NNPM).

As GW was preparing to leave his Headquarters at Yorktown, he was called to Burwell Bassett's home, Eltham, to the bedside of his stepson, Jacky (John Parke Custis), who had been taken seriously ill. In the fall of 1781 Jacky had left Mount Vernon for a stay in the area of Pamunkey, and by 12 Oct. he had written his mother from the "Camp before York" that his health had improved and "the general tho in constant Fatigue looks very well" (ViMtV). He apparently served briefly as a civilian aide during the Yorktown siege. While at Yorktown he was stricken with what appears to have been camp fever and was moved to the Bassett estate of Eltham, some 30 miles from Yorktown, and his mother and wife were summoned. On 6 Nov., GW wrote his aide Jonathan Trumbull, Jr., from Eltham: "I came here in time to see Mr. Custis breathe his last. About Eight o'clock yesterday Evening he expired. The deep and solemn distress of the Mother, and

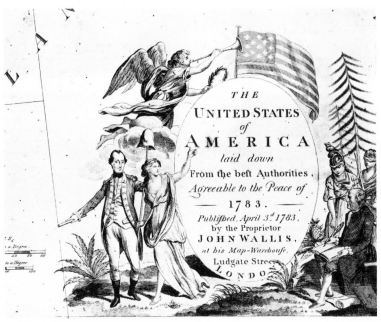

Detail of cartouche from a 1783 map of the United States (Prints Division, New York Public Library)

affliction of the Wife of this amiable young Man, requires every comfort in my power to afford them; the last rights of the deceased I must also see performed; these will take me three or four days; when I shall proceed with Mrs. Washington and Mrs. Custis to Mount Vernon" (WRITINGS, 37:554). See also CUSTIS, 254–55, and Eliza Parke Custis to David Baillie Warden, 20 April 1808, in HOYT, 95.

GW probably left Eltham on 11 Nov. or possibly early on the 12th (see WRITINGS, 23:338 for routes), stopping briefly at Fredericksburg to visit his mother, who proved to be away from home (Mary Ball Washington to GW, 13 Mar. 1782, facsimile, CSmH). By 13 Nov. he was at Mount Vernon and remained there until he left for Philadelphia, probably on 20 Nov., to concert with Congress plans for a 1782 campaign.

Repository Symbols
and Abbreviations

Bibliography

Index

Repository Symbols and Abbreviations

Aff. Etr.	Archives du Ministère des Affaires Etrangères (photostats and microfilm at Library of Congress)
CSmH	Henry Huntington Library, San Marino, Calif.
Ct	Connecticut State Library, Hartford
CtMMCH	Middlesex County Historical Society, Middletown, Conn.
CtY	Yale University, New Haven
DLC	Library of Congress
DLC:GW	George Washington Papers, Library of Congress
DNA	National Archives
DNA:PCC	National Archives, RG 360, Papers of the Continental Congress
ICHi	Chicago Historical Society
M-Ar	Archives Division, Secretary of State, Boston
MdAA	Maryland Hall of Records, Annapolis
MdHi	Maryland Historical Society, Baltimore
MH	Harvard University, Cambridge
MHi	Massachusetts Historical Society, Boston
MiU-C	Clements Library, University of Michigan, Ann Arbor
MnHi	Minnesota Historical Society, Saint Paul
MoSW	Washington University, St. Louis, Mo.
N	New York State Library, Albany
NcD	Duke University, Durham
NHi	New-York Historical Society, New York
NjMoNP	Morristown National Historical Park, Morristown, N.J.
NjP	Princeton University
NN	New York Public Library
NNebgGW	Washington's Headquarters, Jonathan Hasbrouck House, Newburgh, N.Y.
NNMM	Metropolitan Museum of Art, New York
NNPM	Pierpont Morgan Library, New York
PHi	Historical Society of Pennsylvania, Philadelphia
PPiU	University of Pittsburgh
PPRF	Rosenbach Foundation, Philadelphia
P.R.O.	Public Record Office, London
PU	University of Pennsylvania, Philadelphia
Vi	Virginia State Library, Richmond
ViHi	Virginia Historical Society, Richmond
ViMtV	Mount Vernon Ladies' Association of the Union
ViW	College of William and Mary, Williamsburg

Bibliography

ABERNETHY — Thomas Perkins Abernethy. *Western Lands and the American Revolution.* 1937. Reprint, New York: Russell & Russell, 1959.

ADAMS [1] — Lyman Butterfield, ed. *Diary and Autobiography of John Adams.* 4 vols. Cambridge, Mass.: Belknap Press, 1961–62.

ADAMS [2] — Charles Francis Adams, ed. *The Works of John Adams, Second President of the United States: With a Life of the Author, Notes and Illustrations.* 10 vols. Boston: Little, Brown, and Co., 1850–56.

ALDEN — John Richard Alden. *General Charles Lee, Traitor or Patriot?* Baton Rouge: Louisiana State University Press, 1951.

ALLEN — James Allen. "Diary of James Allen, Esq., of Philadelphia, Counsellor-at-Law, 1770–1778." *Pennsylvania Magazine of History and Biography,* 9 (1885), 176–96, 278–96, 424–41.

BAILEY [5] — Kenneth P. Bailey. *Christopher Gist: Colonial Frontiersman, Explorer, and Indian Agent.* Hamden, Conn.: Shoe String Press, 1976.

BAKER — William S. Baker. *Itinerary of General Washington from June 15, 1775, to December 23, 1783.* Philadelphia: J. B. Lippincott Co., 1892.

BALCH [1] — Thomas Willing Balch. *The Philadelphia Assemblies.* Philadelphia: Allen, Lane and Scott, 1916.

BALCH [2] — Thomas Willing Balch. "The English Ancestors of the Shippen Family and Edward Shippen, of Philadelphia." *Pennsylvania Magazine of History and Biography,* 28 (1904), 385–402.

BARBER — A. Richard Barber. "The Tallmadge-Culper Intelligence Ring, a Study of American

Revolutionary Spies." Master's essay, Columbia University, 1963.

BARKER [1] Charles Albro Barker. *The Background of the Revolution in Maryland.* New Haven: Yale University Press, 1940.

BARKER [2] Charles R. Barker. "Colonial Taverns of Lower Merion." *Pennsylvania Magazine of History and Biography,* 52 (1928), 205–28.

BASS Robert D. Bass. *The Green Dragoon: The Lives of Banastre Tarleton and Mary Robinson.* New York: Henry Holt and Co., 1957.

BAURMEISTER Carl Leopold von Baurmeister. *Revolution in America: Confidential Letters and Journals, 1776–1784, of Adjutant General Major Baurmeister of the Hessian Forces.* New Brunswick, N.J.: Rutgers University Press, 1957.

BEALL Fielder Montgomery Magruder Beall. *Colonial Families of the United States Descended from the Immigrants Who Arrived before 1700, Mostly from England and Scotland, and Who Are Now Represented by Citizens of the Following Names, Bell, Beal, Bale, Beale, Beall.* Washington, D.C.: C. H. Potter & Co., 1929.

BEAR James A. Bear, Jr., ed. "Thomas Jefferson Account Books." Vol. 1, 1767–1775, typescript, University of Virginia Library.

BEIRNE Rosamond Randall Beirne and John Henry Scarff. *William Buckland, 1734–1774: Architect of Virginia and Maryand.* Baltimore: Maryland Historical Society, 1958.

BEMIS Samuel Flagg Bemis. *The Diplomacy of the American Revolution.* 1935. Reprint, Bloomington and London: Indiana University Press, 1967.

BERG Fred Anderson Berg. *Encyclopedia of Continental Army Units, Battalions, Regiments, and Independent Corps.* Harrisburg, Pa.: Stackpole Books, 1972.

BERGH Albert Ellery Bergh, ed. *The Writings of Thomas Jefferson.* Memorial Edition. 20 vols. Washington, D.C.: The Thomas Jefferson Memorial Association, 1903–4.

BERKELEY [1] Edmund and Dorothy Smith Berkeley. *John Clayton: Pioneer of American Botany.* Chapel Hill: University of North Carolina Press, 1963.

BERRY'S FERRY "Berry's Ferry, and Old Roads Leading to That Ferry." *Proceedings of the Clarke County Historical Association,* 6 (1946), 8–13.

BETTS [2] Edwin M. Betts, ed. *Thomas Jefferson's Garden Book, 1766–1824.* Philadelphia: American Philosophical Society, 1944.

BLACK [1] R. Alonzo Brock, ed. "Journal of William Black, 1744." *Pennsylvania Magazine of History and Biography,* 1 (1877), 233–49, 404–19; 2 (1878), 40–49.

BOATNER [1] Mark Mayo Boatner III. *Encyclopedia of the American Revolution.* New York: David McKay Co., 1966.

BOATNER [2] Mark Mayo Boatner III. *Landmarks of the American Revolution.* Harrisburg, Pa.: Stackpole Books, 1973.

BOUCHER [1] Jonathan Boucher. *Reminiscenses of an American Loyalist, 1738–1789, Being the Autobiography of the Revd. Jonathan Boucher, Rector of Annapolis in Maryland and Afterwards Vicar of Epsom, Surrey, England.* Boston and New York: Houghton Mifflin Co., 1925.

BOUCHER [2] Jonathan Boucher. *A View of the Causes and Consequences of the American Revolution: in Thirteen Discourses, Preached in North America between the Years 1763 and 1775; with an Historical Preface.* London: G. G. & J. Robinson, 1797.

BOWIE Effie Gwynn Bowie. *Across the Years in Prince George's County.* Richmond: Garrett and Massie, 1947.

BRENT Chester Horton Brent. *The Descendants of Collo. Giles Brent, Capt. George Brent, and Robert Brent, Gent., Immigrants to Maryland and Virginia.* Rutland, Vt.: Tuttle Publishing Co., 1946.

BRIDENBAUGH Carl and Jessica Bridenbaugh. *Rebels and Gentlemen: Philadelphia in the Age of*

Franklin. New York: Reynal & Hitchcock, 1942.

BRITISH
FIELD OFFICERS
A List of the General and Field Officers, As They Rank in the Army. London: J. Millan, 1774.

BROCKETT
Franklin Longdon Brockett. *The Lodge of Washington: A History of the Alexandria Washington Lodge, No. 22, A.F. and A.M. of Alexandria, Va.* Alexandria, Va.: George E. French, 1876.

BRUMBAUGH
Gaius Marcus Brumbaugh. *Maryland Records: Colonial, Revolutionary, County, and Church from Original Sources.* Vol. 1. Baltimore: Williams & Wilkins Co., 1915.

BUCKNERS
William Armstrong Crozier, ed. *The Buckners of Virginia and the Allied Families of Strother and Ashby.* New York: Genealogical Association, 1907.

BURGESS
Louis A. Burgess, ed. *Virginia Soldiers of 1776, Compiled from Documents on File in the Virginia Land Offie; Together with Material Found in the Archives Department of the Virginia State Library, and Other Reliable Sources.* 1927–29. Reprint, Richmond: Richmond Press; Spartanburg, S.C.: Reprint Company, 1973.

BURSON
R. E. Burson. "A Report of the Findings of Mr. R. E. Burson on the George Washington Grist Mill, Situated on Dogue Run Creek, Mount Vernon, Va." Mimeographed Report. Richmond: Virginia Division of Parks, 23 March 1932.

BUSHONG
Millard K. Bushong. *Historic Jefferson County.* Boyce, Va.: Carr Publishing Co., 1972.

BUTLER
Richard Butler. "General Richard Butler's Journal of the Siege of Yorktown." *Historical Magazine,* 8 (1864), 102–12.

CALENDAR [2]
Leon de Valinger, Jr., comp. *Calendar of Kent County, Delaware Probate Records, 1680–1800.* Dover, Del.: Public Archives Commission, 1944.

CAMPBELL [1]
Thomas Elliott Campbell. *Colonial Caroline: A History of Caroline County, Virginia.* Richmond: Dietz Press, 1954.

CAMPBELL [2]   Charles A. Campbell. "Rochambeau's Headquarters in Westchester County, N.Y., 1781." *Magazine of American History,* 4 (1880), 46–48.

CARRINGTON   Henry B. Carrington. *Battles of the American Revolution, 1775–1781; Including Battle Maps and Charts of the American Revolution.* 1877. Reprint, New York: Promontory Press, n.d.

CARROLL   Charles Carroll of Annapolis and Charles Carroll of Carrollton. "Extracts from the Carroll Papers." *Maryland Historical Magazine,* vols. 10–16 (1915–21).

CARSON [1]   George Barr Carson. "The Chevalier de Chastellux, Soldier and Philosophe," Ph.D. diss., University of Chicago, 1942.

CARSON [2]   Jane Carson. *Colonial Virginians at Play.* Williamsburg: Colonial Williamsburg, Inc., 1965.

CARSON [3]   Joseph Carson. *A History of the Medical Department of the University of Pennsylvania, from Its Foundation in 1765; with Sketches of the Lives of Deceased Professors.* Philadelphia: Lindsay and Blakiston, 1869.

CARTER [3]   Jack P. Greene, ed. *The Diary of Colonel Landon Carter of Sabine Hall, 1752–1778.* 2 vols. Charlottesville: University Press of Virginia, 1965.

CARTMELL   Thomas Kemp Cartmell. *Shenandoah Valley Pioneers and Their Descendants: A History of Frederick County, Virginia.* Winchester, Va.: Eddy Press Corp., 1909.

CHAPPELEAR [1]   Curtis Chappelear. "Early Grants of the Site of Berryville and Its Northern Vicinity." *Proceedings of the Clarke County Historical Association,* 8 (1948), 17–38.

CHAPPELEAR [2]   Curtis Chappelear. "A Map of the Original Grants and Early Landmarks in Clarke County, Virginia, and Vicinity." *Proceedings of the Clarke County Historical Association,* 2 (1942), facing p. 56.

CHASE   Philander Dean Chase. "Baron von Steuben in the War of Independence," Ph.D. diss., Duke University, 1972.

[447]

CHASTELLUX

François Jean de Beauvoir, Marquis de Chastellux. *Travels in North America in the Years 1780, 1781 and 1782.* 2 vols. Ed. Howard C. Rice, Jr. Chapel Hill: University of North Carolina Press, 1963.

CLARK [1]

James Alton James, ed. *George Rogers Clark Papers, 1771–1781. Collections of the Illinois State Historical Library,* vol. 8 (Virginia Series, vol. 3). Springfield: Illinois State Historical Library, 1912.

CLARK [2]

Raymond B. Clark, Jr. "The Abbey, or Ringgold House at Chestertown, Maryland." *Maryland Historical Magazine,* 46 (1951), 81–92.

CLINTON

William B. Willcox, ed. *The American Rebellion: Sir Henry Clinton's Narrative of His Campaigns, 1775–1782, with an Appendix of Original Documents.* New Haven: Yale University Press, 1954.

CLOSEN

Evelyn M. Acomb, ed. *The Revolutionary Journal of Baron Ludwig von Closen, 1780–1783.* Chapel Hill: University of North Carolina Press, 1958.

COKE

Daniel Parker Coke. *The Royal Commission on the Losses and Services of American Loyalists, 1783–1785.* Ed. Hugh Edward Egerton. 1915. Reprint, New York: Arno Press, 1969.

COLEMAN

Mary Haldane Coleman. *St. George Tucker, Citizen of No Mean City.* Richmond: Dietz Press, 1938.

COLLES

Christopher Colles. *A Survey of the Roads of the United States of America, 1789.* Ed. Walter W. Ristow. Cambridge, Mass.: Harvard University Press, 1961.

COMBATTANTS FRANÇAIS

Les Combattants français de la guerre américaine, 1778–1783. Paris: Ancienne Maison Quantin, Motteroz, Martinet, 1903.

COPELAND

Pamela C. Copeland and Richard K. Mac-Master. *The Five George Masons: Patriots and Planters of Virginia and Maryland.* Charlottesville: University Press of Virginia, for the Regents of Gunston Hall, 1975.

CORNWALLIS   Charles Ross, ed. *Correspondence of Charles, First Marquis Cornwallis.* 3 vols. London: John Murray, 1859.

CRAIK [1]   David Craik. *The Practical American Millwright and Miller: Comprising the Elementary Principles of Mechanics, Mechanism, and Motive Power, Hydraulics, and Hydraulic Motors, Mill Dams, Saw-Mills, Grist-Mills, the Oat-Meal Mill, the Barley Mill, Wool Carding and Cloth Fulling and Dressing, Windmills, Steam Power, etc.* Philadelphia: Henry Carey Baird, Industrial Publisher, 1870.

CRARY   Catherine Snell Crary. "The Tory and the Spy: The Double Life of James Rivington." *William and Mary Quarterly,* 3d ser., 16 (1959), 61–72.

CRESSWELL   Lincoln MacVeagh, ed. *The Journal of Nicholas Cresswell, 1774–1777.* New York: Dial Press, 1924.

CROFUT   Florence S. Marcy Crofut. *Guide to the History and the Historic Sites of Connecticut.* 2 vols. New Haven: Yale University Press, 1937.

CROMOT DU BOURG   Marie François Joseph Maxime, Baron Cromot du Bourg. "Diary of a French Officer, 1781." *Magazine of American History,* 4 (1880), 205–14, 293–308, 376–85, 441–52; 7 (1881), 283–95.

CROZIER [2]   William Armstrong Crozier, ed. *Spotsylvania County Records, 1721–1800.* Baltimore: Southern Book Co., 1955.

CROZIER [3]   William Armstrong Crozier, ed. *The Buckners of Virginia and Allied Families of Strother and Ashby.* New York: privately printed, 1907.

CURWEN   Andrew Oliver, ed. *The Journal of Samuel Curwen, Loyalist.* 2 vols. Cambridge, Mass.: Harvard University Press, 1972.

CUSTIS   George Washington Parke Custis. *Recollections and Private Memoirs of Washington.* New York: Derby & Jackson, 1860.

CUSTIS ACCOUNT BOOK   GW's Accounts Kept for Martha Parke Custis and John Parke Custis, 1760–1775. Manuscript in Custis Papers, Virginia Historical Society, Richmond.

DAVIES K. G. Davies, ed. *Documents of the American Revolution, 1770–1783 (Colonial Office Series)*. 7 vols. Shannon, Ireland: Irish University Press, 1972–74.

DAY Richard E. Day. "A Summary of the English Period." In vol. 3 of Alexander Clarence Flick, ed. *History of the State of New York.* 10 vols. New York: Columbia University Press, 1933–37.

DELAPLAINE Edward S. Delaplaine. *The Life of Thomas Johnson, Member of the Continental Congress, First Governor of the State of Maryland, and Associate Justice of the United States Supreme Court.* New York: Frederick H. Hitchcock, Grafton Press, 1927.

DESTLER Chester M. Destler. *Connecticut: The Provisions State.* Chester, Conn.: Pequot Press, 1973.

DEUX-PONTS Samuel Abbott Green, ed. *My Campaigns in America: A Journal Kept by Count William de Deux-Ponts, 1780–81.* Boston: J. K. Wiggin and William Parsons Lunt, 1868.

DIARIES John C. Fitzpatrick, ed. *The Diaries of George Washington, 1748–1799.* 4 vols. Boston and New York: Houghton Mifflin Co., 1925.

DONIOL Henri Doniol. *Histoire de la participation de la France à l'établissement des États-Unis d'Amérique: Correspondance diplomatique et documents.* 5 vols. Paris: Imprimerie Nationale, 1886–1892.

DORLAND W. A. Newman Dorland. "The Second Troop Philadelphia City Cavalry." *Pennsylvania Magazine of History and Biography,* 46 (1922), 346–65.

DU BELLET Louise Pecquet du Bellet. *Some Prominent Virginia Families.* 4 vols. Lynchburg, Va.: J. P. Bell Co., 1907.

DUMAS Mathieu Dumas. *Memoirs of His Own Time: Including the Revolution, the Empire, and the Restoration.* 2 vols. Philadelphia: Lea & Blanchard, 1839.

EATON — David W. Eaton. *Historical Atlas of West-moreland County, Virginia; Patents Showing How Lands Were Patented from the Crown & Proprietors of the Northern Neck of Virginia, Including Some History of the Patentees, Indians, Church & State, Parishes, Ministers, Prominent Men, Surveys, Portraits, Maps, Airplane Views, & Other Data.* Richmond: Dietz Press, 1942.

EDDIS — William Eddis. *Letters from America.* Ed. Aubrey C. Land. Cambridge, Mass.: Harvard University Press, 1969.

EDEN — Rosamond Randall Beirne. "Portrait of a Colonial Governor: Robert Eden." *Maryland Historical Magazine,* 45 (1950), 153–75, 294–311.

EGLESTON — Thomas Egleston. *The Life of John Paterson, Major-General in the Revolutionary Army.* New York: G. P. Putnam's Sons, 1894.

FAGGART — Harold L. Faggart. "A Recently Discovered Second Letter from George Washington to John Baker." *Journal of the American Dental Association,* 59 (1959), 549–51.

FAIRFAX — Sally Cary Fairfax. "Diary of a Little Colonial Girl." *Virginia Magazine of History and Biography,* 11 (1903–4), 212–14.

FARQUHAR — Charles Stonehill, ed. *The Complete Works of George Farquhar.* 2 vols. New York: Gordian Press, 1967.

FITHIAN — Hunter Dickinson Farish, ed. *Journal & Letters of Philip Vickers Fithian, 1773–1774: A Plantation Tutor of the Old Dominion.* Williamsburg: Colonial Williamsburg, Inc., 1943.

FORD [4] — Corey Ford. *A Peculiar Service.* New York: Little, Brown, 1965.

FREEMAN — Douglas Southall Freeman. *George Washington.* 7 vols. New York: Charles Scribner's Sons, 1949–57.

GAGE PAPERS — Clarence Edwin Carter, ed. *The Correspondence of General Thomas Gage with the Secretaries of State, and with the War Office and the Treasury.* 1933. Reprint, 2 vols., n.p.: Archon Books, 1969.

GERLACH · Don R. Gerlach. "Philip Schuyler and the New York Frontier in 1781." *New-York Historical Society Quarterly Bulletin,* 53 (1969), 148–81.

GIBBS · Patricia Ann Gibbs. "Taverns in Tidewater Virginia, 1700–1774." Master's thesis, College of William and Mary, 1968.

GLAZEBROOK · Eugenia G. and Preston G. Glazebrook, comp. *Virginia Migration, Hanover County.* 2 vols. Richmond: privately printed, 1943–49.

GOUSSENCOURT · Chevalier de Goussencourt. "A Journal of the Cruise of the Fleet of His Most Christian Majesty under the Command of the Count de Grasse-Tilly, in 1781 and 1782." In J. G. Shea, ed. *The Operations of the French Fleet under the Count de Grasse in 1781–82 as Described in Two Contemporaneous Journals.* New York: Bradford Club, 1864.

GRABOWSKII · Bessie Berry Grabowskii. *The DuVal Family of Virginia, 1701; Descendants of Daniel DuVal, Huguenot, and Allied Families.* Richmond: Dietz Printing Co., 1931.

GRAVES PAPERS · French Ensor Chadwick, ed. *The Graves Papers and Other Documents Relating to the Naval Operations of the Yorktown Campaign.* New York: printed for the Naval History Society by the De Vinne Press, 1916.

GRAYDON · John Stockton Littell, ed. *Memoirs of His Own Time with Reminiscenses of the Men and Events of the Revolution by Alexander Graydon.* Philadelphia: Lindsay & Blackiston, 1846.

GREENE [3] · Katherine Glass Greene. *Winchester, Virginia, and Its Beginnings, 1743–1814, from Its Founding by Colonel James Wood to the Close of the Life of His Son, Brigadier-General and Governor James Wood, with the Publication for the First Time of Valuable Manuscripts, Relics of Their Long Tenure of Public Offices.* Strasburg, Va.: Printed by Shenandoah Publishing House, 1926.

GRIFFIN · Martin I. J. Griffin. *Stephen Moylan.* Philadelphia: privately printed, 1909.

GROOME [1]

Harry C. Groome. *Fauquier during the Proprietorship.* Richmond: Old Dominion Press, 1927.

GW ATLAS

Lawrence Martin, ed. *The George Washington Atlas.* Washington, D.C.: United States George Washington Bicentennial Commission, 1932.

HAMILTON [1]

Stanislaus Murray Hamilton, ed. *Letters to Washington and Accompanying Papers.* 5 vols. Boston and New York: Houghton Mifflin and Co., 1898–1902.

HAMILTON [2]

Harold C. Syrett, ed. *The Papers of Alexander Hamilton.* New York: Columbia University Press, 1961—.

HANSON

George A. Hanson. *Old Kent: The Eastern Shore of Maryland.* Baltimore: John P. Des Forges, 1876.

HARFORD

Portrait and Biographical Record of Harford and Cecil Counties Maryland. New York and Chicago: Chapman Publishing Co., 1897.

HARRISON [1]

Fairfax Harrison. *Landmarks of Old Prince William.* Reprint. Berryville, Va.: Chesapeake Book Co., 1964.

HARRISON [3]

Fairfax Harrison. *Early American Turf Stock, 1730–1830.* 2 vols. Richmond: Old Dominion Press, 1934–35.

HARRISON [4]

Fairfax Harrison. "The Colonial Post Office in Virginia." *William and Mary Quarterly,* 2d ser., 4 (1924), 73–92.

HARRISON [5]

"Harrison of James River." *Virginia Magazine of History and Biography,* 32 (1924), 298–304, 404–10; 33 (1924), 97–103, 205–8, 312–16, 410–19.

HARRISON [6]

"Harrison of Northern Virginia" and "The Harrison Family of Northern Virginia." *Virginia Magazine of History and Biography,* 23 (1915), 214–16, 331–33, 443–45; 24 (1916), 97–99, 211–13, 314–15.

HAYDEN

Horace Edwin Hayden. *Virginia Genealogies. A Genealogy of the Glassell Family of Scotland and Virginia.* 1891. Reprint, Baltimore: Genealogical Publishing Co., 1973.

Bibliography

HAZARD

Fred Shelley, ed. "Ebenezer Hazard's Travels through Maryland in 1777." *Maryland Historical Magazine,* 46 (1951), 44–54.

HEADS OF FAMILIES, VA.

Heads of Families at the First Census of the United States Taken in the Year 1790: Virginia. 1908. Reprint, Baltimore: Genealogical Publishing Co., 1970.

HEATH PAPERS

William Heath. *The Heath Papers,* Parts I, II, III. *Collections of the Massachusetts Historical Society,* 5th ser., 4:1–285; 7th ser., vols. 4 and 5. Boston: Massachusetts Historical Society, 1878–1905.

HEITMAN [1]

Francis Bernard Heitman. *Historical Register of Officers of the Continental Army during the War of the Revolution, April 1775, to December, 1783.* Washington, D.C.: F. B. Heitman, 1893.

HEITMAN [2]

Francis Bernard Heitman. *Historical Register of Officers of the Continental Army during the War of the Revolution, April, 1775, to December, 1783.* Rev. ed. Washington, D.C.: Rare Book Shop Publishing Co., 1914.

HENING

William Waller Hening, ed. *The Statutes at Large; Being a Collection of All the Laws of Virginia from the First Session of the Legislature, in the Year 1619.* 13 vols. New York, Philadelphia, Richmond: various publishers, 1819–23.

HENRY

William Wirt Henry, ed. *Patrick Henry. Life, Correspondence, and Speeches.* 3 vols. New York: Charles Scribner's Sons, 1891.

HILTZHEIMER

Jacob Cox Parsons, ed. *Extracts from the Diary of Jacob Hiltzheimer, of Philadelphia, 1765–1798.* Philadelphia: Press of William F. Bell & Co., 1893.

HONYMAN

Philip Padelford, ed. *Colonial Panorama 1775, Dr. Robert Honyman's Journal for March and April.* San Marino, Calif.: Huntington Library, 1939.

HOOD

David Hannay, ed. *Letters Written by Sir Samuel Hood (Viscount Hood) in 1781, 1782, 1783.* Publications of the Navy Records Society, vol. 3. N.p.: Navy Records Society, 1895.

Bibliography

HOOPER

Robert Hooper. *Lexicon-Medicum or Medical Dictionary: Containing an Explanation of the Terms in Anatomy, Botany, Chemistry, Materia Medica, Midwifery, Mineralogy, Pharmacy, Physiology, Practice of Physic, Surgery, and the Various Branches of Natural Philosophy Connected with Medicine; Selected, Arranged, and Compiled from the Best Authors.* New York: J. & J. Harper, 1826.

H.B.J.

H. R. McIlwaine and John Pendleton Kennedy, eds. *Journals of the House of Burgesses of Virginia.* 13 vols. Richmond: Virginia State Library, 1905–15.

HOYT

William D. Hoyt, Jr. "Self-Portrait: Eliza Custis, 1808." *Virginia Magazine of History and Biography,* 53 (1945), 89–100.

HUFELAND

Otto Hufeland. *Westchester County during the American Revolution, 1775–1783.* White Plains, N.Y.: Westchester County Historical Society, 1926.

JACKSON

Joseph Jackson. "Washington in Philadelphia." *Pennsylvania Magazine of History and Biography,* 56 (1932), 110–55.

JCC

Worthington Chauncey Ford et al., eds. *Journals of the Continental Congress, 1774–1789.* 34 vols. Washington, D.C.: Government Printing Office, 1904–37.

JEFFERSON [1]

Julian P. Boyd, ed. *The Papers of Thomas Jefferson.* Princeton, N.J.: Princeton University Press, 1950—.

JEFFERSON [2]

Paul Leicester Ford, ed. *The Writings of Thomas Jefferson.* 10 vols. New York: G. P. Putnam's Sons, 1892–99.

JETT

Dora C. Jett. *Minor Sketches of Major Folk and Where They Sleep: The Old Masonic Burying Ground, Fredericksburg, Virginia.* Richmond: Old Dominion Press, 1928.

JOHNSTON [1]

Christopher Johnston. "The Tilghman Family." *Maryland Historical Magazine,* 1 (1906), 181–84, 280–84, 369–76.

JOHNSTON [3]

Henry P. Johnston. *The Yorktown Campaign and the Surrender of Cornwallis, 1781.* New York: Da Capo Press, 1971.

JONES [1]
Hugh Jones. *The Present State of Virginia from Whence Is Inferred a Short View of Maryland and North Carolina.* Ed. Richard L. Morton. Chapel Hill: University of North Carolina Press, 1956.

JOURNAL OF AN OFFICER
"Journal of an Officer in the Naval Army in America." In J. G. Shea, ed. *The Operations of the French Fleet under the Count de Grasse in 1781–82, As Described in Two Contemporaneous Journals.* New York: Bradford Club, 1864.

KEIM
DeBenneville Randolph Keim. *Rochambeau, a Commemoration by the Congress of the United States of America of the Services of the French Auxiliary Forces in the War of Independence.* Washington, D.C.: Government Printing Office, 1907.

KEITH [2]
Charles P. Keith. "Andrew Allen." *Pennsylvania Magazine of History and Biography,* 10 (1886), 361–65.

KELLY [1]
J. Reaney Kelly. "Cedar Park, Its People and Its History." *Maryland Historical Magazine,* 58 (1963), 30–53.

KING [2]
George H. S. King. "General George Weedon." *William and Mary Quarterly,* 2d ser., 20 (1940), 237–52.

KING [3]
George H. S. King. "Some Notes on the Coleman Family of Caroline County, Virginia." *Virginia Magazine of History and Biography,* 54 (1946), 258–60.

KING [6]
J. Estelle Stewart King, comp. *Abstracts of Wills, Inventories, and Administration Accounts of Loudoun County, Virginia, 1757–1800.* Beverly Hills, Calif.: J. Estelle Stewart King, 1940.

KNIGHT
Helen Cross Knight, comp. *Lady Huntington and Her Friends; or, The Revival of the Work of God in the Days of Wesley, Whitefield, Romaine, Venn, and Others in the Last Century.* New York: American Tract Society, 1853.

KONWISER
Harry M. Konwiser. *Colonial and Revolutionary Posts: A History of the American Postal System, Colonial and Revolutionary*

Periods. Richmond: Dietz Printing Co., 1931.

LABAREE [3]   Leonard W. Labaree et al., eds. *The Papers of Benjamin Franklin.* New Haven, Conn.: Yale University Press, 1959—.

LAND   Aubrey C. Land. *The Dulanys of Maryland: A Biographical Study of Daniel Dulany, the Elder (1685–1753) and Daniel Dulany, the Younger (1722–1797).* Baltimore: Maryland Historical Society, 1955.

LANDIS   Charles I. Landis. "The History of the Philadelphia and Lancaster Turnpike." *Pennsylvania Magazine of History and Biography,* 42 (1918), 1–28, 127–40; 43 (1919), 84–90.

LEDGER A   Manuscript Ledger in George Washington Papers, Library of Congress.

LEDGER B   Manuscript Ledger in George Washington Papers, Library of Congress.

LEDGER C   Manuscript Ledger in Morristown National Historical Park.

LEE [1]   Cazenove Gardner Lee, Jr. *Lee Chronicle.* Ed. Dorothy Mills Parker. New York: New York University Press, 1957.

LEE [2]   Worthington Chauncey Ford, ed. *Letters of William Lee.* 3 vols. Brooklyn, N.Y.: Historical Printing Club, 1891.

LEE [3]   Ida J. Lee, comp. "Land Taxed in King William County in 1782." *William and Mary Quarterly,* 2d ser., 6 (1926), 326–28.

LEE [4]   Henry Lee. *Memoirs of the War in the Southern Department of the United States.* Rev. ed. Ed. Robert E. Lee. New York: University Publishing Co., 1870.

LMCC   Edmund C. Burnett, ed. *Letters of Members of the Continental Congress.* 8 vols. 1921–38. Reprint, Gloucester, Mass.: Peter Smith, 1963.

LINCOLN   Anna T. Lincoln. *Wilmington, Delaware: Three Centuries under Four Flags, 1609–1937.* Rutland, Vt.: Tuttle Publishing Co., 1937.

LIVERMORE   Shaw Livermore. *Early American Land Companies: Their Influence on Corporate*

Development. London: Oxford University Press, 1939.

LOSSING

Benson J. Lossing. *The Pictorial Field-Book of the Revolution.* 2 vols. New York: Harper & Brothers, Publishers, 1851.

LOWER NORFOLK

The Lower Norfolk County, Virginia, Antiquary. Ed. Edward W. James. Vols. 1–5. 1895–1906. Reprint, New York: Peter Smith, 1951.

LOYALIST

"A Loyalist's Account of Certain Occurrences in Philadelphia after Cornwallis's Surrender at Yorktown." *Pennsylvania Magazine of History and Biography,* 16 (1892), 103–7.

LUCAS

Silas Emmett Lucas, Jr. *The Powell Families of Virginia and the South, Being an Encyclopedia of the Eight (8) Major Powell Families of Virginia and the South in General.* Vidalia, Ga.: Silas Emmett Lucas, Jr., Publisher, for Georgia Genealogical Reprints, 1969.

LUDLUM

David M. Ludlum. *Early American Winters.* 2 vols. Boston: American Meteorological Society, 1966.

LYLE

Maria Cook Nourse Lyle. "James Nourse of Virginia." *Virginia Magazine of History and Biography,* 8 (1900–1901), 199–202.

MACAULAY

Alexander Macaulay. "Journal of Alexander Macaulay." *William and Mary Quarterly,* 1st ser., 11 (1902–3), 180–91.

MCDONALD

Cornelia McDonald. *A Diary with Reminiscences of the War and Refugee Life in the Shenandoah Valley, 1860–1865.* Nashville: Cullon & Ghertner Co., 1935.

MCGRATH

Francis Sims McGrath. *Pillars of Maryland.* Richmond: Dietz Press, 1950.

MACKENZIE [2]

Frederick Mackenzie. *Diary of Frederick Mackenzie, Giving a Daily Narrative of His Military Service as an Officer of the Regiment of Royal Welch Fusiliers during the Years 1775–1781 in Massachusetts, Rhode Island, and New York.* 2 vols. Cambridge, Mass.: Harvard University Press, 1930.

MACKESY — Piers Mackesy. *The War for America, 1775–1783.* Cambridge, Mass.: Harvard University Press, 1964.

MACMASTER — Richard K. MacMaster and David C. Skaggs, eds. "The Letterbooks of Alexander Hamilton, Piscataway Factor." *Maryland Historical Magazine,* 61 (1966), 146–66, 305–28; 62 (1967), 135–69.

MALONE [2] — Dumas Malone. *Jefferson and His Time.* Boston: Little, Brown and Co., 1948—.

MARSHALL [1] — Christopher Marshall. *Extracts from the Diary of Christopher Marshall, Kept in Philadelphia and Lancaster during the American Revolution, 1774–1781.* Ed. William Duane. Albany: Joel Munsell, 1877.

MD. ARCHIVES — *Archives of Maryland.* Baltimore: Maryland Historical Society, 1883—.

MD. RED BOOKS — *Calendar of Maryland State Papers. No. 4, Part 2, The Red Books.* Annapolis: Hall of Records Commission, 1953.

MASON [1] — Frances Norton Mason, ed. *John Norton & Sons, Merchants of London and Virginia: Being the Papers from Their Counting House for the Years 1750 to 1795.* New York: Augustus M. Kelley, Publishers, 1968.

MASON [2] — Robert A. Rutland, ed. *The Papers of George Mason, 1725–1792.* 3 vols. Chapel Hill: University of North Carolina Press, 1970.

MASONS — "Williamsburg Lodge of Masons." *William and Mary Quarterly,* 1st ser., 25 (1916–17), 149–56.

MAYS — David John Mays. *Edmund Pendleton, 1721–1803: A Biography.* 2 vols. Cambridge, Mass.: Harvard University Press, 1952.

MEADE [1] — William Meade. *Old Churches, Ministers, and Families of Virginia.* 2 vols. Philadelphia: J. B. Lippincott Co., 1910.

MERRENS — Harry Roy Merrens. *Colonial North Carolina in the Eighteenth Century; A Study in Historical Geography.* Chapel Hill: University of North Carolina Press, 1964.

MOFFETT — Lee Moffett. *Water Powered Mills of Fauquier County, Virginia.* N.p., n.d.

MONAGHAN   Frank and Lowenthal Marvin Monaghan. *This Was New York, the Nation's Capital in 1789.* Garden City, N.Y.: Doubleday, Doran & Co., 1943.

MOORE [2]   Frank Moore. *Diary of the American Revolution.* 2 vols. New York: Charles Scribner, 1859.

MORDECAI   Samuel Mordecai. *Virginia, Especially Richmond, in By-Gone Days; with a Glance at the Present: Being Reminiscences and Last Words of an Old Citizen.* 2d ed. Richmond: West & Johnston, 1860.

MORGAN [1]   John Hill Morgan and Mantle Fielding. *The Life Portraits of Washington and Their Replicas.* Philadelphia: by the authors, 1931.

MORRIS   Richard B. Morris. *The Peacemakers: The Great Powers and American Independence.* 1965. Reprint, New York: Harper Torchbooks, 1970.

MORTON [1]   Louis Morton. *Robert Carter of Nomini Hall, a Virginia Tobacco Planter of the Eighteenth Century.* Williamsburg, Va.: Colonial Williamsburg, Inc., 1941.

NEILL   Edward Duffield Neill. *The Fairfaxes of England and America in the Seventeenth and Eighteenth Centuries, Including Letters from and to Hon. William Fairfax, President of Council of Virginia, and His Sons, Col. George William Fairfax and Rev. Bryan, Eighth Lord Fairfax, the Neighbors and Friends of George Washington.* Albany: Joel Munsell, 1868.

NEWMAN   Harry Wright Newman. *The Maryland Dents: A Genealogical History of the Descendants of Judge Thomas Dent and Captain John Dent Who Settled Early in the Province of Maryland.* Richmond: Dietz Press, 1963.

NICKLIN [2]   J. B. Calvert Nicklin. "The Calvert Family." *Maryland Historical Magazine,* 16 (1921), 50–59, 189–204, 313–18, 389–94.

NORRIS [1]   J. E. Norris, ed. *History of the Lower Shenandoah Valley.* 1890. Reprint, Berryville: Virginia Book Co., 1972.

NORRIS [2]

Walter B. Norris. *Annapolis: Its Colonial and Naval History.* New York: Thomas Y. Crowell Co., 1925.

N.C. COL. REC.

Willam L. Saunders, ed. *The Colonial Records of North Carolina.* 10 vols. Raleigh: State of North Carolina, 1886–90.

PALMER

John McAuley Palmer. *General Von Steuben.* New Haven: Yale University Press, 1937.

PALTSITS

Victor Hugo Paltsits, ed. *Minutes of the Commissioners for Detecting and Defeating Conspiracies in the State of New York, Albany County Sessions, 1778–1781.* 3 vols. Albany: State of New York, 1909–10.

PAULLIN

Charles Oscar Paullin. *Commodore John Rodgers.* Cleveland: Arthur H. Clark Co., 1910.

PENNYPACKER

Morton Pennypacker. *General Washington's Spies on Long Island and in New York.* Brooklyn, N.Y.: Long Island Historical Society, 1939.

POWELL

Mary G. Powell. *The History of Old Alexandria, Virginia, from July 13, 1749 to May 24, 1861.* Richmond: William Byrd Press, 1928.

PRICE

Jacob M. Price. "Who Was John Norton? A Note on the Historical Character of Some Eighteenth-Century London Virginia Firms." *William and Mary Quarterly,* 3d ser., 19 (1962), 400–407.

PURVIANCE

Robert Purviance. *A Narrative of Events Which Occurred in Baltimore Town during the Revolutionary War.* Baltimore: Jos. Robinson, 1849.

RAMSBURGH

Edith Roberts Ramsburgh. "Sir Dudley Digges, His English Ancestry and the Digges Line in America." *Daughters of the American Revolution Magazine,* 57 (1923), 125–39.

RANKIN

Hugh F. Rankin. *The Theater in Colonial America.* Chapel Hill: University of North Carolina Press, 1960.

RAWLINGS

James Scott Rawlings. *Virginia's Colonial Churches: An Architectural Guide.* Richmond: Garrett & Massie, 1963.

REPS — John W. Reps. *Tidewater Towns: City Planning in Colonial Virginia and Maryland.* Williamsburg, Va.: Colonial Williamsburg Foundation, Inc., 1972.

RICE — Howard C. Rice, Jr., and Anne S. K. Brown, eds. *The American Campaigns of Rochambeau's Army, 1780, 1781, 1782, 1783.* 2 vols. Princeton, N.J., and Providence: Princeton University Press and Brown University Press, 1972.

RICHARDSON [1] — William E. Richardson. "Colonial Homes in West River Hundred." *Records of the Columbia Historical Society of Washington, D.C.* Vols. 44–45, 103–25. Washington, D.C.: Columbia Historical Society, 1944.

RICHARDSON [2] — Hester Dorsey Richardson. *Side-Lights on Maryland History with Sketches of Early Maryland Families.* 2 vols. Baltimore: Williams and Wilkins Co., 1913.

RIEDESEL — Marvin L. Brown, ed. *Baroness von Riedesel and the American Revolution: Journal and Correspondence of a Tour of Duty, 1776–1783.* Chapel Hill: University of North Carolina Press, 1965.

RIGHTMYER — Nelson Waite Rightmyer. *Maryland's Established Church.* Baltimore: Church Historical Society for the Diocese of Maryland, 1956.

RILEY [2] — Elihu Samuel Riley. *Riley's Historic Map of Annapolis.* Annapolis: Arundel Press, 1909.

ROCHAMBEAU — Jean Baptiste Donatien, comte de Rochambeau. *Memoires, militaires, historiques, et politiques de Rochambeau.* 2 vols. Paris: Fain, 1809.

ROTHERY — Agnes Rothery. *Houses Virginians Have Loved.* New York: Bonanza Books, 1954.

ROWLAND [1] — Kate Mason Rowland, ed. *The Life of Charles Carroll of Carrollton, 1737–1832, with His Correspondence and Public Papers.* 2 vols. New York: G. P. Putnam's Sons, 1898.

ROWLAND [2] — Kate Mason Rowland, ed. *The Life of George Mason, 1725–1792.* 2 vols. New York: G. P. Putnam's Sons, 1892.

ST. PAUL'S | George H. S. King, comp. *The Register of Saint Paul's Parish, 1715–1798.* Fredericksburg, Va.: George Harrison Sanford King, 1960.

SAYERS | R. S. Sayers. *Lloyds Bank in the History of English Banking.* Oxford, Eng.: Clarendon Press, 1957.

SCHARF [1] | J. Thomas Scharf and Thompson Westcott. *History of Philadelphia, 1609–1884.* 3 vols. Philadelphia: L. H. Everts & Co., 1884.

SCHARF [2] | John Thomas Scharf. *The Chronicles of Baltimore; Being a Complete History of "Baltimore Town" and Baltimore City from the Earliest Period to the Present Time.* Baltimore: Turnbull Brothers, 1874.

SCHARF [3] | John Thomas Scharf. *History of Western Maryland.* 2 vols. Philadelphia: Louis H. Everts, 1882.

SCHOEPF | Johann David Schoepf. *Travels in the Confederation.* Ed. and trans. Alfred J. Morrison. 2 vols. Philadelphia: William J. Campbell, 1911.

SCOTT | Mary Wingfield Scott. *Houses of Old Richmond.* Richmond: Valentine Museum, 1941.

SELLERS | Charles Coleman Sellers. *Charles Willson Peale.* 2 vols. Philadelphia: American Philosophical Society, 1947.

SERLE | Edward H. Tatum, ed. *The American Journal of Ambrose Serle, Secretary to Lord Howe, 1776–1778.* San Marino, Calif.: Huntington Library, 1940.

SHIPPEN | "Military Letters of Captain Joseph Shippen of the Provincial Service, 1756–1758." *Pennsylvania Magazine of History and Biography,* 36 (1912), 367–78, 385–463.

SHONNARD | Frederic Shonnard and W. W. Spooner. *History of Westchester County.* 1900. Reprint, New York: Harbor Hill Books, 1974.

SIMCOE | John Graves Simcoe. *Simcoe's Military Journal: A History of the Operations of a Partisan Corps, Called the Queen's Rangers, Commanded by Lieut. Col. J. G. Simcoe, during the War of the American Revolution.* New York: Bartlett & Welford, 1844.

[463]

Bibliography

SKAGGS

David C. Skaggs and Richard K. MacMaster, eds. "Post-Revolutionary Letters of Alexander Hamilton, Piscataway Merchant." *Maryland Historical Magazine,* 63 (1968), 22–54; 65 (1970), 18–35.

SLAUGHTER [1]

Philip Slaughter. *The History of Truro Parish in Virginia.* Philadelphia: G. W. Jacobs & Co., 1908.

SLAUGHTER [2]

Philip Slaughter. *A History of St. Mark's Parish, Culpeper County, Virginia, with Notes of Old Churches and Old Families and Illustrations of the Manners and Customs of the Olden Time.* Baltimore: Innes & Co., 1877.

SMITH [1]

William Smith. "The Colonial Post-Office." *American Historical Review,* 21 (1915–16), 258–75.

SMITH [2]

Elizabeth W. Smith. "A Reminiscence." *Pennsylvania Magazine of History and Biography,* 46 (1922), 39–56.

SMYTH

John Ferdinand Dalziel Smyth. *A Tour in the United States of America; Containing an Account of the Present Situation of That Country; the Population, Agriculture, Commerce, Customs, and Manners of the Inhabitants. . . .* 2 vols. London: printed for G. Robinson, J. Robson, and J. Stewell, 1784.

SPARKS

Jared Sparks, ed. *The Writings of George Washington: Being His Correspondence, Addresses, Messages, and Other Papers, Official and Private, Selected and Published from the Original Manuscripts.* 12 vols. Boston: John B. Russell, 1833–37.

SPRAGUE

William B. Sprague. *Annals of the American Pulpit or Commemorative Notices of Distinguished American Clergymen of Various Denominations.* 9 vols. New York: Robert Carter & Brothers, 1859.

SPROUSE [3]

Edith Moore Sprouse. *Colchester: Colonial Port on the Potomac.* Fairfax, Va.: Fairfax County Office of Comprehensive Planning, 1975.

Bibliography

STANARD [1]   William G. Stanard and Mary Newton. *The Colonial Virginia Register*. Baltimore: Genealogical Publishing Co., 1965.

STETSON [1]   Charles W. Stetson. *Four Mile Run Land Grants*. Washington, D.C.: Mimeoform Press, 1935.

STETSON [2]   Charles W. Stetson. *Washington and His Neighbors*. Richmond: Garrett and Massie, 1956.

STEVENS [1]   William Oliver Stevens. *Annapolis: Anne Arundel's Town*. New York: Dodd, Mead & Co., 1937.

STEVENS [3]   John Austin Stevens. "The Operations of the Allied Armies before New York, 1781." *Magazine of American History*, 4 (1880), 1–45.

STEVENS [4]   Benjamin Franklin Stevens, ed. *The Campaign in Virginia, 1781. An Exact Reprint of Six Rare Pamphlets on the Clinton-Cornwallis Controversy*. 2 vols. London, 1888.

STEWART   Mrs. Catesby Willis Stewart. *The Life of Brigadier General William Woodford of the American Revolution*. 2 vols. Richmond: Whittet & Shepperson, 1973.

TARLETON   Banastre Tarleton. *A History of the Campaigns of 1780 and 1781, in the Southern Provinces of North America*. 1787. Reprint, Spartanburg, S.C.: Reprint Co., 1967.

TAYLOE   Benjamin Ogle Tayloe. "American Gentlemen of the Olden Time, Especially in Maryland and Virginia." *Tyler's Quarterly Magazine*, 2 (1920–21), 85–97.

THACHER   James Thacher. *Military Journal of the American Revolution*. Hartford: Hurlburt, Williams & Co., 1862.

TILGHMAN [1]   Tench Francis Tilghman. "The Founding of St. John's College, 1784–1789." *Maryland Historical Magazine*, 44 (1949), 75–92.

TILGHMAN [2]   Oswald Tilghman. *History of Talbot County, Maryland, 1661–1861*. 2 vols. Baltimore: Regional Publishing Co., 1967.

TILGHMAN [3]   Tench Francis Tilghman. *Memoir of Lieut. Col. Tench Tilghman, Secretary and Aid*

[465]

Bibliography

to *Washington, Together with an Appendix, Containing Revolutionary Journals and Letters, Hitherto Unpublished.* Albany: J. Munsell, 1876.

TRUMBULL [1]   Jonathan Trumbull, Jr. "Minutes of Occurrences Respecting the Siege and Capture of York in Virginia, Extracted from the Journal of Colonel Jonathan Trumbull, Secretary to the General, 1781." *Proceedings of the Massachusetts Historical Society*, 1st ser., 14 (1876), 331–38.

TRUMBULL PAPERS   *The Trumbull Papers. Collections of the Massachusetts Historical Society*, 7th ser., vol. 1. Boston: Massachusetts Historical Society, 1902.

TUCKER   Edward M. Riley, ed. "St. George Tucker Journal of the Siege of Yorktown, 1781." *William and Mary Quarterly*, 3d ser., 5 (1948), 375–95.

TYLER [2]   Lyon G. Tyler. "The Smiths of Virginia." *William and Mary Quarterly*, 1st ser., 4 (1895–96), 46–52, 95–103, 183–87.

VAN SCHREEVEN   William J. Van Schreeven et al., eds. *Revolutionary Virginia: The Road to Independence.* Charlottesville: University Press of Virginia, for the Virginia Independence Bicentennial Commission, 1973—) .

VA. EXEC. JLS.   H. R. McIlwaine, Wilmer L. Hall, and Benjamin Hillman, eds. *Executive Journals of the Council of Colonial Virginia.* 6 vols. Richmond: Virginia State Library, 1925–66.

VSP   William P. Palmer et al., eds. *Calendar of Virginia State Papers and Other Manuscripts.* 11 vols. Richmond: various publishers, 1875–93.

VERME   Elizabeth Cometti, ed. *Seeing America and Its Great Men: The Journal and Letters of Count Francesco dal Verme, 1783–1784.* Charlottesville: University Press of Virginia, 1969.

WALKER [3]   Lewis Burd Walker. "Life of Margaret Shippen, Wife of Benedict Arnold." *Pennsylvania Magazine of History and Biography*, 24 (1900), 401–29.

WARD [1]

Townsend Ward. "A Walk to Darby." *Pennsylvania Magazine of History and Biography*, 3 (1879), 150–66.

WASHINGTON AND DE GRASSE

Institut Français de Washington. *Correspondence of General Washington and Comte de Grasse, 1781, Aug. 17–November 4*. Washington, D.C.: Government Printing Office, 1931.

WATERMAN

Thomas Tileston Waterman. *The Mansions of Virginia, 1706–1776*. Chapel Hill: University of North Carolina Press, 1946.

WAYLAND [1]

John Walter Wayland. *The Washingtons and Their Homes*. 1944. Reprint, Berryville: Virginia Book Co., 1973.

WEAKS

Mabel Clare Weaks, ed. *Calendar of the Kentucky Papers of the Draper Collection of Manuscripts*. Madison: State Historical Society of Wisconsin, 1925.

WEBB [2]

Worthington Chauncey Ford, ed. *Correspondence and Journals of Samuel Blachley Webb*. 3 vols. New York: Wickersham Press, 1893.

WEELEN

Jean-Edmond Weelen. *Rochambeau, Father and Son: A Life of the Marechal de Rochambeau*. New York: Henry Holt & Co., 1936.

WHARTON

Francis Wharton, ed. *The Revolutionary Diplomatic Correspondence of the United States*. 6 vols. Washington, D.C.: Government Printing Office, 1889.

WHARTON LETTER BOOK

"Selections from the Letter-Books of Thomas Wharton, of Philadelphia, 1773–1783." *Pennsylvania Magazine of History and Biography*, 33 (1909), 319–39, 432–53; 34 (1910), 41–61.

WHITRIDGE

Arnold Whitridge. *Rochambeau*. New York: Macmillan Co., 1965.

WICKWIRE

Franklin and Mary Wickwire. *Cornwallis: The American Adventure*. Boston: Houghton Mifflin Co., 1970.

WILLCOX [2]

William B. Willcox. "The British Road to Yorktown: A Study in Divided Command." *American Historical Review*, 52 (1946–47), 1–35.

WILLCOX [3]

William B. Willcox. *Portrait of a General: Sir Henry Clinton in the American War of Independence.* New York: Alfred A. Knopf, 1964.

WMQ

The William and Mary Quarterly: A Magazine of Early American History. Williamsburg, Va.: Published by the Institute of Early American History and Culture.

WILLIAMS [1]

Harrison Williams. *Legends of Loudoun.* Richmond: Garrett and Massie, 1938.

WILLIAMSBURG

Colonial Williamsburg Official Guidebook: Containing a Brief History of the City and Descriptions of More Than One Hundred Dwelling-Houses, Shops & Publick Buildings, Fully Illustrated. Also a Large Guide Map. Williamsburg: Colonial Williamsburg Foundation, 1970.

WILLISON

George F. Willison. *Patrick Henry and His World.* Garden City, N.Y.: Doubleday & Co., 1969.

W.P.A. [1]

W.P.A. Writers' Project. *Prince William: The Story of Its People and Its Places.* Manassas, Va.: Bethlehem Good Housekeeping Club, 1941.

W.P.A. [2]

W.P.A. Writers' Project. *Maryland: A Guide to the Old Line State.* New York: Oxford University Press, 1940.

W.P.A. [3]

W.P.A. Writers' Project. *Delaware: A Guide to the First State.* American Guide Series. New York: Viking Press, 1938.

WRITINGS

John C. Fitzpatrick, ed. *The Writings of George Washington from the Original Manuscript Sources, 1745–1799.* 39 vols. Washington, D.C.: Government Printing Office, 1931–44.

WYLIE

T. W. J. Wylie. "Franklin County One Hundred Years Ago: A Settler's Experience Told in a Letter Written by Alexander Thomson in 1773." *Pennsylvania Magazine of History and Biography,* 8 (1884), 313–27.

Index

Individuals and places mentioned for the first time in this volume have been identified in the footnotes; identification notes for those which previously appeared in the first two volumes may be located by consulting the indexes for those volumes. A cumulative index will be included in the last volume of the *Diaries*.

Index

Evans, Sarah, 113
Ewell, Bertrand, 71
Ewell, Charles, 71
Ewell, Frances. *See* Ballendine, Frances Ewell
Ewell, Mariamne. *See* Craik, Mariamne Ewell
Ewell, Solomon, 71

Fairfax, Ann. *See* Lee, Ann Fairfax Washington
Fairfax, Bryan (illus., 82), 69, 81, 82; at Mount Vernon, 15, 81, 82, 132, 147, 159, 160, 162, 194, 228, 231, 234, 235, 291, 325; as trustee of Margaret Green Savage, 81; hunting with GW, 81, 82, 147, 159, 162; and Dr. William Savage, 81, 88, 89; debt to GW, 88, 89, 110, 132; GW visits, 109; land of, 110, 132; and politics, 260, 261
Fairfax, Elizabeth Cary, 119
Fairfax, George William, 124, 157, 160, 162, 194, 319; at Mount Vernon, 1, 2, 19, 33, 45, 71, 75, 114, 119, 135, 149, 153, 154, 167, 174, 188; GW visits, 46, 76, 133, 161; family of, 70, 168; as churchwarden, 113; travels, 119, 132, 193; land deals with GW, 132, 199; correspondence with GW, 154, 351; leaves Virginia, 192, 193; rental and sale of Belvoir, 204, 226, 269, 270, 296
Fairfax, Sally Cary (daughter of Bryan Fairfax), 69, 71
Fairfax, Sarah ("Sally") Cary (wife of George William Fairfax), 1, 2, 21, 33, 46, 70, 71, 103, 114, 119, 171, 178, 188, 192
Fairfax, William (d. 1759), 110
Fairfax (brig or brigantine). *See Farmer*
Fairfax of Cameron, Robert Fairfax, seventh Baron, 1, 2, 9, 15, 19, 25
Fairfax of Cameron, Thomas Fairfax, sixth Baron, 1, 12, 14, 19, 114, 174, 322
Fairfax's (Belvoir) Neck, 157
Fairfield (Frederick County), 292
Fairfield (Gloucester County), 48

Fair Hill, 278
Fairmont Park, 335
Fantasque (ship), 384, 385
Farmer (of New York City), 181
Farmer (Anne and Elizabeth, Fairfax; brig or brigantine), 120, 226, 240, 241, 304, 320, 321, 322, 323
The Farmer's Compleat Guide through All Articles of His Profession (book), 50
Farquhar, George, 3
Fendall, Philip Richard, 204, 205
Fendall, Sarah Lettice Lee, 204
Ferry Farm (Rappahannock River), 52
Fish, Nicholas, 407, 411, 428
Fisher, William, 279
Fitzgerald, John, 174, 175, 225, 238, 270, 297, 320
Fitzhugh (Mount Vernon visitor), 60, 61, 133, 270
Fitzhugh, John (Mount Vernon visitor), 133, 135, 136
Fitzhugh, John (of Bell Air), 133
Fitzhugh, John (of Marmion, Mount Vernon visitor), 147
Fitzhugh, John (of Marmion, d. 1733), 147
Fitzhugh, John (son of John Fitzhugh of Marmion, who d. 1733), 147
Fitzhugh, John (son of William Fitzhugh of Marmion), 133, 147
Fitzhugh, Sarah. *See* Thornton, Sarah Fitzhugh
Fitzhugh, William (of Chatham), 144
Fitzhugh, William (of Marmion), 147
Flagg, Ebenezer, 364, 365
Fleming, Bridget ("Biddy"), 132
Fleming, Thomas, 132, 152
Fleming, William, 75, 76
Flood, John, 360, 361
Flowing Springs Farm, 6
Forbes, John, 334
Forman, David, 367, 398, 408, 409, 418, 435
Fort Augusta, 380, 381
Fort Charles (Fort Prince Charles), 399, 401

Index